THE Sunset
ESSENTIAL WESTERN
COOKBOOK

Best-loved classics and fresh new favorites

Oxmoor House.

Sunset

©2012 by Time Home Entertainment Inc.
135 West 50th Street, New York, NY 10020

ISBN-10: 0-376-02799-1
ISBN-13: 978-0-376-02799-3
Library of Congress Control Number: 2012938010
First printing 2012
Printed in the United States of America

OXMOOR HOUSE

VP, Publishing Director: Jim Childs
Editorial Director: Leah McLaughlin
Creative Director: Felicity Keane
Brand Manager: Fonda Hitchcock
Managing Editor: Rebecca Benton

SUNSET PUBLISHING

President: Barb Newton
VP, Editor-in-Chief: Kitty Morgan
Creative Director: Mia Daminato
Photography Director: Yvonne Stender
Food Editor: Margo True

CONTRIBUTORS TO THIS BOOK

Editor: Tam Putnam
Art Director: Tonya Sutfin
Production Manager: Linda M. Bouchard
Project Editor: Sarah H. Doss
Photo Coordinator: Danielle Johnson
Senior Imaging Specialist: Kimberley Navabpour
Proofreader: Denise Griffiths
Indexer: Ken DellaPenta

To order additional publications, call 1-800-765-6400

For more books to enrich your life, visit **oxmoorhouse.com**

Visit *Sunset* online at **sunset.com**

For the most comprehensive selection of *Sunset* books, visit **sunsetbooks.com**

To search, savor, and share thousands of recipes, visit **myrecipes.com**

SPECIAL THANKS

Associate Food Editor Elaine Johnson, Recipe Editor Amy Machnak, Test Kitchen Coordinator Stephanie Dean, former food editors Jerry Anne DiVecchio and Sara Schneider, and previous staff writers, including Linda Anusasananan, Amy Traverso, and Molly Watson; plus the *Sunset* recipe retesters—Kevyn Allard, Angela Brassinga, April Cooper, Dorothy Decker, Sarah Epstein, Lenore Grant, Doni Jackson, Melissa Kaiser, Marlene Kawahata, Eve F. Lynch, Rebecca Parker, Bunnie Russell, Laura Shafsky, Vicki Sousa, Linda Tebben, and Sue Turner

We would also like to thank Erika Ehmsen, Mark Hawkins, Catherine Jacobes, Charla Lawhon, Julia Lee, Laura Martin, Haley Minick, Marie Pence, Alan Phinney, Lorraine Reno, Margaret Sloan, Sue B. Smith, and Katie Tamony

FRONT-COVER PHOTO Cola Shredded-Beef Tacos (recipe on page 81)

PHOTOGRAPHY CREDITS

Quentin Bacon: 214; **Iain Bagwell:** 51, 70, 94, 97, 160, 225, 246; **Edmund Barr:** 104; **Leigh Beisch:** 1, 3, 36, 64, 72, 111, 113, 118, 121, 180, 198, 204, 235; **Annabelle Breakey:** front cover, 4, 7, 8, 10, 11, 15, 16, 18, 19, 20, 25, 26, 27, 28, 31, 32, 35, 39, 41, 43, 44, 46, 48 right, 52, 55, 56, 59, 63, 67, 68, 71, 75, 79, 80, 82, 83, 84, 85, 89, 91, 93, 98, 101, 107, 108, 110, 116, 117 both, 123, 125, 126, 128, 130, 134, 137, 138, 143, 145, 146, 149, 150, 152, 153, 154, 157, 161, 162, 165, 166, 168, 171, 172, 174, 177, 178, 181, 182, 184, 190, 193, 195, 197, 203, 207, 208 left, 209, 212, 215, 216, 217, 218, 222, 227, 228, 231, 239, 240, 244, 245, 247, back cover top left and top middle right and bottom; **Maren Caruso:** 200; **Jeffery Cross:** 23; **Alex Farnum:** 90, 133 all, 164, 201; **David Fenton:** 139 all; **Dan Goldberg:** 76, 132, 194, 224, 246 left; **Leo Gong:** 14, 50, 57, 232, back cover top right; **Thayer Allyson Gowdy:** 12, 86, 135 both, 208 right, 211; **Jim Henkens:** 186; **Yunhee Kim:** 103, 114, 167, 202; **Ngoc Minh Ngo:** 48 left; **Scott Peterson:** 236; **David Prince:** 60; **Lisa Romerein:** 185; **Thomas J. Story:** 42, 58, 96, 100, 122, 141, 142 all, 158, 163, 188, 206, 221, 242 all, 243 all, 248, back cover top middle left

BLOOMING SALAD
recipe on page 37

DELFINA'S
BROCCOLI RABE
PIZZA *recipe on page 142*

Contents

6 Introduction

9 Apps & First Courses

21 Drinks

33 Salads

53 Soups & Stews

73 Main Courses

74 Beef
86 Pork
96 Lamb
100 Bison/Venison
102 Poultry
118 Fish
132 Seafood
142 Vegetarian

155 Side Dishes

179 Desserts

219 Breakfast & Brunch

237 Preserves & Pantry

250 Metric Equivalents

251 Index

Introduction

Fragrant, juicy Meyer lemons, flawless avocados, and lettuces so crisp and gorgeous they seem to still be growing: During all the years that I lived in other places, whenever I'd return to California I'd have these three things as often as possible. The sight and smell and taste of them meant I was home.

This book is about the ingredients and dishes that have that sense of place. They're the ones that most precisely capture the flavors of the West—which, for *Sunset*, spans the Rockies to the Pacific, from Alaska and British Columbia down through Baja California. They're foods like the huckleberry cobbler on page 189, baked up in an iron skillet at a cabin in Washington's magnificent Cascade mountains, or chorizo-spiked pinto beans (page 164) at a taco stand in Santa Barbara, where the lines go out the door. Or like a steaming bowl of red chile stew on a cold night in Santa Fe, full of the fruity heat of New Mexico's most famous crop (turn to page 71 for that recipe). For me, it's the salads chapter, where you can find just about everything grown under Western skies—including your own backyard produce.

Throughout the book, you'll glimpse the bigger picture of Western food. Short essays on each major region briskly whisk you through the centuries, from Native American ways of eating to those of pioneers and immigrants and, more recently, chefs and restaurants—describing the ground from which all its recipes spring. Somehow you appreciate salmon more once you've seen it through Lewis and Clark's eyes, swimming in a flashing tumult up the Columbia River.

Some of the recipes in these pages are icons of the Western kitchen: California's Caesar salad, or its tangy sourdough bread, for instance. Other classics aren't as well known, but definitely should be—like rich, chocolaty Nanaimo bars from the town of Nanaimo, in British Columbia (page 214); airy, honey-drizzled Southwestern *sopaipillas* (page 216); and Basque sheepherder's bread, which anticipated today's wildly popular no-knead bread (page 177).

The other pleasure of digging deep into the foods of the West is the stories and surprises you'll find. Who knew that the popsicle came from an experimental 11-year-old San Franciscan in 1905, or that Baja California's fish taco probably started out as tempura? Read (and cook) on, and you'll unearth the original Aztec name for the avocado (it will make you either laugh or frown), the artichoke's ties to the Mafia, and the sad and compelling saga behind the sunniest of fruits, the navel orange.

Above all else, you'll understand that a recipe is never invented—it evolves. What we eat in the West has been shaped by the traditions, techniques, and flavor preferences of the cultures that have settled here. Some dishes have remained basically unchanged, like *pho*, the iconic Vietnamese noodle soup; others are brilliant fusions, like the kimchi quesadilla or the California roll. Yet all of them are shaped, as inexorably as the Grand Canyon by the Colorado River, by what is grown, fished, and ranched here.

This book is an appreciation for all that we have in the West, and is a delicious reminder of who we are.

Margo True
Food Editor, *Sunset* magazine

CLASSIC CIOPPINO
recipe on page 62

BEAN AND CHICKEN
TAQUITOS *recipe on page 10*

Apps & First Courses

Among the ideas born in the West are suave ahi *poke* from Hawaii, taquitos from San Diego, barbecued oysters from just north of San Francisco, and that 1950s West Coast "aha" moment, onion dip. Any one of the innovations in this chapter will launch a meal brilliantly.

Avocados with warm bacon parsley vinaigrette

Crunchy bacon brings out the smokiness of a good Hass avocado, and the sharp vinaigrette helps cut its richness.

SERVES 4 as a first course | 20 minutes

⅓ lb. thin-sliced bacon
2 firm-ripe avocados, pitted, peeled, and each cut into
    4 to 6 wedges
3 garlic cloves, minced
2 tbsp. lemon juice
1 tsp. sugar
Kosher salt and pepper
2 tbsp. chopped flat-leaf parsley

1. Cook bacon in a large frying pan over medium-low heat until crisp. Drain on paper towels; let cool. Remove pan from heat and discard all but 2 tbsp. bacon fat. Divide avocado wedges among plates.

2. Heat reserved bacon fat over medium heat. Add garlic, ¼ cup water (carefully, because it will sputter a little), the lemon juice, and sugar and simmer 1 minute, stirring. Season with salt and pepper. Stir in parsley and crumble in bacon. Immediately pour over avocado wedges and serve.

PER SERVING 270 CAL., 83% (225 CAL.) FROM FAT; 5.2 G PROTEIN; 25 G FAT (5.7 G SAT.); 8.6 G CARBO (2.5 G FIBER); 211 MG SODIUM; 14 MG CHOL.

Bean and chicken taquitos

El Indio restaurant, in San Diego, is credited with inventing taquitos, also known in Southern California as rolled tacos. In the 1940s, when El Indio was a tortilla factory, the owner's mother adapted the flauta, a fried filled cylinder of tortilla, to create taquitos. For variety's sake, we fill some with beans and some with chicken, using mostly store-bought ingredients so they're a snap to prepare. You'll need 40 toothpicks to hold the taquitos together as they fry. (Photo on page 8.)

MAKES 40 taquitos | 1 hour

20 flour or thin, pliable corn tortillas (8-in. size),
    each cut in half
About 1½ cups canned refried black beans
About 2½ cups (10 oz.) shredded Mexican cheese blend
About 1½ cups shredded rotisserie chicken (from half
    a 3-lb. chicken)
Vegetable oil for frying
Red or green salsa (store-bought, or see page 14 for a recipe)
Guacamole (see page 13 for a recipe)

1. Lay 1 tortilla half on a work surface. Spoon about 1 tbsp. beans onto an end. Sprinkle filling with about 1 tbsp. cheese. Roll taquito into a tight cylinder, starting with the filled end, and skewer seam with a toothpick. Repeat to make 19 more bean taquitos, and then, using chicken, to make 20 chicken taquitos.

2. Heat 1 in. oil in a large wide pot over medium heat to 375° on a deep-fry thermometer. Cook 4 taquitos at a time, turning often, until golden brown, 2 minutes. Using a slotted spoon, transfer taquitos to a rimmed baking sheet lined with paper towels. When cool, remove toothpicks. Serve with salsa and guacamole on the side.

PER TAQUITO (AVERAGE OF BEAN AND CHICKEN) 144 CAL., 49% (71 CAL.) FROM FAT; 5.1 G PROTEIN; 8 G FAT (2.3 G SAT.); 13 G CARBO (1.2 G FIBER); 227 MG SODIUM; 12 MG CHOL.

Roasted baby artichokes with spring salsa

Toasted almonds, stir-fried favas, and parmesan curls add layers of richness to the artichokes in this first course from Jeremy Fox, former chef of Ubuntu restaurant in Napa.

SERVES 4 as a first course | 2¼ hours

20 baby artichokes
About ⅔ cup extra-virgin olive oil, divided
6 to 8 thyme sprigs
2 tsp. chopped rosemary
2 tbsp. finely shredded Meyer or regular lemon zest, divided
About ½ tsp. kosher salt
About 1 cup shelled fava beans (from 1 lb. whole pods)*
½ tsp. red chile flakes
1½ tsp. minced garlic
1½ tbsp. Meyer or regular lemon juice
¼ cup blanched almonds, toasted* and finely chopped
½ cup loosely packed dill fronds, chopped
¾ cup mild green olives, such as Castelvetrano, pitted and torn in half
Chunk of parmesan cheese (at least 2 oz.), at room temperature
15 to 20 miner's lettuce* or baby arugula leaves

1. Preheat oven to 300°. Snap off leaves of artichokes down to the yellow-green layer. Trim green tips of remaining leaves and tough outer layer from stems; trim stems to 1 in.

2. Pour ¼ cup oil into a small rimmed baking pan. Add artichokes, herbs, 4 tsp. lemon zest, and ½ tsp. salt; turn to coat artichokes. Cover pan with foil and roast artichokes until tender when pierced with tip of a knife, 30 to 45 minutes.

3. Uncover pan and set oven to broil. Broil artichokes, turning every minute or so, until browned all over, about 8 minutes. Transfer artichokes to a cutting board. Pour any oil from pan into a measuring cup and add enough extra oil to equal ½ cup; pour into a large cast-iron or nonstick frying pan.

4. Make salsa: Heat artichoke oil over medium-high heat. Add shelled fava beans and cook, stirring often, until favas are heated through, 3 to 4 minutes. Add chile flakes, garlic, and remaining 2 tsp. lemon zest and cook 1 minute. Transfer mixture to a bowl and gently toss with lemon juice, chopped almonds, dill, and salt to taste. Add extra oil to loosen salsa if you like.

5. Cut some artichokes in half and, along with whole artichokes, divide among 4 plates (or arrange on a platter). Spoon salsa over and around artichokes and scatter olives here and there. Using a vegetable peeler, generously shave wide curls of parmesan over each plate. Top with miner's lettuce.

*To shell favas, shuck whole pods. Blanch beans 2 minutes in boiling water, dunk in cold water, and pop out of skins by slitting with a knife or your fingernail. To toast nuts, spread them out in a baking pan and toast in a 350° oven until golden, 8 to 12 minutes. Find the mild, delicate green called miner's lettuce at farmers' markets from late winter to early spring.

PER SERVING 697 CAL., 77% (535 CAL.) FROM FAT; 20 G PROTEIN; 61 G FAT (9.4 G SAT.); 30 G CARBO (15 G FIBER); 894 MG SODIUM; 9.6 MG CHOL.

CARAMELIZED
MAUI ONION DIP

Caramelized Maui onion dip

Remember onion-soup-mix dip? This is similar, but infinitely better. In 1954, when an unknown California cook combined sour cream with onion soup mix, the recipe became so popular that Lipton soup company began to print it on its packages. We gave the dip a Hawaiian accent. Make it a couple of hours ahead of time to let flavors develop, and serve with lots of potato chips.

MAKES 2 cups | 30 minutes, plus 2 hours to chill

2 tbsp. olive oil
2 Maui onions (or other sweet onions), halved and
    thinly sliced (about 5 cups)
1 cup sour cream
½ cup buttermilk
1 tsp. kosher salt

1. Heat oil in a large nonstick frying pan over medium heat. Add onions and cook, stirring occasionally, until brown, sticky, and caramelized, about 20 minutes. If the pan starts to burn, reduce heat to medium-low and add 1 tbsp. water, stirring well. Transfer onions to a small bowl and chill until cold, about 1 hour.
2. Reserve 1 tbsp. onions. In a food processor, pulse remaining onions, sour cream, buttermilk, and salt just until combined. Transfer to a serving dish, top with reserved onions, and chill at least 1 hour.

PER 2-TBSP. SERVING 69 CAL., 62% (43 CAL.) FROM FAT; 1.5 G PROTEIN; 4.8 G FAT (2.1 G SAT.); 5.6 G CARBO (0.8 G FIBER); 94 MG SODIUM; 6.6 MG CHOL.

From the orchard: Hass avocados

Avocados are Central American natives (the name is from the Aztec word *ahuacatl*—meaning, of all things, "testicle"). Green-skinned, mild-tasting Fuerte was the main North American variety in 1926, when Rudolph Hass, postman and amateur horticulturist, bought an avocado seedling of unknown origin to plant in his grove in La Habra Heights, California, near L.A. To his surprise, the tree bore a weird, almost black, pebbly skinned fruit with unusually deep, rich flavor. Hass never made much money on his namesake discovery—he died in 1952 having earned $5,000 from it—but his tree's offspring now account for 80 percent of avocados sold commercially worldwide.

Gabriel's guacamole

At Gabriel's, in Santa Fe, the guacamole—made table-side in a Mexican *molcajete* (stone mortar)—is seasoned as diners direct. This recipe is a jumping-off point; add more garlic, jalapeño, onion, salt, lime juice, or cilantro to your taste. (We prefer extra jalapeño, onion, and lime.) Serve with tortilla chips.

MAKES 2 cups | 10 minutes

2 firm-ripe medium Hass avocados, pitted, peeled,
    and diced
¼ tsp. *each* minced garlic and jalapeño, plus more to taste
¼ cup chopped tomato
1 tsp. finely chopped onion, plus more to taste
Salt
2 tsp. *each* lime juice and finely chopped cilantro,
    plus more to taste

Coarsely mash avocados, garlic, and jalapeño in a bowl or a molcajete with a wooden spoon until avocados are creamy but still very chunky. Add tomato, onion, and salt to taste, and stir together. Sprinkle with lime juice and cilantro, then stir and taste once more. Add more seasonings if you like.

PER ¼-CUP SERVING 75 CAL., 80% (60 CAL.) FROM FAT; 1 G PROTEIN; 6.7 G FAT (0.9 G SAT.); 4.3 G CARBO (3 G FIBER); 17 MG SODIUM; 0 MG CHOL.

Hot artichoke dip

Classic, creamy artichoke dip, hot from the oven, is a party pleaser. Scoop it up with toasted baguette slices and, if you like, cooked artichoke leaves.

MAKES 3 cups; 16 to 18 servings | 1 hour

1 cup grated parmesan cheese, divided
1 package (8 oz.) cream cheese, at room temperature
1 cup sour cream or mayonnaise
1 tsp. finely chopped dill
1 can (13.75 oz.) artichoke hearts, drained, or 1 package (10 oz.)
    frozen artichoke hearts, thawed

1. Set aside 1 tbsp. parmesan. In a bowl with a mixer, beat remaining parmesan, the cream cheese, sour cream, and dill until well blended and creamy. Finely chop artichoke hearts and stir in.
2. Preheat oven to 325°. Spoon mixture into a small, shallow baking dish. Sprinkle with remaining parmesan. Bake, uncovered, until lightly browned, 30 to 45 minutes.

PER SERVING (ABOUT 2½ TBSP.) 110 CAL., 77% (85 CAL.) FROM FAT; 4.5 G PROTEIN; 9.4 G FAT (5.1 G SAT.); 2.4 G CARBO; 192 MG SODIUM; 27 MG CHOL.

Roasted poblano chipotle salsa

This smoky, tangy salsa is versatile—good as a dip for chips and for dolloping on quesadillas and tacos—and it's quick to make.

MAKES 2 cups | 20 minutes

1 white onion, peeled and quartered
1 fresh poblano chile or 2 Anaheim chiles (5 oz. total)
1 lb. fresh tomatillos, husked
3 large garlic cloves, peeled
2 or 3 canned chipotle chiles in adobo sauce, plus 1 tbsp. sauce
1/4 cup cilantro leaves
1 tbsp. lime juice
Salt

1. Put onion, fresh chile, tomatillos, and garlic on a baking sheet. Broil 4 to 5 in. from heat, turning once, until blackened, 8 to 10 minutes total. Let cool.
2. Peel, stem, and seed broiled fresh chile and cut into chunks. In a blender or food processor, purée broiled onion, chile, tomatillos, garlic, chipotle chiles with sauce, cilantro, and lime juice until coarsely puréed. Season to taste with salt.

PER 1/4-CUP SERVING 40 CAL., 16% (6.3 CAL.) FROM FAT; 1.5 G PROTEIN; 0.7 G FAT (0.1 G SAT.); 8.2 G CARBO (1.9 G FIBER); 165 MG SODIUM; 0 MG CHOL.

Classic crabcakes

These simple, delicious crabcakes, from Nicholas Petti, owner of Mendo Bistro in Fort Bragg, California, won the Mendocino Crab & Wine Days Crabcake Cook-off in both 2002 and 2003.

SERVES 8 as a first course | 45 minutes

1 lb. shelled cooked crab (about 2 3/4 cups)
1 3/4 cups *panko* (Japanese-style bread crumbs) or other fine dried bread crumbs, divided
1/2 cup finely chopped green onions
Tarragon Aioli (recipe below)
About 1/2 cup vegetable oil, divided
Champagne Cabbage Salad (recipe below)

1. Combine crab, 3/4 cup panko, and the onions in a bowl. Gently mix in 1/2 cup aioli.
2. Press mixture firmly into 8 patties about 3 in. wide; set, separated, on waxed paper or foil. Pour remaining 1 cup panko into a shallow bowl.
3. Preheat oven to 200°. Pour 1/3 cup oil into a large frying pan over medium-high heat. When hot, set each crabcake in panko; using a slotted spatula, turn, pressing gently to coat. Cook in small batches, adding more oil as needed, until golden brown on bottom, 3 to 4 minutes; turn gently and cook until browned on other side, 3 to 4 minutes longer. Transfer to a baking sheet and keep warm in oven. Serve with aioli and salad.

PER CRABCAKE 138 CAL., 31% (43 CAL.) FROM FAT; 13 G PROTEIN; 4.8 G FAT (0.6 G SAT.); 9.2 G CARBO (0.6 G FIBER); 197 MG SODIUM; 57 MG CHOL.

Tarragon aioli Blend 2 **egg yolks***, 3 peeled **garlic cloves,** 1/3 cup **lemon juice,** and 1/2 tsp. **salt** in a blender until smooth. With machine running, gradually pour in 1 cup **vegetable oil** and 1/2 cup **extra-virgin olive oil** in a slow stream until smooth, 1 to 1 1/2 minutes. Stir in 1/4 cup chopped **tarragon,** 1/4 to 1/2 tsp. **hot sauce,** and more lemon juice and salt to taste. *****If you're concerned about raw eggs or are short on time, use this shortcut: Combine 1 1/2 cups **mayonnaise,** 1/4 cup chopped **tarragon,** 1 1/2 to 2 tbsp. minced **garlic,** and 2 tbsp. **lemon juice;** mix with **hot sauce** and **salt** to taste.

PER TBSP. 117 CAL., 100% (117 CAL.) FROM FAT; 0.3 G PROTEIN; 13 G FAT (1.8 G SAT.); 0.4 G CARBO (0 G FIBER); 47 MG SODIUM; 16 MG CHOL.

Champagne cabbage salad Mix 3 qts. shredded **cabbage** (about 1 1/4 lbs.) with 1 1/2 tsp. **salt;** let stand 30 minutes. Mix with 1/3 cup chopped **chives** and 1/4 cup **Champagne vinegar.**

PER 3/4-CUP SERVING 19 CAL., 5% (0.9 CAL.) FROM FAT; 0.9 G PROTEIN; 0.1 G FAT (0 G SAT.); 4.1 G CARBO (1.8 G FIBER); 449 MG SODIUM; 0 MG CHOL.

CLASSIC CRABCAKES

Barbecued oysters with chipotle glaze

Grilled oysters get a tequila-laced chile glaze in a recipe from Dory Ford, former chef at the Monterey Bay Aquarium's restaurant and now at Point Pinos Grill in Pacific Grove, California. Seafood Watch (*montereybayaquarium.org/cr/ seafoodwatch.aspx*), the aquarium's guide to sustainable seafood, recommends farmed oysters.

SERVES 8 as an appetizer | 30 minutes, plus 30 minutes to marinate

2 tbsp. plus 2 tsp. lime juice
2 tbsp. olive oil
1 tbsp. tequila
1 tsp. minced cilantro
1 tsp. coarse sea salt or kosher salt, divided
1/4 tsp. pepper
2 dozen oysters on the half-shell, with their juices*
1/4 cup unsalted butter, softened
2 tbsp. mayonnaise
1 canned chipotle chile in adobo sauce, minced,
    plus 1 1/2 tsp. sauce
1 tsp. minced lime zest
At least 2 cups rock salt for lining platter
Canola-oil cooking spray

1. Whisk 2 tbsp. lime juice with oil, tequila, cilantro, 1/2 tsp. sea salt, and the pepper in a medium bowl. Add oysters and their juices, reserving bottom shells. Marinate oysters 30 to 45 minutes in refrigerator; drain, reserving about 1 1/2 cups marinade.

2. Meanwhile, soak shells in water for 30 minutes. Drain on a kitchen towel and pat dry.

3. Prepare a charcoal or gas grill for very high direct heat (see "How-to: Grilling," page 83).

4. In a small heatproof bowl, whisk together butter, mayonnaise, chile and sauce, lime zest, remaining 2 tsp. lime juice, and remaining 1/2 tsp. sea salt. Set glaze aside.

5. Spread rock salt on a platter large enough to hold oysters in a single layer. Arrange oyster shells on a large baking pan and spray insides lightly with cooking spray.

6. Set half the shells on cooking grate (balance on bars so they won't roll over). Heat shells 30 seconds. Spoon 1 oyster into each shell with 1 tbsp. reserved marinade and cook (close lid on gas grill) until juices are bubbling, 2 to 3 minutes. Drizzle 1 tsp. glaze onto each oyster and cook 30 seconds more. (If the glaze stiffens, set it on the hot cooking grate for a minute.) Using tongs, transfer oysters to platter, keeping them level so juices don't spill, and nestle them in the salt. Grill remaining oysters the same way.
*Have your fishmonger shuck the oysters; ask that the juices stay in the shells to keep oysters moist. Keep them cold and as level as possible in transport to avoid losing the liquid, and use the oysters as soon as you can.

PER 3-OYSTER SERVING 146 CAL., 86% (126 CAL.) FROM FAT; 3.3 G PROTEIN; 14 G FAT (4.7 G SAT.); 2.9 G CARBO (0.2 G FIBER); 320 MG SODIUM; 41 MG CHOL.

From the Pacific: Oysters

Though the oysters at raw bars and in fish markets bear a wide variety of intriguing names (Hama Hama, Yaquina, Naked Roy's Beach), every oyster raised in North America is one of only five species. And chances are, the species you're enjoying is a Pacific, as most of the oysters cultivated on the West Coast are Pacifics. The names oysters are called, though, are usually geographical—that's because nutrients and minerals from the waters washing over them give the bivalves their distinctive flavors. A Hama Hama Pacific, from Washington, will taste different from a Pacific raised in Oregon's Yaquina Bay. (Oysters not named after a place are given a trade name by the grower.)

PACIFIC A native of Japan that has been grown along the West Coast since 1919, the Pacific often has a flavor described as cucumber-like.

KUMAMOTO Also originally a Japanese import; tastes sweet and buttery.

OLYMPIA A tiny oyster with a metallic tang, it's the only species native to the West Coast. Slow-growing, so less attractive to oyster farmers and thus found less in markets and on menus.

EUROPEAN FLAT (OR BELON) The European flat has a pleasantly metallic flavor; West Coast growers cultivate fewer of these than other varieties.

Anchovy fries with smoked paprika mayo

Fresh anchovies are mild, sweet, and totally different from canned ones—and they're addictive when fried. Small fish are increasingly the best choice when it comes to eating fish. They're plentiful, flavorful, and they don't tend to accumulate toxins in their bodies the way larger fish can. And the oilier ones—like anchovies—have lots of good-for-you omega-3s. Little fish are a good source of calcium, since you eat them bones and all. (The bones are too small to notice, and the heads taste mild.)

SERVES 8 to 10 | 1¼ hours

3/4 cup olive-oil mayonnaise
2 tbsp. lemon juice
1 garlic clove, minced
1½ tsp. *each* Hungarian hot paprika and Spanish sweet
    smoked paprika
1 lb. whole anchovies, smelt, or sardines*
Vegetable oil for frying
½ cup flour
1 tsp. kosher salt, divided
1¾ cups *panko* (Japanese-style bread crumbs)

3 large eggs
Lemon wedges

1. Stir mayonnaise, lemon juice, garlic, and paprikas together in a bowl. Chill paprika mayo until serving.
2. Clean fish*, if your fishmonger didn't. (If using sardines, discard heads and tails and cut bodies into 2-in. pieces.)
3. Preheat oven to 200°. Line a rimmed baking sheet with paper towels and keep warm in oven. Fill a large pot with 1 in. oil, insert a deep-fry thermometer, and bring oil to 375° over medium-high heat.
4. Combine flour and ½ tsp. salt in a pie pan, and panko and remaining ½ tsp. salt in another pie pan. In a shallow bowl, whisk eggs to blend. Dip fish in flour, shaking off excess, then in egg, then in panko, turning to coat; set on another baking sheet.
5. Fry one-quarter of fish at a time until golden, 1 to 1½ minutes. Transfer to baking sheet in oven. Serve with paprika mayo and lemon. (If using sardines, cut cooked meat from bones.)
*Find at some grocery stores, fish markets (you might need to order them), and Asian markets. Look for fish with bright eyes, shiny skin, and a mild aroma. They're very perishable, so cook them the same day. To clean, scrape off scales gently with fingertips. Cut through both sides of belly ¼ in. from edge, from collar to tail. Pull out the guts; rinse fish. Snip off fins.

PER SERVING 224 CAL., 59% (133 CAL.) FROM FAT; 11 G PROTEIN; 15 G FAT (2.5 G SAT.); 11 G CARBO (0.5 G FIBER); 239 MG SODIUM; 78 MG CHOL.

Sesame ahi *poke*

Poke, the much-loved Hawaiian raw-fish salad, has many variations; this is a relatively simple one. Use the highest-quality fish you can get your hands on—that's often found at Japanese markets. Serve with taro chips.

SERVES 4 | 25 minutes

1½ lbs. sashimi-grade ahi tuna steaks, cut into ½-in. dice*
1 tbsp. *each* minced fresh ginger and Asian (toasted) sesame oil
1/3 cup sliced green onions
3 tbsp. low-sodium soy sauce
2 tsp. sesame seeds, toasted*

Combine all ingredients in a medium bowl. Serve immediately.
*Ahi is not prone to parasites, so can safely be eaten raw without special handling. Still, seek out sashimi grade for the best quality. To toast sesame seeds, heat them in a dry pan over medium heat until golden, stirring occasionally.

PER ½-CUP SERVING 58 CAL., 22% (13 CAL.) FROM FAT; 10 G PROTEIN; 1.4 G FAT (0.3 G SAT.); 0.5 G CARBO (0.1 G FIBER); 118 MG SODIUM; 19 MG CHOL.

SESAME AHI POKE

PEACH COLLINS
recipe on page 25

Drinks

From the fruit-rich morning smoothie to the cocktail that gives a party its sparkle, an inspired Western drink takes on every occasion. In this chapter, we're muddling all manner of herbs, fruits, and vegetables with liquor; and relatively new drinks (like Asian bubble teas) join longtime favorites (like the SoCal date shake and the classic mai tai).

Green gin

Herbs and celery underscore gin's juniper aroma in a refreshing combo. To extract vivid color from the herbs, don't hold back when muddling them.

SERVES 2 | 5 minutes

¼ cup *each* parsley and mint leaves
⅓ cup gin
2 tbsp. Simple Syrup made with celery (recipe below)
1 cup club soda
Celery sticks and mint sprigs

Using a wooden spoon or muddler, vigorously bruise parsley and mint leaves with gin in a cocktail shaker. Add celery simple syrup. Strain into two small ice-filled glasses. Stir half the club soda into each. Garnish with celery and mint sprigs.

PER SERVING 135 CAL., 0.2% (0.3 CAL.) FROM FAT; 0.2 G PROTEIN; 0 G FAT; 9.8 G CARBO (0.3 G FIBER); 28 MG SODIUM; 0 MG CHOL.

Simple syrup Stir together ¾ cup *each* sugar and water in a small saucepan. Add flavoring (below) if you like. Bring to a gentle simmer over medium heat. When bubbles first appear, reduce heat to medium-low and simmer 5 minutes. Cool, then strain. Makes about 1 cup.
Celery Add 2 celery stalks, coarsely chopped.
Make ahead 1 week, chilled.

Lime-chile beer

The British shandy, a traditional mixture of beer and lemonade, travels West.

SERVES 2 | 10 minutes

⅓ cup lime juice, plus 2 lime wedges
2½ tsp. sugar
1 (12-oz.) bottle light-bodied wheat beer, such as
    New Belgium's Sunshine Wheat
¼ tsp. *each* coarse kosher salt and chili powder

1. In a glass measuring cup, stir lime juice, sugar, and ⅓ cup water together until sugar dissolves. Fill two beer mugs with ice and pour half the beer into each. Top with lime mixture.
2. Sprinkle one side of each lime wedge with salt and the other with chili powder. Serve with beer.

PER SERVING 108 CAL., 1% (0.9 CAL.) FROM FAT; 0.8 G PROTEIN; 0.1 G FAT (0 G SAT.); 16 G CARBO (1 G FIBER); 253 MG SODIUM; 0 MG CHOL.

Pineapple cosmo

Give the cosmo a Hawaiian spin with pineapple vodka.

SERVES 1 | 2 minutes

3 tbsp. Fresh Pineapple Vodka (recipe below)
1 tbsp. triple sec
Juice from ½ lime
1 tbsp. cranberry juice
Lime twist and/or pineapple slice

Pour all the ingredients (except garnish) into a cocktail shaker filled with ice. Shake well, then strain into a martini glass. Garnish with a lime twist, a pineapple slice, or both.

PER SERVING 96 CAL., 0% FROM FAT; 0.2 G PROTEIN; 0 G FAT; 9.6 G CARBO (0.1 G FIBER); 0.9 MG SODIUM; 0 MG CHOL.

Fresh pineapple vodka

Homemade infused vodka bests the commercially bottled brands.

MAKES 1½ cups | 5 minutes, plus 5 days to chill

1 lb. pineapple slices
1½ cups vodka

Put pineapple slices in a 1-qt. jar. Pour in vodka, cover, and chill at least 5 days and up to 3 weeks.

PER 3-TBSP. SERVING 32 CAL., 0% FROM FAT; 0 G PROTEIN; 0 G FAT; 0.3 G CARBO (0 G FIBER); 0.2 MG SODIUM; 0 MG CHOL.

From the brewery: Beer

Especially in the West, small brewers began in the mid-1960s to challenge the bland beer that had earned the United States a reputation for insipid brew but dynamite beer commercials. Fritz Maytag bought San Francisco's Anchor Brewing Company in 1965 with an agenda of preserving old beermaking traditions. A decade after that, New Albion Brewery was founded in Sonoma, California; it closed seven years later, but not before inspiring a spate of homebrewers to follow suit—in effect launching a movement of full-flavored artisan beers. Today, when it comes to the number of breweries per capita, three of the top five states are in the West: Colorado, Oregon, and Montana.

FRESH PINEAPPLE VODKA

PINEAPPLE COSMO

From the vineyard: Wine

For most of the world, **NAPA VALLEY** is shorthand for all California wines, in the same way that Hollywood means American movies. And in Napa, Cabernet Sauvignon is king. The heart of the valley, around Rutherford, produces some of the most sought-after, wonderful Cabs in the world. The seeds of the valley's current golden age were planted in 1864, when General George Yount presented his granddaughter and her soon-to-be husband, Thomas Rutherford, with about 1,000 acres of land. The vineyards that Rutherford cultivated became the estates of Inglenook and Beaulieu Vineyard (known as BV).

SONOMA COUNTY'S wine history reaches even further back. The first vineyard was planted at Mission San Francisco de Solano in 1824 (and was where Yount later got the vines he planted in Napa). Sonoma is now home to about half as many wine producers as Napa Valley, though at more than 1,500 square miles (as opposed to Napa's 788), it's as big as Rhode Island. Its geography is wildly varied: Breezes off San Pablo Bay cool the southern Carneros region, while warmer-weather grapes thrive in Sonoma Valley proper. In toasty Alexander Valley, gentle Cabs and Merlots reign. To the west, the Petaluma Gap allows cool air inland, making the Russian River Valley a home for Pinot Noir and Chardonnay; follow the Russian River north into Dry Creek Valley, and Cab and Zin rule.

Possibly the most newsworthy wineries in **MENDOCINO COUNTY** are in remote Anderson Valley. Where the Navarro River breaks through, ocean fog rolls in, establishing the valley as Pinot Noir and cool-weather white (Riesling, Gewürztraminer, Pinot Gris) territory. Among the oak-studded hills of **LAKE COUNTY,** a landscape dominated by an extinct volcano, Mt. Konocti, nuanced microclimates and soils produce notable Sauvignon Blancs and Tempranillos. The Zins of the **SIERRA FOOTHILLS** are almost pruny ripe and earthy, with high alcohol—but the best are spectacular, balanced wines. Though many of **SANTA CRUZ MOUNTAINS'** wineries lie just 15 miles from Silicon Valley, the wines—led by Chardonnay and Pinot

Noir—are full of the complexities induced by stony soils, mountain elevations, and fog-driven hang time. Most of the best wine in **MONTEREY COUNTY** (most of the worst too) comes from the Salinas Valley east of the Santa Lucia Range, where the wind pulls in ocean chill from Monterey Bay. Cool-weather lovers like Pinot Noir and Chardonnay grow in the north valley and grapes with warmer-weather needs in the south.

A few decades ago, **SAN LUIS OBISPO COUNTY'S** Paso Robles AVA was cattle country. Now, large producers make Cabs in the hot, dry land east of the Salinas River, blocked from ocean air by the Santa Lucia Range. The range's Templeton Gap lets maritime breezes funnel into the west side of the AVA, where small producers craft fine Syrahs and other Rhône varieties. Mountain ranges surround three sides of **SANTA BARBARA COUNTY,** while the west side fronts the Pacific. Santa Maria, the Santa Rita Hills, and Santa Ynez are the beneficiaries of the marine influence—the first two areas focusing on Pinot Noir and Chard, the last on Cabernet Sauvignon and other Bordeaux varieties. Riverside County's **TEMECULA VALLEY** may be far south, but it's just 25 miles from the Pacific, at an elevation of 1,500 feet. Days are warm and nights cool, allowing it to support disparate varieties such as Gewürztraminer and Merlot.

Although Oregon's **WILLAMETTE VALLEY** produces Pinot Gris and other varietals, Pinot Noir is the star. Famously damp and gray, the valley supplies barely enough light and heat to ripen grapes. In a bad year, that results in underripe, thin wines; in good years, those conditions nurture concentrated, complex Pinots. Most Washington grapes grow east of the Cascades, where summer nighttime temps drop after scorching days, keeping grapes' acid levels high. Vineyards get about an hour more sun a day than in Napa Valley, allowing grapes to develop intense flavors. Appellations such as **YAKIMA VALLEY** and **WALLA WALLA VALLEY** as well as subregions like Horse Heaven Hills produce superbly structured Cabernets, Syrahs, and Rieslings.

Sunset margaritas

A drizzle of pomegranate juice down the side of the glass makes a margarita (which had its origin in 1930s Mexico) look at least faintly like a sky at sunset. We created this for *Sunset's* Celebration Weekend, our annual open house in June.

SERVES 2 | 5 minutes

⅓ cup *each* **tequila and triple sec**
3 tbsp. orange juice
2 tbsp. lime juice
4 tbsp. pomegranate juice
2 twists lime

1. Put 1 cup ice cubes in a pitcher. Pour in tequila, triple sec, orange juice, and lime juice. Stir well; divide between glasses.
2. Using a spouted pourer or a large spoon, carefully pour 2 tbsp. pomegranate juice down the side of each glass. Garnish with slightly crushed lime twists.

PER SERVING 225 CAL., 0% (1.4 CAL.) FROM FAT; 0.3 G PROTEIN; 0.2 G FAT (0 G SAT.); 20 G CARBO (0.2 G FIBER); 3.8 MG SODIUM; 0 MG CHOL.

Peach Collins

The culinary cocktail is a delicious way to get your vitamins. In this play on the pre-Prohibition classic Tom Collins, we muddle ripe peaches and shake them up with peach-flavored vodka. (Photo on page 20.)

SERVES 2 | 10 minutes

¼ cup *each* **Simple Syrup* and lemon juice**
½ cup chopped ripe peaches, divided
½ cup peach-flavored vodka
½ cup club soda
2 peach slices

1. Mix simple syrup, lemon juice, ¼ cup chopped peaches, and about ½ cup ice in a cocktail shaker or plastic cup. Using the end of a wooden spoon, muddle (mash) mixture until peaches start to break up. Pour in vodka, cover shaker with top (or the cup with plastic wrap), and shake until blended.
2. Divide unstrained mixture between two glasses. Add half the remaining chopped peaches to each; fill glasses with ice. Top each glass with ¼ cup club soda and garnish with a peach slice.
*Find simple syrup next to the cocktail mixes at a well-stocked beverage store, or see recipe on page 22 (make an unflavored version).

PER SERVING 266 CAL., 0% (0.9 CAL.) FROM FAT; 0.5 G PROTEIN; 0.1 G FAT (0 G SAT.); 32 G CARBO (0.7 G FIBER); 13 MG SODIUM; 0 MG CHOL.

CLASSIC TIKI MAI TAI

Classic tiki mai tai

The mai tai is a creation of the West, invented in the 1940s in Oakland by Victor Bergeron of Trader Vic's fame. It features rum, lime juice, and orange liqueur, with a bit of orgeat (almond-flavored syrup). Go as fanciful as you like with the garnishes.

SERVES 1 | 5 minutes

2 tbsp. *each* **white (light) rum and gold rum**
1 tbsp. *each* **orange curaçao, orgeat*, rock candy syrup*, and lime juice**
2 tbsp. dark rum

1. Pour white and gold rums, curaçao, orgeat, rock candy syrup, and lime juice into a cocktail shaker. Fill with ice cubes, cover, and shake vigorously.
2. Strain into an ice-filled 8- to 12-oz. glass. Slowly pour dark rum onto top of drink.
*Rock candy syrup is simple syrup with a hint of vanilla; look for it and orgeat where cordial syrups are sold.

PER SERVING 320 CAL., 0% FROM FAT; 0 G PROTEIN; 0 G FAT; 27 G CARBO (0 G FIBER); 15 MG SODIUM; 0 MG CHOL.

WATERMELON
SIDECAR

Fresh Bloody Mary

A Bloody Mary can be deeply tomatoey, especially if you use summer-ripe heirloom tomatoes. Look for varieties like Kellogg's Breakfast, which is OJ-yellow and has lots of juice and a bright, tart flavor. Ripe red tomatoes work beautifully too.

MAKES 1 generous or 2 smaller servings | 10 minutes

½ lb. ripe tomatoes
¼ cup gin or vodka
1 tbsp. lemon juice
¼ tsp. Worcestershire
About ¼ tsp. salt
1 pinch to ⅛ tsp. celery seeds
Hot sauce
Leafy celery sticks and green onions, trimmed
Pepper

1. Cut tomatoes in half crosswise. Press tomatoes, cut side down, through a colander or a coarse-mesh strainer set over a bowl to collect juice (you'll need about ¾ cup); discard skins.
2. Mix the ¾ cup tomato juice, gin, lemon juice, and Worcestershire with salt, celery seeds, and hot sauce to taste. Pour into an ice-filled glass or two. Garnish with celery, onions, and pepper.

PER GENEROUS SERVING 182 CAL., 2% (4.5 CAL.) FROM FAT; 2.1 G PROTEIN; 0.5 G FAT (0.1 G SAT.); 13 G CARBO (3.8 G FIBER); 665 MG SODIUM; 0 MG CHOL.

Watermelon sidecar

The sunshine and heat of Arizona and inland California produce extra-sweet melons. Our version of the classic sidecar transforms watermelon into a colorful summer drink.

SERVES 1 | 7 minutes

1½ cups peeled watermelon cubes, plus watermelon wedge
    for garnish
1 tbsp. sugar
Lemon wedge, plus 1 tbsp. lemon juice
2 tbsp. brandy
2 tbsp. Cointreau or other orange-flavored liqueur

1. Blend watermelon flesh in a food processor until puréed; strain. Put sugar on a plate. Rub the rim of a martini glass with lemon wedge, then dip rim in sugar.
2. Pour brandy, lemon juice, Cointreau, and 3 tbsp. melon juice into a cocktail shaker filled with ice. Shake thoroughly, then strain into glass. Garnish with melon wedge.

PER SERVING 226 CAL., 0% FROM FAT; 0.7 G PROTEIN; 0.2 G FAT (0 G SAT.); 29 G CARBO (1.7 G FIBER); 1.8 MG SODIUM; 0 MG CHOL.

Melon-berry *aguas frescas*

Sweet-tart *aguas frescas*, served all over Mexico, cool off a summer day. Use a very ripe melon—and add the sugar gradually so you don't oversweeten.

SERVES 4 | 20 minutes

2 cups peeled, seeded honeydew melon chunks*
1 cup sliced strawberries
1 cup raspberries
About ⅓ cup *each* sugar and lime juice

1. Combine melon, berries, and 2 cups cold water in a blender. Blend until puréed. Add sugar and lime juice to taste.
2. Pour mixture through a fine-mesh strainer into a serving pitcher. Serve cold or over ice.
***Or substitute seeded cantaloupe or watermelon chunks.

PER SERVING 124 CAL., 2.9% (3.6 CAL.) FROM FAT; 0.9 G PROTEIN; 0.4 G FAT (0 G SAT.); 32 G CARBO (0 G FIBER); 12 MG SODIUM; 0 MG CHOL.

PERSIMMON
SMOOTHIE

Persimmon smoothies

Hachiya persimmons bring a subtle cinnamony flavor to these smoothies. The Hachiya is an elongated acorn-shaped persimmon that's eaten when jelly-soft. Fuyu, in contrast, is a squat, tomato-shaped variety eaten when firm. Occasionally, at farmers' markets, you'll see the rarer types: Hyakume (cinnamon persimmon), a crisp fruit with flesh flecked with brown; the varieties referred to as chocolate, which have dark flesh and a slight chocolate flavor; and the deep reddish orange Giant Fuyu.

SERVES 2 | 5 minutes

2 Hachiya persimmons, chilled
¾ cup plain low-fat yogurt
½ cup milk
¾ cup orange juice

Cut tops off persimmons and scoop out pulp (you should get about 1 cup). Purée persimmon pulp in a blender with yogurt, milk, orange juice, and 1 cup ice cubes until smooth.

PER SERVING 253 CAL., 14% (36 CAL.) FROM FAT; 8.5 G PROTEIN; 4 G FAT (2.1 G SAT.); 50 G CARBO (6.2 G FIBER); 91 MG SODIUM; 12 MG CHOL.

Citrus smoothies

Fruit smoothies probably arrived in California with Latin American immigrants, and then provided inspiration for the frothy, creamy Orange Julius, which made its debut in Los Angeles in 1929. Our citrus smoothies are rich with Greek yogurt and banana, and tangy with tangerine and Meyer lemon.

SERVES 2 | 10 minutes

1 frozen banana
1½ to 2 tbsp. Meyer lemon juice
½ cup tangerine juice
1 to 2 tbsp. honey
½ cup low-fat Greek yogurt
½ to ⅔ cup ice cubes
Tangerine slices, from 1 peeled tangerine

Blend banana in a blender with lemon juice, tangerine juice, honey, yogurt, and ice cubes. Blend in a little more lemon juice or honey to taste. Divide between glasses. Float tangerine slices in each smoothie.

PER SERVING 192 CAL., 7% (14 CAL.) FROM FAT; 6 G PROTEIN; 1.6 G FAT (0.9 G SAT.); 42 G CARBO (2.4 G FIBER); 21 MG SODIUM; 3.8 MG CHOL.

California date shake

One of the great foods of the Golden State, the date shake is exactly what you want to be slurping while visiting baking-hot date country near Palm Springs. Our favorite shake is the one at Shields Date Gardens, in Indio. Shields uses date "crystals"—dehydrated Deglet Noor and Blonde dates. Order them online (*shieldsdategarden.com*), or substitute fresh, as we've done here.

MAKES 1 shake (1⅓ cups) | 10 minutes

4 pitted Medjool dates (about 3 oz.), coarsely chopped
¼ cup very cold milk
1¼ cups high-quality vanilla ice cream

Blend dates in a blender with milk until smooth and super-frothy. Add ice cream and pulse a few times, until just blended.

PER SERVING 614 CAL., 30% (182 CAL.) FROM FAT; 9.2 G PROTEIN; 20 G FAT (12 G SAT.); 105 G CARBO (6.8 G FIBER); 157 MG SODIUM; 79 MG CHOL.

From the desert: Dates

Spanish missionaries brought dates to California in the 1700s, but the U.S. date industry really began about a century ago, in the ferocious heat of the Coachella Valley and in southwestern Arizona.

Dates grow there in huge clusters dangling below the canopy of each date palm, and nurturing them involves shrouding the clusters in bags to protect them from rain, dust, birds, and insects. If the tree is tall, its fruit is picked by a worker balanced on a mobile steel tower. Most dates are harvested fully ripe and sold dried (the tamar stage), but some Arizona and Southern California farmers' markets and Middle Eastern markets sell them at the yellow, firm, faintly astringent khalal stage, and the caramelly ripe, but not fully dried, rutab stage (order at *oasisdate.com*).

BARHI This variety is small, plump, and soft (especially at rutab stage), with tastes of caramel and honey.

DAYRI (OR DHERRI) Slender, dark; rich molasses flavor.

KHALASA Small, soft; cinnamon and clove notes.

MEDJOOL Largest of the dates, with finely wrinkled, delicate skin and chewy-tender, dense flesh.

Rhubarb-rose bubble tea

Bubble tea, a drink partly filled with plump, chewy "bubbles" made from tapioca starch, originated in Taiwan in the 1980s and quickly spread around the globe. The drink found a thirsty audience in many parts of the West—especially the Asian-style cafes of California, where its makers came up with all kinds of flavor combinations. Ours is a bit less sweet than the cafe standard and uses fresh ingredients rather than powders. Buy extra-wide straws, so the bubbles can shoot up into your mouth.

SERVES 2 | 30 minutes

1½ cups sliced rhubarb
½ cup sugar
½ cup green tea–flavored or black tapioca pearls*
½ cup cool double-strength jasmine tea
½ to 1 tbsp. rose water or orange-blossom water,
    such as Monteux*

1. Mix rhubarb and sugar with 1 tbsp. water in a small saucepan. Cook, covered, over medium heat, stirring occasionally, until rhubarb is very soft, about 10 minutes. Purée in a blender and leave there to cool slightly.
2. Meanwhile, in a medium saucepan, cook the tapioca pearls in about 4 cups boiling water according to package directions until soft but still chewy, about 6 minutes. Drain, rinse, and drain again. Divide between two large glasses (14 oz. each).
3. Add 2 cups ice cubes, the tea, and rose water to the rhubarb mixture in blender; purée. Pour into glasses and add a fat straw* to each.
*Look for tapioca pearls and wide straws at Asian markets and well-stocked grocery stores. Find rose or orange-blossom water at specialty-foods stores.

PER SERVING 350 CAL., 1% (1.7 CAL.) FROM FAT; 0.9 G PROTEIN; 0.2 G FAT (0.1 G SAT.); 88 G CARBO (2 G FIBER); 4.2 MG SODIUM; 0 MG CHOL.

Mango-coconut bubble tea

This is a bubble-tea twist on mango *lassi*, a traditional Indian drink made with mango and yogurt. If you can't find a good fresh mango, use canned mango pulp (Alphonse mango pulp, available at Indian markets, is the best). If your fresh mango is very fibrous, purée it first, then strain and purée again with the ice cubes, tea, coconut milk, and sugar.

SERVES 2 | 15 minutes

½ cup black tapioca pearls*
3 cups diced peeled fresh mango
½ cup cool double-strength black tea
¼ cup canned coconut milk
4 tbsp. sugar

1. Cook tapioca pearls in a small pan with about 4 cups boiling water according to package directions until soft but still chewy, about 6 minutes. Drain, rinse, and drain again. Divide between two large glasses (16 oz. each).
2. Chop 1 cup ice cubes in a blender; purée ice with half of each of the remaining ingredients. Pour into one of the glasses with pearls. Repeat for second drink. Add a fat straw to each drink.
*Find tapioca pearls and wide straws at Asian markets and well-stocked grocery stores.

PER SERVING 463 CAL., 15% (70 CAL.) FROM FAT; 2 G PROTEIN; 7.8 G FAT (6.5 G SAT.); 103 G CARBO (5.5 G FIBER); 9.8 MG SODIUM; 0 MG CHOL.

Keoke coffee

A simple, warming coffee drink is an ideal end to a big meal (a little chocolate on the side can complete the sweet finish). Keoke coffee was invented by George Bullington at his restaurant, Bully's, in La Jolla, California, in the late 1960s. His staff dubbed it "George's coffee" until one of the cooks, a Hawaiian, came up with the name that stuck: *Keoke* is Hawaiian for "George."

SERVES 2 | 5 minutes

4 tbsp. *each* brandy, Kahlúa, and crème de cacao
3 cups freshly brewed hot coffee
4 tbsp. whipped cream (optional)

Divide brandy, Kahlúa, and crème de cacao between two mugs. Add half the coffee to each. Top with whipped cream if you like.

PER SERVING 245 CAL., 0% FROM FAT; 0.4 G PROTEIN; 0 G FAT; 19 G CARBO (0 G FIBER); 7.1 MG SODIUM; 0 MG CHOL.

KEOKE COFFEE

RUBY GRAPEFRUIT, AVOCADO, AND SPINACH SALAD *recipe on page 50*

Salads

In California, the nation's Salad Bowl, leafy greens are just the jumping-off point for salads. They're topped with goat cheese, crowned with crabmeat, strewn with fruit. In the Northwest, berries and hazelnuts are in the mix, while the Southwest adds roasted chiles and avocados.

Hazelnut herb salad

Tarragon, chives, and parsley temper the richness of the hazelnuts in this salad from Maria Hines, chef and owner of Tilth and the Golden Beetle, both in Seattle.

SERVES 10 to 12 | 35 minutes

1 cup hazelnuts, toasted
About ¾ tsp. salt, divided
1 bunch chives
Leaves from 5 tarragon sprigs
Leaves from 3 flat-leaf parsley sprigs
¼ cup *each* roasted hazelnut oil and extra-virgin
   olive oil
1 large egg yolk
¼ tsp. dry mustard
1 tbsp. lemon juice
About ¼ tsp. pepper
3 heads butter lettuce, such as Bibb

1. Roughly chop hazelnuts and set aside.
2. Fill a medium saucepan with water and bring to a boil. Add ½ tsp. salt, the chives, tarragon, and parsley. Cook 30 seconds; drain. Rinse herbs with very cold water and use your hands to squeeze out as much water from them as possible. Chop herbs and put in a blender.
3. Add both oils to blender and purée until mixture is smooth, 2 to 3 minutes.
4. In a small bowl, whisk together egg yolk and mustard. Add a drop of the herb-oil mixture and whisk until fully incorporated. Repeat with the remaining herb-oil mixture, adding only ½ tsp. at a time, to create a thick, mayonnaise-like dressing. Whisk in remaining ¼ tsp. salt, the lemon juice, and pepper. Add more salt and pepper to taste if you like.
5. Tear lettuce leaves into bite-size pieces and put in a large bowl. Toss gently but thoroughly with dressing. Garnish with reserved hazelnuts.
Make ahead Dressing, up to 2 days, chilled; hazelnuts, up to 2 days, airtight at room temperature.

PER SERVING 152 CAL., 95% (144 CAL.) FROM FAT; 2.1 G PROTEIN; 16 G FAT (1.5 G SAT.); 2.6 G CARBO (1.2 G FIBER); 197 MG SODIUM; 18 MG CHOL.

Chez Panisse's baked goat cheese with spring lettuce salad

This salad was on the cafe menu at Chez Panisse, in Berkeley, for more than 25 years. Owner Alice Waters met pioneering cheesemaker Laura Chenel in 1981, just as Chenel, based in Sonoma County, was figuring out how to market her fresh goat cheeses. Waters snapped them up. The French-style salad, with its beautiful greens and savory marinated disks of warm cheese, was a fresh idea that became a classic—another of the ground-breaking contributions that Waters has made to the way we think about food, flavor, and farming today.

SERVES 4 | 30 minutes, plus 12 hours to marinate

¾ lb. fresh mild goat cheese
Leaves from 4 thyme sprigs, chopped
Leaves from 1 small rosemary sprig, chopped
1½ cups extra-virgin olive oil
1 cup *panko* (Japanese-style bread crumbs)
½ baguette, cut into eight ¼-in.-thick slices
1 tsp. sherry vinegar
½ tsp. kosher or sea salt
¼ tsp. pepper
2½ tbsp. roasted walnut or extra-virgin olive oil
½ lb. baby lettuces or salad mix
½ cup walnuts, toasted and coarsely chopped

1. Cut goat cheese into eight 1-in.-thick disks and put in a container just big enough to hold them in a single layer. Sprinkle cheese with thyme and rosemary and pour olive oil on top. Cover and chill at least 12 hours. One hour before baking, pop them in the freezer to firm up.
2. Preheat oven to 400°. Remove cheese from marinade and roll all sides in panko, pressing gently so crumbs adhere. Put on a large baking sheet and bake until golden, about 15 minutes, turning over halfway through. Add baguette slices for last 5 minutes of baking.
3. Whisk together vinegar, salt, pepper, and walnut oil. Put lettuces in a large bowl, drizzle with just enough dressing to coat, and toss gently and thoroughly.
4. Divide lettuces among salad plates, sprinkle with walnuts, and to each plate add two goat cheese disks and a baguette slice or two. Serve immediately.
Make ahead Goat cheese can marinate for up to 1 week, chilled.

PER SERVING 703 CAL., 65% (459 CAL.) FROM FAT; 25 G PROTEIN; 51 G FAT (16 G SAT.); 38 G CARBO (3 G FIBER); 804 MG SODIUM; 39 MG CHOL.

CHEZ PANISSE'S
BAKED GOAT CHEESE
WITH SPRING LETTUCE
SALAD

BLOOMING SALAD

Classic Cobb salad

Late one night in 1937, a hungry Bob Cobb, manager of Hollywood's Brown Derby, wandered into the restaurant's kitchen. Scrounging from the refrigerator—or so the story goes—he created what would become the Derby's signature salad. Theater promotor Sid Grauman, who was with him that night, liked the greens topped with chopped chicken, roquefort cheese, and bacon and soon began requesting it. The Cobb was added to the menu and became a huge hit with customers. The original restaurant (a conspicuous Bunyan-size domed hat) is now closed, but the salad lives on at restaurants across the country.

SERVES 4 to 6 as a main course | 1½ hours

1 lb. sliced bacon, preferably applewood smoked, coarsely chopped
⅓ cup extra-virgin olive oil
¼ cup tarragon vinegar
1 tbsp. *each* Dijon mustard and minced shallot
½ tsp. pepper
¼ tsp. salt
1 qt. lightly packed watercress sprigs (¼ lb.), tough stems removed*
4 qts. finely shredded lettuce (half butter lettuce and half iceberg or all iceberg)
2 firm-ripe tomatoes (⅔ lb. total), cored and chopped
1½ cups thinly sliced skinned cooked chicken
⅔ cup crumbled (3 oz.) pungent blue cheese, such as Oregon Blue, roquefort, or gorgonzola
2 hard-cooked eggs, peeled and chopped
1 firm-ripe avocado (½ lb.), halved, pitted, peeled, and thinly sliced crosswise

1. In a large frying pan over medium-high heat, cook bacon, stirring often, until browned and crisp, 10 to 15 minutes; spoon out and discard fat in pan as it accumulates. With a slotted spoon, transfer bacon to paper towels to drain; discard remaining fat.
2. In a 1-cup glass measure or small bowl, mix oil, vinegar, mustard, shallot, pepper, and salt.
3. Set aside 4 to 6 watercress sprigs; coarsely chop remaining sprigs. Combine chopped watercress and lettuce in a very large bowl. Add all but ¼ cup dressing and mix gently to coat.
4. Divide lettuce mixture among wide, shallow bowls. On each, in wedges shaped like pie slices, arrange portions of bacon, tomatoes, chicken, blue cheese, eggs, and avocado.
5. Spoon remaining dressing over toppings. Garnish salads with reserved watercress sprigs.

*To trim tough stems from a watercress bunch, hold it upside down and run a sharp knife down the sides of the bunch. Reserve the shaved leaves. Remove the now-exposed tough stems from outside of the bunch, then slice off all lower stems and discard. Mainly tender stems will be left; pick out the few remaining tough stems.

PER SERVING 458 CAL., 71% (324 CAL.) FROM FAT; 25 G PROTEIN; 36 G FAT (10 G SAT.); 12 G CARBO (3.5 G FIBER); 768 MG SODIUM; 129 MG CHOL.

Blooming salad

Tender greens—a mix of mild and spicy—and flowers, preferably picked from the garden, take salad to a whole new level. It makes a beautiful case for growing your own food.

SERVES 6 | 20 minutes

2½ tbsp. grapeseed, safflower, or canola oil
1 tbsp. unseasoned rice vinegar
½ tsp. kosher salt
¼ tsp. pepper
1 tsp. minced tarragon
1 Persian cucumber or ⅓ English cucumber
About 50 sugar snap peas
¼ cup lightly packed chervil sprigs (optional)
3 oz. mâche clusters (about 3 lightly packed cups)
4 oz. mesclun (about 6 lightly packed cups)
4 medium radishes, sliced in half lengthwise
Bachelor's buttons (whole and petals), calendula and carnation petals, whole Johnny-jump-ups, nasturtium petals, pansy petals, and/or stock florets (15 to 20 whole flowers total)*

1. Whisk together oil, vinegar, salt, pepper, and tarragon in a small bowl.
2. Thinly slice cucumber. Split 30 of the fatter pea pods and remove the peas; set aside. Gently rinse chervil, mâche, and mesclun and gently spin twice in a salad spinner to thoroughly dry leaves. Put greens in a large bowl and toss gently but thoroughly with 3 tbsp. dressing (leaves should be barely coated), adding more dressing if necessary.
3. Divide greens among plates. Top with cucumber, sugar snap peas (both whole pods and peas), and radishes. Drizzle with any remaining dressing if you like, and top with flowers.
*Use only unsprayed, organic flowers. If you're growing your own flowers from seedlings, be sure to buy organic plants; don't spray as they grow. To buy edible flowers, try gourmet grocery stores and farmers' markets; avoid blooms from florists and nurseries.

PER SERVING 67 CAL., 77% (51 CAL.) FROM FAT; 1 G PROTEIN; 5.7 G FAT (0.5 G SAT.); 3.2 G CARBO (0.5 G FIBER); 101 MG SODIUM; 0 MG CHOL.

Celery Victor with watercress and capers

This simple, delicious poached vegetable dish hails from the days before raw greens defined a salad; we've added watercress and capers. With a red fez set atop his head and a persona larger than life, chef Victor Hirtzler—a native of Strasbourg, France; a former taster for Czar Nicholas II; and once chef to King Carlos I of Portugal—reigned over the kitchen at the Hotel St. Francis in San Francisco from 1904 to 1926. Of the many creations Hirtzler named after himself, Celery Victor is the most enduring.

SERVES 6 | 30 minutes, plus 2 hours to chill

3 celery hearts* (each about 2½ in. wide)
3½ cups chicken broth
⅓ cup *each* extra-virgin olive oil and tarragon vinegar
    or white wine vinegar
1 qt. lightly packed watercress sprigs (¼ lb.), tough stems
    removed*
2 tbsp. drained capers
Salt and pepper

1. Trim and discard tough stem ends from celery hearts, keeping stalks attached to bases. Trim tops to make stalks about 8 in. long; discard tops. With a vegetable peeler, pare coarse strings from backs of outer stalks. Cut each heart in half lengthwise; tie each half tightly around the center with cotton string.
2. Combine celery and broth in a 5- to 6-qt. pan (at least 10 in. wide). Bring to a boil over high heat; cover, reduce heat, and simmer until celery is tender when pierced, 12 to 15 minutes, turning bundles over halfway through cooking.
3. Combine oil and tarragon vinegar in a 1-gal. resealable plastic freezer bag. With tongs, transfer celery from broth to bag (save broth for other uses). Set upright and let cool, unsealed.
4. Seal bag and turn to coat celery with dressing. Chill until cold, at least 2 hours, turning bag occasionally.
5. Divide watercress among plates. Lift celery bundles from dressing; remove and discard strings. Place a bundle on each mound of watercress and sprinkle with capers. Spoon remaining dressing over salads if you like, and add salt and pepper to taste.
*Many supermarkets sell hearts of celery; you can also pull off outer stalks from regular bunches of celery and use the tender, pale green inner stalks (save outer stalks for other uses). For trimming watercress, see note at end of Classic Cobb Salad, page 37.

PER SERVING 138 CAL., 82% (113 CAL.) FROM FAT; 3.4 G PROTEIN; 13 G FAT (1.9 G SAT.); 3.1 G CARBO (1.6 G FIBER); 248 MG SODIUM; 15 MG CHOL.

Deviled crab Louis

Whoever Louis—or Louie—was (no one's quite sure), San Francisco's Hotel St. Francis was serving his addictive combination of Dungeness crab, iceberg lettuce, and chili-mayo dressing in 1910. Our updated recipe reflects a broader selection of greens, with salsa and smoky chipotle chiles replacing the chili sauce for a more interesting interplay of flavors. But a little mountain of sweet, fresh crab—a far pricier ingredient now than a century ago—is still the final flourish.

SERVES 4 as a main course | 1¼ hours

8 romaine or iceberg lettuce leaves (10 in. long)
1 head Belgian endive (white or red; 3 oz.), leaves separated
2 qts. finely shredded romaine or iceberg lettuce, or a
    combination*
¼ cup chopped flat-leaf parsley
Deviled Louis Dressing (recipe below)
1 lb. shelled cooked Dungeness or Alaska king crab
2 firm-ripe tomatoes (¾ lb. total), cored and each cut
    into 8 wedges
2 hard-cooked eggs, peeled and each cut into 4 wedges
Salt and pepper
2 tbsp. chopped chives
Lemon wedges

1. Line dinner plates or wide bowls with whole lettuce leaves, and then Belgian endive leaves.
2. In a large bowl, combine shredded lettuce and parsley. Add ⅔ cup deviled Louis dressing and mix gently. Divide among lettuce-lined plates.
3. Mound crab in center of shredded lettuce mixture; arrange tomato and egg wedges around edges. Sprinkle salads with salt, pepper, and chopped chives. Serve with lemon wedges and remaining dressing.
*To cut fine shreds of iceberg lettuce, cut head in half through core; cut out and discard core. Cut each half in half again lengthwise, then set each quarter on one cut side and slice thinly lengthwise. To cut fine shreds of romaine, stack a few leaves at a time, roll lengthwise into a cylinder, and slice thinly crosswise.

PER SERVING 297 CAL., 37% (109 CAL.) FROM FAT; 31 G PROTEIN; 12 G FAT (2.2 G SAT.); 16 G CARBO (4.4 G FIBER); 713 MG SODIUM; 198 MG CHOL.

Deviled Louis dressing Purée 1 cup **tomato salsa** (medium to hot) and 3 to 4 tsp. chopped **canned chipotle chiles** in a blender until smooth. Pour into a bowl and stir in 2 cups **mayonnaise**, 6 tbsp. **lemon juice,** and 1 tbsp. **sugar.** Season with **salt** and **pepper** to taste. Makes 3½ cups.

DEVILED CRAB LOUIS

Green bean Caesar salad with baby romaine lettuces

In Tijuana, Mexico, on July 4, 1924, as Caesar's Place filled with diners, its Italian-born chef and owner, Caesar Cardini, ran short of ingredients for the day's salad. He improvised with what was on hand: romaine leaves, parmesan, olive oil, lemon juice, a raw egg, Worcestershire, and croutons (anchovies came later). The salad was a hit with the Hollywood set who frequented Cardini's restaurant, and they took their fervor back home. The salad, served plain or topped with everything from grilled chicken to fried ginger, became a hallmark of California cuisine.

The Caesar variation below is based on a recipe in *Crave: The Feast of the Five Senses*, by Los Angeles chef Ludo Lefebvre.

SERVES 8 | 45 minutes

DRESSING
2 anchovy fillets in oil, drained and minced
1 large egg yolk*
1 garlic clove, minced
1 tsp. Dijon mustard
1 tbsp. finely grated parmesan cheese
2 tbsp. lemon juice
2 tsp. chopped fresh tarragon
1/4 tsp. hot sauce
1/3 cup extra-virgin olive oil
1/2 tsp. *each* fine sea salt and pepper

SALAD
1 lb. French green beans (haricots verts), trimmed
4 slices bacon, cut crosswise into 1/4-in.-thick strips*
2 tbsp. olive oil
1 cup 1/2-in. cubes day-old rustic white bread, crusts trimmed
Fine sea salt and pepper
10 oz. (10 cups lightly packed) mixed baby red romaine and baby green romaine lettuce leaves
2 garlic cloves, cut lengthwise into paper-thin slices
2 tbsp. fresh tarragon leaves

1. Make dressing: Shake all dressing ingredients together in a medium glass jar. Chill until ready to use.
2. Make salad: Boil green beans until crisp-tender, about 3 minutes. Drain. Dip into a bowl of ice water to cool; drain again. Cook bacon in a large frying pan over medium heat until crisp, about 10 minutes, and drain on paper towels. Pour out bacon fat and wipe pan clean. Swirl in oil, then add bread cubes and toast, stirring often, until golden brown, about 5 minutes. Drain the croutons on paper towels and season with salt and pepper.

3. Put green beans, lettuces, garlic slices, and tarragon leaves in a large bowl and toss with just enough dressing to coat well. Top with bacon and croutons.
***** If you're serving the salad to people with compromised immune systems, use pasteurized yolks (find them in the egg case at the grocery store) or omit. Freezing the bacon for 20 minutes will make it easier to cut into thin strips.

PER SERVING 184 CAL., 71% (131 CAL.) FROM FAT; 3.7 G PROTEIN; 15 G FAT (2.6 G SAT.); 7.9 G CARBO (2.3 G FIBER); 260 MG SODIUM; 31 MG CHOL.

Green salad with papaya-seed dressing

The creamy-looking dressing on this version of a classic Hawaiian salad gets its texture and zing from sweet Maui onions and peppery, crunchy papaya seeds. Greg and Lynn Boyer, of Oahu, gave us the recipe; Greg, a landscape architect, and Lynn like to host multicultural luaus in their dreamlike tropical garden.

SERVES 10 to 12 | 15 minutes

1/3 cup *each* unseasoned rice vinegar and canola oil
1/2 small sweet onion, such as Maui, chopped, plus 1 large sweet onion thinly sliced into rings and rinsed with cold water
1 1/2 tsp. sugar
1/2 tsp. *each* salt and dry mustard
1 1/2 tbsp. papaya seeds
1 lb. mixed salad greens
2 firm-ripe avocados, pitted, peeled, and sliced

1. Blend vinegar, oil, chopped onion, sugar, salt, and mustard in a blender until smooth. Add papaya seeds and pulse until seeds look like coarsely ground peppercorns.
2. Combine onion rings in a large bowl with salad greens and three-quarters of avocado slices; pour dressing over salad and toss gently to coat. Arrange salad on a large platter and top with remaining slices of avocado.

PER SERVING 145 CAL., 74% (108 CAL.) FROM FAT; 1.8 G PROTEIN; 12 G FAT (1.4 G SAT.); 8.4 G CARBO (1.7 G FIBER); 122 MG SODIUM; 0 MG CHOL.

GREEN SALAD WITH
PAPAYA-SEED DRESSING

Cantaloupe and prosciutto salad

A twist on the traditional Spanish pairing of prosciutto and melon, this salad combines prosciutto slices, baked until crisp, then broken into pieces and strewn over ribbons of juicy melon. Cantaloupe, grown in California and, to a lesser extent, Arizona, is at its fragrant best between June and September.

SERVES 8 | 30 minutes

4 thin slices prosciutto (1 oz.)
1 ripe cantaloupe, halved, seeded, and rind cut off
8 to 10 large mint leaves, thinly sliced
2 tbsp. extra-virgin olive oil

1. Preheat oven to 350°. Set a rack over a rimmed baking sheet. Lay prosciutto on rack and bake until crisp, 8 to 10 minutes. Let cool, then break into shards and chips.

2. Shave off ribbons of cantaloupe onto plates or a serving platter, using a vegetable peeler, mandoline, or very sharp knife. Sprinkle prosciutto and mint over melon shavings. Drizzle oil over salad.

PER ¾-CUP SERVING 62 CAL., 56% (35 CAL.) FROM FAT; 1.6 G PROTEIN; 4 G FAT (0.7 G SAT.); 5.8 G CARBO (0.7 G FIBER); 108 MG SODIUM; 1.9 MG CHOL.

Spicy avocado-poblano salad

Roasted chiles, crunchy jicama and radishes, silky avocado, crumbly cheese, and a spicy-sweet dressing make this salad an explosion of flavors and textures.

SERVES 4 | 50 minutes

4 medium poblano chiles (about ¾ lb. total)
2 tbsp. lime juice, divided
1 tsp. kosher salt
¼ tsp. honey
⅛ tsp. cayenne
3 tbsp. avocado, safflower, or canola oil
2 large firm-ripe avocados
½ lb. jicama, peeled, halved, and thinly sliced into semicircles
¼ cup crumbled cotija (dry, salty white Mexican cheese; sometimes called queso añejo) or parmesan cheese
¼ cup pumpkin seeds (pepitas), toasted*
4 radishes, cut into matchsticks

1. Preheat oven to broil. Broil poblanos 4 in. from heat in a rimmed baking pan, turning as needed, until blackened all over, about 10 minutes. Let poblanos rest on pan until skins are loosened, 15 to 20 minutes.
2. Whisk together 1 tbsp. lime juice, salt, honey, cayenne, and oil.
3. Halve, pit, and peel avocados. Set each avocado half cut side down, rest your hand gently on top, and slide knife through avocado horizontally to make ¼-in.-thick slices. Drizzle with remaining 1 tbsp. lime juice.
4. Skin, stem, and seed poblano chiles. Cut into irregular 1- to 2-in. pieces.
5. On salad plates, arrange a layer each of poblanos, avocados, and jicama; drizzle with some dressing. Add another layer each of poblanos and avocados, drizzle with dressing, and tuck remaining jicama into salads from the side. Sprinkle with cheese, pumpkin seeds, and radishes.
***Toast pumpkin seeds in a small (not nonstick) frying pan over medium heat until popped and golden brown, stirring occasionally, 2 to 4 minutes.

PER SERVING 327 CAL., 74% (243 CAL.) FROM FAT; 5.5 G PROTEIN; 27 G FAT (4.4 G SAT.); 20 G CARBO (6.1 G FIBER); 397 MG SODIUM; 4 MG CHOL.

CANTALOUPE AND PROSCIUTTO SALAD

FRESH CORN AND
AVOCADO SALAD

Fresh corn and avocado salad

This recipe from reader Kathy Kane, of Menlo Park, California, is a celebration of summer: corn, tomatoes, and intoxicating fresh basil, tied together with the buttery smoothness of avocado.

SERVES 6 | 30 minutes

6 ears corn, husked
2 cups halved cherry tomatoes
½ cup thinly sliced red onion
1 large firm-ripe avocado, pitted, peeled, and cut into ½-in. cubes
⅓ cup chopped basil leaves
2 tbsp. Champagne vinegar
1 tsp. Dijon mustard
¼ cup extra-virgin olive oil
¼ tsp. *each* kosher salt and pepper

1. In a large pot of boiling water, cook corn until warmed through, 3 to 5 minutes. Drain and rinse under cold water until cool.
2. Meanwhile, combine tomatoes, onion, avocado, and basil in a large bowl. In a small bowl, whisk vinegar, mustard, oil, salt, and pepper until blended.
3. Cut corn kernels off cobs and add to salad, then pour in vinaigrette and toss gently to combine.

PER SERVING 245 CAL., 62% (153 CAL.) FROM FAT; 4.5 G PROTEIN; 17 G FAT (2.5 G SAT.); 25 G CARBO (4.4 G FIBER); 92 MG SODIUM; 0 MG CHOL.

Marionberry, blue cheese, and arugula salad

Marionberries, with their deep tangy-sweet flavor, are the berries against which all other blackberries are judged. Named for Marion County, Oregon, marionberries are grown only in the Beaver State.

SERVES 4 | 15 minutes

3 tbsp. extra-virgin olive oil
1 tbsp. lemon juice
1 tbsp. thyme leaves, divided
¼ tsp. dry mustard
About ¼ tsp. *each* salt and pepper
6 oz. arugula (about 13 cups)
6 oz. (1½ cups) marionberries or other blackberries
2 oz. mild blue cheese

Whisk together oil, lemon juice, 1 tsp. thyme leaves, the mustard, ¼ tsp. salt, and ¼ tsp. pepper in a salad bowl. Add arugula and gently toss until coated with dressing. Add berries and gently toss. Divide among salad plates. Crumble cheese on salads. Sprinkle with remaining thyme and salt and pepper to taste.

PER SERVING 175 CAL., 77% (135 CAL.) FROM FAT; 4.5 G PROTEIN; 15 G FAT (4.2 G SAT.); 7.8 G CARBO (2.7 G FIBER); 353 MG SODIUM; 11 MG CHOL.

California

California has always provided a well-stocked larder. The land is so generous that before Europeans arrived, few tribes, other than those in the southern desert, turned to agriculture—the Chumash, for example, in what's now coastal Southern California, lived on fish and game, as well as acorns, berries, and cattail roots. The Spanish padres who established missions up and down California—the first in San Diego in 1769— brought European nuts, fruit, wheat, and Latin American chiles, corn, and tomatoes. Wealthy Spaniards and Mexicans ran enormous cattle ranchos, where a celebration meant a blowout barbecue.

European immigrants poured in with the Gold Rush, and many Italians among them later turned to fishing and farming. Chinese miners and railroad workers began to farm in the 1860s, as did Japanese laborers in the following decades. Luther Burbank bred new fruits and vegetables in Santa Rosa. Grand-scale irrigation watered the land, iced railroad cars kept produce fresh, and California went from growing grain to vegetables, fruit, and nuts (and today, half of all U.S. produce comes from the state). Farmers banded together in co-ops, canneries bought up farmland around World War II, and the tractor, fertilizer, and industrial feedlot arrived.

In 1971, Alice Waters opened Chez Panisse in Berkeley, with a vision of local, ingredient-inspired cuisine that shifted the way we cook and eat today. California also brings to the table all manner of Latino, Asian, and other cultural identities expressed in both authentic dishes and multicultural mashups.

Asparagus herb salad

At its luscious, grassy-flavored peak from March to June, asparagus is wonderful with red onion, pine nuts, and herbs.

SERVES 6 | 20 minutes

2 lbs. thick asparagus, cut into 2-in. pieces
2 tbsp. *each* **lemon juice and Dijon mustard**
3 tbsp. olive oil
¼ cup *each* **chopped fresh basil, chives, and cilantro**
1 cup thinly sliced red onion
¾ cup toasted pine nuts
2 oz. feta cheese, crumbled (½ cup)
½ tsp. *each* **salt and pepper**

1. Bring a large saucepan of water to a boil. Drop asparagus into water and cook until bright green and slightly softened, 1 to 2 minutes. Drain asparagus and rinse with very cold water until cool.
2. Whisk juice in a large bowl with mustard, oil, and basil, chives, and cilantro. Add asparagus, onion, nuts, feta, salt, and pepper; stir to combine.

PER SERVING 227 CAL., 71% (162 CAL.) FROM FAT; 9.7 G PROTEIN; 18 G FAT (3.7 G SAT.); 10 G CARBO (2.7 G FIBER); 425 MG SODIUM; 8.4 MG CHOL.

ASPARAGUS HERB SALAD

Green Goddess salad

The play *The Green Goddess* opened in San Francisco in 1923. In its honor, the chef at the grand Palace Hotel created a special salad dressing to spoon over artichoke bottoms filled with shrimp, chicken, or crab. In keeping with the era's tastes, the dressing incorporated just a suggestion of herbs and anchovies, and plenty of mayonnaise. The dressing eventually became more famous than the play. Our version, from Peter DeMarais, the Palace Hotel's chef from 1993 to 2005 (his great-grandfather was also a chef there), adds fresh herbs with a bolder hand than did the original.

SERVES 6 as a main course | 45 minutes

1 head iceberg lettuce (1 lb.)
1 head radicchio (⅓ lb.)
1 can (15 oz.) artichoke bottoms, drained
1¼ lbs. cooked bay shrimp
1½ cups cherry or pear tomatoes (red, yellow, or
 a combination), halved if larger than 1 in.
Green Goddess Dressing (recipe below)
Paper-thin red onion rings and tarragon sprigs

1. Cut iceberg lettuce lengthwise through core into six equal wedges. Cut radicchio lengthwise into six equal wedges. Arrange a lettuce wedge and a radicchio wedge on each plate.
2. Place an artichoke bottom, cup side up, beside lettuce on each plate (reserve extra for other uses). Mound shrimp in artichokes, letting shrimp spill over edges. Arrange tomatoes alongside.
3. Spoon about half the dressing over salads. Top with onion rings and tarragon sprigs. Serve remaining dressing on the side.

PER SERVING 446 CAL., 63% (279 CAL.) FROM FAT; 27 G PROTEIN; 31 G FAT (4.8 G SAT.); 15 G CARBO (3.7 G FIBER); 944 MG SODIUM; 210 MG CHOL.

Green Goddess dressing Put 1 cup **mayonnaise** or sour cream in a blender with 5 cups loosely packed **spinach leaves,** 1 cup loosely packed **parsley leaves,** ½ cup loosely packed **tarragon leaves,** ½ cup loosely packed **chervil leaves** (optional; if not using, increase tarragon to 1 cup), 1 tbsp. *each* **lemon juice** and chopped **shallot,** and 1 can (2 oz.) **anchovies,** drained. Blend until very smooth. Makes 2 cups.

PER TBSP. 56 CAL., 89% (50 CAL.) FROM FAT; 0.8 G PROTEIN; 5.6 G FAT (0.8 G SAT.); 0.9 G CARBO (0.3 G FIBER); 96 MG SODIUM; 4.8 MG CHOL.

Heirloom tomato salad with pomegranate drizzle

Pomegranate molasses brings out the best in vine-ripened tomatoes—it's not unlike balsamic vinegar. A tart-sweet syrup, it's concentrated pomegranate juice and is a staple in Middle Eastern cooking. A variety of tomato colors makes the salad pop.

SERVES 6 | 10 minutes

3 tbsp. extra-virgin olive oil
2 tbsp. pomegranate molasses*
2 lbs. mixed heirloom tomatoes, sliced ¼ in. thick
Sea salt, such as Maldon*
½ tsp. pepper
2 tbsp. oregano leaves

Whisk together oil and molasses. Arrange tomatoes on a platter. Drizzle with oil-molasses dressing. Sprinkle with salt and pepper and scatter oregano on top.

*Find pomegranate molasses and Maldon sea salt at well-stocked grocery stores and specialty-foods shops.

PER SERVING 135 CAL., 51% (69 CAL.) FROM FAT; 1.4 G PROTEIN; 7.6 G FAT (1.1 G SAT.); 17 G CARBO (2.2 G FIBER); 40 MG SODIUM; 0 MG CHOL.

Endive apple salad

Crisp, sweet Fuji apples pair wonderfully with rich gorgonzola and toasted walnuts in an autumn salad. We're fans of Oregonzola, a creamy, tangy blue cheese from Rogue Creamery in Southern Oregon.

SERVES 4 | 25 minutes

4 oz. gorgonzola cheese, divided
2 tbsp. Champagne vinegar
¼ cup olive oil
Kosher salt and pepper
2 Fuji apples, thinly sliced
4 heads Belgian endive, separated
½ cup toasted walnuts

1. In a medium bowl, combine 2 oz. cheese with vinegar and oil, mashing cheese with a fork. Season to taste with salt and pepper.
2. In another bowl, toss apples and endive with half the dressing, then divide among plates. Crumble remaining 2 oz. cheese over each salad; top with walnuts. Drizzle with remaining dressing.

PER SERVING 376 CAL., 77% (290 CAL.) FROM FAT; 8.8 G PROTEIN; 32 G FAT (8.7 G SAT.); 18 G CARBO (3.8 G FIBER); 395 MG SODIUM; 25 MG CHOL.

From the orchard: Apples

The first apple seeds were carried to the Northwest in the 1820s by an officer in the Hudson Bay Company, and planted at Fort Vancouver, Washington. A few decades later, Oregon Trail settlers headed West with apple trees and scions—because grafting, rather than sowing seed, is the only sure way to grow apples resembling those on the parent tree. Hard cider, rather than apple pies, was the goal.

Nowadays, Washington is the source of more than half the apples in the country. The state's largest growing region is the Yakima Valley, producer—along with the Columbia Basin—of the Fuji, a cross between two American apples that was bred in Japan in the 1930s.

We like to buy organic, because conventional apples are likely to have pesticide residue, even after you wash and peel them—more, according to studies, than almost any other fruit or vegetable.

Here are a few of our favorite varieties:

BRAEBURN Sweet, with rich flavors of pear and spice. Holds up well in cooking—good for apple cakes or savory dishes like pork stew.

CRIPPS PINK (aka Pink Lady) One of the best for baking whole: The skin keeps its color, and the flesh, with strawberry and lemon notes, holds together well.

GALA Crisp, mild, and juicy, the Gala doesn't turn brown as fast as other apples when cut—so it's great for salads. Not as good for baking.

GRANNY SMITH Firm and tart; its lemony acidity stands up to rich piecrusts and crisps. It makes a good sorbet (see Green Apple Sauvignon Blanc Sorbet, page 206).

JONAGOLD A cross between Jonathan and Golden Delicious; works well with Granny Smiths in pie, thanks to sweet melon and honey notes and firm, juicy flesh.

Grilled lettuces with manchego

Small, crisp Little Gem, a type of miniature romaine lettuce, is ideal for this recipe, but hearts of regular romaine work too. Barbecues in the West, once decidedly meat-oriented (with a few vegetables thrown on for side dishes), now welcome all manner of leafy greens to the grill.

SERVES 4 | 20 minutes

3 canned anchovy fillets, drained and finely chopped
2 to 2½ tbsp. extra-virgin olive oil
1 tbsp. lemon juice
Salt and pepper
2 whole small Little Gem lettuces or 4 hearts of romaine, rinsed and patted dry
⅛ lb. manchego cheese, shaved into thin curls with a vegetable peeler
1 lemon, cut into wedges

1. With the flat side of a knife, mash the anchovies to a paste. In a small bowl, whisk together olive oil, lemon juice, anchovy paste, and salt and pepper to taste.
2. Cut lettuces in half lengthwise, keeping leaves attached to cores. Brush all over with 1½ to 2 tbsp. anchovy dressing.
3. Prepare a grill for medium-high heat (see "How-to: Grilling," page 83). Lay lettuces on cooking grate and close lid on gas grill. Cook, turning once, until lettuces are softened and streaked brown, about 8 minutes.
4. Place lettuces cut side up on a platter. Drizzle lettuces with remaining dressing and top with manchego curls. Serve with lemon wedges.

PER SERVING 149 CAL., 79% (117 CAL.) FROM FAT; 6.2 G PROTEIN; 13 G FAT (4.8 G SAT.); 5.2 G CARBO (2.7 G FIBER); 206 MG SODIUM; 17 MG CHOL.

GRILLED LETTUCES
WITH MANCHEGO

SPINACH, MUSHROOM, AND
FENNEL SALAD WITH WARM
BACON VINAIGRETTE

Spinach, mushroom, and fennel salad with warm bacon vinaigrette

"Every hippie menu in the '70s had a spinach and mushroom salad," Mark Peel says about this recipe, inspired by a restaurant from his college days in Isla Vista, California. Chef at Campanile Restaurant in Los Angeles, Peel wrote *New Classic Family Dinners* with Martha Rose Shulman, from which this recipe is adapted.

SERVES 8 | 45 minutes

3 qts. (7 to 8 oz.) lightly packed baby spinach
3 large eggs, hard-cooked and cut into wedges
5 oz. mushrooms, thinly sliced
5 oz. good-quality thick-cut bacon
2 tbsp. *each* canola oil and extra-virgin olive oil
1 large fennel head (about 4 in. wide), trimmed and
    thinly sliced
2½ tbsp. minced shallot
1½ tsp. roughly chopped thyme leaves
2½ tbsp. sherry vinegar
2 tsp. Dijon mustard
About ½ tsp. *each* kosher salt and pepper

1. Combine spinach, eggs, and mushrooms in a large shallow serving bowl.

2. Cut bacon on the diagonal into strips about ¼ in. thick and 1½ in. long. Cook bacon with ⅓ cup water in a large frying pan over medium heat, stirring occasionally, until water disappears, 8 to 12 minutes. Add oils and cook until bacon is light golden but still supple, 3 to 5 minutes more. Transfer bacon with a slotted spoon to paper towels to drain.

3. Add fennel to pan and cook, stirring occasionally, until slightly softened, about 2 minutes. Transfer with a slotted spoon to more paper towels.

4. Stir shallot and thyme into fat in pan and cook until softened, about 2 minutes. Remove pan from heat and whisk in vinegar to deglaze pan. Whisk in mustard, ½ tsp. *each* salt and pepper, and 2 tsp. water.

5. Add bacon and fennel to salad. Spoon out dressing or scrape out with a rubber spatula and add to salad; toss gently to coat. Season to taste with salt and pepper.

PER SERVING 201 CAL., 75% (151 CAL.) FROM FAT; 5.9 G PROTEIN; 17 G FAT (4 G SAT.); 6.9 G CARBO (2.3 G FIBER); 380 MG SODIUM; 92 MG CHOL.

From the orchard: Olive oil

The West produces some of the best olive oil in the world. Virtually all of it is cultivated in California, which has the Mediterranean climate that olives love. The first trees planted in the state were brought by Spanish missionaries in the late 1700s, and it's an enduring legacy—one of the most common varieties in California today is the Mission olive, descended from those original trees.

California's olives and olive oils were significant products until the turn of the last century, when production dropped after an influx of cheaper imported oils. A few oil makers stuck it out. In the 1980s, when olive oil was rediscovered as a healthy, monounsaturated fat, public demand for it began to rise. Interest in high-quality olive oil increased as well. In 1992, the California Olive Oil Council (COOC) was founded to elevate the standards for the state's olive oil. Now, trained tasters sip and sniff hundreds of oils every year for the council, and only the flawless ones are certified as extra-virgin. Any oil with the COOC label, if properly stored, will be reliably good.

Olive oil is made by crushing the fruit of olive trees into a paste—pits and all—in a mill. Most producers use a giant tank mixer and a centrifuge to extract the oil from the paste. Extra-virgin oil is produced from the first pressing of a batch of olives; additional pressings, often with heat or chemicals, produce lesser-quality oils.

Store oil airtight in a cool, dark place, as heat and light can degrade its quality. Olive oil should be kept no more than a year at room temperature, although peppery varieties can last longer (the best oils will have a harvest date on the bottle). And don't use really good extra-virgin olive oil for cooking; heat destroys its subtle flavors. Instead, drizzle it over food just before serving, or add it to salad dressings.

Watermelon salad with lime dressing

At now-closed Stars in San Francisco, chef Jeremiah Tower used to serve savory watermelon salad, inspiring a constellation of others to do the same—including us.

SERVES 6 | 15 minutes

1 lime
1/4 cup sugar
4 cups cubed watermelon

Zest lime, then trim outer white membrane. Chop lime into bits, reserving juice. Combine lime zest, bits, and juice with sugar and 1/4 cup water in a small saucepan. Cook over high heat until boiling. Cool slightly. Gently mix with watermelon.

PER 1½-CUP SERVING 63 CAL., 0% (0 CAL.) FROM FAT; 0.3 G PROTEIN; 17 G CARBO (0.7 G FIBER); 0.1 MG SODIUM; 0 MG CHOL.

WATERMELON SALAD
WITH LIME DRESSING

Ruby grapefruit, avocado, and spinach salad

Fresh ginger, fish sauce, and rice vinegar add a Southeast Asian twist to a classic California salad. (Photo on page 32.)

SERVES 4 | 10 minutes

3½ cups baby spinach
3 ruby grapefruit (1 lb. each), cut into segments, juice reserved
1 firm-ripe avocado (about 1/2 lb.), pitted, peeled, and thinly sliced
2 tbsp. *each* unseasoned rice vinegar and Vietnamese fish sauce
2 tsp. minced fresh ginger
2½ tsp. sugar

1. Arrange spinach, grapefruit segments, and avocado slices on salad plates.
2. Measure 3 tbsp. grapefruit juice (save any extra for other uses) into a small bowl and whisk with vinegar, fish sauce, ginger, and sugar to blend. Spoon dressing over salads.

PER SERVING 173 CAL., 39% (67 CAL.) FROM FAT; 4.2 G PROTEIN; 7.4 G FAT (1.2 G SAT.); 26 G CARBO (4.8 G FIBER); 395 MG SODIUM; 0 MG CHOL.

Persimmon salad with dates, cashews, and honey

Western persimmons were introduced to California from Japan (by way of Commodore Matthew Perry) in the 1870s. Tomato-shaped Fuyu persimmons, eaten when firm, ripen just in time for a bright autumnal orange salad. (See Persimmon Smoothies, page 29, for more on the fruit.)

SERVES 6 | 15 minutes

6 small or 4 large Fuyu persimmons (about 1½ lbs.),
    cut into wedges
5 Medjool dates, pitted and cut into slivers
1/2 cup salted cashews, very roughly chopped
1 tbsp. finely chopped crystallized ginger
1/4 cup honey
1/4 tsp. kosher salt
Lime wedges

Toss persimmons with dates and cashews in a medium bowl. In a small microwave-safe bowl, whisk together ginger, honey, and salt. Microwave until honey is thin enough to drizzle, about 20 seconds. Whisk again, then drizzle on salad and toss to coat. Serve with lime wedges to squeeze on top.

PER 1-CUP SERVING 573 CAL., 8.4% (48 CAL.) FROM FAT; 5 G PROTEIN; 5.3 G FAT (1.1 G SAT.); 133 G CARBO (10 G FIBER); 183 MG SODIUM; 0 MG CHOL.

PERSIMMON SALAD
WITH DATES, CASHEWS,
AND HONEY

LENTIL STEW
WITH WINTER
VEGETABLES
recipe on page 65

Soups & Stews

Some of the West's soups and stews are practically tourist attractions—cioppino says San Francisco as surely as fog over the Golden Gate Bridge does, while *chile verde* is as Southwestern as a saguaro. Their main ingredients also vividly convey the spirit of place: From the fields of Montana, Idaho, and Washington, for example, come the nation's largest crop of lentils, which we cook into a chill-chasing stew.

Creamy artichoke soup

Duarte's Tavern, an unprepossessing landmark an hour's drive south of San Francisco, in the town of Pescadero, opened in 1894 and still serves great food. This is our take on its famous artichoke soup.

SERVES 4 | 45 minutes

6 artichokes
2 tbsp. lemon juice
2 tbsp. olive oil
About 1 tbsp. salt
3 tbsp. butter
1 onion, chopped
2 tbsp. flour
6 cups chicken broth
3 tbsp. whipping cream
Pepper
Chervil or parsley

1. Trim leaves, stems, and fuzzy chokes from artichokes (save leaves for other uses); as you trim, drop artichoke hearts into a bowl of ice water mixed with lemon juice and olive oil. Bring a large pot of water to a boil and add 1 tbsp. salt. Drain artichoke hearts and add to boiling water; cook until tender. Drain.
2. Melt butter in a pan over medium-high heat. Add onion and stir until golden. Stir in flour; cook, stirring often, 3 to 5 minutes.
3. Add chicken broth and artichoke hearts; cook, stirring, until mixture boils and thickens, 15 to 20 minutes. Blend mixture in a blender until smooth. Return to pan and heat through. Add whipping cream and salt and pepper to taste.
4. Ladle soup into bowls and garnish with chervil or parsley, in sprigs or chopped.

PER SERVING 243 CAL., 55% (133 CAL.) FROM FAT; 13 G PROTEIN; 15 G FAT (8.2 G SAT.); 16 G CARBO (8.1 G FIBER); 880 MG SODIUM; 38 MG CHOL.

Tiered tomato soup

This eye-popping chilled soup floats a red stratum of tomato soup on a green layer of avocado soup. Clear straight-sided glasses or wineglasses show off the soup's layers.

SERVES 6 to 8 as a first course | 30 minutes, plus 1 hour to chill

2 lbs. ripe tomatoes
3 to 4 tbsp. white wine vinegar, divided
Salt
2 firm-ripe avocados (8 oz. each)
¾ cup reduced-sodium chicken broth
¼ cup sour cream
3 tbsp. lime juice
1 cucumber (12 oz.)
3 tbsp. minced shallots
1 tsp. minced tarragon

1. Core tomatoes; cut into chunks. Blend in a blender or food processor until smooth, then rub through a fine-mesh strainer into a bowl; you should have about 3 cups. Discard residue. Season purée with 2 to 3 tbsp. vinegar and salt to taste. Cover and chill until cold, at least 1 hour.
2. Pit and peel avocados; cut into chunks. Blend avocados, broth, sour cream, and lime juice until smooth in a blender or food processor. Add salt to taste. Cover surface with plastic wrap (to prevent discoloration) and chill until cold, at least 1 hour.
3. Peel cucumber; cut in half lengthwise and scoop out and discard seeds. Cut into ⅛-in. dice; you should have about 1 cup. In a small bowl, mix cucumber, shallots, 1 tbsp. vinegar, and tarragon. Cover and chill until cold, at least 30 minutes.
4. Stir avocado soup and pour into glasses. Whisk tomato soup and gently pour over avocado. Top with cucumber mixture.

PER SERVING 117 CAL., 65% (76 CAL.) FROM FAT; 2.5 G PROTEIN; 8.4 G FAT (2.1 G SAT.); 11 G CARBO (2.4 G FIBER); 31 MG SODIUM; 3.5 MG CHOL.

From the field: Tomatoes

The tomato, whose tiny-fruited ancestor was born in South America, made its way up to Mexico—where the Mayans cultivated it—and from there, by way of 16th-century Spanish colonizers, to Europe. Though the *pomodoro*, or "golden apple," was slow to catch on in Europe (it had a reputation in some quarters as poisonous), British colonists carried the plants to North America. The tomato's crisis in flavor and texture began in the 1950s, when a botanist at the University of California, Davis, bred a tomato specifically for machine harvesting. While hard, pale supermarket tomatoes are grown today mainly in Florida and Mexico, more flavorful tomatoes for processing (into ketchup and pizza sauce or put into cans) are California's specialty. The current boom in locally grown vine-ripened tomatoes takes us back to the flavors of an earlier time, when the fruit was bred for taste, not shipping.

Pumpkin soup with pumpkin seed–mint pesto

Not quite enough pumpkin for you? Serve it in Mini Pumpkin Bowls (as in photo; the recipe follows).

SERVES 4 or 5 | 50 minutes

SOUP
1 large onion, chopped
1½ tbsp. chopped fresh ginger
2 tbsp. olive oil
4 large garlic cloves, chopped
2 tsp. ground coriander
4½ cups peeled 1-in. chunks pumpkin or other
    orange-fleshed squash (from a 2½-lb. squash)*
4½ cups reduced-sodium chicken broth
¾ tsp. kosher salt
½ tsp. pepper

PUMPKIN SOUP
WITH PUMPKIN SEED–
MINT PESTO

PESTO
1 small garlic clove
⅓ cup mint leaves, plus slivered leaves
⅛ tsp. kosher salt
¼ cup extra-virgin olive oil, divided
¼ cup salted roasted pumpkin seeds

1. Make soup: Sauté onion and ginger in oil in a pot over medium-high heat until golden, 5 minutes. Add garlic and coriander and cook until softened, 1 minute, then add pumpkin, broth, salt, and pepper. Simmer, covered, until pumpkin is very tender, 8 to 10 minutes. Purée in batches in a blender until very smooth.
2. Make pesto: Pound garlic, whole mint leaves, salt, and 1 tbsp. oil into a coarse paste in a mortar (or use a food processor). Add remaining 3 tbsp. oil and pumpkin seeds and pound (or pulse) until coarsely crushed.
3. Drop small spoonfuls of pesto over bowls of soup, garnish with slivered mint, and serve remaining pesto on the side.
*Use a variety with dense, deep orange flesh, such as Sugar Pie or Jarrahdale (or kabocha or other squash).

PER 1½-CUP SERVING 263 CAL., 70% (185 CAL.) FROM FAT; 8.3 G PROTEIN; 21 G FAT (3.4 G SAT.); 13 G CARBO (2.6 G FIBER); 406 MG SODIUM; 23 MG CHOL.

Mini pumpkin bowls Cut a thin slice from bases of 4 or 5 **mini pumpkins** so they sit flat. Set on a rimmed baking sheet and rub with **olive oil.** Bake pumpkins in a 400° oven until tender, 40 to 45 minutes. Cut off 2-in. lids. Carefully scrape out the seeds with a small spoon. (If you get a hole, line pumpkin with a piece of foil.)

Tepary bean and fennel ragout

This earthy stew is also delicious made with other unusual Southwest heirloom varieties (see "From the Field: Heirloom Beans," at far right), or regular pintos.

SERVES 4 | 2¼ hours, plus at least 4 hours to soak

½ lb. (1¼ cups) tepary, Anasazi, or Rio Zape beans*,
    sorted for debris and rinsed
1 fennel head, trimmed, feathery tops reserved
2 tbsp. olive oil, divided
1 large carrot, diced
1 medium onion, chopped
1½ tsp. kosher salt
2½ tsp. chopped thyme leaves, divided

1. Soak beans overnight in a medium bowl with 1 qt. water; or boil beans in a medium pot with 1 qt. water 2 minutes, then remove pot from the heat and let stand, covered, 4 hours.

2. Halve fennel lengthwise, then thinly slice lengthwise, discarding core. In a medium saucepan, sauté fennel with 1 tbsp. oil over medium heat until edges brown, 7 to 10 minutes. Pour into a bowl; chill until used.

3. Add remaining 1 tbsp. oil, the carrot, and onion to pan; sauté until starting to brown, about 8 minutes. Add beans and their liquid, cover, and bring to a boil. Reduce heat and simmer until tender, 1½ to 1¾ hours, stirring occasionally and adding a little more water if beans start to look dry. Stir in salt, 2 tsp. thyme, and the fennel slices; return to a simmer and cook about 10 minutes more.

4. Chop enough fennel fronds to make 1 tbsp. and stir into beans with remaining ½ tsp. thyme.

*Buy from *nativeseeds.org, ranchogordo.com,* or *anasazibeans.com*

PER SERVING 302 CAL., 23% (68 CAL.) FROM FAT; 14 G PROTEIN; 7.7 G FAT (1.1 G SAT.); 46 G CARBO (12 G FIBER); 785 MG SODIUM; 0 MG CHOL.

Carrot soup with Dungeness crab

Serve this soup, a showcase for Dungeness crab, to brighten a winter day.

SERVES 4 | 50 minutes

2½ tbsp. butter
1 medium onion, chopped
1 lb. carrots, sliced
1 large bay leaf (or 2 small)
2 tbsp. white rice
1 tsp. salt
½ tsp. pepper
½ tsp. lemon zest
6 oz. shelled cooked Dungeness crab (from a 1½-lb. crab)
1 tbsp. lemon juice
1 tbsp. minced chives, plus chopped chives for garnish

1. Melt butter in a 5-qt. pot over medium-high heat. Add onion, carrots, bay leaf, rice, salt, and pepper. Cook, stirring, until onion is light golden, about 6 minutes. Add 5 cups water and bring mixture to a boil, then reduce heat and simmer 25 minutes. Remove bay leaf. Working in batches, purée soup in a blender until smooth. Return soup to pot, stir in zest, and keep warm.

2. Toss crab in a small bowl with lemon juice and minced chives. Put a mound of crab mixture in each soup bowl, then ladle soup around crab. Garnish with chopped chives.

PER SERVING 188 CAL., 38% (72 CAL.) FROM FAT; 11 G PROTEIN; 8 G FAT (4.7 G SAT.); 18 G CARBO (3.6 G FIBER); 864 MG SODIUM; 51 MG CHOL.

CARROT SOUP
WITH DUNGENESS
CRAB

From the field: Heirloom beans

Tepary beans sustained native peoples for thousands of years in the Sonoran Desert, and then nearly disappeared. The sweet, creamy bean is no longer impossible to find, thanks to seed savers and growers like New Mexico's "Bean Queen," Elizabeth Berry; Seed Bank in Petaluma, California; and Seed Savers Exchange in Iowa. Other heirlooms we love:

BLACK VALENTINE Meaty texture and neutral flavor.
FLAGEOLET Slender bean, white to pale green, with a mild taste and buttery texture.
FLOR DE MAYO Small red bean, with medium-firm but creamy texture and subtly sweet flavor.
NEW MEXICO APPALOOSA Red or black mottled with white; creamy texture and mild, earthy flavor.
SCARLET RUNNER Purple bean with black markings; a meaty, starchy texture; and a sweet chestnut flavor.

Chilled corn soup

A summer soup that is pure essence of corn. For a smoky flavor, roast or grill the corn in its husk rather than boil it.

MAKES About 6 cups; 4 servings | 20 minutes, plus 3 hours to chill

9 medium ears fresh yellow corn, husked
Salt
½ cup tightly packed basil leaves
¼ cup extra-virgin olive oil

1. Plunge ears of corn into a pot of boiling water and boil, covered, 2 to 3 minutes, until heated. Remove from water; when ears are cool enough to handle, slice off kernels. In two batches, purée kernels in a blender with 4 cups water total. Strain into a bowl, pressing to squeeze out liquid; discard the kernel mash. Add salt to taste and chill soup until cold, at least 3 hours.
2. Meanwhile, plunge basil into boiling water for 2 or 3 seconds. Drain immediately, plunge leaves into ice water, and drain again. Purée basil in a blender with ½ tsp. salt and the oil.
3. Serve soup cold, drizzled with basil oil.

PER SERVING 337 CAL, 44% (147 CAL.) FROM FAT; 8.4 G PROTEIN; 17 G FAT (2.3 G SAT.); 48 G CARBO (6.9 G FIBER); 38 MG SODIUM; 0 MG CHOL.

CHILLED CORN SOUP

Chicken *laksa*

The spicy Malaysian soup may have a long list of ingredients, but it's super easy. Malaysian kitchens (in Southeast Asia, in Southern California, and elsewhere) weave Chinese, Indian, and Malay culinary strands into a complex cuisine.

SERVES 4 to 6 | 1 hour

2 tbsp. coriander seeds
1 tsp. *each* black peppercorns, cumin seeds, and fennel seeds
4 cloves
¼ tsp. ground turmeric
5 to 8 dried arbol chiles, stemmed
2 lemongrass stalks
3 tbsp. vegetable oil
1 lb. boned, skinned chicken thighs, cubed
1 tsp. shrimp paste*
3 large shallots, thinly sliced
1 can (13.5 oz.) coconut milk
1 qt. reduced-sodium chicken broth
2 tsp. sugar
3 tsp. kosher salt
1 cinnamon stick
6 oz. mung bean sprouts, rinsed
8 oz. wide rice noodles
⅓ cup *each* mint and cilantro leaves, torn
Lime wedges
Sambal oelek* chili paste

1. Grind coriander, peppercorns, cumin seeds, fennel seeds, cloves, turmeric, and chiles coarsely in a spice grinder; set aside. Peel tough outer layers from lemongrass, then mash core with a meat mallet or small, heavy frying pan.
2. Heat oil in a large pot over medium heat. Add chicken, shrimp paste, shallots, and reserved ground spices and cook, stirring constantly, until fragrant, 2 minutes.
3. Pour in coconut milk, broth, sugar, and salt; add cinnamon stick and lemongrass. Bring to a boil, then simmer, covered, 20 minutes.
4. Boil bean sprouts in a large pot of boiling water until softened, 2 minutes. Transfer sprouts to a bowl. Add noodles to pot and cook until firm, 4 minutes. Drain; rinse well.
5. Divide sprouts and noodles among bowls. Ladle in soup (remove cinnamon and lemongrass) and top with mint and cilantro. Serve with limes and sambal.
***Find in the Asian-foods aisle of a well-stocked grocery store or at an Asian market.

PER 1½-CUP SERVING 494 CAL., 46% (225 CAL.) FROM FAT; 27 G PROTEIN; 25 G FAT (14 G SAT.); 39 G CARBO (2.7 G FIBER); 1,455 MG SODIUM; 81 MG CHOL.

CHICKEN *LAKSA*

TORTILLA SOUP

Tortilla soup

To get to know her neighbors in Berkeley better, Johanna Sedman started hosting a monthly soup night. With tortilla soup, guests can customize their own toppings. The recipe is Sedman's take on the Mexican soup, which traveled north by at least the mid–20th century (a version appears in *Elena's Famous Mexican and Spanish Recipes*, published in San Francisco in 1944).

MAKES About 4½ qts.; 12 servings | 1 hour

1 tbsp. vegetable oil, plus more for frying
2 large onions, chopped
8 garlic cloves, minced
1½ tbsp. kosher salt, divided
1 tsp. ground cumin
½ tsp. red chile flakes
12 cups reduced-sodium chicken broth
1 can (28 oz.) diced tomatoes
Juice of 2 limes, divided
1 package (8 oz.) small corn tortillas, cut into ¼-in.-thick strips*
2 lbs. boned, skinned chicken breasts, cut into ¼-in.-thick strips
1 cup chopped cilantro
Sliced avocado, sour cream, shredded Monterey jack cheese, additional chopped cilantro, and/or sliced green onions for topping

1. Heat 1 tbsp. oil in a large pot (at least 5 qts.) over medium heat. Add onions and cook, stirring a few times, until translucent, 5 to 7 minutes. Stir in two-thirds of garlic, 1 tbsp. salt, the cumin, and red chile flakes and cook 2 minutes. Add broth, tomatoes (with their juice), and half the lime juice and increase heat to a gentle simmer; cook 20 minutes.

2. Meanwhile, pour about 1 in. of oil into a small frying pan over medium-high heat. When oil is hot but not smoking, add a third of the tortilla strips and cook until golden brown and crisp, about 2 minutes. With a slotted spoon, transfer strips to a paper towel–lined baking pan. Repeat with remaining tortilla strips in two batches. Sprinkle with 1 tsp. salt. Set aside.

3. Purée soup in batches in a blender until smooth. Return soup to pot and resume simmering. In a bowl, toss chicken with remaining lime juice, garlic, and ½ tsp. salt. Marinate at room temperature 10 minutes, then add to soup and simmer until chicken is just cooked through, about 5 minutes. Stir in cilantro.

4. Serve with bowls of tortilla strips and toppings for guests to add as they like.

*No time to make tortilla strips? Store-bought chips will do in a pinch.

PER SERVING 243 CAL., 32% (78 CAL.) FROM FAT; 21 G PROTEIN; 8.9 G FAT (1.3 G SAT.); 21 G CARBO (1.8 G FIBER); 1,565 MG SODIUM; 37 MG CHOL.

Frito pie

It's often been said that Frito pie was born in New Mexico, at the Woolworth's lunch counter in Santa Fe, but history favors Texas. Charles Elmer Doolin of San Antonio founded the Frito Company in 1932, and a couple of years later, Frito pie appeared. This humble but delicious concoction of chili poured over Frito chips—often right in the bag, with shredded cheese, lettuce, tomato, and onion on top—may or may not have been invented by Elmer's mom, Daisy Dean Doolin, but one thing is sure: Generations of Texans knew Frito pie before it surfaced in New Mexico in the early 1960s.

You can argue, though, that Santa Fe has put its own stamp on the dish, making it with green or red chiles from the state's prize crop.

The recipe here is from the Diner, a once-popular stop (now closed) in Tres Piedras, near Taos, New Mexico. Former owner Barbara Cozart prepared her chili using local red chiles, from the Espanola Valley.

SERVES 6 | 30 minutes

2 lbs. ground lean (7% fat) beef
1 tbsp. garlic powder
About 1 tsp. salt
2 tbsp. flour
1 can (15 oz.) black beans (optional), rinsed and drained
3 tbsp. ground dried New Mexico chiles or chili powder
About 4½ cups Fritos corn chips (15-oz. bag)
6 tbsp. finely chopped onion
1½ cups shredded longhorn cheddar cheese
2 cups finely shredded iceberg lettuce
¾ cup chopped tomato

1. Cook ground beef, garlic powder, and 1 tsp. salt in a large pan over medium-high heat, stirring, until beef is crumbly and well browned, 6 to 8 minutes.

2. Push beef mixture to one side of pan with a large slotted spoon and tilt pan so liquid runs to opposite side. Stir flour into liquid until well blended, then mix with beef mixture. Add 2 cups water, black beans if using, and dried chiles; stir until mixture boils and thickens, about 8 minutes.

3. Spread about ¾ cup Fritos in each of 6 wide, shallow bowls and sprinkle chopped onion on top of each portion. Divide chili among bowls and top with cheese, lettuce, and tomato. Add more salt to taste.

PER SERVING 776 CAL., 53% (414 CAL.) FROM FAT; 44 G PROTEIN; 46 G FAT (14 G SAT.); 45 G CARBO (3.9 G FIBER); 1,088 MG SODIUM; 117 MG CHOL.

Smoky beef-and-bacon chili

Bacon, fire-roasted tomatoes, and spicy smoked paprika give an easy-to-make chili a deep, complex flavor. While it's great right after you make it, it's even better the next day. Warm cornbread is a good companion.

SERVES 6 | 1 hour, 10 minutes

2 slices thick-cut bacon, finely chopped
1 large onion, finely chopped
1 large garlic clove, minced
1½ lbs. ground lean beef
1½ tbsp. chili powder
1½ tsp. *each* ground cumin and sweet smoked
    Spanish paprika*
½ tsp. to 1½ tsp. cayenne
About 1 tsp. salt
1 can (14.5 oz.) crushed fire-roasted tomatoes*
    or regular crushed tomatoes
1 can (8 oz.) tomato sauce
1 cup beer (India Pale Ale or pilsner)
1 tsp. Worcestershire
1 can (14.5 oz.) pinto beans, drained and rinsed
Sour cream, sliced green onions, and/or shredded
    cheddar cheese for topping

1. Cook bacon in a large, heavy-bottomed pot over medium-high heat, stirring until it just begins to brown, about 4 minutes. Add onion, lower heat to medium, cover, and cook, stirring occasionally, until translucent, 4 to 7 minutes. Uncover pot, stir in garlic, and cook 1 minute.
2. Increase heat to medium-high and add ground beef; cook, breaking up meat with a wooden spoon and stirring gently, until beef loses its raw color, 6 to 8 minutes. Stir in chili powder, cumin, paprika, cayenne, and 1 tsp. salt and cook 1 minute. Add tomatoes, tomato sauce, beer, and Worcestershire and bring to a boil. Reduce heat to medium-low, cover partially, and cook 30 minutes.
3. Add beans and cook 10 minutes, uncovered. Season to taste with more salt. Serve with toppings on the side.
*Smoked Spanish paprika and fire-roasted tomatoes are available at well-stocked and specialty grocery stores.

PER SERVING 465 CAL., 62% (288 CAL.) FROM FAT; 26 G PROTEIN; 32 G FAT (12 G SAT.); 19 G CARBO (4.3 G FIBER); 1,078 MG SODIUM; 94 MG CHOL.

Cioppino

During the mid-1800s, San Francisco's immigrant Italian fishermen cooked up what was left of the day's catch in a purée of vegetables, much as they had in their home port city of Genoa. They called it *ciuppin,* dialect for "little soup." Over time, Sicilians replaced the Genoese on the fishing boats—and in their cooking pots, *cioppino,* as it came to be called, acquired peppers and tomatoes, which were left in chunks. Today, the sumptuous stew has far transcended its origins as a poor man's dish.

SERVES 4 to 6 | 1 hour

1 fennel head (¾ lb.)
3 tbsp. olive oil
1 onion (½ lb.), chopped
2 garlic cloves, minced
¼ cup chopped flat-leaf parsley, divided
3 cans (14.5 oz. each) diced tomatoes
2 cups dry white wine
⅓ cup tomato paste
1 tbsp. dried basil
½ tsp. *each* dried oregano and red chile flakes
1 dozen clams in the shell (discard any that are not closed),
    well scrubbed
2 cooked Dungeness crabs (about 2 lbs. each), cleaned and
    cracked (see "How-to: Dungeness Crab," page 133)
1 lb. large shrimp (21 to 30 per lb.), peeled and deveined
Salt and pepper

1. Trim off and discard tough stalks and base of fennel head. Core and chop bulb.
2. Cook fennel, oil, onion, garlic, and 2 tbsp. parsley in a medium pan over medium-high heat, stirring, until onion is limp, 8 to 10 minutes.
3. Add diced tomatoes (with their juice), wine, tomato paste, basil, oregano, and chile flakes. Bring to a boil over high heat. Cover and simmer over low heat until flavors are well blended, about 15 minutes.
4. Add clams and crabs. Cover and bring to a boil over high heat, then reduce heat and simmer, covered, for 5 minutes (transfer any opened clams to a bowl and cover to keep warm). Stir in shrimp, cover, and simmer until clams finish popping open, shrimp turn pink, and crab is hot, 6 to 9 minutes longer; remove seafood as it finishes cooking. Discard any clams that have not opened.
5. Season cioppino with salt and pepper and ladle into bowls with seafood. Serve sprinkled with remaining 2 tbsp. parsley.

PER SERVING 309 CAL., 29% (90 CAL.) FROM FAT; 35 G PROTEIN; 10 G FAT (1.4 G SAT.); 21 G CARBO (4.3 G FIBER); 798 MG SODIUM; 176 MG CHOL.

SPEEDY CHICKEN
POSOLE WITH
AVOCADO AND LIME

Speedy chicken posole with avocado and lime

For an era shorter on time than that of the Aztecs—who brought us posole—we came up with a recipe using canned hominy and boned chicken. Serve the stew with warm corn tortillas alongside.

SERVES 4 or 5 | 45 minutes

3 large poblano chiles (1 lb. total)
6 garlic cloves
1 large onion
2 cans (14½ oz. each) white hominy
1½ lbs. boned, skinned chicken thighs
½ tsp. kosher salt
2 tsp. dried Mexican oregano*, divided
2 tbsp. olive oil
3 cups reduced-sodium chicken broth
3 tbsp. ground red New Mexico chiles*
Sliced avocado, lime wedges, cilantro sprigs, and
    sour cream for topping

1. Preheat broiler. When hot, broil poblanos on a baking sheet until blackened, turning as needed, about 15 minutes.
2. Meanwhile, mince garlic in a food processor. Cut onion in chunks and pulse with garlic until chopped; set aside. Drain hominy; set aside.
3. Cut chicken into 1- to 1½-in. chunks and sprinkle with salt and 1 tsp. oregano. Heat oil in a medium pan over high heat. Brown half the chicken lightly, stirring occasionally, about 5 minutes. With a slotted spoon, transfer meat to a plate. Repeat with remaining chicken; transfer to plate.
4. Reduce heat to medium-high. Add onion mixture and remaining 1 tsp. oregano to pan and sauté until onion is softened, 3 minutes. Meanwhile, in a microwave-safe bowl, microwave broth until steaming, about 3 minutes. Add ground chiles to onion mixture in pan and cook, stirring, about 30 seconds.
5. Add broth, hominy, and chicken to pan. Cover and bring to a boil, then reduce heat and simmer to blend flavors, 10 minutes.
6. Meanwhile, remove stems, skins, and seeds from poblanos and discard; chop poblanos.
7. Stir poblanos into posole and cook 1 minute. Ladle into bowls and top with avocado, lime, cilantro, and sour cream.
*Find Mexican oregano at well-stocked grocery stores, along with ground red New Mexico chiles (for online sources, see "From the Field: New Mexico Chiles," page 104).

PER SERVING 436 CAL., 39% (169 CAL.) FROM FAT; 32 G PROTEIN; 19 G FAT (4.2 G SAT.); 36 G CARBO (7.2 G FIBER); 715 MG SODIUM; 89 MG CHOL.

Lentil stew with winter vegetables

The Palouse, a piece of the West cut out of Montana, Idaho, and Washington, is America's lentil land. The name derives from the French word *pelouse,* meaning "grassy lawn," and in spring, the lentil fields confirm that label. By late summer, the land is honey-colored, and hundreds of combines scoop up millions of thumb-size pods, each holding only two or three lentils. Western farmers grow all manner of lentils, including the green ones called French or *lentilles du Puy,* which cook up firm and nutty. Combine them with root vegetables, kale, and squash for a deeply satisfying winter meal. (Photo on page 52.)

SERVES 4 | 1 hour

2 tbsp. olive oil
1 medium onion, chopped
3 garlic cloves, minced
1 cup French green lentils, sorted for debris and rinsed
1 tsp. salt
¼ tsp. pepper
2 thyme sprigs
2 small turnips, cut into ½-in. cubes (about 1 cup)
1 bunch (about 5) baby golden or Chioggia beets, peeled
    (or 3 large beets, peeled and halved)
1 cup cubed peeled butternut squash (½-in. cubes)
4 cups chopped stemmed kale
1 bunch (about 5) baby carrots
½ cup minced flat-leaf parsley
3 oz. aged goat cheese, such as Le Chevrot or Bûcheron*,
    cut into small pieces

1. Heat oil in a medium pot over medium-high heat until hot. Add onion and cook, stirring, until translucent, about 3 minutes. Add garlic, lentils, salt, pepper, thyme, and 4 cups water. Bring to a boil, then reduce heat to medium-low. Add turnips, beets, and squash and simmer gently, stirring occasionally, 20 minutes.
2. Add kale and carrots and cook until vegetables are tender and most of the liquid has been absorbed, about 10 minutes.
3. Remove from heat; stir in parsley and goat cheese.
*Semi-firm aged goat cheese, at most cheese counters, has an assertive flavor that pairs well with winter greens and root vegetables, and a firm texture that holds up when heated.

PER SERVING 416 CAL., 30% (126 CAL.) FROM FAT; 23 G PROTEIN; 14 G FAT (5.4 G SAT.); 55 G CARBO (10 G FIBER); 813 MG SODIUM; 17 MG CHOL.

Broccolini and chickpea dal

With the right seasonings, a potentially plain bowl of legumes becomes supremely flavorful. Broccolini, not at all traditional to India, adds an appealing mildly peppery note. America grows its chickpeas in Idaho, Washington, and California.

SERVES 6 | 1¼ hours, plus at least 2 hours to soak

2 cups dried chickpeas (garbanzos), cleaned of debris
    and rinsed
2 to 3 serrano chiles, coarsely chopped
1 qt. vegetable broth or reduced-sodium chicken broth
1½ tsp. turmeric
1 tsp. ground cumin
About 1 tsp. kosher salt, divided
2 medium onions, thinly sliced
3 tbsp. vegetable oil
1 bunch broccolini (¾ lb.), stems sliced ½ in. thick and
    tops cut into 1½-in. florets
4 tsp. black mustard seeds
1½ tsp. cumin seeds
Hot cooked quinoa or basmati rice

1. Put chickpeas in a large pot, add water to cover by 2 in., and soak overnight. (Or bring to a boil over high heat, then turn off heat and soak about 2 hours.) Drain.
2. Pulse half the chickpeas in a food processor with ¼ cup fresh water until coarsely chopped. Pour into pot used for soaking. Repeat with remaining chickpeas, more water, and the chiles. Add broth, 1 cup water, the turmeric, ground cumin, and ¾ tsp. salt to pot.
3. Cover and bring to a boil over high heat, then reduce heat and simmer until chickpeas are tender, stirring occasionally, 40 to 50 minutes. Meanwhile, cook onions in oil in a large frying pan over medium heat, stirring occasionally, until deep golden, 12 to 15 minutes. Remove from heat.
4. Stir broccolini into chickpeas, return to simmering, and cook until tender, about 12 minutes.
5. Stir mustard and cumin seeds and remaining ¼ tsp. salt into onions and cook over medium-high heat, stirring, until cumin turns a shade darker, 2 minutes. Set aside about one-third of mixture and stir the rest into dal. Ladle dal and quinoa next to each other in bowls and top with reserved onion mixture. Add more salt to taste.

PER SERVING 369 CAL., 28% (105 CAL.) FROM FAT; 16 G PROTEIN; 12 G FAT (1.3 G SAT.); 52 G CARBO (14 G FIBER); 656 MG SODIUM; 0 MG CHOL.

Fresh herb and tofu curry

This fragrant coconut-milk curry is based on a dish served at Hawker Fare, the Thai-inspired eatery in Oakland from chef James Syhabout. Accompany the curry with rice or crusty bread.

SERVES 4 | 50 minutes

14 to 16 oz. firm tofu
1 tsp. salt
2 to 3 tbsp. canola oil
½ cup thinly sliced shallots
1 large garlic clove, finely chopped
6 to 8 fresh curry leaves (optional)*
1½ tsp. curry powder, preferably Madras
1 can (13.5 oz.) coconut milk
½ cup thinly sliced canned bamboo shoots, drained and rinsed
2 to 3 tsp. packed shaved light palm sugar* or light brown sugar
4 or 5 small heads baby bok choy, cut crosswise into 1-in. pieces
1 tsp. Thai or Vietnamese fish sauce
½ cup coarsely chopped fresh herbs, such as mint, cilantro,
    Thai basil, or Vietnamese coriander (*rau ram*)

1. Cut tofu into 16 rectangles shaped like husky dominoes (each about 1 in. wide, 1½ in. long, and 1 in. thick). Put in a wide, shallow bowl. Mix salt with 2 cups very hot or just-boiled water and pour over tofu to just cover. Let sit 15 minutes. Transfer to a double layer of paper towels on a plate and let drain 10 minutes.
2. Meanwhile, heat 2 tbsp. oil in a medium nonstick frying pan over medium heat. Fry shallots, stirring occasionally, until light golden, 9 to 10 minutes. Add garlic and curry leaves and fry 2 to 3 minutes, stirring constantly, until crisp. Add curry powder, remove from heat, and stir to aromatize spices. Using a slotted spoon, transfer seasonings to a bowl, leaving most of oil in pan.
3. Blot tofu dry. Add more oil to pan, if needed, to film bottom and heat to medium-high. Fry tofu, turning once, until golden, 4 to 5 minutes (it won't be crisp).
4. Lower heat slightly and return all but 1 tbsp. shallot mixture to pan. Add coconut milk, bamboo shoots, and palm sugar. Bring to a simmer and cook 2 to 3 minutes. Add bok choy and cook until tender, 3 to 5 minutes. Gently stir in fish sauce.
5. Transfer to a bowl and top with herbs and rest of shallots.
*Find curry leaves at Indian markets. Palm sugar has a musky, slightly molasses-like flavor; slice off shavings with a sharp knife before measuring. Find it at well-stocked grocery stores and Asian or Latino markets (in Indian markets, it's called jaggery, and in Latino markets, *piloncillo*).

PER SERVING 406 CAL., 76% (307 CAL.) FROM FAT; 15 G PROTEIN; 34 G FAT (19 G SAT.); 16 G CARBO (3.2 G FIBER); 324 MG SODIUM; 0 MG CHOL.

VIETNAMESE BEEF
NOODLE SOUP
(PHO BO)

Vietnamese beef noodle soup (Pho bo)

Pho, the beloved meat-and-noodle soup of Vietnam, has firmly established itself in the United States—particularly in the West, where large numbers of Vietnamese have settled. Noodle shops that sell huge, steaming bowls of pho abound in urban areas like Los Angeles, Seattle, San Francisco, and San Jose, and in many rural areas as well. Pho originated in Hanoi at the turn of the last century, possibly inspired by *pot-au-feu*, the beef stew of Vietnam's French colonial rulers, and incorporated Chinese-style rice noodles.

In those early days, it was a beef broth embellished only with noodles and sliced beef. As it spread to South Vietnam, pho took on spices and herbs and other ingredients—and it's this bounteous style of pho that crossed the ocean to the United States, brought by immigrants fleeing the fall of Saigon in 1975. Traditionally a breakfast dish, pho is in such demand that it now appears day and night here and in Vietnam.

For a streamlined *pho bo*, see Simpler Version and Make Ahead at right.

SERVES 6 | 2¼ to 2½ hours

½ cup thinly sliced fresh ginger
1 cup thinly sliced shallots
3 star anise pods (or 2 tsp. pieces) or 1 tsp. anise seeds
1 cinnamon stick (3 in. long)
1½ lbs. boned beef chuck, fat trimmed
2½ qts. beef broth
About ¼ cup Thai or Vietnamese fish sauce
1 tbsp. sugar
Salt
2 cups bean sprouts (5 to 6 oz.), rinsed
¼ cup very thinly sliced red or green chiles, such as Thai, serrano, or jalapeño
½ cup Thai or small regular basil leaves
½ cup cilantro leaves
3 limes, cut into wedges
½ lb. boned beef sirloin steak, fat trimmed and very thinly sliced*
6 cups Cooked Rice Noodles (recipe at right)
½ cup thinly sliced yellow onion
¾ cup thinly sliced green onions
Hoisin sauce and Asian red chili paste or sauce (optional)

1. Wrap ginger, shallots, star anise, and cinnamon stick in two layers of cheesecloth (about 17 in. square); tie with heavy cotton string. Combine beef chuck, broth, 2½ qts. water, ¼ cup fish sauce, sugar, and spice bundle in a large pot. Cover and bring to a boil over high heat; uncover, reduce heat, and simmer until beef is tender when pierced, 1½ to 1¾ hours.

2. Transfer meat to a board with a slotted spoon. Remove and discard spice bundle. Skim and discard fat from broth. Add salt and more fish sauce to taste. Return broth to a simmer.

3. Meanwhile, arrange bean sprouts, sliced chiles, basil, cilantro, and lime wedges on a platter. When beef chuck is cool enough to handle, thinly slice across the grain.

4. Immerse sliced sirloin in simmering broth (use a wire basket or strainer, if available) and cook just until brown on the outside but still pink in the center, 30 seconds to 1 minute; lift out (with basket or a slotted spoon).

5. Mound hot noodles in deep bowls (at least 3-cup capacity). Top with beef chuck, sirloin, and onions. Ladle broth over portions to cover generously.

6. Serve with platter of accompaniments and hoisin sauce and chili paste (if using) to add to taste.

*****To slice the sirloin as thin as possible, freeze it flat for 30 to 45 minutes, then cut it crosswise into 2- to 3-in.-long strips.

Simpler version To simplify the recipe, omit the beef chuck, increase the boned sirloin steak to 2 lbs., and increase the beef broth to 3 qts.; for steps 1 and 2, simmer broth (omit water) with the spice bundle and add fish sauce, sugar, and salt to taste.

Make ahead Sliced meat, up to 6 hours, chilled; broth (steps 1 and 2), up to 1 day, chilled (cover beef chuck and broth separately). Bring broth to a boil before serving.

PER SERVING 592 CAL., 17% (99 CAL.) FROM FAT; 42 G PROTEIN; 11 G FAT (4 G SAT.); 81 G CARBO (1.3 G FIBER); 768 MG SODIUM; 97 MG CHOL.

Cooked rice noodles (*Bun*) Dried rice noodles (*mai fun*, rice sticks, or rice vermicelli) range in width from about 1/16 to ¼ in.; for the pho bo, choose ⅛ in. wide. Bring 3 to 4 qts. water to a boil in a medium pan over high heat. Add 12 to 14 oz. **dried rice noodles** and stir to separate; cook until barely tender to the bite, 2 to 3 minutes. Drain. If not using immediately, rinse well to keep noodles from sticking together and drain again. Makes 6 to 8 cups; 6 to 8 servings.

PER SERVING 144 CAL., 0% FROM FAT; 0 G PROTEIN; 0 G FAT; 36 G CARBO (0 G FIBER); 75 MG SODIUM; 0 MG CHOL.

Warm soba noodle bowl

In this popular Japanese winter dish, soba, shiitakes, and other savory items are adrift in broth made with *dashi*—a soup base whose umami goodness comes from dried bonito tuna flakes and *kombu* seaweed. Warming soups like this are on menus in San Francisco's Japantown and L.A.'s Little Osaka, where the noodle shops and izakaya eateries are next to toy-and-manga stores.

SERVES 4 | 40 minutes

2 large eggs
6 cups liquid *dashi* (or use concentrate)*
4 shiitake mushrooms, stemmed and thinly sliced
1 tbsp. *each* mirin and soy sauce
16 oz. dried soba noodles
20 thin slices daikon, peeled
1 sheet nori seaweed, cut into ¼- by 1-in. strips
2 green onions, finely sliced diagonally

1. Put eggs in a small pot of cold water. Bring to a boil, remove from heat, cover, and let sit 15 minutes. Drain; rinse with cold water.

2. Bring dashi to a boil. Reduce heat to low and add mushrooms, mirin, and soy sauce.

3. Bring a 3-qt. saucepan of water to a boil. Add soba and cook, stirring to separate noodles, until softened, about 5 minutes. Drain but don't rinse. Divide noodles among serving bowls.

4. Pour 1½ cups of dashi over noodles in each bowl. Arrange mushrooms and daikon over noodles, dividing so each bowl has a neat row of both. Peel hard-cooked eggs and cut each in half lengthwise, placing a half in each bowl. Divide nori and green onions among bowls.

*Find liquid dashi in containers in Japanese groceries and some gourmet stores. It's more widely available as a dry concentrate called *dashi-no-moto*; reconstitute according to the package directions.

PER SERVING 436 CAL., 6.9% (30 CAL.) FROM FAT; 20 G PROTEIN; 3.3 G FAT (0.9 G SAT.); 88 G CARBO (0.4 G FIBER); 1,534 MG SODIUM; 106 MG CHOL.

WARM SOBA NOODLE BOWL

Green chile pork stew
(Chile verde)

This spicy, long-simmered pork dish is a fixture in New Mexico, Arizona, and Colorado cooking, and each state has its own version. (New Mexicans use their famous green chiles, naturally.) Ours is a bit of a combination.

SERVES 6 to 8 | 2½ hours

4 lbs. boned pork shoulder (butt), fat trimmed and
    cut into 2-in. cubes
2 to 3 tbsp. vegetable oil, if needed
3 onions (2 lbs. total), cut into ¼-in. wedges
5 large garlic cloves, minced
3 tbsp. ground cumin
1 can (28 oz.) peeled whole tomatoes
1 can (14.5 oz.) chicken broth
1½ lbs. Anaheim or poblano chiles (about 10), peeled*
    and chopped; or 4 cans (7 oz. each) whole green chiles,
    drained and chopped
2 tbsp. chopped oregano leaves
Salt and pepper
Chopped cilantro
Lime wedges

1. Put pork with ⅓ cup water in medium pan. Cover and cook over medium-high heat, stirring occasionally, until meat is very juicy, 15 to 20 minutes. Uncover, increase heat to high, and cook, stirring often, until the liquid has evaporated and meat is browned, 20 to 30 minutes. Lift out meat and set aside.

2. Reduce heat to medium. If you have leftover rendered pork fat in the pan, discard all but 3 tbsp.; if not, add oil. Add onions, garlic, and cumin; stir and cover. Cook, stirring occasionally, until onions are soft, about 8 minutes.

3. Return meat and any juices to pan. Add tomatoes (with their juice) and broth. Break up tomatoes with a spoon. Bring almost to a boil, then reduce to a gentle simmer, cover, and cook 1 hour.

4. Stir in chiles and oregano. Cover and cook until pork is very tender when pierced and flavors are blended, about 15 minutes. Season to taste with salt and pepper. Sprinkle with cilantro and serve with lime wedges to squeeze over stew.

*To peel chiles, remove stems, slice in half lengthwise, then remove ribs and seeds. Lay cut side down on a baking sheet and broil 4 to 5 in. from heat until black and blistered, 5 to 8 minutes. Let chiles cool, then peel.

PER SERVING 454 CAL., 38% (171 CAL.) FROM FAT; 50 G PROTEIN; 19 G FAT (6.2 G SAT.); 21 G CARBO (3.6 G FIBER); 362 MG SODIUM; 152 MG CHOL.

Red chile and pork stew
(Carne adovada)

In New Mexico, ground dried red chiles are used to thicken as well as season sauces. They are sold according to heat level, from mild and sweet to quite spicy, so be sure to buy a batch that suits your taste. And don't be put off by the large quantity called for in this recipe; the ingredient is nothing like cayenne or supermarket "chili powder." Ground Chimayo chiles have a particularly intense, flowery aroma (for sources, see below, right). Serve the stew with warm corn or flour tortillas if you like.

SERVES 6 | 2¾ hours

3 tbsp. vegetable oil, divided
2 medium onions, chopped
6 large garlic cloves, minced
3 tbsp. flour
1½ tsp. *each* salt and ground cumin
1 tsp. pepper
3½ lbs. boned pork shoulder (butt), fat trimmed and
    cut into 1½-in. cubes
1 cup ground dried mild red New Mexico chiles,
    preferably Chimayo*
4 cups reduced-sodium chicken broth
1 bay leaf

1. Preheat oven to 350°. Heat 2 tbsp. oil in a large, heavy-bottomed, ovenproof pot over medium-high heat. Add onions

RED CHILE AND PORK STEW
(*CARNE ADOVADA*)

and garlic and cook, stirring, until onions are golden, about 6 minutes. Remove from heat and transfer onions and garlic to a bowl with a slotted spoon.

2. Stir together flour, salt, cumin, and pepper in a large bowl. Add pork and toss to coat. Return pot to medium-high heat, add remaining 1 tbsp. oil, and, working in batches, lightly brown meat on all sides, 5 to 7 minutes per batch. Transfer meat to a separate bowl as you go.

3. Return onions and garlic to pot. Sprinkle with ground chiles and cook, stirring, 2 minutes (mixture will be thick). Add broth and, using a wooden spoon or spatula, scrape up any browned bits from bottom of pot.

4. Transfer contents of pot to a blender (in batches if needed) and purée until smooth. Return sauce to pot and add bay leaf and reserved pork.

5. Cover pot, put in oven, and cook 1 hour.

6. Set lid slightly ajar and continue cooking until pork is fork-tender, about 1 hour more.

*Find ground dried red Chimayo chile powder at Latino markets or online at *cibolojunction.com* or *santafeschoolofcooking.com*

PER SERVING 577 CAL., 47% (270 CAL.) FROM FAT; 57 G PROTEIN; 30 G FAT (8.5 G SAT.); 20 G CARBO (5.4 G FIBER); 1,171 MG SODIUM; 177 MG CHOL.

GRILLED SALMON
WITH CUCUMBER
SALAD *recipe on page 120*

Main Courses

Think of the West's foods as a pot-luck of contributions from regional kitchens. On that crowded buffet table, the recipes here are the main attractions—from the Northwest's cedar-planked salmon, the Rockies' bison burgers, and New Mexico's chile enchiladas to California's fish tacos and greens-topped pizza.

Santa Maria–style grilled tri-tip

When Spanish settlers came to California, missions weren't all they established. In the Central Coast valley of Santa Maria, *rancheros*—the owners of huge cattle spreads—would, after the annual calf branding, host Spanish-style cookouts to feed family, friends, and *vaqueros* (the original American cowboys). Besides beef, the menu included salsa, bread, and tiny local pinquito beans. Those dishes are at the heart of what has become Santa Maria–style barbecue, served along the Central Coast and its inland valleys. The meat is either a thick cut of boned top sirloin or a tri-tip, usually seasoned with nothing more than salt, garlic salt, and black pepper and grilled over local red oak on a massive black grate.

The red oak gives the meat a wonderful, rustic flavor. Using chips, which are easier to obtain if you're outside the area, isn't quite the same as grilling over logs, but it's close. Serve the tri-tip with pinquito beans and salsa (recipes at right) and grilled garlic bread.

SERVES 8 | 45 minutes, plus at least 45 minutes to stand

2 tbsp. garlic powder
1½ tbsp. kosher salt
1 tsp. pepper
2 tsp. dried parsley
1 beef tri-tip (2 to 2½ lbs.), preferably with some fat on one side
2 cups red oak chips*, soaked in water for at least 20 minutes

1. Mix garlic powder, salt, pepper, and parsley together in a small bowl; rub over and into meat. Let stand 30 minutes at room temperature.
2. Meanwhile, prepare a grill for indirect medium-high heat (see "How-to: Grilling," page 83) and add chips to the grill. Set beef tri-tip over direct heat, with the fat side up, and sear until nicely browned (close lid on gas grill), 3 to 5 minutes; turn meat over and sear other side.
3. Move tri-tip over indirect-heat area and grill, turning every 10 minutes or so, until an instant-read thermometer inserted into thickest part registers 125° to 130°, 25 to 35 minutes.
4. Transfer tri-tip to a cutting board and let rest at least 15 minutes (keep grill going if you are making grilled garlic bread). Slice meat across the grain as thin or as thick as you like.
*You can order red oak chips online from Susy Q's Brand (*susieqbrand.com*).

PER SERVING 290 CAL., 50% (146 CAL.) FROM FAT; 32 G PROTEIN; 16 G FAT (6.1 G SAT.); 1.8 G CARBO (0.3 G FIBER); 1,158 MG SODIUM; 72 MG CHOL.

Santa Maria–style pinquito beans
Some Santa Maria cooks use diced ham instead of bacon, which is really good too.

SERVES 8 generously | 2½ to 3 hours

1 lb. dried pinquito (small pink) beans*
8 slices (about ½ lb.) bacon, chopped
2 onions, chopped
2 garlic cloves, minced
½ cup *each* tomato purée and canned red chile or red enchilada sauce
1 tbsp. *each* firmly packed brown sugar and stone-ground mustard
1 tsp. salt

1. Pick over and rinse beans. Put in a 6-qt. pot and cover with water. Bring to a boil, cover, take off heat, and let stand 1 hour.
2. Drain beans. Cover with fresh water, bring to a boil, lower heat to a simmer, and cook, covered, until tender, anywhere from 40 to 90 minutes, depending on freshness of beans. Drain, reserving 1 cup cooking liquid along with beans.
3. In a 5-qt. pot over medium-high heat, cook bacon until crisp, stirring a few times. Pour off all but 1 tbsp. fat from pan. Add onions and garlic and cook, stirring, until onions just start to brown, about 4 minutes. Add tomato purée, red chile sauce, brown sugar, mustard, salt, beans, and reserved cooking liquid. Bring to a boil, stirring often, then lower heat and simmer for about 10 minutes to blend flavors.
*Find pinquito beans at grocery stores throughout Central California. You can also order them online from Susie Q's Brand (*susieqbrand.com*).

PER 1-CUP SERVING 296 CAL., 19% (57 CAL.) FROM FAT; 16 G PROTEIN; 6.4 G FAT (2.1 G SAT.); 44 G CARBO (8.2 G FIBER); 678 MG SODIUM; 12 MG CHOL.

Santa Maria salsa Fresh and uncomplicated, this salsa goes with just about anything grilled. In a medium bowl, mix 4 chopped **ripe tomatoes** (1 lb. total); ½ cup *each* thinly sliced **green onions** and chopped **poblano chiles**; ¼ cup diced **celery**; 3 tbsp. chopped **cilantro**; 4 tsp. **red wine vinegar**; 1½ tsp. **kosher salt**; ¼ tsp. **dried oregano**; and a dash *each* **Tabasco** and **Worcestershire**. Taste and add more salt, if needed. Makes about 3½ cups.

PER ½-CUP SERVING 16 CAL., 9% (1.5 CAL.) FROM FAT; 0.8 G PROTEIN; 0.2 G FAT (0 G SAT.); 3.5 G CARBO (1 G FIBER); 368 MG SODIUM; 0 MG CHOL.

GRILLED RIB-EYE
STEAKS WITH MISO
BUTTER AND SWEET
ONIONS

Grilled rib-eye steaks with miso butter and sweet onions

Add Japanese miso paste to butter to emphasize the savory umami quality. Walla Walla onions are a mellow accompaniment; Washington farmers bred the onions for sweetness after planting seeds brought to the state from Corsica by a French immigrant in 1900.

SERVES 4 generously | 40 minutes, plus 30 minutes to freeze butter

½ cup unsalted butter, softened
2 tbsp. plus 1 tsp. white or yellow miso paste
1 tbsp. finely minced chives
1½ tsp. minced garlic
4 boned rib-eye steaks (¾ to 1 in. thick)
Salt and pepper
4 sweet onions, such as Walla Walla or Maui
About 3 tbsp. olive oil

1. Stir together butter, miso, chives, and garlic in a small bowl. Spoon butter mixture onto a square of plastic wrap or waxed paper, fold plastic or paper over butter from top and bottom, and form into a log about 1½ in. thick. Twist ends of plastic or paper to close. Put in freezer until firm, about 30 minutes.
2. Meanwhile, pat steaks dry and season well with salt and pepper; let stand at room temperature 15 to 25 minutes. Cut onions in half crosswise. Trim about ½ in. from the rounded side of each onion half so that sides will lie flat on the grill. Rub onions with some oil and salt and pepper to taste.
3. Prepare a grill for direct medium-high heat (see "How-to: Grilling," page 83). Grill onions 2 minutes, then add steaks and grill until browned, 3 to 4 minutes. Turn everything over. Onions will need another 6 to 8 minutes, until they're softened and browned. For steaks, cook an additional 2 to 4 minutes for rare, 5 to 7 minutes for medium-rare, and 8 to 15 minutes for well done (cut to test).
4. Remove wrapping from miso butter; top each steak with 2 tsp. miso butter (you will have some butter left over). Serve with grilled onions.

PER SERVING 1,030 CAL., 71% (729 CAL.) FROM FAT; 57 G PROTEIN; 81 G FAT (35 G SAT.); 19 G CARBO (3.3 G FIBER); 521 MG SODIUM; 237 MG CHOL.

Grilled skirt steak (Arracheras)

Mexican *arracheras*, like Tex-Mex fajitas, are marinated skirt steaks cooked quickly over high heat to produce a nicely browned crust and pink interior. This recipe is from Santa Fe barbecue experts Bill Jamison and Cheryl Alters Jamison.

SERVES 6 to 8 | 40 minutes, plus at least 5 hours to marinate

2 beef skirt steaks (1 to 1¼ lbs. each), fat and membrane trimmed
1 bottle or can (12 oz.) beer
¼ cup *each* orange juice and lime juice
2 to 3 tbsp. chipotle hot sauce, such as Tabasco Chipotle Pepper Sauce, plus more for serving
2 tbsp. minced garlic
1½ tbsp. kosher salt
1½ tsp. ground cumin
3 large red onions, cut into ½-in.-thick slices
Vegetable-oil cooking spray
12 flour tortillas (8 in. wide), warmed
Lime wedges

1. Cut each steak in half crosswise. Put in a large resealable plastic bag. Stir together beer, orange juice, lime juice, hot sauce, and garlic, then pour over steaks. Seal bag and refrigerate at least 5 hours and up to overnight.
2. Prepare a grill for direct medium-high heat (see "How-to: Grilling," page 83). Drain meat and discard marinade. Blot dry with paper towels. Mix salt and cumin and rub into meat.
3. Spray onions lightly with oil and set, with steaks, on cooking grate. Do not cover. Turn steaks at least once while grilling (more if juice starts to pool on surface). For medium-rare to medium (cut to test), grill steaks 3 to 4 minutes per side if less than ½ in. thick; add 1 minute more per side if more than ½ in. thick. Grill onions, turning once, until browned on both sides and cooked through, 8 to 10 minutes total.
4. Transfer steaks to a platter and let rest 5 minutes. With a sharp knife at a slight diagonal, cut across the meat's grain into thin strips. Serve steak and onions with tortillas, lime wedges, and hot sauce.

PER SERVING 463 CAL., 33% (153 CAL.) FROM FAT; 32 G PROTEIN; 17 G FAT (5.1 G SAT.); 43 G CARBO (3.4 G FIBER); 1,345 MG SODIUM; 58 MG CHOL.

Dutch oven–braised beef and summer vegetables

After a day of hiking or swimming at Lost Lake, near Mt. Hood, Adam Sappington—chef at the Country Cat, in Portland—likes the simplicity of this one-pot meal. The frozen marinated meat acts as a handy ice block in the ice chest.

SERVES 6 | 3 hours (about 2½ hours in camp)

BEEF
6 garlic cloves, minced
2 tbsp. roughly chopped rosemary leaves
2 tbsp. olive oil
About 1 tsp. kosher salt
About ½ tsp. pepper
1 boneless beef chuck roast (about 2 lbs.)

VEGETABLES & COOKING
1 pt. cherry tomatoes, stems removed
2 ears corn, cleaned and cut into thirds
1 onion, cut into 6 wedges
½ lb. green beans, ends trimmed, cut in half
6 baby zucchini (½ lb. total), ends trimmed, or regular zucchini cut into chunks
¾ lb. thin-skinned potatoes (about 1 in. wide)

2 tbsp. butter
About 3 cups chicken broth, divided

1. At home, prepare the beef: In a bowl, combine garlic, rosemary, oil, 1 tsp. salt, and ½ tsp. pepper. Rub all over beef and pack in a resealable plastic bag. Chill up to 2 days, or freeze.
2. At home, prepare the vegetables: Put tomatoes, corn, and onion in a resealable plastic bag, and green beans and zucchini in another; chill up to 2 days. Don't chill potatoes.
3. In camp: Set up a fire for top and bottom dutch-oven cooking (see "How-to: Dutch Oven," step 2, below). Put a 4- to 6-qt. cast-iron camp dutch oven in place, add butter, and melt. Add beef; cook until browned on one side, 10 minutes. Turn meat over, add 2 cups broth, and cover. Arrange coals on top of pot, then add more fuel every 30 minutes (see "Start Cooking," below); cook 1 hour.
4. Turn meat over, add 1 cup broth, tomatoes, corn, onion, and potatoes; cook, covered, 1 hour. Turn meat and corn, add beans and zucchini, and more broth if pot is getting dry; cook, covered, until meat is very tender, 15 to 30 minutes. Season with more salt and pepper to taste.

PER SERVING 442 CAL., 42% (187 CAL.) FROM FAT; 38 G PROTEIN; 21 G FAT (6.9 G SAT.); 26 G CARBO (5.7 G FIBER); 582 MG SODIUM; 102 MG CHOL.

How-to: Dutch oven

You can cook practically anything in this versatile cast-iron pot—it's a stewpot, a frying pan, and an oven in one. All you need is an open fire.

Dutch ovens traveled west with the pioneers and explorers, including Lewis and Clark in 1805, and were indispensable to cowboys on the range. (The ovens are not actually Dutch, but acquired the name because superior ones were produced in the Netherlands.) The dutch oven is still much loved in the West, especially in Utah, where it's an official state symbol.

Sources for buying include Lodge Manufacturing Company (*lodgemfg.com*). The best model is the camp dutch oven, which has little pointy legs to raise it over, not right on top of, the coals (this keeps the food from burning). It also has a rimmed lid to hold coals—which inverts to become a griddle.

1. Prepare the fire
If you have a campfire going, move any large pieces of still-burning wood to the side and level out the hot coals into a circle the diameter of the dutch oven. If the campground doesn't allow wood fires, burn 50 charcoal briquets until they're mostly gray, 10 to 15 minutes, and spread into an even layer that's the diameter of the dutch oven.

2. Set up the oven
For many recipes, just set the dutch oven over the hot coals. Occasionally, though, heat should come from above as well as below: Scrape about half the coals to the side and arrange the rest in a circle the size of the dutch oven's outer edge. Set the oven on top of the circle of coals, then pile the rest of the coals evenly on top of the lid. Add or remove coals (2 coals from the lid for every 1 from below) to raise and lower the temperature, keeping the coals evenly spaced.

3. Start cooking
Lift the dutch-oven lid occasionally to check the food and temperature. To decrease the heat, scrape away some fuel. To increase the heat, or to cook longer than 45 minutes, add 6 to 10 new briquets or more wood embers (from that still-burning wood you moved to the side of your firepit) every 30 minutes.

GREEN CHILES
STUFFED WITH BEEF,
ALMONDS, AND
RAISINS

Green chiles stuffed with beef, almonds, and raisins

Raisins, nuts, and a slightly sweet tomato sauce soften the citrusy heat of the chiles.

SERVES 5 or 6 | 1¾ hours

⅓ cup plus ¾ cup slivered almonds
15 to 18 green New Mexico or Anaheim chiles*
1 tbsp. olive oil
8 large garlic cloves, minced, divided
¾ cup chopped onion
1 lb. ground beef
1½ tsp. salt, divided
1 tsp. *each* cinnamon, ground cumin, and pepper
⅓ cup raisins
½ cup fine dried bread crumbs
2 tbsp. chopped oregano leaves
½ lb. *queso fresco*, crumbled
1 can (28 oz.) crushed tomatoes
2 tbsp. honey

1. Preheat oven to 350°. Spread nuts in a baking pan and toast until golden, 8 to 12 minutes. Meanwhile, slice off chile stems. With a spoon or melon baller, scoop out and discard seeds and white membranes (avoid slitting chiles). Raise oven to 375°.
2. Add oil to a frying pan over medium-high heat. Add half the garlic and the onion and cook, stirring often, until onion is translucent, 3 minutes. Add beef, 1 tsp. salt, the cinnamon, cumin, and pepper and cook, breaking up beef, until it's cooked through, about 10 minutes. Add raisins and cook, stirring, 3 minutes. Add bread crumbs, oregano, ⅓ cup almonds, and the queso fresco. Cook, stirring, 2 minutes; remove from heat.
3. Carefully pack each chile with beef filling. Put chiles in a large baking pan and bake until chiles are browned and beginning to blister, 35 to 45 minutes.
4. Meanwhile, make sauce: In a large frying pan over medium heat, bring tomatoes, honey, remaining garlic, and ½ tsp. salt to a gentle simmer. Cook until most of liquid has evaporated, about 15 minutes. Stir in remaining ¾ cup toasted almonds. Transfer sauce to a blender, add ½ cup water, and blend until very smooth, about 1 minute. Drizzle sauce over chiles.
*For sources, see "From the Field: New Mexico Chiles," page 104. Queso fresco is a mild, crumbly Mexican cheese sold in Latino markets and some supermarkets; if you can't find it, substitute farmer's cheese or feta.

PER 3-CHILE SERVING 568 CAL., 52% (297 CAL.) FROM FAT; 31 G PROTEIN; 33 G FAT (11 G SAT.); 40 G CARBO (4.4 G FIBER); 1,202 MG SODIUM; 76 MG CHOL.

Cola shredded-beef tacos

The cola tempers the chiles' heat and adds a delicious sweetness to the sauce in this recipe, adapted from *Amor y Tacos*, by San Diego chef Deborah Schneider. (Photo on front cover.)

MAKES 12 tacos; 6 servings | 4¼ hours

3 medium dried ancho chiles*
2 large dried guajillo chiles*
2 tbsp. canola oil, divided
¼ cup finely chopped red onion
2 large garlic cloves, sliced
½ tsp. cumin seeds
1 cup canned diced tomatoes
1 tsp. dried oregano, preferably Mexican*
2 tsp. kosher salt, divided
2 lbs. chuck roast, fat trimmed and cut into 4 pieces
1 bay leaf
1½ cups Mexican Coca-Cola (cane-sugar sweetened)*
    or another cola (not diet)
12 or 24 corn tortillas (6 in. wide; use 24 if they're thin)*
Chopped avocado, red onion, and cilantro; thinly sliced pickled
    jalapeños; and *crema* (Mexican cultured cream)* or sour cream

1. Wipe chiles clean with a damp cloth; stem, seed, and tear into pieces. Heat 1 tbsp. oil in a heavy saucepan over medium heat. Add onion and garlic and cook, stirring, until softened, 2 minutes. Add chiles and cook, stirring, until fragrant, 1 to 2 minutes. Add 1½ cups water, the cumin seeds, tomatoes, oregano, and 1 tsp. salt. Bring to a boil; reduce heat and simmer, covered, until chiles are softened, 10 minutes. Purée in a blender until smooth.
2. Meanwhile, season beef with remaining 1 tsp. salt. Heat remaining 1 tbsp. oil in a 5- to 6-qt. pot over medium-high heat. Brown beef all over, 10 to 14 minutes. Discard fat, if any.
3. Pour chile sauce into pot and add bay leaf, cola, and a little water if needed to barely cover meat. Cover, reduce heat, and simmer until beef is very tender, about 3 hours.
4. With a slotted spoon, transfer beef to a plate. Let cool slightly; tear into shreds, discarding any fat or gristle. Meanwhile, boil sauce over medium-high heat, stirring occasionally, until slightly thickened and reduced to about 3 cups, 10 to 30 minutes. Stir in beef and heat a few minutes until hot. Remove bay leaf.
5. Transfer beef with some sauce to a bowl. Spoon beef into tortillas, tuck in accompaniments, and serve with more sauce.
*Find dried chiles, Mexican oregano, Mexican Coca-Cola, and *crema* at a Latino market. To heat tortillas, wrap in a kitchen towel and microwave until warm and soft, about 1 minute.

PER 2-TACO SERVING 587 CAL., 54% (315 CAL.) FROM FAT; 32 G PROTEIN; 35 G FAT (11 G SAT.); 40 G CARBO (6.5 G FIBER); 607 MG SODIUM; 107 MG CHOL.

Korean kimchi burgers

The Korean fusion wave continues to crest—and these zesty burgers with a fresh kimchi-style topping might help explain why. For a shortcut, omit the recipe's cabbage relish and use kimchi from the supermarket or Asian market; the recipe will be saltier, though. Pair the burgers with a beer with balanced malt and hops, like Saigon Export.

MAKES 4 burgers | 35 minutes

3 cups finely shredded napa cabbage
½ cup thinly sliced green onions, divided
3 tbsp. seasoned rice vinegar
4 tsp. *each* minced garlic and fresh ginger, divided
1 tbsp. toasted sesame oil, divided
1½ tsp. Asian chili garlic sauce, divided
¼ cup mayonnaise
1½ lbs. ground beef chuck

KOREAN KIMCHI
BURGERS

2 tbsp. soy sauce
4 hamburger buns, split

1. Prepare grill for high heat (see "How-to: Grilling," below, right).
2. Meanwhile, mix cabbage, ¼ cup green onions, the vinegar, 1 tsp. *each* garlic and ginger, 2 tsp. sesame oil, and ½ tsp. chili sauce in a large bowl. Set relish aside, stirring occasionally. In another bowl, mix mayonnaise with remaining 1 tsp. chili sauce.
3. Combine beef, soy sauce, and remaining ¼ cup green onions, 1 tbsp. *each* garlic and ginger, and 1 tsp. sesame oil. Shape into 4 patties, each about ½ in. thick.
4. Oil cooking grate, using tongs and a wad of oiled paper towels. Grill burgers, covered, turning once, 7 to 8 minutes total for medium. In the final minutes, toast buns.
5. Spread bun bottoms with chili mayonnaise. Set burgers on buns. With a slotted spoon, put some cabbage relish on each. Serve with remaining relish.

PER SERVING 607 CAL., 55% (336 CAL.) FROM FAT; 35 G PROTEIN; 37 G FAT (10 G SAT.); 27 G CARBO (1.8 G FIBER); 1,049 MG SODIUM; 110 MG CHOL.

Grass-fed burgers with chipotle barbecue sauce

Grass-fed operations are easier on the environment than grain feedlots, and easier on the animals (grass is, after all, a cow's natural diet). Grass-feeding gives a truer beef flavor, not masked by fat marbling, and the beef is lower in saturated fat and higher in omega-3s. Just don't overcook it, as the meat cooks faster than grain-fed. A side note about burgers: Who knew in 1940, when the McDonald brothers opened their first restaurant in San Bernardino, California, that it would dramatically affect the way Americans eat? Here's our redo of an iconic fast food.

MAKES 4 burgers | 35 minutes

CHIPOTLE BARBECUE SAUCE
¼ cup firmly packed light brown sugar
½ cup ketchup
2 tbsp. canned chipotle chiles in adobo sauce
    (about 3 chiles), plus 1 tbsp. sauce
1 tbsp. Worcestershire
2 tbsp. *each* molasses and thawed orange juice concentrate
1 tsp. minced garlic

BURGERS
1¼ lbs. grass-fed ground beef
2 tsp. *each* kosher salt and pepper, divided
1 red onion, cut ¼ to ½ in. thick crosswise
3 tsp. vegetable oil, divided
4 slices Swiss cheese

4 sesame-seed hamburger buns
4 slices ripe tomato
4 butter or romaine lettuce leaves

1. Make chipotle barbecue sauce: Purée all sauce ingredients in a blender or food processor until very smooth.
2. Make burgers: In a medium bowl, combine beef and 1½ tsp. *each* salt and pepper. Form into 4 patties, each about ¾ in. thick and slightly thinner in the center (burgers will even out while cooking). Put on a plate, cover, and chill until ready to grill.
3. Prepare a grill for direct medium heat (see "How-to: Grilling," below). Sprinkle onion slices with remaining ½ tsp. *each* salt and pepper and 1 tsp. oil. Grill, covered, until softened, turning once, about 8 minutes total.
4. Meanwhile, rub burgers with remaining 2 tsp. oil and set on grill. Close lid on grill and cook burgers, turning once, about 6 minutes total for medium-rare. In last few minutes of cooking, lay a slice of cheese on each burger. Toast bun halves on grill.
5. Transfer buns to a platter; put burgers and onions on bun bottoms. Spoon about 1½ tbsp. barbecue sauce on top of each and add a slice of tomato, a lettuce leaf, and bun tops.

PER BURGER, WITH 1½ TBSP. SAUCE AND TRIMMINGS 612 CAL., 50% (306 CAL.) FROM FAT; 36 G PROTEIN; 34 G FAT (14 G SAT.); 41 G CARBO (2.3 G FIBER); 1,175 MG SODIUM; 112 MG CHOL.

GRASS-FED BURGERS WITH CHIPOTLE BARBECUE SAUCE

How-to: Grilling

Direct heat
With a gas grill Follow your grill's lighting instructions and turn all burners to high. Close the lid, and wait for the grill to get hot. Then adjust the burners for the temperature range you need. As you cook, keep the lid closed as much as possible.
With a charcoal grill Our favorite way to ignite coals is with a chimney starter: Stuff a few pieces of crumpled newspaper into its base, then fill with charcoal. Set the chimney on the firegrate and open the vents underneath the grill. Ignite the paper and let the chimney burn until all the charcoal ignites, 7 to 20 minutes depending on the coals (grooved burn faster). Spread charcoal out with tongs. Put the cooking grate in place to preheat and let the coals burn to the heat specified in the recipe. Grill with the lid on (and its vents open) for the most even cooking, or keep the lid off for easy access. If you need to reduce the fire's temperature, partially close the vents in the lid and at firegrate level.

Indirect heat
With a gas grill Put a drip pan in place under one part of the cooking grate (the indirect-heat area), then light only the burner or burners on the rest of the grill (the direct-heat area).
With a charcoal grill Bank ignited coals on opposite sides of the firegrate, leaving a cleared area in the middle. Set a drip pan in the cleared area. Let coals burn down to the temperature that's specified in the recipe. Maintain temperature by adding 10 to 12 briquets to fire every 30 minutes; if fire gets too hot, partially close vents under grill and on lid.

Taking the temperature
If your grill doesn't have a built-in thermometer, use the following "hand test." On a charcoal grill, especially, temps can fluctuate quite a bit (your cue to move the food to a hotter or cooler spot, or to add coals). Hold your hand 5 in. above the cooking grate to determine temperature level:
Very high 550° to 650°; you can hold your hand 5 in. above the cooking grate only 1 to 2 seconds.
High 450° to 550°; only 2 to 4 seconds.
Medium 350° to 450°; only 5 to 7 seconds.
Low 250° to 350°; only 8 to 10 seconds.

Vietnamese-style steak salad

We tested this salad using grass-fed beef, which is leaner than regular beef and cooks a lot faster. Because it's so lean, don't cook the meat beyond medium-rare—otherwise it will be tough. The clean taste of grass-fed beef is complemented by lemongrass.

SERVES 4 | 1¾ hours, plus 1 hour to marinate

RUB & STEAKS

3 stalks fresh lemongrass
2 quarter-size slices fresh ginger
1 garlic clove, quartered
1 medium shallot, sliced
1 tbsp. vegetable oil
1¼ tsp. kosher salt, divided
2 New York beef strip steaks (½ lb. each), fat trimmed, or 1 beef skirt steak (1 lb. total), preferably grass-fed

VINAIGRETTE

½ cup vegetable oil
8 large garlic cloves, very thinly sliced
⅓ cup lime juice (from 3 or 4 large limes)
2 tsp. sugar
2 tbsp. Thai or Vietnamese fish sauce

SALAD

¼ lb. thin rice-stick noodles
½ cup shredded carrot
1 cup thinly sliced cucumber
2 qts. chopped napa cabbage
¼ cup *each* chopped cilantro, mint leaves, and green onions

1. Make rub: Pull off tough outer layers of lemongrass and cut off stem end and coarse leaves. Chop tender inner stalk and then very finely chop in a food processor, scraping down bowl side as needed. Add ginger, garlic, and shallot and process into a paste, 2 to 3 minutes more. Add oil and ¼ tsp. salt; pulse to combine.

2. Sprinkle steaks with remaining 1 tsp. salt, then cover both sides with lemongrass rub. Chill at least 1 hour and up to 6.

3. Make vinaigrette: Heat oil in a medium frying pan over medium heat. Add garlic and cook until light golden, stirring gently, being careful not to burn (it will continue to darken off the heat). Pour garlic and oil through a strainer into a small, heatproof mixing bowl. Lift out garlic chips, reserving oil, and drain chips on paper towels. After oil has cooled slightly, whisk in lime juice, sugar, and fish sauce.

4. Make salad: In a medium saucepan, bring 2 qts. water to a boil and add rice noodles. Cook until tender, 3 to 5 minutes. Drain and put in a large bowl. Add carrot, cucumber, cabbage, cilantro, mint, and green onions.

5. Prepare a grill for direct high heat (see "How-to: Grilling," page 83). Grill steaks (close lid on gas grill), using a wide spatula to turn once (keeping as much of crust on steaks as possible), about 8 minutes total for medium-rare. Transfer steaks to a cutting board, tent with foil, and let rest at least 5 minutes.

6. Pour vinaigrette over salad and toss thoroughly. Divide salad among bowls. Slice steaks (trying to keep crust on slices) and arrange over salads. Sprinkle with garlic chips.

Make ahead Rub, vinaigrette, and salad, several hours ahead; toss salad together while steaks grill.

PER SERVING 584 CAL., 59% (342 CAL.) FROM FAT; 24 G PROTEIN; 38 G FAT (6.5 G SAT.); 37 G CARBO (3.5 G FIBER); 729 MG SODIUM; 49 MG CHOL.

VIETNAMESE-STYLE
STEAK SALAD

Chorizo-beef dinner nachos

Our super-stacked version of nachos has chorizo, juicy chopped steak, black beans, guacamole, and crisp lettuce. The ultimate crowd-pleaser, nachos were invented in 1943 by a maître d' at the Victory Club in Piedras Negras, Mexico (just across the border from Eagle Pass, Texas). Ignacio "Nacho" Anaya was the only restaurant employee on-site when a group of U.S. military wives came in for a snack. With no cooks around, he cobbled together a pile of tortilla chips topped with melted cheese and jalapeños. His creation, quickly imitated by others, became hugely popular, paving the way for massive concession-stand revenues across America.

SERVES 6 | 45 minutes

5 oz. beef skirt steak, chopped; or ground lean beef
5 oz. Mexican-style firm chorizo sausage*, casings removed and finely crumbled
1 medium onion
1 large garlic clove
1 tsp. ground cumin, divided
1½ cups plus 1 tbsp. salsa verde, store-bought or homemade (for a recipe, see Roasted Poblano Chipotle Salsa, page 14)
1 can (15 oz.) black beans, drained and rinsed
½ tsp. dried oregano
1 can (4 oz.) diced green chiles, drained
1 large firm-ripe avocado
1 tbsp. lime juice
2 tbsp. chopped cilantro, divided
Kosher salt
9 cups tortilla chips
2 cups (½ lb.) shredded jack cheese
4 cups finely shredded iceberg lettuce

1. Preheat oven to 400°. Brown steak and chorizo in a large frying pan over medium-high heat, stirring, about 5 minutes. Meanwhile, chop onion and mince garlic. Add onion and all but ⅛ tsp. cumin to pan. Cook, stirring often, until onion is soft, 4 to 5 minutes. Reduce heat to medium, then stir in 1½ cups salsa. Simmer until mixture is thick, 8 to 10 minutes, stirring occasionally.

2. While steak mixture simmers, combine black beans, ¾ cup water, oregano, 1 tsp. garlic, and the chiles in a small saucepan. Bring to a boil over high heat; reduce heat and simmer until all but about ¼ cup liquid has evaporated, about 10 minutes.

3. Meanwhile, make guacamole: Pit and peel avocado. In a bowl, mash the avocado with remaining 1 tbsp. salsa and ⅛ tsp. cumin, remaining garlic, and the lime juice. Stir 1 tbsp. cilantro into guacamole and add salt to taste.

CHORIZO-BEEF
DINNER NACHOS

4. Line a large rimmed baking sheet with parchment paper. Arrange chips in a 12-in. circle. Sprinkle with jack cheese. Bake until cheese melts, 3 to 4 minutes.

5. While chips are baking, arrange lettuce around rim of a large serving platter (at least 16 in. wide). With a wide spatula, loosen chips from parchment. Carefully lift parchment from pan, then slide chips off paper into center of platter. Spoon meat mixture over chips. With a slotted spoon, top with beans. Spoon guacamole over center of nachos and sprinkle with remaining 1 tbsp. cilantro.

*Buy firm, fresh chorizo in natural casings at well-stocked supermarkets or Latino markets. Very soft, bright red chorizo in plastic casings isn't nearly as good.

PER SERVING 795 CAL., 55% (441 CAL.) FROM FAT; 29 G PROTEIN; 49 G FAT (16 G SAT.); 63 G CARBO (8.4 G FIBER); 1,271 MG SODIUM; 75 MG CHOL.

Char siu–glazed pork and pineapple buns

Chinese-style barbecued pork, or *char siu*, is popular throughout the Hawaiian Islands. We like to serve the tangy-sweet meat in soft rolls (Hawaiian sweet rolls, if possible) at a cocktail-party twist on the luau. You might start with Pineapple Cosmos (page 22) and Caramelized Maui Onion Dip (page 13), followed by Green Salad with Papaya-Seed Dressing (page 40) and these little buns, and end with Chocolate Liliko'i Parfaits (page 210).

SERVES 12 | 1 hour, plus 3 hours to brine

¼ cup *each* kosher salt and packed light brown sugar
1 tbsp. Hawaiian vanilla extract*
2 pork tenderloins (about 1 lb. each)
½ cup *each* ketchup and hoisin sauce
2 tbsp. *each* Asian (toasted) sesame oil, minced garlic, minced fresh ginger, and low-sodium soy sauce
12 slices peeled, cored fresh pineapple
24 King's Hawaiian sweet rolls or other small soft rolls, warmed on the grill if you like
1 cup cilantro sprigs

1. Make brine: In a large pot, bring 3½ cups water to a boil. Stir in salt, brown sugar, and vanilla. Chill until cool.

2. Put pork in a 9- by 13-in. pan and pour on brine. Chill at least 3 hours and up to 12.

3. Make char siu glaze: In a small bowl, mix together ketchup, hoisin, sesame oil, garlic, ginger, and soy sauce. Pour half of sauce into another small bowl.

4. Prepare a grill for indirect medium heat (see "How-to: Grilling," page 83). Lay pork over indirect-heat area, close lid on grill, and cook until an instant-read thermometer inserted into thickest part registers 135°, 15 to 20 minutes.

5. Using a pastry brush and one bowl of glaze, cover pork with glaze, reserving 2 tbsp. for pineapple. Cook pork (if you're using charcoal, add 6 to 8 briquets to maintain temperature), turning occasionally, until glaze has caramelized slightly and meat registers 145°. Transfer grilled pork to a cutting board, tent with foil, and let rest 15 minutes.

6. Lay pineapple on direct-heat area of grill, brush with reserved glaze, and cook, turning once, until grill marks appear. Remove slices from grill and cut each in half.

7. Cut pork into ½-in.-thick slices. Cut a deep diagonal slit across top of each roll. Fill each roll with a piece of pork, a grilled pineapple slice, a cilantro sprig, and ½ tsp. glaze from second bowl. Serve rolls with remaining glaze for drizzling.

*Find aromatic Hawaiian vanilla extract at specialty-foods stores and *hawaiianvanilla.com*; vanilla extract from elsewhere works too.
Make ahead Brine pork and make char siu glaze up to 1 day ahead and chill.

PER 2-BUN SERVING 424 CAL., 25% (108 CAL.) FROM FAT; 26 G PROTEIN; 12 G FAT (5.2 G SAT.); 53 G CARBO (3.2 G FIBER); 823 MG SODIUM; 87 MG CHOL.

The Hawaiian luau

Huge celebratory feasts have long been a tradition in Polynesia, of which Hawaii is geographically and culturally a part. And the luau—originally known as 'aha'aina ("gathering")—was the way 19th-century Hawaiian royalty showed hospitality to guests.

At early luaus, guests helped themselves from large platters of food and ate with their hands—a key part of the pleasure of the feast. In fact, the luau staple of poi, a glutinous porridge of pounded taro, was described in terms of how many fingers it took to scoop it up: three-, two-, or one-finger poi. The best-known item at today's luau is *kalua* pig. Kalua, meaning "the hole," refers to an underground oven. Making a kalua involves digging the hole, laying a wood fire, and adding rocks to retain heat. A whole pig is set in the kalua, damp banana or ti leaves are layered into the pit to create steam, and everything is covered with wet burlap bags and soil. The cooking process can take up to two days, but the succulent results are well worth the wait.

Other luau foods include *lomi* salmon (fish crushed with tomatoes and sweet Maui onions), *laulau* (pork and/or fish steamed in taro or ti leaves), and *haupia* (coconut custard; see our recipe, page 209). Despite Hawaii's last 130 years of melting-pot cuisine—in which Chinese, Japanese, Portuguese, German, Filipino, and Korean flavors and foods have mingled—the luau is still popular. Beyond the tourist versions, it remains a meaningful way to celebrate a special event.

Sunset's burritos grandes

San Franciscans love giant burritos packed with a dinner plate's worth of food, and these are outstanding. For less indulgent burritos, omit the guacamole, sour cream, and cheese, and make six instead of four. For grilling the meat, you'll need two 18-in.-long metal skewers or four 10-in. ones.

MAKES 4 large or 6 regular-size burritos | 1 hour, plus 15 minutes to marinate

2 oz. (4 to 6) dried ancho, New Mexico, or California chiles*
⅓ cup tequila
¼ cup lemon juice
3 garlic cloves, peeled
1 tbsp. olive oil
½ tsp. dried oregano
1 tsp. salt, divided
1¼ lbs. pork shoulder (butt), fat trimmed
½ cup long-grain white rice
¼ cup canned tomato sauce
1 can (15 oz.) pinto or red beans
4 large (13 in.) or 6 regular-size (10 in.) flour tortillas
1¼ cups Basic Guacamole (recipe at right), or store-bought guacamole
⅓ cup *crema** (Mexican cultured cream) or sour cream
1 cup crumbled *cotija* cheese* (also called *queso añejo*) or shredded jack cheese
½ cup chopped cilantro
1⅔ cups Classic Salsa Fresca (recipe at right) or store-bought red salsa, divided

1. Wipe chiles clean with a damp cloth and remove stems and seeds. Chop in a blender until finely ground. Add tequila, lemon juice, ¼ cup water, garlic, oil, oregano, and ¾ tsp. salt; blend until smooth.

2. Cut pork across grain into slices ½ in. thick and 3 to 4 in. long. In a bowl, add meat to marinade. Chill at least 15 minutes and up to 24 hours.

3. Lift meat from marinade and thread strips onto skewers. Lay skewers parallel and about 2 in. apart on a baking sheet. Pat marinade onto meat.

4. Prepare a grill for direct medium-high heat (see "How-to: Grilling," page 83). Lay skewered meat on oiled cooking grate (close lid on gas grill). Cook, turning often, until meat is well browned and crusty, about 20 minutes.

5. Meanwhile, bring ¾ cup water, the rice, tomato sauce, and remaining ¼ tsp. salt to a boil in a small pan over high heat. Reduce heat and simmer, covered, until liquid is absorbed, 15 to 20 minutes.

6. About 5 minutes before meat is done, put beans and their liquid in a 1-qt. pan and cook over medium-high heat until bubbling, about 5 minutes.

7. Lift cooked meat to a platter and cover with foil. Heat 1 or 2 tortillas at a time on the grill until lightly browned but still soft, turning once, 30 to 40 seconds. Stack tortillas on platter beneath foil to keep warm.

8. Preheat oven to 200°. Warm serving plates in oven. Remove meat from skewers to a board and cut into ¼-in.-wide strips. Lay tortillas flat. Toward one side of each, fill with guacamole, crema, pork, beans (including most of liquid), rice, cheese, and cilantro; divide 1 cup salsa among burritos. Fold over sides and roll up tightly to enclose. Work quickly during assembly to keep burritos hot, and serve on warm plates; if burritos cool off, you can wrap each one in lightly oiled foil and heat in a 350° oven for 10 to 20 minutes. Serve remaining salsa on the side.
*Buy ancho chiles, *crema*, and *cotija* cheese at a Mexican market or other specialty-foods store.

PER LARGE BURRITO 930 CAL., 41% (378 CAL.) FROM FAT; 45 G PROTEIN; 42 G FAT (9.9 G SAT.); 81 G CARBO; 1,250 MG SODIUM; 114 MG CHOL.

Basic guacamole Pit and peel 2 firm-ripe **avocados** (1 lb. total). In a bowl, coarsely mash avocados with a fork or pastry blender. Stir in 1½ tbsp. **lime juice,** 1 tbsp. chopped **cilantro,** and ½ tsp. ground **cumin.** Add **garlic salt** to taste. Makes about 1¼ cups.

PER TBSP. 27 CAL., 85% (23 CAL.) FROM FAT; 0.3 G PROTEIN; 2.6 G FAT (0.4 G SAT.); 1.3 G CARBO; 1.9 MG SODIUM; 0 MG CHOL.

Classic salsa fresca Combine 1½ cups chopped **ripe tomatoes,** ¼ cup sliced **green onions,** 1½ to 2 tbsp. minced **jalapeño chile,** and 1 tsp. **lemon juice** in a bowl. Season to taste with **salt.** Makes 1⅔ cups.

PER TBSP. 2.7 CAL., 0% FROM FAT; 0.1 G PROTEIN; 0 G FAT; 0.6 G CARBO; 1.1 MG SODIUM; 0 MG CHOL.

Sizzling Saigon crêpes
(Bánh xèo)

Mai Pham, chef and owner of Lemon Grass restaurant in Sacramento, gave us her version of a classic Saigon street snack. Wrap pieces of hot, smoky crêpe in lettuces and aromatic herbs and dip into a salty, tangy sauce.

MAKES 4 crêpes | 1¼ hours

1½ cups Asian rice flour*
½ cup unsweetened coconut milk
¼ tsp. turmeric
1 tsp. curry powder
About ½ tsp. salt
2 tsp. sugar
3 green onions, thinly sliced
5 tbsp. vegetable oil, divided
6 shiitake mushrooms, cut into ¼-in.-thick slices
⅓ yellow onion, slivered
8 oz. pork shoulder, cut into thin bite-size pieces
3½ cups bean sprouts
Table salad*
1 cup Vietnamese Dipping Sauce (recipe below right)

1. Whisk together rice flour, coconut milk, 1½ cups water, the turmeric, curry powder, ½ tsp. salt, the sugar, and green onions.
2. Heat 1 tbsp. oil in a large nonstick pan over medium heat. Add mushrooms and a pinch of salt and sauté until soft, about 10 minutes. Transfer to a bowl, discarding any juices.
3. Preheat oven to 200°. Wipe out pan and heat 1 tbsp. oil over medium-high heat. Add a quarter of onions and a quarter of pork. Cook, stirring, until fragrant, 2 minutes.
4. Whisk batter and ladle about ¾ cup into center of pan. Immediately tilt and rotate pan so batter covers whole surface. Pile a quarter of bean sprouts and a quarter of mushrooms on one side of crêpe, close to center. Cover; reduce heat to medium. Cook until edges pull away from the pan, about 2 minutes.
5. Reduce heat to low, uncover, and cook crêpe until browned on bottom, 7 minutes. Fold over and slide onto a plate. Cover with foil; keep warm in oven. Make remaining crêpes the same way.
* Buy rice flour from an Asian market; the kind sold in supermarkets is too coarse. For table salad, or *rau song*, use lettuce, thinly sliced cucumber, and any combo of aromatic herb sprigs.

PER CRÊPE 607 CAL., 43% (259 CAL.) FROM FAT; 22 G PROTEIN; 30 G FAT (9.7 G SAT.); 69 G CARBO (6 G FIBER); 389 MG SODIUM; 37 MG CHOL.

Vietnamese dipping sauce *(Nu'o'·c châ´m)* Cut 3 **Thai bird chiles** or 1 serrano chile into thin rings and set aside a third for garnish. Mince remaining chiles; put in a mortar with 1 minced **garlic clove** and 3 tbsp. **sugar** and pound into a coarse, wet paste. Transfer chile mixture to a small bowl and add ⅔ cup warm water, 1½ tbsp. **lime juice,** and 5 tbsp. **fish sauce.** Stir well to dissolve. Add reserved chiles and 2 tbsp. finely shredded **carrots** and set aside at least 10 minutes and up to 3 hours before serving. Makes 1 cup.

PER TBSP. 13 CAL., 1% (0.1 CAL.) FROM FAT; 0.3 G PROTEIN; 0 G FAT; 2.9 G CARBO (0 G FIBER); 435 MG SODIUM; 0 MG CHOL.

Chinese glazed riblets with garlic and Thai basil

These crisp, garlicky ribs, so dark and shiny that they look almost lacquered, are from Alexander Ong, chef of Betelnut restaurant in San Francisco.

SERVES 6 | 2¾ hours, plus 4 hours to marinate

RIBS & MARINADE

4 lbs. pork spareribs trimmed St. Louis–style, membrane removed, cut in half across the bone*
¾ cup mushroom soy sauce*, or regular soy sauce plus 1½ tbsp. molasses
6 tbsp. Shaoxing rice wine* or dry sherry
3 star anise pods
½ tsp. Chinese five-spice powder
¾ cup coarsely chopped unpeeled fresh ginger

CHINESE GLAZED RIBLETS WITH GARLIC AND THAI BASIL

SAUCE & SERVING

6 tbsp. *each* sugar and reduced-sodium soy sauce
½ cup Chinese red vinegar* or unseasoned rice vinegar
1 tbsp. Thai or Vietnamese fish sauce
Vegetable oil for deep frying, plus ¼ cup oil for cooking in wok
1 cup cornstarch, divided
3 tbsp. minced garlic
½ cup Thai basil leaves* or small regular basil leaves, plus a few basil sprigs

1. Prepare ribs: Cut apart between bones. Rinse and put in a 6- to 8-qt. pot. Add 2½ qts. water, cover, and bring to a boil. Skim and discard any foam. Add mushroom soy sauce, rice wine, star anise, five-spice, and ginger. Return to a boil, then reduce heat and simmer, covered, until meat is tender, 45 minutes to 1 hour.

2. Strain rib mixture through a colander set over a large bowl. Set bowl of braising liquid in a larger bowl of ice water. Let ribs and seasonings cool in colander, then return to liquid and chill, covered, at least 4 and up to 12 hours.

3. Meanwhile, make sauce: In a small bowl, stir together sugar, soy sauce, vinegar, and fish sauce until sugar dissolves. Set aside.

4. Preheat oven to 250° and set a rimmed baking sheet in it. Pour 1½ in. oil into a 5- to 6-qt. pot. Insert a deep-fry thermometer and heat oil over high heat to 350°. Meanwhile, skim and discard fat from braising liquid. Transfer ribs to a colander and discard ginger. Working with one-quarter of ribs at a time, toss in a medium bowl with ¼ cup cornstarch. Gently add ribs to oil. Cook until bones are browned and meat is crisp, 2 to 3 minutes. Transfer ribs to baking sheet in oven.

5. Heat a wok or 12-in. frying pan over medium heat. Add 1 tbsp. of remaining ¼ cup oil. When it's hot, stir in one-quarter of garlic; cook about 15 seconds, then add one-quarter *each* of ribs and sauce. Cook, stirring with tongs (or a wide metal spatula, if using a frying pan), until sauce thickens and coats ribs well, 1 to 2 minutes. Stir in one-quarter of basil leaves; cook and toss ribs until basil turns bright green, about 15 seconds. Transfer to a platter. Scrape out excess sauce from wok and spoon over ribs.

6. Cook remaining ribs the same way, adding a splash of water and reducing heat if pan starts to scorch.

*Ask a butcher to trim and cut the ribs. To remove membrane, slide a meat thermometer underneath to loosen; pull membrane off with a paper towel. Find mushroom soy sauce, Shaoxing rice wine, Chinese red vinegar, and Thai basil at Asian markets.

Make ahead Up to 1 day through step 3 (drain ribs after 12 hours).

PER SERVING 832 CAL., 61% (511 CAL.) FROM FAT; 43 G PROTEIN; 57 G FAT (17 G SAT.); 32 G CARBO (0.4 G FIBER); 1,124 MG SODIUM; 171 MG CHOL.

Hoi An–style oven-crisped pork sandwiches (Bánh mì thit Hoi An)

Especially in regions with large Vietnamese populations—like California's San Gabriel Valley and the cities of San Jose, Seattle, and Portland—bánh mì, the Vietnamese sandwich on a baguette, has become a standby. It always has pork in some form, chiles, fresh herbs, spices, and usually marinated vegetables. Bánh mì can also include a layer of chicken-liver or pork pâté. This version comes from Hoi An, a fishing village in central Vietnam.

MAKES 6 sandwiches | 45 minutes

1 tsp. **Chinese five-spice powder**
1 tbsp. **vegetable oil**
¼ cup **chopped shallots**
1 **garlic clove, minced**
¾ lb. **ground lean pork**
3 tbsp. **soy sauce**
1½ tsp. **sugar**
Salt
3 **baguettes*** (½ lb. each)
2 tbsp. **Asian red chili paste or Sriracha sauce, plus**
   more to taste
½ lb. **roasted, boned, fat-trimmed pork loin or cooked ham**
   or chicken, thinly sliced
2 cups **thinly sliced English cucumbers** (about ½ lb.)
3 cups **salad mix** (¼ lb.)
½ cup **Thai or regular basil leaves, cut into 1-in. pieces**
½ cup **Fried Sliced Shallots** (optional; recipe below right)

1. Cook five-spice powder, stirring, in an 8- to 10-in. frying pan over medium-high heat until fragrant, about 30 seconds. Stir in oil, shallots, and garlic. Add ground pork and cook, stirring often and breaking apart with a spoon, until meat is crumbly and no longer pink, about 15 minutes. Add soy sauce, sugar, and salt to taste.

2. Preheat oven to 375°. Cut baguettes in half crosswise, then split lengthwise almost all the way through, leaving halves attached at one side. Spread 1 tsp. chili paste on one cut side of each baguette section. Spoon about a sixth of warm ground pork mixture, including juice, over chili paste. Tuck a sixth of pork slices into each sandwich. Set sandwiches, slightly separated, on a 12- by 15-in. baking sheet.

3. Bake just until filling is warm and crust is crisp, about 5 minutes. Remove sandwiches from oven and fill each with a sixth of the cucumbers, salad mix, basil, and fried shallots if using. Add more chili paste and salt to taste.

HOI AN-STYLE OVEN-CRISPED PORK SANDWICHES (BÁNH MÌ THIT HOI AN)

*Choose a sweet baguette with a light, slightly soft interior and a thin, crisp crust.
Make ahead Through step 2, up to 1 hour, covered loosely and kept at room temperature.

PER SANDWICH 596 CAL., 29% (171 CAL.) FROM FAT; 35 G PROTEIN; 19 G FAT (4.2 G SAT.); 70 G CARBO (4.3 G FIBER); 1,290 MG SODIUM; 64 MG CHOL.

Fried sliced shallots Thinly slice enough **shallots** lengthwise to fill 1 cup. Heat ⅓ cup **olive oil** over medium heat in a medium frying pan. Add the shallots and fry until just golden, 6 to 10 minutes. Using a slotted spoon, transfer shallots to paper towels to drain. Makes about about ½ cup shallots.

Lupe's pork tamales

Every Christmas, Lupe Coronel and her family, residents of La Quinta, California, make these fantastic tamales, based on a traditional recipe from Durango, Mexico. (We're not the only ones who think they're exceptional: They won first prize at the Indio International Tamale Festival in Indio, California, in 1994.) When you make the tamales, remember two things: Don't cut back on the salt or the lard (and don't substitute shortening for lard), or the taste and texture will suffer; and do have a few other people help you assemble the tamales, because it's time-consuming. The good news is you can make a big batch and freeze part of it for later.

MAKES 4 to 4½ dozen tamales | 6 hours (with 3 people helping to assemble)

4 lbs. boned pork shoulder (butt), most of fat trimmed
3 oz. dried California or New Mexico chiles*
1½ oz. dried pasilla chiles
¼ cup flour
2 large garlic cloves
2 tsp. *each* coriander seeds and dried oregano
1 tsp. cumin seeds
²⁄₃ cup *each* chopped tomato and onion
½ cup *each* chopped green bell pepper and chopped seeded
 Anaheim chiles
3 cups (1⅓ lbs.) fresh, unhydrogenated lard, divided
2 tbsp. instant beef bouillon
2 tsp. garlic salt
½ cup *each* chopped cilantro sprigs and sliced green onions
5 lbs. fresh masa (*masa fresca*, dough made from ground dried
 corn and no lard or salt); or 8 cups dehydrated masa (also
 sold as corn flour, masa harina, or instant corn masa mix),
 mixed with 5¼ cups warm water until smooth
2 tsp. baking powder
2 tbsp. salt
1½ lbs. russet potatoes
¾ lb. dried cornhusks*
1 jar (10 oz.) small pimiento-stuffed green olives, drained
2 cans (7 oz. each) sliced pickled jalapeño chiles, drained
Salsa, store-bought or homemade (such as Roasted Poblano
 Chipotle Salsa, page 14, or Classic Salsa Fresca, page 88)

1. Put pork in a 5- to 6-qt. pan with 3 qts. water; bring to a boil. Reduce heat; simmer, covered, until meat is tender when pierced, about 2 hours. Drain and reserve broth; skim off fat. Let meat stand until cool; tear into chunks, discarding fat. Return to pan.
2. Meanwhile, discard stems and seeds from all the dried chiles, then rinse well. Put in a medium pan with 1 qt. water and bring

to a boil over high heat. Cover, reduce heat, and simmer, stirring often, until chiles are soft when pressed, 20 to 25 minutes. Drain, reserving 2 cups liquid. In a blender, purée chiles with liquid until very smooth; set aside.
3. Cook flour in a small pan over medium heat, stirring, until deep tan, 5 to 6 minutes; pour into a bowl. When pork is cooked, stir ½ cup reserved broth into flour; scrape into pan with meat.
4. Blend garlic, coriander seeds, oregano, cumin, and 1½ cups reserved broth in a blender until seasonings are finely ground. Pour through a fine-mesh strainer into pan with meat, pushing on solids to extract as much liquid as possible. Discard seasonings.
5. Add 1½ cups chile purée, the tomato, onion, bell pepper, Anaheim chiles, ¼ cup lard, the bouillon, and garlic salt to meat. Bring to a simmer over medium-high heat, stirring. Cook, stirring often, for 10 minutes to blend flavors. Stir in cilantro and green onions. With a fork, break any meat chunks into shreds.
6. Prepare masa: In a large bowl, break up masa with your hands. Add baking powder and salt; mix well. Heat remaining 2¾ cups lard in a small pan over medium-high heat until melted; let stand until cool enough to touch. Pour into masa, add remaining chile purée, and mix with hands or a heavy spoon. Mix masa vigorously with a spoon (or beat half at a time with a mixer) until very smooth and no lumps of masa remain.
7. Peel potatoes and cut into 48 sticks, each 4 to 5 in. long and ¼ to ⅓ in. thick. Put sticks in a medium pan with water to cover. Bring to a boil over high heat; reduce heat and simmer, covered, until tender-crisp, about 3 minutes. Drain and set aside.
8. Separate cornhusks and discard any silks. Select 5½ dozen large outer husks (5 to 6 in. wide across middle and 7 to 8 in. long; trim larger husks to this size). Soak husks in a sink with hot water to cover until they are pliable, about 20 minutes. Rinse, removing any grit; drain and put in a large bowl. Tear about 12 of the husks into long, thin strips. (If assembly takes more than a few hours and husks dry out, briefly resoak.)
9. Assemble tamales: On a large work surface, arrange masa and whole husks at one end, followed by fillings (meat, potatoes, olives, and jalapeños) and husk strips, leaving space at the other end for tying and stacking tamales.
10. For each tamale, lay a husk fairly flat with smooth side up. Spoon ¼ cup masa in center. Hold husk with one hand; using quick flicks of back of a soup spoon or a small spatula, evenly spread half of masa from center to one long edge (leave a 1-in. border bare at edge of husk). Repeat on other half of husk, again leaving a 1-in. border bare at edge. Spread 2 to 3 tbsp. meat filling in a band 1 in. from one long edge of masa. Place a potato piece, 2 olives, and a jalapeño piece over meat. Fold long edge of husk

closest to fillings over them, then roll up snugly. If husk doesn't quite meet to enclose filling, patch with a piece of another husk. Using husk strips, tie tamale as tightly as possible at both ends, then add a tie in center. (If needed, knot two strips together to make a longer tie.) Repeat to make remaining tamales.

11. To steam 2 dozen tamales, set a rack on supports at least 1½ in. above bottom of an 8- to 10-qt. pot. Fill pot with 1 in. reserved pork broth or water. Arrange first layer of tamales in one direction on rack; change direction of tamales 90° with each additional layer.

12. Cover and bring to a boil over high heat, then simmer until masa no longer sticks to husks, 1 to 1¼ hours, occasionally adding boiling water to maintain level of liquid. Serve with salsa.

*Find dried chiles, cornhusks, and fresh masa at a Mexican market or well-stocked grocery store. You can also buy fresh masa from a tortilla company.

Make ahead Pork, through step 5, up to 2 days, chilled. Masa (step 6), up to 4 hours, covered at room temperature; up to 2 days, chilled (bring to room temp before using, 4 to 5 hours). Uncooked tamales, frozen up to 2 months; no need to thaw before cooking, but increase steaming time to 1½ to 1¾ hours.

PER TAMALE 245 CAL., 59% (144 CAL.) FROM FAT; 8.9 G PROTEIN; 16 G FAT (5.5 G SAT.); 18 G CARBO; 673 MG SODIUM; 33 MG CHOL.

Peach and ginger glazed riblets

Sweet and spicy, these pork ribs are enticing party food or, served with rice and salad, dinner. California produces the majority of U.S. peaches—but, if you live elsewhere, buy local.

SERVES 4 | 1 hour, plus 1 hour to marinate

1 tbsp. minced garlic
4 tsp. minced fresh ginger, divided
¼ cup soy sauce
2½ lbs. baby back ribs, cut into riblets*
½ cup peach preserves
1½ tsp. hoisin sauce
2 tsp. unseasoned rice vinegar
1 tbsp. halved and sliced red jalapeño chile
½ cup chopped peeled peaches
1 tbsp. chopped green onion

1. Marinate meat: Mix garlic, 1 tbsp. ginger, and the soy sauce in a bowl. Add riblets to bowl, tossing to coat. Chill at least 1 hour and up to overnight, stirring occasionally.

2. Make glaze: Combine preserves, hoisin, vinegar, jalapeño, and remaining 1 tsp. ginger in a small saucepan. Cook over medium heat, stirring often, until bubbling. Remove from heat; set aside.

PEACH AND GINGER
GLAZED RIBLETS

3. Cook ribs: Prepare a grill for medium indirect heat (see "How-to: Grilling," page 83). Grill ribs over direct-heat portion of grill, covered, turning once, 15 minutes or until browned.

4. Reduce heat to very low (200° to 250°; for charcoal, partially close air vents to lower heat, and check temperature with an oven thermometer set on indirect-heat area). Move ribs to indirect-heat area and cook, covered, until tender and meat is starting to pull away from edges of bones, about 30 minutes.

5. Brush ribs generously with glaze and cook, covered, turning once, until glaze is bubbling, about 8 minutes total.

6. Toss riblets in a large bowl with peaches and remaining glaze. Transfer to a platter and sprinkle with green onions.

*Ask a butcher to cut a rack of ribs in half lengthwise, then slice between each rib to make 26 to 32 bite-size riblets.

PER SERVING 652 CAL., 55% (361 CAL.) FROM FAT; 40 G PROTEIN; 40 G FAT (15 G SAT.); 32 G CARBO (0.6 G FIBER); 1,098 MG SODIUM; 160 MG CHOL.

PORK SHOULDER ROAST
WITH FIGS, GARLIC, AND
PINOT NOIR

Pork shoulder roast with figs, garlic, and Pinot Noir

Stuffing this roast with figs and garlic slivers will make you feel like a modern-day Julia Child, and the results are stunning: mosaic-like meat slices infused with rich fruit and wine flavors.

SERVES 6 or 7 | 3¼ hours

1½ cups (10 oz.) dried Mission figs, stemmed and halved lengthwise
1 tbsp. sugar
½ tsp. anise seeds
2 tbsp. plus ½ tsp. chopped thyme leaves, divided, plus thyme sprigs
1 bottle (750 ml.) Pinot Noir, divided
1 boned pork shoulder (butt roast; about 3½ lbs.)
8 garlic cloves, cut into large slivers
About 1½ tsp. kosher salt
About ½ tsp. pepper
3 tbsp. olive oil
About 1 tsp. lemon juice (optional)

1. Put figs, sugar, anise seeds, 1 tbsp. thyme, and 1 cup wine in a medium saucepan. Cover and bring to a boil over high heat. Reduce heat and simmer, covered, until figs are just tender when pierced, 10 to 12 minutes. Let cool.

2. With a small, sharp knife, make 16 evenly spaced lengthwise cuts into roast, each about 1 in. long and 1 in. deep. Insert a garlic sliver, then a fig half into each cut, closing meat over figs; make cuts a little bigger if needed. Set aside remaining garlic and figs and their liquid.

3. Preheat oven to 325°. Using kitchen twine, tie pork crosswise at 1½-in. intervals and lengthwise twice to form a neat roast. In a small bowl, combine 1 tbsp. thyme, 1½ tsp. salt, ½ tsp. pepper, and the oil. Rub all over roast. Heat a 12-in. frying pan over medium-high heat. Brown pork all over, turning as needed, 8 to 10 minutes total; adjust heat if needed to keep meat from scorching. Transfer pork, fat side up, to a 9- by 13-in. baking pan.

4. Reduce heat to medium. Add reserved garlic to frying pan; cook, stirring often, until light golden, about 1 minute. Pour in remaining wine from bottle and bring to a boil, scraping browned bits from bottom of pan with a wooden spoon. Pour mixture over pork and cover tightly with foil. Bake pork until almost tender when pierced, 2½ hours. Stir reserved fig mixture into pan juices; bake, covered, until meat is tender, 15 to 20 minutes more.

5. Spoon pan juices over pork to moisten, then transfer meat to a cutting board and tent loosely with foil. Skim fat from pan juices. Pour juices with figs into a large frying pan and boil over high heat until reduced to 2 cups, about 5 minutes. Stir in remaining ½ tsp. thyme. Taste and season with lemon juice if using and more salt and pepper. Remove twine from pork, then cut meat crosswise into thick slices. Garnish with thyme sprigs and serve with sauce.

PER SERVING 498 CAL., 50% (247 CAL.) FROM FAT; 32 G PROTEIN; 28 G FAT (8.4 G SAT.); 32 G CARBO (4.2 G FIBER); 526 MG SODIUM; 107 MG CHOL.

Shot-and-a-beer pork stew

Tacolicious, a restaurant as well as a taco stand at San Francisco's Ferry Plaza Farmers Market, serves this braised pork in tacos, but owner Joe Hargrave also makes it at home as a stew. The chiles fall apart during cooking, giving the meat a mellow, earthy spiciness. Hargrave likes it with a side of cabbage-cilantro slaw.

SERVES 6 | 3¾ hours

2 large dried chipotle chiles*
2 large dried ancho chiles*
12 oz. Mexican lager, such as Tecate
¼ cup white (silver) tequila
3½ lbs. pork shoulder, cut into 2-in. cubes
2 tsp. kosher salt
1 tbsp. vegetable oil
1 medium onion, chopped
3 garlic cloves, chopped
¾ lb. tomatoes, chopped
2 tsp. *each* dried Mexican oregano* and ground cumin
Lime wedges, crumbled *cotija* cheese, and tortilla chips

1. Preheat oven to 350°. Wipe chiles clean with a damp cloth. In a dry, heavy saucepan over medium heat, toast chiles until fragrant and puffy, turning occasionally to keep them from burning, 3 to 5 minutes. Let cool slightly, then remove stems, seeds, and membranes. Pour beer and tequila over chiles to soften.

2. Meanwhile, season pork with salt. Heat oil in a heavy, large ovenproof pot such as a dutch oven over medium-high heat. Brown half the pork at a time, turning as needed, 8 to 10 minutes per batch. Transfer browned pork to a bowl.

3. Add onion and garlic to pot; cook until soft, stirring often, 5 minutes. Stir in chile-beer mixture, tomatoes, oregano, cumin, and pork. Add water if needed to barely cover pork. Bring to a boil over high heat; cover.

4. Bake stew until pork is falling-apart tender, 3 hours. Skim fat. Ladle stew into bowls and serve with lime, cheese, and chips.
*Find in the Latino-foods aisle or spice aisle of a supermarket, or at a Latino market.

PER SERVING 618 CAL., 58% (360 CAL.) FROM FAT; 50 G PROTEIN; 40 G FAT (14 G SAT.); 15 G CARBO (4.4 G FIBER); 517 MG SODIUM; 186 MG CHOL.

Grilled apricot-stuffed leg of lamb

A Moroccan spice mix and dried California apricots come together with lamb in a savory-sweet dish. Use intensely flavorful Blenheim apricots if possible (find at *brfarms.com*).

SERVES 8 to 10 | About 3 hours, plus at least 6 hours to marinate

1 boneless leg of lamb (4 to 5 lbs.), butterflied and trimmed
   of excess fat
1 tbsp. coarse kosher salt, divided
½ cup plus 3 tbsp. olive oil
2 small onions, roughly chopped (about 2½ cups)
5 garlic cloves, roughly chopped
2 tbsp. *ras el hanout**
1¼ to 1¾ cups dried apricot halves, preferably Blenheim

1. Unfold lamb, rinse, and pat dry. Slash ½-in.-deep cuts about 1 in. apart all over both sides of lamb. Season all over with 1½ tsp. salt. Put in a baking dish just large enough to hold meat unfolded.
2. Pour ½ cup water and ½ cup oil into a blender; add onions, garlic, ras el hanout, and remaining 1½ tsp. salt. Pulse to blend into a loose paste and pour over lamb. Cover and refrigerate at least 6 hours and up to 1 day. Let lamb come to room temperature before grilling, about 45 minutes.
3. Prepare a grill for low indirect heat (see "How-to: Grilling," page 83). Or preheat oven to 325°.
4. Wipe marinade off lamb and arrange apricot halves in a single layer over meat, leaving about ½-in. border on all sides. Roll up meat jelly-roll style and tie tightly with kitchen twine. Trim ends of twine. Rub lamb with remaining 3 tbsp. olive oil. If cooking on grill, rub grill well with oil-soaked paper towels.
5. Grill lamb over indirect-heat area, or roast in oven, set in a V-rack in a large roasting pan. Cook meat, turning over once halfway through, until an instant-read thermometer registers 140° for medium-rare, 1½ to 2½ hours. Let lamb rest, covered with foil, 15 to 20 minutes. Slice and serve.
*Find ras el hanout, a Moroccan spice mix, at well-stocked grocery stores or Middle Eastern markets. Or make your own blend: Whisk 1 tsp. *each* ground cardamom, coriander, ginger, and turmeric; ½ tsp. *each* pepper, cinnamon, nutmeg, and saffron (optional); and ¼ tsp. *each* ground allspice, cloves, and mace.

PER SERVING 390 CAL., 37% (144 CAL.) FROM FAT; 44 G PROTEIN; 16 G FAT (4.8 G SAT.); 16 G CARBO (2 G FIBER); 431 MG SODIUM; 135 MG CHOL.

GRILLED APRICOT-
STUFFED LEG OF LAMB

Grilled lamb shoulder chops with *pimentón* rub

A shortcut to deliciousness: Rub chops with smoky *pimentón*. The recipe comes from cookbook author Janet Fletcher.

SERVES 4 | 15 minutes, plus at least 2 hours to chill

4 bone-in lamb shoulder chops (preferably grass-fed),
   about ½ lb. each
1½ tbsp. extra-virgin olive oil
1 tbsp. plus 1 tsp. dried oregano, crumbled fine
2 tsp. kosher salt
1 tsp. garlic powder
1 tsp. bittersweet or sweet smoked Spanish paprika *(pimentón)*
4 lemon wedges

1. Coat lamb all over with oil. In a small bowl, combine oregano, salt, garlic powder, and paprika. Sprinkle evenly all over lamb, pressing into place. Chill chops on a rack set on a tray, uncovered, 2 to 8 hours. Bring to room temperature during the last hour.
2. Prepare a grill for high heat (see "How-to: Grilling," page 83). Grill chops, covered, turning once, about 8 minutes total for medium-rare. Serve with lemon wedges.

PER SERVING 421 CAL., 63% (267 CAL.) FROM FAT; 34 G PROTEIN; 30 G FAT (12 G SAT.); 3.5 G CARBO (1.6 G FIBER); 1,068 MG SODIUM; 132 MG CHOL.

GRILLED LAMB
SHOULDER CHOPS
WITH *PIMENTÓN* RUB

LAMB STEW WITH
ROASTED RED PEPPERS

Lamb stew with roasted red peppers

We were inspired by the lamb stews at Basque restaurants in towns like Bakersfield, California. These places date to the turn of the last century, and catered to Basque immigrants who had gravitated to Idaho, Nevada, and California to work as sheepherders.

SERVES 6 | 2¼ to 2½ hours

3 lbs. lamb shoulder or other lamb stew meat, fat trimmed, cut into 1½-in. chunks
Salt and pepper
About 1 tbsp. olive oil
1 medium onion, chopped
2 tbsp. *each* minced garlic and paprika
2 tsp. ground cumin
1 cup Syrah or other dry red wine
About 1½ cups reduced-sodium beef broth
3 tbsp. tomato paste
3 red bell peppers, halved, stemmed, and seeded
¼ cup chopped flat-leaf parsley
3 tbsp. *each* chopped pitted kalamata olives and chopped drained capers

1. Sprinkle lamb with salt and pepper. Pour olive oil into a large pot over medium-high heat. Working in batches, add lamb in a single layer; cook, turning, until browned all over, 12 minutes per batch. Transfer to a bowl; add oil between batches if necessary.

From California: Garlic

"The Garlic Capital of the World"—that's what Gilroy, California, proudly calls itself. Although China leads in global production, sunny little Gilroy processes more garlic than anywhere else on Earth, and it certainly grows the most garlic in America. Locals revel in the deep, pungent aroma that hangs over the town as freshly picked garlic is pickled, minced, and powdered into umpteen different garlic products.

At the end of the harvest, for three days in July, more than 100,000 garlic lovers pour into Gilroy to watch the Great Garlic Cook-off (winners are crowned with garlic wreaths), snack on concoctions from garlic fries to garlic ice cream, meet Miss Gilroy Garlic, listen to music—and buy garlands of exceptionally fresh, juicy garlic.

2. Reduce heat to medium; if pan is dry, add a little more oil. Add onion and cook, stirring occasionally, until soft, 5 minutes. Add garlic, paprika, and cumin and cook until fragrant, 2 minutes. Add wine, 1½ cups broth, and the tomato paste; bring to a boil, stirring to scrape up browned bits. Add lamb and juices; cover and simmer, stirring occasionally, until lamb is very tender when pierced, 1½ to 1¾ hours. Add more broth if mixture gets too dry.
3. Meanwhile, preheat broiler. Set pepper halves skin side up on a baking sheet. Broil 4 to 6 in. from heat until blackened all over, 8 minutes. Remove from oven and let stand 10 minutes; peel and thinly slice lengthwise. Mix parsley, olives, and capers in a bowl.
4. Stir roasted peppers into lamb mixture. If stew is too thick, add a little broth. Cook, uncovered, until heated through. Season to taste with salt and pepper and top with parsley mixture.

PER SERVING 352 CAL., 43% (153 CAL.) FROM FAT; 39 G PROTEIN; 17 G FAT (5 G SAT.); 11 G CARBO (1.7 G FIBER); 578 MG SODIUM; 123 MG CHOL.

Armenian-style kebabs

Private chefs in Hollywood (and sisters) Jewels and Jill Elmore like to serve these kebabs alongside bulgur pilaf and Greek salad.

SERVES 8, plus leftovers | 30 minutes, plus chilling time

3 lbs. ground lamb or sirloin
1 large yellow onion, very finely chopped (about 2 cups)
¼ cup finely chopped flat-leaf parsley, plus more for garnish
1 tbsp. finely chopped mint leaves
1 large egg
2 tsp. ground cumin
1 tbsp. paprika
½ tsp. garlic powder
2 tsp. kosher salt
1 tsp. pepper
2 tbsp. tomato paste
Juice of ½ lemon

1. Line a baking sheet with parchment paper. Using your hands, mix all ingredients (except garnish) in a large bowl just until combined (overmixing may toughen the meat).
2. Gently squeeze meat around 10-in. metal skewers to form log-shaped kebabs, each about 8 in. long. Put kebabs on a baking sheet. Cover sheet with plastic wrap or waxed paper and, if you have time, chill 30 minutes to let flavors meld and firm up meat.
3. Prepare a grill for high heat (see "How-to: Grilling," page 83) and grill kebabs, turning twice, until grill marks appear and meat feels firm, 8 minutes total. Sprinkle with parsley.

PER SERVING 326 CAL., 58% (189 CAL.) FROM FAT; 27 G PROTEIN; 21 G FAT (8.7 G SAT.); 5 G CARBO (0.9 G FIBER); 383 MG SODIUM; 125 MG CHOL.

Roast bison with velvety pan gravy

Despite the impressive size and burliness of bison (also called buffalo), its meat is mild and very lean.

SERVES 8 | 1½ hours

1 tsp. ground cumin
2 tsp. paprika
3 garlic cloves, minced
1 tsp. ground coriander
About 1½ tsp. kosher salt
3 lbs. bison sirloin tip roast*
4 tbsp. olive oil, divided
2 tbsp. *each* flour and tomato paste
2 cups beef broth

1. Preheat oven to 325°. Whisk together cumin, paprika, garlic, coriander, and 1½ tsp. salt in a small bowl. Rub roast with 1 tbsp. oil and pat spice mixture all over roast.

2. Heat 1 tbsp. oil in a dutch oven or other heavy 5- to 6-qt. pot over medium heat. Brown roast on all sides, about 4 minutes per side, adding another ½ tbsp. oil halfway through browning.

3. Transfer roast to a plate and wipe pot clean with a paper towel. Add ½ tbsp. oil to pot, put roast back in pot, and roast until a meat thermometer inserted in the thickest part registers 135°, about 50 minutes.

4. Transfer roast to a rimmed cutting board and tent with foil. Add remaining 1 tbsp. oil and the flour to pot and, over medium heat, whisk 1 to 2 minutes to cook flour. Whisk in tomato paste. Slowly whisk in beef broth and bring to a simmer. Cook gravy until thickened slightly, whisking frequently, 7 to 9 minutes. Season to taste with salt.

5. Slice roast thinly and serve with pan gravy.

*Available at Whole Foods Market and other well-stocked grocery stores, or by request from a butcher.

PER SERVING 244 CAL., 33% (81 CAL.) FROM FAT; 38 G PROTEIN; 9.1 G FAT (1.7 G SAT.); 3.3 G CARBO (0.5 G FIBER); 472 MG SODIUM; 0 MG CHOL.

ROAST BISON WITH VELVETY PAN GRAVY

From the ranch: Bison

Bison meat, from the massive, shaggy-headed icon of the West (also known as American buffalo), is leaner and more delicate in flavor than beef. It's also higher in protein and lower in fat and cholesterol (lower, actually, than skinless chicken).

Once plentiful, bison were nearly driven to extinction by European settlers, who took the herds from an estimated 30 million head to a few hundred by the 19th century. It's been a long time coming, but bison have been making a resurgence over the past decade. Ranchers in the West are raising more of the animals, particularly in the Mountain states, and the population is now at about 500,000 (with a protected herd of about 3,000 in Yellowstone National Park).

Antibiotics are prohibited in the bison industry, and the animals are mostly grass-fed, making bison meat an attractive choice for both eco- and health-conscious consumers. Many grocery stores and butcher shops now carry a variety of roasts, steaks, and ground bison. A key point: Because it's so lean, bison cooks much more quickly than beef, so watch to prevent overcooking.

Beer-and-bison burgers with pub cheese

Oats help bind the bison meat together. Monitor the burgers during grilling, as bison is faster-cooking than beef.

SERVES 4 | 30 minutes

1 lb. ground bison or beef
¼ cup quick-cooking rolled oats
¼ cup amber ale, such as Fat Tire, divided
1 tsp. kosher salt
½ tsp. pepper
2 tsp. olive oil
1 large garlic clove
4 oz. cream cheese
1 cup shredded sharp white cheddar cheese
4 whole-wheat hamburger buns
2 cups alfalfa sprouts

1. Prepare a grill for medium heat (see "How-to: Grilling," page 83). Mix meat, oats, 2 tbsp. ale, the salt, and pepper in a bowl until just combined. Form into four ½-in.-thick patties with a slight depression in the center of each. Brush with oil.
2. Chop garlic in a food processor until minced. Add cheeses and remaining 2 tbsp. ale and blend until smooth.
3. Grill burgers, turning once, until cooked the way you like, 6 minutes total for medium. In last few minutes, grill split buns, turning once, about 2 minutes total.
4. Put burgers on bottom of buns and top with sprouts. Spread bun tops with cheese mixture.

PER BURGER 531 CAL., 53% (280 CAL.) FROM FAT; 36 G PROTEIN; 31 G FAT (15 G SAT.); 29 G CARBO (4.2 G FIBER); 1,020 MG SODIUM; 121 MG CHOL.

Venison loin roast

Venison is relatively easy to order from a butcher or online. Pan-brown the venison first to caramelize the surface.

SERVES 6 | 30 minutes

2 venison tenderloins (about 1½ lbs. total), fat and membrane trimmed
2 tsp. canola or safflower oil
Blackberry-Orange or Brandy-Peppercorn Sauce (recipes at right)

1. Preheat oven to 450°. Pat tenderloins dry. Heat oil in a 10- to 12-in. ovenproof frying pan over medium-high heat until hot. Add venison and brown well on all sides, 4 to 5 minutes total.
2. Roast venison in frying pan in oven until done to your liking (125° on a thermometer for rare, 6 to 9 minutes), turning meat

BEER-AND-BISON BURGERS WITH PUB CHEESE

once. Transfer to a platter and let rest 5 minutes. Make sauce.
3. Slice meat, adding juices to sauce. Serve meat with sauce.

PER SERVING WITHOUT SAUCE 136 CAL., 18% (24 CAL.) FROM FAT; 26 G PROTEIN; 2.7 G FAT (1.1 G SAT.); 0 G CARBO; 58 MG SODIUM; 96 MG CHOL.

Blackberry-orange sauce Set frying pan with drippings over high heat. Add 1½ cups **beef broth,** 3 tbsp. **seedless blackberry jam,** 2 tbsp. **balsamic vinegar,** 1 tbsp. minced **orange zest,** and 2 tsp. prepared **horseradish.** Boil, stirring, until reduced to ⅔ cup, 8 minutes, and add **salt** to taste.

PER TBSP. 19 CAL., 0% FROM FAT; 0.8 G PROTEIN; 0 G FAT; 4.2 G CARBO (0.1 G FIBER); 14 MG SODIUM; 0 MG CHOL.

Brandy-peppercorn sauce Set frying pan with drippings over high heat. Add 1 tbsp. **butter,** ⅔ cup minced **shallots,** and 1½ tbsp. **jarred green peppercorns** (rinsed, drained, and crushed with the bottom of a skillet). Cook, stirring, over high heat until shallots are lightly browned, 2 minutes. Add ¾ cup **reduced-sodium beef broth** and ¼ cup *each* **brandy** and **whipping cream.** Boil, stirring, until reduced to ⅔ cup, 3 minutes.

PER TBSP. 102 CAL., 66% (67 CAL.) FROM FAT; 3.1 G PROTEIN; 7.4 G FAT (4.6 G SAT.); 2.6 G CARBO; 82 MG SODIUM; 31 MG CHOL.

Green chile chicken enchiladas

A hearty, rustic dish that's quintessentially New Mexican. Adjust the heat level with the chile variety you choose; go with Anaheims if you scorch easily. You can also substitute New Mexico Green Chile Sauce for step 1 of this recipe if you like. (Or try the Red Chile Sauce; both recipes on page 105.)

MAKES 10 enchiladas; 5 servings | 50 minutes

1 lb. roasted, skin-on green New Mexico, poblano,
    or Anaheim chiles*
2 tbsp. olive oil
1 tbsp. butter
5 large garlic cloves, finely chopped
½ tsp. *each* salt and pepper
3 cups reduced-sodium chicken broth, divided
10 corn tortillas (7 to 8 in. wide)
2 cups coarsely shredded cheddar or jack cheese, divided
2½ cups shredded cooked chicken*
Sour cream

1. Peel, seed, and chop chiles. Heat oil and butter in a large frying pan over medium heat. Add garlic and cook until fragrant, about 30 seconds. Add chiles, salt, and pepper. Cook, stirring occasionally, 3 minutes. Add 1 cup broth and simmer until reduced by a third, about 10 minutes.

2. Meanwhile, preheat oven to 400°. Prepare tortillas: In a small frying pan, bring remaining 2 cups broth to a gentle simmer. Very briefly dip a tortilla into broth to barely soften, then transfer it to a large baking sheet; repeat with remaining tortillas (you may need two or three baking sheets). Do not overlap or tortillas will stick.

3. Divide 1¼ cups cheese among tortillas and top each with the shredded chicken. Wrap each tortilla around filling and transfer, seam side down, to a 9- by 13-in. baking dish.

4. Pour chile sauce over enchiladas and top with remaining ¾ cup cheese. Bake until cheese is bubbling and browned, 15 to 20 minutes. Serve with sour cream.

*Order fresh or frozen New Mexico chiles from New Mexican Connection (*newmexicanconnection.com*). (See also "From the Field: New Mexico Chiles," page 104.) If the chiles aren't roasted, broil the chiles until blackened all over; let stand until cool, then peel off skin with the help of a paper towel (don't wash it off; rinsing dilutes the flavor). For the chicken, you'll need about half the meat from a roasted 2½- to 3-lb. bird. **Make ahead** Up to 1 month, frozen.

PER 2-ENCHILADA SERVING 526 CAL., 50% (261 CAL.) FROM FAT; 32 G PROTEIN; 29 G FAT (13 G SAT.); 38 G CARBO (4.2 G FIBER); 1,402 MG SODIUM; 117 MG CHOL.

Bengali five-spice roasted chicken and vegetables

Once-hard-to-find spice blends are popping up in grocery and specialized spice stores these days—like *panch phoron* ("five spices" in Bengali), popular in Northeast India and Bangladesh. It's made from cumin, fennel, fenugreek, brown mustard, and nigella seeds and has a bittersweet, licoricey flavor. Baked in a very hot oven, the sauce in this recipe reduces until the panch phoron seeds cling to the chicken and vegetables in flavorful nubbins.

SERVES 4 to 6 | 1 hour, plus at least 2 hours to marinate

2½ tbsp. vegetable oil
2 tbsp. *panch phoron*
2 dried bay leaves
2½ tbsp. *each* grated fresh ginger and minced garlic
2½ tsp. ground coriander
1½ tsp. kosher salt
1¼ cups plain whole-milk yogurt mixed with 1½ tsp. flour
4 *each* bone-in chicken legs and thighs (separated; 2 lbs. total)
1 *each* red and yellow bell peppers, cut into chunks
2 large carrots, quartered lengthwise, cut into 3-in. pieces
1 lb. Yukon Gold potatoes, peeled and cut into chunks

1. Heat oil in a small frying pan over medium-high heat. Add panch phoron and cook, stirring, until seeds begin to pop, about 30 seconds. Reduce heat to medium. All at once, add bay leaves, ginger, and garlic; cook, stirring, until ginger softens, about 3 minutes. Remove from heat, stir in coriander and salt, and let stand until fragrant, about 30 seconds. Add yogurt-flour mixture and stir to loosen browned bits. Let marinade cool.

2. Marinate ingredients: Put chicken, bell peppers, and carrots in a 1-gal. resealable plastic bag, then add yogurt mixture. Seal bag and squish to coat. Chill at least 2 hours or overnight.

3. Bake chicken: Preheat oven to 475° with a rack set in upper third of oven. Put potatoes on a large rimmed baking sheet and squeeze contents of bag over them. Mix to coat, then pat all the ingredients into a single layer. Bake, turning food with a wide spatula every 15 to 20 minutes and ending with chicken skin side up, until browned, 40 to 45 minutes.

*Find at well-stocked grocery stores, specialty shops, and online (we like *worldspice.com* and *savoryspiceshop*).

PER SERVING 377 CAL., 45% (171 CAL.) FROM FAT; 25 G PROTEIN; 19 G FAT (4.6 G SAT.); 23 G CARBO (3.2 G FIBER); 595 MG SODIUM; 78 MG CHOL.

From the field: New Mexico chiles

Why are the chiles grown in New Mexico so good? High altitude, warm days, cool nights, and intense light create their unusually robust flavors. Picked green, the chiles taste fresh and lively, with a good kick. Left on the plant to fully mature, they turn red, developing a complex, earthy flavor and mellow heat as they dry. They are at the heart of traditional New Mexican cooking.

SOUTH The south of the state, from Hatch to Las Cruces, is home to New Mexico's largest chile-growing region. The dry valleys are best known for their meaty green chiles—high-yielding hybrids such as Sandia, Hatch, and NuMex Big Jim, developed for consistent flavor and thick, straight pods that are easy to peel after roasting. The chiles are used fresh or frozen in sauces and stews.

NORTH A smaller growing area, known for its landrace chiles (strains or varieties adapted to specific geographic locations), lies north of Santa Fe. The skinnier, more twisted native chiles are especially appreciated at the red stage, when they develop a more intense flavor with flowery aromas and varying heat levels. Smaller and thinner-fleshed than southern varieties, they dry more easily. These are the ones traditionally strung on *ristras*, or ropes, to last throughout the year. Locals name the chiles for the farming towns they come from: Dixon, Chimayo, Española. They're usually simmered in braises and used whole or ground for sauces.

RED OR GREEN *Chile colorado* and *chile verde*, the two sauces on the opposite page, are near-ubiquitous in New Mexico, in everything from stews to enchiladas. In New Mexico's restaurants, the offer of a choice of green chile or red chile as a condiment is standard.

Stock up on chiles if you're in the state during the summer-to-fall harvest season, or order chiles online any time of year. You can buy frozen roasted green chiles as well as whole and ground dried red chiles at *new mexicanconnection.com*; dried red chiles and ristras at *cibolojunction.com*; and ristras at *madeinnewmexico.com*

New Mexico red chile sauce
(Chile colorado)

Red chiles make an earthy-sweet and intensely flavored sauce. For a richer flavor, some cooks soften the chiles in pork or chicken broth instead of water. To shave 20 minutes from the prep time, use the shortcut version that follows this recipe. If you have sensitive skin, wear gloves while working with chiles.

MAKES 1¼ cups | 1 hour

3 oz. (7 to 12) dried New Mexico red chiles or California red chiles, stemmed, seeded, and rinsed
½ medium onion, chopped
2 garlic cloves, minced
1 tbsp. *each* vegetable or olive oil and flour
½ tsp. dried Mexican oregano
¼ tsp. ground cumin
About ½ tsp. salt

1. Heat a wide 5- to 6-qt. pot over medium heat. Toast half the chiles at a time, turning occasionally, just until fragrant, about 2 minutes. Transfer chiles to a heatproof bowl, add 2 cups boiling water, and submerge chiles with a plate. Let stand until softened, 15 to 20 minutes. Drain, reserving water.
2. Meanwhile, in a medium saucepan, cook onion and garlic in oil over medium heat, stirring often, until onion is golden, 8 to 10 minutes. Sprinkle flour over onion and continue to cook, stirring, until mixture smells toasty, about 2 minutes. Remove from heat and stir in oregano, cumin, and ½ tsp. salt.
3. Purée chiles in a blender with half the soaking liquid. Set a fine strainer over pan with onion mixture. Rub puréed chiles through strainer into pan. Discard contents of strainer.
4. Bring mixture to a simmer over medium heat, then reduce heat and simmer, uncovered, stirring occasionally, until flavors are well blended, 12 to 15 minutes; add more soaking liquid and water as needed (sauce should be thick enough to coat a spoon). Taste and add more salt if you like.
Make ahead Up to 3 days, chilled; or freeze.

PER ¼-CUP SERVING 43 CAL., 58% (25 CAL.) FROM FAT; 0.7 G PROTEIN; 2.9 G FAT (0.3 G SAT.); 4 G CARBO (0.6 G FIBER); 235 MG SODIUM; 0 MG CHOL.

Quick New Mexico red chile sauce Follow the directions above, but replace whole chile pods with ½ cup **ground New Mexico chiles** (see opposite page) and stir until smooth with 2 cups cold water. Omit steps 1 and 3. Stir chile mixture into onion mixture and proceed with step 4. Makes 1⅓ cups.

PER ¼-CUP SERVING 98 CAL., 45% (44 CAL.) FROM FAT; 2.7 G PROTEIN; 5 G FAT (0.3 G SAT.); 11 G CARBO (6.7 G FIBER); 240 MG SODIUM; 0 MG CHOL.

New Mexico green chile sauce
(Chile verde)

New Mexico produces more chiles than any other state, and devotees swear there are none better. However, most hot peppers must be hand-harvested, allowing cheaper chiles from Latin America and China to take a bite out of New Mexico's crop in the past decade. The good news for aficionados is that in recent years, the state's chile acreage has gone up again. A cooking caveat: When preparing chiles, wear kitchen gloves if you have sensitive skin.

MAKES 2½ cups | 40 minutes

½ cup chopped onion
2 garlic cloves, minced
2 tbsp. *each* vegetable or olive oil and flour
1½ cups chicken broth or water
1½ cups chopped stemmed, seeded roasted green chiles, preferably New Mexico or poblano* (from about 1¾ lbs. chiles)
About ½ tsp. salt

1. In a medium saucepan, cook onion and garlic in oil over medium heat, stirring often, until onion is golden, 8 to 10 minutes. Sprinkle flour over onion and continue to cook, stirring, until mixture smells toasty, about 2 minutes. Whisk in broth until smooth, then stir in chiles and ½ tsp. salt.
2. Simmer sauce, uncovered, stirring occasionally, until flavors are blended, 15 to 20 minutes; add water if sauce gets too thick. For a smoother sauce, purée in a blender. Taste and add more salt if you like.
*Buy frozen roasted New Mexico green chiles (see opposite page) or roast your own: Put 2 lbs. fresh New Mexico green chiles or poblano chiles in a shallow pan. Broil, turning as needed, until chiles are charred all over, 10 to 15 minutes. Cool, then skin, seed, and chop.
Make ahead Up to 3 days, chilled; or freeze.

PER ¼-CUP SERVING 62 CAL., 44% (27 CAL.) FROM FAT; 2.2 G PROTEIN; 3.2 G FAT (0.5 G SAT.); 7.6 G CARBO (1.1 G FIBER); 140 MG SODIUM; 3.8 MG CHOL.

Roast chicken with Meyer lemon–shallot sauce

Shallots roast alongside the chicken; then they're puréed and browned with lemony pan juices to make a fragrant and naturally thick gravy—no flour or cornstarch necessary. (See "From the Orchard: Meyer Lemons," page 194, for the story of how the juicy, vivid fruit arrived in the West.)

SERVES 6 to 8 | 2 hours, plus 3 hours to cure

1 chicken (4 to 5 lbs.)
1 tbsp. kosher salt
2 medium Meyer or regular (Eureka) lemons
2½ tbsp. olive oil, divided
1½ tsp. dried thyme
1 lb. shallots, unpeeled
¾ to 1 cup reduced-sodium chicken broth
⅓ cup dry white wine

1. Remove giblets from chicken and save for another use. Pull off and discard lumps of fat, then pat chicken dry. Loosen skin of breast and thighs and work some salt under skin. Rub remaining salt all over chicken and in cavity. Chill, uncovered, at least 3 hours and up to overnight.*

2. Preheat oven to 400°. Finely shred zest of lemons. Slice 1 lemon; juice half the other and reserve.

3. Pat chicken dry, inside and out. Rub zest under as much of skin as possible and rub any remaining zest inside cavity. Rub chicken all over with 1 tbsp. oil and the thyme. Put lemon slices in cavity.

4. Set a V-shaped rack in a heavy roasting pan large enough to hold shallots. Put chicken in rack, breast side up. Add unpeeled shallots to pan and drizzle with remaining 1½ tbsp. oil, turning them to coat.

5. Roast chicken, basting with pan juices every 30 minutes or so, until chicken leg moves easily, skin is brown and crisp, and a thermometer registers 170° when inserted through thickest part of breast to bone or 180° through thickest part of thigh at joint, 1 to 1½ hours (remove shallots after 1 hour and set aside). Tip chicken so juices from cavity pour into roasting pan. Transfer chicken to a carving board and let rest, covered with foil.

6. Meanwhile, make sauce: Pour pan drippings into a measuring cup with a pouring lip. Trim tops from shallots and squeeze soft insides into a blender. Discard all but about 1 tbsp. fat from pan drippings and add drippings to blender. Add ¾ cup broth and the wine and pulse until smooth.

7. Pour sauce into roasting pan. Cook over medium-high heat on the biggest burner (or straddling two burners), scraping any browned bits off bottom of pan and adding more broth if you want a thinner sauce, until sauce turns a nutty brown, about 10 minutes. Stir in 1 tbsp. reserved lemon juice, or more to taste. Pour sauce through a fine-mesh strainer into a serving bowl. Carve chicken, discarding lemon slices; serve with sauce.
*Salting the chicken hours ahead rather than just before cooking makes the meat more flavorful.

PER SERVING WITH 2 TBSP. GRAVY 388 CAL., 56% (216 CAL.) FROM FAT; 33 G PROTEIN; 24 G FAT (6 G SAT.); 11 G CARBO (1.2 G FIBER); 700 MG SODIUM; 101 MG CHOL.

Easy chicken adobo

Most of the country's Filipino communities are clustered on the West Coast—in Seattle, the Bay Area, and Los Angeles, as well as Hawaii—and this recipe pays tribute to the Philippine national dish. Adobo, whether of meat, poultry, or seafood, blends garlic, vinegar, and soy sauce to create a zingy, full-flavored dish. Traditional adobo sauces are usually enriched with coconut milk, but for everyday cooking, we like this lighter, simpler version. Serve with rice.

SERVES 4 | 45 minutes

1 tbsp. vegetable oil
6 bone-in, skinless chicken thighs
3 cloves garlic, minced
⅔ cup apple cider vinegar
⅓ cup soy sauce
1 tsp. whole black peppercorns
1 bay leaf

1. Heat oil in a medium frying pan over medium-high heat. Add chicken and cook until lightly browned, about 5 minutes, then turn over and cook an additional 5 minutes. Transfer chicken to a plate and set aside.

2. Pour off all but 1 tbsp. of pan drippings and return pan to low heat. Add garlic and sauté until soft, about 1 minute. Add remaining ingredients and stir to incorporate. Return chicken to pan and cook, covered, for 20 minutes.

3. Uncover, increase heat to medium-low and cook 15 to 20 minutes more, occasionally spooning sauce over chicken, until sauce thickens a bit and chicken is tender and nicely glazed with sauce. Remove bay leaf before eating.

PER SERVING 251 CAL., 35% (89 CAL.) FROM FAT; 34 G PROTEIN; 9.9 G FAT (2.1 G SAT.); 5.7 G CARBO (0.2 G FIBER); 1,501 MG SODIUM; 138 MG CHOL.

ROAST CHICKEN
WITH MEYER LEMON–
SHALLOT SAUCE

Best-ever Chinese chicken salad

Our update has all the great flavor of the original, with more from-the-garden ingredients. Historians surmise that the first appearance of Chinese chicken salad was in California. In 1938, the *Los Angeles Times* published a recipe calling for chicken, bean sprouts, celery, French dressing, mayo, and soy sauce. At Kan's in San Francisco, which opened in 1940, Johnny Kan served a version with lettuce and chile flakes. Chef Lee of New Moon Cafe, a 1950s L.A. establishment that's still going, claimed to have brought the recipe from Hong Kong. A decade later, San Francisco's Cecilia Chiang—often credited with introducing America to the food of northern China—offered the salad at the Mandarin. No matter what its origins, the dish has become an American classic.

SERVES 6 to 8 | 45 minutes

½ lb. asparagus, trimmed and cut diagonally into 1-in. pieces
2 navel oranges
About 1½ cups vegetable oil
4 fresh won ton wrappers, cut into ¼-in.-wide strips*
6 cups finely shredded cabbage
2 cups cubed cooked chicken
Spicy Soy-Ginger Dressing (recipe at right)
1 large avocado, cubed
4 green onions (including green tops), sliced diagonally
2 tbsp. toasted sesame seeds

1. Bring about 1 qt. water to a boil in a 2- to 3-qt. pan over high heat. Add asparagus and cook until crisp-tender, 2 to 3 minutes. Drain, then plunge asparagus into ice water to stop the cooking. Drain and set aside.

2. Cut off and discard ends from oranges. Following the curve of the fruit, cut off peel and outer membrane. Slice oranges crosswise into ¼-in.-thick rounds, then cut these rounds into quarters. Set aside.

3. Pour oil into a 3- to 4-qt. pan (the oil should be about ½ in. deep) and set over medium-high heat. When oil reaches 350°, add won ton strips and fry, stirring, until golden brown on both sides, about 30 seconds total. Lift out with a slotted spoon and transfer to paper towels to drain.

4. Toss the cabbage, chicken, and asparagus with the dressing in a serving bowl or on plates. Top with avocado, orange slices, and wonton strips, then garnish with green onions and sesame seeds.

*To save time, you can use store-bought crispy won tons or chow mein noodles instead of frying your own.

PER SERVING 308 CAL., 56% (171 CAL.) FROM FAT; 15 G PROTEIN; 19 G FAT (3.1 G SAT.); 20 G CARBO (4 G FIBER); 317 MG SODIUM; 36 MG CHOL.

Spicy soy-ginger dressing Whisk together 2 tbsp. **rice wine vinegar,** 2 tbsp. **brown sugar,** 1½ tbsp. **soy sauce,** 1 tbsp. **red chili sauce** (such as Sriracha), and 1½ tsp. grated **fresh ginger** in a medium bowl. Slowly drizzle in ¼ cup **vegetable oil** or grapeseed oil, whisking constantly. Season with **salt** to taste.

From the orchard: Navel oranges

Both the summer-ripening Valencia orange and the seedless winter navel orange arrived in California in the 1870s. The navel made its appearance when Luther and Eliza Tibbets, newly settled in Riverside, asked the USDA for plants suitable to the warm California climate and were sent a few orange trees from Brazil that the USDA had been nurturing. After several years, two trees bore oranges with astonishing sweet, juicy seedlessness. Word spread, and the Tibbetses gave away or sold at low price hundreds of grafts, reasoning that they shouldn't profit from trees the government had given them free.

Other people, however, made millions. Within a few years, thousands of acres of cattle-grazing land had been planted to oranges, using trees budded from the Tibbets navels. People poured into Southern California to get in on the orange action, and an orange-driven boom created Pomona, Redlands, Tustin, and other towns in and around what came to be called Orange County. California navels were shipped across the country and became a strong part of the state's economy. As for the Tibbetses, Eliza succumbed to illness; and Luther, his money drained from traveling with Eliza at the end of her life and from battling litigation over water rights, lost his property to foreclosure. Yet one of the original trees still survives, in a park in Riverside.

In the 1960s, when real estate prices soared, citrus ranchers sold out all over Southern California, and groves were replaced by houses and malls. Some determined growers, however, such as those in the Inland Orange Conservancy, have begun to take up the fight to preserve California's sunny oranges.

Pinot-braised duck with spicy greens

Michael Wild, chef and co-owner of Bay Wolf restaurant in Oakland, loves duck and Pinot Noir, and here he pairs them. Wild recommends getting two bottles of wine for this dish: a reasonably priced Pinot Noir to cook with and the best Pinot you can find—or a good red Burgundy—to drink with it. For a lighter sauce, and because it's easier to find, we've substituted chicken broth for the rich duck stock he uses.

SERVES 4 | 2¼ hours

4 duck legs (about ½ lb. each)
Salt and pepper
1 tsp. herbes de Provence
About 1 bottle (750 ml.) Pinot Noir
2 tbsp. olive oil, divided

¼ cup minced shallots
4 cups reduced-sodium chicken broth
1 thyme sprig
1 bay leaf
1 tbsp. butter
1 onion (about ½ lb.), chopped
1 lb. broccoli rabe (rapini), trimmed and cut into
    about 1-in. pieces, or 1½ lbs. mustard greens,
    trimmed and sliced crosswise
2 garlic cloves, minced
1 flat anchovy (optional), minced
¼ tsp. cayenne
1 tbsp. lemon juice

1. Preheat oven to 375°. Lay duck legs skin side up in a roasting pan that just holds them comfortably. Sprinkle with salt, pepper, and the herbes de Provence. Roast 1 hour.

2. Spoon fat from pan and save for other uses or discard. Pour wine over duck; the wine should be deep enough so meat is immersed but not so deep as to cover skin (skin should be exposed). Continue roasting until skin is golden red, about 30 minutes more.

3. Meanwhile, pour 1 tbsp. oil into a 1½- to 2-qt. pan over medium-high heat; add shallots and cook, stirring often, until they begin to brown, about 2 minutes. Add broth, thyme, and bay leaf; boil, stirring occasionally, until reduced to about 1½ cups, about 45 minutes. When the duck is done, add 1 cup of its braising liquid to broth mixture and boil, stirring often, until mixture has been reduced by a fourth, about 15 minutes. Pour through a fine-mesh strainer into a small pitcher or bowl.

4. While broth reduces, prepare broccoli rabe: In a 12- to 14-in. frying pan over medium-high heat, melt butter with remaining 1 tbsp. oil. Add onion and cook, stirring often, until it begins to brown, about 7 minutes. Add broccoli rabe and cook, stirring often, until tender to the bite, 3 to 5 minutes (if using mustard greens, add half, stir until wilted, then add remaining). Add garlic and anchovy if using and cook until fragrant, about 1 minute more. Remove from heat and season to taste with salt, pepper, cayenne, and lemon juice.

5. Mound greens on plates and set duck legs on top. Serve pan juices alongside.

PER SERVING 370 CAL., 47% (175 CAL.) FROM FAT; 33 G PROTEIN; 20 G FAT (5.4 G SAT.); 16 G CARBO (1.1 G FIBER); 537 MG SODIUM; 106 MG CHOL.

PINOT-BRAISED DUCK
WITH SPICY GREENS

Barbecued glazed turkey

One method, three distinctive glaze possibilities: Just pick the seasonings that go best with the rest of your feast. Grilling gives the bird a really crisp, brown skin—plus it frees up your oven to cook everything else.

SERVES 12 to 24, depending on size of turkey, with ample leftovers | 2 to 3 hours, plus 15 to 30 minutes to rest

1 turkey (12 to 24 lbs.; see "How-to: Turkey Basics," page 115)
Olive or vegetable oil
Glaze (recipes below)

1. Remove and discard leg truss from turkey. Pull off and discard any lumps of fat. Remove giblets and neck. Rinse bird inside and out and pat dry. Rub skin with oil. Insert a meat thermometer straight down through thickest part of breast to bone (if using an instant-read thermometer, insert later).
2. Prepare a grill for indirect medium heat, using a drip pan (see "How-to: Grilling," page 83).
3. Set turkey, breast up, on cooking grate over drip pan and close lid on grill. Cook turkey according to glaze directions. (If drippings flare when lid is open, add some water to drip pan.)
4. Using two large spatulas, transfer cooked turkey to a platter. Cover loosely with foil and let rest 15 to 30 minutes.
5. Carve bird. If thighs are still pink at the joint, microwave them until pinkness disappears, 1 to 3 minutes.

Brown sugar crackle glaze Mix 2 cups firmly packed **light brown sugar,** 5 tbsp. **Dijon mustard,** and 2 tsp. **coarsely ground pepper** in a small bowl. When turkey has about 45 minutes more to cook (breast temperature at bone will be about 135° for birds up to 18 lbs. and about 145° for larger ones), spread with half the glaze. Cook 20 minutes. Brush with remaining glaze and cook, sliding folded strips of foil between bird and grate if edges of turkey begin to get too dark, and draping any other dark areas with foil, until an instant-read thermometer registers 160°.

PER ¼-LB. SERVING (WHITE AND DARK MEAT WITH SKIN AND BROWN SUGAR CRACKLE GLAZE) 265 CAL., 34% (90 CAL.) FROM FAT; 32 G PROTEIN; 10 G FAT (3 G SAT.); 9 G CARBO (0 G FIBER); 123 MG SODIUM; 93 MG CHOL.

Chile-orange glaze Combine 3 tbsp. **ground dried New Mexico** or California **chiles,** 1 can (12 oz.; 1½ cups) thawed **orange juice concentrate,** 2 tbsp. finely shredded **orange zest,** and 1 tsp. **ground cumin** in a small bowl. When turkey has about 20 minutes more to cook (breast temperature at bone will be about 150° for birds up to 18 lbs. and about 155° for

BARBECUED GLAZED
TURKEY WITH CHILE-
ORANGE GLAZE

larger ones), coat generously with glaze. Cook, sliding folded strips of foil between bird and grate if edges of turkey begin to get too dark, and draping any other dark areas with foil, until an instant-read thermometer registers 160°.

PER ¼-LB. SERVING (WHITE AND DARK MEAT WITH SKIN AND CHILE-ORANGE GLAZE) 245 CAL., 37% (90 CAL.) FROM FAT; 32 G PROTEIN; 10 G FAT (3 G SAT.); 3.7 G CARBO (0.2 G FIBER); 87 MG SODIUM; 93 MG CHOL.

Sage butter glaze Mix ¼ cup melted **butter,** 2 tbsp. **lemon juice,** and 1 tsp. minced **sage leaves** in a small bowl. When turkey has about 45 minutes more to cook (breast temperature at bone will be about 135° for birds up to 18 lbs. and about 145° for larger ones), baste often with sage butter. Cook, sliding folded strips of foil between bird and grate if edges of turkey begin to get too dark, until an instant-read thermometer registers 160°.

PER ¼-LB. SERVING (WHITE AND DARK MEAT WITH SKIN AND SAGE BUTTER GLAZE) 243 CAL., 44% (108 CAL.) FROM FAT; 32 G PROTEIN; 12 G FAT (3.9 G SAT.); 0.1 G CARBO (0 G FIBER); 97 MG SODIUM; 97 MG CHOL.

Wine-smoked turkey

A recipe inspired by California wine country, this is the one you want to serve visitors from the East Coast—preferably outside, for a full-on Western-style Thanksgiving. Wine-infused wood chips and a heady herbal marinade give crisp-skinned grilled turkey fantastic flavor.

SERVES 16 to 18, with ample leftovers | 3 to 3½ hours

4 to 6 cups lightly packed wine-infused wood chips or shavings*
3 tbsp. olive oil
2 tbsp. minced sage leaves or 2 tsp. dried sage
1 tbsp. minced parsley
2 tsp. minced marjoram leaves or ½ tsp. dried marjoram
½ tsp. pepper
1 turkey (16 to 18 lbs.; see "How-to: Turkey Basics," page 115)
1 Golden Delicious apple, cored
1 medium onion, peeled
Zinfandel Gravy (recipe at right)
Sage or marjoram sprigs

1. Soak wine-infused chips or shavings in water at least 20 minutes. In a small bowl, mix oil with minced herbs and pepper.
2. To prepare turkey, remove and discard leg truss. Pull off and discard any lumps of fat; remove giblets and neck and set aside for gravy. Rinse bird inside and out and pat dry. Brush all over with 2 tbsp. oil mixture. Cut apple and onion into 1-in. chunks, stir into remaining oil mixture, and spoon apple mixture into body cavity. Put foil caps on drumstick tips and wing tips. Insert a meat thermometer straight down through thickest part of breast to bone (if using an instant-read thermometer, insert later).
3. Prepare a grill for indirect medium-low heat (see "How-to: Grilling," page 83). **For a charcoal grill,** when banked briquets have burned to medium, place a drip pan filled halfway with warm water between banks of coals. To each mound of coals, add 5 briquets and ½ cup soaked wood chips or shavings now and every 30 minutes while cooking; if needed, keep grill uncovered for a few minutes to help briquets ignite. **For a gas grill,** remove cooking grate and turn all burners to high. Put 1 cup soaked wood chips or shavings in grill's metal smoking box or in a small, shallow foil pan set directly on burner in a corner. Close lid and heat 10 minutes. Then turn off one burner and lower other(s) to medium. Set a metal or sturdy foil drip pan, filled halfway with water, on turned-off burner. Add another 1 cup wood chips or shavings now if first ones have burned away (add 1 cup chips every hour or so while cooking). Replace cooking grate.
4. Set turkey, breast up, on cooking grate over drip pan and close lid on grill. Cook until an instant-read thermometer inserted straight down through thickest part of breast to bone registers 160°, 2½ to 3 hours; during cooking, loosely tent turkey with foil if it starts to get too dark.
5. Drain juices and remove apple and onion from cavity; reserve for gravy. Place turkey on a platter and let rest 15 to 30 minutes. Remove drip pan from grill; skim and discard fat from juices. Reserve juices for gravy. Garnish platter with herb sprigs.
*Buy wine-infused chips through *amazon.com;* or soak mesquite or applewood chips in equal parts red wine and water and omit soaking in step 1.

PER ¼-LB. SERVING (WHITE AND DARK MEAT WITH SKIN) 250 CAL., 43% (108 CAL.) FROM FAT; 32 G PROTEIN; 12 G FAT (3.2 G SAT.); 1.4 G CARBO (0 G FIBER); 82 MG SODIUM; 93 MG CHOL.

Zinfandel gravy

Make this gravy with what you plan to drink with dinner.

MAKES 6 cups; 18 servings | 2 hours

Giblets and neck from a 16- to 18-lb. turkey
2 large onions, quartered
2 large carrots, cut into chunks
1 cup sliced celery
4½ cups reduced-sodium chicken broth, divided
2¾ cups Zinfandel, divided
2 strips orange zest (3 in. each)
½ tsp. pepper
Apple mixture and pan juices from Wine-Smoked Turkey (left)
½ cup cornstarch
Salt

1. Combine giblets, neck, onions, carrots, celery, and ½ cup broth in a large pan. Cook, covered, over medium-high heat, 20 minutes. Uncover; cook over high heat, stirring often as liquid evaporates, until vegetables are browned and browned bits stick to bottom of pan, 5 to 8 minutes. Add another ½ cup broth; stir to loosen browned bits. Cook and brown, uncovered, as before.
2. Add remaining 3½ cups broth, 2 cups Zinfandel, the zest, and pepper to pan. Cover and simmer over low heat for 1 to 1½ hours.
3. Add cooked apple mixture from turkey cavity; bring to a boil. Lower heat and simmer, covered, 5 minutes.
4. Pour broth mixture through a fine-mesh strainer into a bowl. Discard contents of strainer. Measure broth; if needed, add turkey pan juices to make 5½ cups. In pan, mix cornstarch with ¼ cup water and ¾ cup wine. Stir in broth mixture and cook, stirring, over high heat until boiling, about 5 minutes. Season with salt.

PER ⅓-CUP SERVING 34 CAL., 5% (1.8 CAL.) FROM FAT; 1.8 G PROTEIN; 0.2 G FAT (0 G SAT.); 6.1 G CARBO (0 G FIBER); 163 MG SODIUM; 3.8 MG CHOL.

Heritage turkey with crisped pancetta and rosemary

Heritage turkeys are breeds (such as Bourbon Red and Standard Bronze) that predate the Broad-Breasted White, the ubiquitous grocery-store turkey. The thighs and legs have rich, amazing flavor, but can be tough, so for best results, we braise legs and thighs and roast the breast.

SERVES 10, with leftovers | 4 hours, plus at least 1 day to brine

1 heritage turkey (12 to 14 lbs.), truss removed and giblets
    removed (use for gravy if you like)
3 tbsp. kosher salt
2 tbsp. finely chopped fresh rosemary
5 oz. thinly sliced pancetta (not lean)
1/2 tsp. pepper
About 1 tbsp. canola oil
2 carrots, peeled and diced
2 celery stalks, diced
1 onion, diced
1 bay leaf
3 to 4 cups reduced-sodium or homemade turkey or chicken stock
Rich Brown Gravy (recipe at right)

1. Rinse turkey, pat dry, and cut off drumsticks and thighs.

2. Mix salt and rosemary together in a small bowl. Sprinkle all over turkey pieces, including inside the cavity. Put all pieces in a roasting pan, slide into a large plastic bag, and loosely tie top. Chill at least 1 day and up to 3.

3. Let turkey stand at room temperature 1 hour. Remove top rack of oven and preheat to 350°. Pat turkey dry with paper towels. Cover breast with pancetta (keep slices in their circle shapes and overlap slightly), then sprinkle with pepper. Rub wings with a bit of canola oil and set turkey body with breast on a V-rack in a large roasting pan.

4. Roast turkey body until an instant-read thermometer, inserted straight down through the breast until it touches the bone, registers 160°, 2 to 2½ hours. Tent with foil after 45 minutes to keep pancetta from burning.

5. Meanwhile, heat 1 tbsp. oil in a 12-in.-wide frying pan with at least 2-in. sides or in a wide stockpot over medium-high heat. Add turkey legs and thighs, skin side down, in a single layer and let cook undisturbed until skin is deep golden brown, 8 to 10 minutes. Turn over and brown 4 minutes.

6. Put turkey legs and thighs on a plate. Reduce heat to medium and pour off all but 1 tbsp. fat from pan. Add carrots, celery, onion, and giblets, if using, and cook, stirring occasionally, until softened and lightly browned, 7 minutes. Add bay leaf. Return

legs and thighs (and juices) to pan, skin side up, and pour in enough stock to come halfway up turkey. Cover pan; reduce heat to low. Cook until an instant-read thermometer inserted in thickest part of a thigh registers 160°, 50 minutes to 1 hour.

7. Transfer legs and thighs to a rimmed baking sheet, skin side up; cover with foil. Strain stock through a fine-mesh strainer, discarding solids, and use to make gravy.

8. Remove turkey from oven and let rest 20 minutes. Meanwhile, increase heat to broil and broil legs and thighs until skin is crispy, 10 minutes. Transfer to a warmed serving platter.

9. Cut each breast half from the turkey in one piece, slicing on either side of breastbone and as close to the bone as possible. Make a horizontal cut just above wing joint to release bottom part of each breast half; cut off wings. Transfer meat to platter.

PER SERVING WITH 2 TBSP. GRAVY 771 CAL., 45% (346 CAL.) FROM FAT; 98 G PROTEIN; 38 G FAT (11 G SAT.); 1.6 G CARBO (0.2 G FIBER); 818 MG SODIUM; 293 MG CHOL.

Rich brown gravy Toast ½ cup **flour** in a 5- to 6-qt. pot over medium heat, whisking constantly, until deep golden brown, 7 to 10 minutes. Pour in 2 cups **reduced-sodium chicken broth** and whisk into a smooth paste. Add 3½ to 4 cups **turkey** or chicken **stock** and 1½ tbsp. minced **fresh rosemary.** Bring to a boil; simmer about 10 minutes, whisking often. Makes 5 cups.

How-to: Turkey basics

Turkey weight with giblets*	Oven/grill temperature	Desired internal temperature**	Cooking time***
10–13 lbs.	350°	160°	1½–2¼ hours
14–23 lbs.	325°	160°	2–3 hours
24–27 lbs.	325°	160°	3–3¾ hours
28–30 lbs.	325°	160°	3½–4½ hours

*Allow 1 lb. (16 oz.) turkey per person (raw weight with bones) to yield ¼ lb. (4 oz.) neatly sliced meat per person, plus leftovers.

**To measure, insert a thermometer through the thickest part of breast until it touches the bone, where the temperature is most consistent (it will continue to rise after you remove the bird from the oven). For turkey with stuffing, use an instant-read thermometer to check in several places; it should reach at least 165°.

***Times are for unstuffed birds. A stuffed bird may cook at same rate as an unstuffed one, but be ready to allow 30 to 50 minutes more. Turkeys take about the same amount of time to roast as they do to grill, but a grill browns the bird more fully.

Sunset turkey Tetrazzini

We took classic Tetrazzini—a dish said to have been invented in San Francisco in the early 1900s to honor soprano Luisa Tetrazzini, who lived in the city for a time—and punched it up with fresh leeks, portabella mushrooms, and radicchio.

SERVES 8 | 1 hour

3 leeks
5 tbsp. butter, divided
2 portabella mushroom caps, cubed
1½ cups (¼ lb.) sliced button mushrooms
5 tsp. salt, divided
¼ tsp. nutmeg
1 lb. medium egg noodles
3 tbsp. flour
2 cups chicken broth
½ cup dry sherry
1 cup half-and-half
½ cup grated parmesan cheese
2 cups cubed or shredded (½-in. pieces) cooked turkey
About ⅓ cup chopped flat-leaf parsley
¾ cup chopped radicchio leaves

1. Cut off and discard root ends and dark green leaves of leeks. Cut leeks in half lengthwise and swish around in a large bowl of water to rinse; transfer to a colander, leaving dirt behind, and rinse again in fresh water if necessary. Thinly slice crosswise into semicircles.
2. Melt 2 tbsp. butter in a 14-in. frying pan or 5-qt. saucepan over medium heat. Add leeks, mushrooms, 1 tsp. salt, and the nutmeg; cook, stirring often, until vegetables are soft and beginning to brown, 12 minutes. Using a slotted spoon, transfer leek mixture to a bowl and set aside. Set aside pan with cooking juices in it.
3. Bring a large pot of water to a boil. Add 3 tsp. salt and the egg noodles and cook until they are barely tender to the bite. Drain noodles and set aside, covered.
4. While noodles are cooking, melt remaining 3 tbsp. butter in same frying pan or saucepan. Sprinkle in flour and cook, stirring, until mixture looks glossy and golden brown, about 3 minutes. Whisk in broth and sherry and simmer until thickened, about 3 minutes. Remove from heat and whisk in half-and-half, parmesan, and remaining 1 tsp. salt. Reduce heat to low, return pan to heat, and stir in leek mixture, turkey, and ⅓ cup parsley.
5. Just before serving, stir in radicchio. Serve over cooked noodles and garnish with more chopped parsley.

PER SERVING 455 CAL., 32% (144 CAL.) FROM FAT; 24 G PROTEIN; 16 G FAT (8.6 G SAT.); 53 G CARBO (2.8 G FIBER); 1,148 MG SODIUM; 115 MG CHOL.

TURKEY TETRAZZINI

Turkey enchiladas

The original recipe for these rich and easy enchiladas came from the 1969 edition of the *Sunset Cook Book of Favorite Recipes*. Reader Donna Barasch, of Villa Park, California, adapted it recently with timesaving tricks, replacing the homemade chile-tomato sauce with a jar of medium-hot salsa. We tried both red and green salsas in our tests, as well as our New Mexico Red and Green Chile Sauces (recipes on page 105), and they were all delicious. The enchiladas are a great way to use up leftover holiday turkey; shredded cooked chicken can be substituted if you like.

SERVES 6 | 40 minutes

3 cups shredded cooked turkey
2 cups sour cream
About 2 cups shredded (½ lb.) sharp cheddar cheese
1 tsp. salt
⅓ cup vegetable oil
12 corn tortillas (8 in. wide)
1 jar (16 oz.) medium-hot salsa

1. Preheat oven to 350°. In a large bowl, mix turkey, sour cream, 2 cups cheddar cheese, and the salt.

TURKEY ENCHILADAS

2. Heat oil in an 8- to 10-in. frying pan over low heat. Dip 1 tortilla at a time in hot oil just until limp, about 5 seconds each.
3. Fill tortillas with turkey mixture, roll up, and arrange side by side, seam down, in a 9- by 13-in. baking dish. Pour salsa over the top. Bake until heated through, about 20 minutes.
4. Sprinkle more shredded cheese over hot enchiladas.

PER SERVING 677 CAL., 60% (405 CAL.) FROM FAT; 35 G PROTEIN; 45 G FAT (21 G SAT.); 32 G CARBO (2.6 G FIBER); 1,308 MG SODIUM; 128 MG CHOL.

Golden Gate grilled turkey and cheese

The sandwich from reader Britta Glade of Orinda, California, is like a Monte Cristo—only better. The parmesan crust is genius.

MAKES 2 sandwiches | 30 minutes

2 tbsp. butter, softened
1 tsp. minced garlic
½ tsp. red chile flakes
1 large egg, lightly beaten
¼ cup milk

1 cup coarsely shredded parmesan cheese
4 freshly cut slices from a sourdough loaf
6 oz. thinly sliced turkey
½ firm-ripe avocado, pitted, peeled, and thinly sliced
1 tbsp. chopped cilantro
2 slices muenster cheese

1. Combine butter, garlic, and chile flakes in a small bowl. Whisk egg and milk in a medium bowl. Spread parmesan on a plate.
2. Melt half the garlic butter in a large frying pan over medium heat. Dip 1 bread slice in egg mixture, coating one side only. Dip coated side into parmesan. Put in frying pan, cheese side down. Repeat with 1 more bread slice. Arrange turkey, avocado, cilantro, and muenster evenly on both slices.
3. Dip remaining bread slices into egg on one side and then into parmesan. Set on sandwiches in pan, cheese side up. Continue cooking sandwiches over medium heat until undersides are golden brown, 3 to 4 minutes. Lift sandwiches and add remaining garlic butter to pan; flip and cook until second side is golden brown, another 3 to 4 minutes.

PER SANDWICH 866 CAL., 54% (468 CAL.) FROM FAT; 62 G PROTEIN; 52 G FAT (26 G SAT.); 38 G CARBO (2.7 G FIBER); 1,668 MG SODIUM; 272 MG CHOL.

GRILLED KING SALMON
WITH ASPARAGUS,
MORELS, AND LEEKS

Grilled king salmon with asparagus, morels, and leeks

Steelhead Diner sits above Seattle's Pike Place Market, and its chef, Kevin Davis, came up with this splurge-worthy combo when local salmon, asparagus, and morels all showed up downstairs.

SERVES 6 | 1¼ hours

1 lb. slender asparagus, trimmed and cut in half on a diagonal
1 large leek (white part only), thinly sliced and rinsed well
3 tbsp. butter
2 tsp. chopped thyme leaves
¾ tsp. kosher salt, divided
½ tsp. pepper, divided
½ lb. fresh morel mushrooms, rinsed well and halved
    lengthwise, or ¾ oz. dried morels*
¼ cup fino sherry or dry white wine
1 tbsp. olive oil
1 king or coho salmon fillet (1½ lbs., 1 in. thick), with skin
1 cup whipping cream

1. Boil asparagus until barely tender-crisp, 2 minutes; drain and rinse in cold water. Prepare a grill for medium-high heat (see "How-to: Grilling," page 83).

2. Sauté leek in butter in a frying pan over medium heat until soft, 5 minutes. Add thyme, ½ tsp. salt, ¼ tsp. pepper, and the morels; cook, stirring occasionally, until morels are tender, 5 minutes. Stir in sherry and reduce by half, 30 to 45 seconds. Set aside.

3. Fold a 12- by 17-in. sheet of heavy-duty foil in half crosswise. With a knife tip, poke dime-size holes through foil about 2 in. apart. Oil one side of foil. Rub fish on both sides with oil and put skin side down on foil. Sprinkle with ¼ tsp. *each* salt and pepper.

4. Set salmon on foil on cooking grate; grill, covered, until fish is barely cooked through, about 10 minutes. With 2 wide spatulas, slide fish from skin to a warm platter; tent with foil. If you want crisp skin, continue to cook skin on foil until crisp, 1 to 3 minutes more. Remove foil from grill, then gently peel off skin, using fingers or a wide spatula (skin may break into pieces).

5. Add cream and asparagus to mushrooms and boil over high heat, stirring; boil longer to thicken if you like. Set salmon skin, if using, on a platter. With 2 spatulas, set fish on skin. Spoon half the vegetable sauce over salmon and serve the rest on the side.

*Soak dried morels in hot water until softened, 8 minutes. Squeeze out water; cut in half.

PER SERVING 448 CAL., 71% (316 CAL.) FROM FAT; 25 G PROTEIN; 35 G FAT (15 G SAT.); 8.7 G CARBO (2.7 G FIBER); 366 MG SODIUM; 132 MG CHOL.

Cedar-planked salmon

A technique developed by Northwest Native Americans, grilling salmon on a cedar plank gives the fish a deep, woodsy taste and keeps it moist by protecting it from the flames. You'll need an untreated cedar board, ½ to ¾ in. thick and large enough to accommodate your fish. Find planks at a well-stocked fish shop, a barbecue store, or online.

SERVES 6 | 45 minutes, plus 2 hours to soak plank

2 tbsp. table salt
1 tsp. vegetable oil
1 skin-on, boned salmon fillet* (2 to 2½ lbs.)
½ tsp. kosher or sea salt
¼ tsp. pepper
1 tsp. butter

1. Put 8 cups hot water and table salt in a pan large enough to hold the plank; stir to dissolve salt. Soak plank at least 2 hours.

2. Meanwhile, prepare a grill for indirect medium-high heat (see "How-to: Grilling," page 83).

3. Wipe water off plank and rub it with vegetable oil. Set plank over direct heat and toast it, covered, until it starts to smoke and char, 5 to 10 minutes.

4. Meanwhile, season salmon fillet with salt and pepper. Turn plank over, set over indirect heat, and set fillet, skin side down, on charred side. Dot with butter. Close lid on grill and cook salmon until center of fillet flakes, 30 to 40 minutes.

*Buy a long, narrow fillet that fits your board; or, with a short, wide fillet, divide it down the center and lay the pieces end to end.

PER SERVING 322 CAL., 55% (176 CAL.) FROM FAT; 34 G PROTEIN; 20 G FAT (4.3 G SAT.); 0.1 G CARBO (0 G FIBER); 258 MG SODIUM; 98 MG CHOL.

From the Pacific: Salmon

Ever since the last Ice Age, adult salmon have left the ocean and battled their way up Western rivers—in some cases more than a thousand miles—to spawn and die where they were born. Today, however, the runs of wild salmon are disappearing; Alaska is the one remaining Western fishery that's well managed, with relatively healthy and abundant salmon populations. Many fish-farming practices pollute the ocean and harm wild fish—but techniques are being improved, and new land-based facilities may reduce some of the problems. For now, though, wild salmon is the best choice.

Grilled salmon with cucumber salad

Pair hot with cool: Top fish just off the grill with a refreshing salad. Maria Hines, chef of Tilth and Golden Beetle restaurants in Seattle, serves this dish with couscous seasoned with fresh herbs, lemon zest, and grilled cucumber slices. (Photo on page 72.)

SERVES 4 | 35 minutes

SAUCE
1 cup plain whole-milk yogurt
1 tbsp. *each* chopped fresh dill and extra-virgin olive oil
2 tsp. lemon juice
¼ tsp. kosher salt
⅛ tsp. pepper

CUCUMBER SALAD
½ lb. Persian or English cucumbers
2 tsp. *each* chopped chives and flat-leaf parsley
1½ tsp. minced shallot
2 tsp. extra-virgin olive oil
¾ tsp. lemon juice
⅛ tsp. *each* kosher salt and pepper

SALMON & SERVING
4 sockeye salmon fillets (each 5 to 6 oz., ½ to 1 in. thick), with skin
1 tbsp. olive oil
¼ tsp. *each* kosher salt and pepper
Dill sprigs

1. Make sauce: Combine yogurt, dill, oil, lemon juice, salt, and pepper in a bowl. Cover and chill until used.
2. Prepare a grill for medium-high heat (see "How-to: Grilling," page 83).
3. Make salad: Cut cucumbers lengthwise into paper-thin strips, preferably with a mandoline. Put in a bowl with herbs and shallot; chill until used. In another bowl, mix oil, lemon juice, salt, and pepper; set dressing aside.
4. Prepare salmon: Rub fish all over with oil and sprinkle all over with salt and pepper. Fold a 12- by 20-in. sheet of heavy-duty foil in half crosswise. With a knife tip, poke dime-size holes through foil about 2 in. apart. Oil one side of foil.
5. Set foil with oiled side up on cooking grate. Set fillets slightly separated, skin side down, on foil. Grill, covered, until fish is barely cooked through, 7 to 12 minutes. With a wide spatula, slide fish from skin to a platter and tent with foil. If you want crisp skin, continue to cook skin on foil until crisp, 2 to 3 minutes more. Remove foil from grill, then gently peel off skin, using your fingers or a wide spatula (skin may break into pieces).

6. Set crisp skin, if using, on plates and set the salmon on top. Discard any liquid from cucumber mixture in bowl, then quickly toss mixture with dressing and mound on fish. Garnish with dill sprigs. Serve immediately with yogurt sauce (salmon skin will soften as it stands).

PER SERVING 380 CAL., 56% (213 CAL.) FROM FAT; 34 G PROTEIN; 24 G FAT (4.8 G SAT.); 5.6 G CARBO (0.4 G FIBER); 409 MG SODIUM; 109 MG CHOL.

Salmon *shioyaki*

Add *shioyaki*—Japanese for "salt-grilled"—to your repertoire. The technique creates salmon with an umami-rich crust and a crispy skin. Taichi Kitamura, chef of Kappo Tamura restaurant in Seattle, shared the recipe—it's been his favorite way to eat fish since his childhood in Kyoto, Japan.

SERVES 4 | 15 minutes, plus 2 hours to salt

4 sockeye salmon fillets (each 5 to 6 oz., ½ to 1 in. thick), with skin
1½ tsp. fine sea salt
1 tbsp. vegetable oil
Hot cooked sushi rice, such as Nishiki or other short- to medium-grain rice
4 sheets nori (about 8 in. square), each cut into 6 pieces
Lemon wedges
*Furikake** (Japanese rice seasoning)

1. Set salmon on a cooling rack in a rimmed pan, sprinkle fillets all over with sea salt, and chill uncovered at least 2 hours and as long as 5 hours.
2. Heat a grill to medium-high (see "How-to: Grilling," page 83). Fold a 12- by 20-in. sheet of heavy-duty foil in half crosswise. With a knife tip, poke dime-size holes through foil about 2 in. apart. Oil one side of foil. Rub fish all over with oil.
3. Set foil with oiled side up on cooking grate. Set fillets slightly separated, skin side down, on foil. Grill, covered, until fish is barely cooked through, 7 to 12 minutes. With a wide spatula, slide fish from skin to a platter and tent with foil. Cook skin on foil until crisp, 2 to 3 minutes more. Remove foil from grill, then gently peel off skin, using fingers or a wide spatula (skin may break into pieces).
4. Serve salmon immediately with crispy skin, rice, nori, lemon, and furikake.
*A salty-sweet condiment, sold at Asian-foods stores and at *asianfoodgrocer.com*

PER SERVING 292 CAL., 50% (145 CAL.) FROM FAT; 33 G PROTEIN; 16 G FAT (2.6 G SAT.); 1 G CARBO (0.5 G FIBER); 967 MG SODIUM; 101 MG CHOL.

SALMON *SHIOYAKI*

CHILLED POACHED
HALIBUT WITH FRESH
APRICOT SALSA

Chilled poached halibut with fresh apricot salsa

Pacific halibut, whose range extends from offshore Canada and Alaska across to Russia, is a sustainably fished species that's in season from March through mid-November. Try to find fresh tangy-sweet Blenheim apricots, in season in June, to complement the delicately flavored poached halibut. (See "From the Orchard: Blenheim Apricots," page 180.) If you use supermarket apricots, mix in a little honey and extra lemon juice.

SERVES 4 | 30 minutes, plus 30 minutes to chill

2 tbsp. vegetable oil
2 tsp. brown mustard seeds*
1 lb. apricots, preferably Blenheim*
2 tbsp. lemon juice
½ cup diced red onion, rinsed and drained
¼ cup coarsely chopped cilantro
¼ to ½ red jalapeño, seeds and ribs removed and cut
   into rings crosswise as thinly as possible,
   or ¼ to 1 tsp. minced seeded habanero chile
About 1 tbsp. kosher salt, divided
½ lemon, thinly sliced
4 skinned, boned halibut fillets, ¾ in. thick (6 oz. each)

1. Put oil and mustard seeds in a skillet, cover, and heat over medium-high heat. The seeds will start popping wildly. When popping sounds die down, remove from heat. Let cool slightly, uncovered.
2. Halve and pit apricots; cut into ½-in. dice. Put diced apricots in a large bowl and toss gently with lemon juice, onion, cilantro, jalapeño, and mustard seeds with oil. Stir in 2 tsp. salt and chill for at least 30 minutes and up to 2 hours.
3. Meanwhile, wipe skillet clean with paper towels and fill half-full with water. Add remaining 1 tsp. salt and the lemon slices. Heat water over medium heat until gently simmering. Add fish and cook, covered, until just opaque in center (cut to check), 5 to 8 minutes.
4. Transfer fish with a spatula to a platter and chill at least 20 minutes. Season fish with salt to taste and serve it cold with apricot salsa.
*Find brown mustard seeds at Middle Eastern, South Asian, and well-stocked grocery stores. If using supermarket apricots, increase lemon juice to 2½ tbsp. and mix it with 1½ tsp. honey before adding to salsa.

PER SERVING 347 CAL., 39% (135 CAL.) FROM FAT; 38 G PROTEIN; 15 G FAT (1.9 G SAT.); 15 G CARBO (2 G FIBER); 586 MG SODIUM; 54 MG CHOL.

Halibut kebabs with grilled bread and pancetta

With its big flakes, halibut holds up well on the grill; it's "basted" by the pancetta. You'll need four 10-in. skewers (soaked if wood).

SERVES 4 | 25 minutes

¼ cup olive oil
1 tbsp. coarsely chopped rosemary leaves
1 tsp. *each* salt and pepper
1½ lbs. boned and skinned halibut, cut into 2-in. chunks
4 cups crusty bread, such as ciabatta, cut into 1½-in. cubes
3 oz. pancetta, sliced paper-thin

1. Prepare a grill for medium heat (see "How-to: Grilling," page 83). Combine oil, rosemary, salt, and pepper in a large bowl; add halibut and bread; toss to coat. Set aside 5 minutes.
2. Cut pancetta into 2-in.-wide strips. Skewer an end of 1 strip, then alternate fish and bread cubes, weaving pancetta between them. Repeat with 3 more skewers. Grill kebabs, turning often, until fish is cooked through and bread is browned, 6 minutes.

PER SERVING 516 CAL., 56% (288 CAL.) FROM FAT; 42 G PROTEIN; 32 G FAT (6.9 G SAT.); 22 G CARBO (1.2 G FIBER); 1,117 MG SODIUM; 66 MG CHOL.

HALIBUT KEBABS
WITH GRILLED BREAD
AND PANCETTA

Sake and birch syrup–roasted sablefish with fresh peas and chard

Sablefish—also called black cod—is sweet and moist, with fat, pearly white flakes. Heighten the sweetness with birch syrup (you can substitute maple syrup) and *sake kasu* (the lees left after making sake). Abundant in the Pacific from California to Alaska, the sablefish in the waters off Alaska and British Columbia are caught sustainably.

SERVES 4 | 1¼ hours, plus 2 hours to marinate

7 tbsp. tamari or soy sauce
7 tbsp. birch syrup* or maple syrup
¼ to ½ fresh or dried Thai chile, minced
1-in.-piece fresh ginger, peeled and thinly sliced
2 smashed, peeled garlic cloves, plus 2 minced garlic cloves
2 sprigs thyme, plus 1 tsp. leaves
2 tbsp. *sake kasu** (sake lees) or white miso
4 skinned sablefish fillets, ¾ in. thick (6 oz. each)
5 tbsp. butter or olive oil, divided
½ white onion, finely diced
1 cup shelled fresh peas
½ bunch rainbow Swiss chard, leaves stripped from ribs and torn into pieces; ribs and stems diced

1. Marinate fish: In a small pot, combine tamari, birch syrup, chile, ginger, smashed garlic, 2 sprigs thyme, the sake kasu or miso, and ⅔ cup water (⅓ cup if using miso). Bring to a simmer and cook, whisking occasionally, 5 minutes (or, for miso, just bring to a simmer, then remove from heat without further cooking). Let cool. Pour into a 1-gal. resealable plastic bag. Add fish, seal, and chill, about 2 hours.

2. Remove fish from marinade and pat dry. Prepare a grill for medium-high heat (see "How-to: Grilling," page 83); or cook on the stove. Heat 2 tbsp. butter in a large heavy frying pan or 2 smaller pans. Add fish and sauté, turning once, until crisp-edged and opaque in center, 10 to 15 minutes. Set pan aside, covered and wrapped in a towel to keep warm. If using a charcoal grill, add 10 to 12 briquets to fire.

3. Melt 2 tbsp. butter in a medium saucepan, add onion and thyme leaves, and cook over grill or on stove, stirring often, until onion starts to soften, 3 to 5 minutes. Stir in minced garlic, ¼ cup water, the peas, and chard ribs and stems and cook, covered and stirring often, until tender, about 5 minutes. Stir in chard leaves; cook, covered, until wilted, about 2 minutes more. Stir remaining 1 tbsp. butter into vegetables and serve with fish.

*Order birch syrup through Kahiltna Birchworks (*alaskabirch syrup.com*). Find sake kasu at Japanese markets.

PER SERVING 482 CAL., 68% (364 CAL.) FROM FAT; 27 G PROTEIN; 41 G FAT (15 G SAT.); 15 G CARBO (2.7 G FIBER); 760 MG SODIUM; 122 MG CHOL.

The Northwest

You might say that geology set the Northwest table. Cataclysmic volcano eruptions and flooding from melting glaciers made the rich land of the Willamette Valley and the Columbia Basin. The Cascade Range contains the clouds drifting in from the Pacific, sending rain down into what's now western Washington and Oregon. To the dry east of the range, sunny plains and hills run on into Idaho. Before Europeans arrived, Native Americans dined on fish and shellfish, nettles and other greens, berries, and sweet potato–like camas bulbs. Clark, navigating the Columbia with Lewis in 1805, wrote that the river's Celilo Falls were "a great emporium … where all the neighboring nations assemble" to fish the salmon run. In the 1840s, Oregon Trail settlers began to roll in, bringing seeds and recipes and establishing farms. The Northwest's harvest then included potatoes, beans, huckleberries, pears, apples, cherries, and hazelnuts; its catch, salmon, clams, halibut, sablefish, and trout. From there, 100 years or so take us through the arrival of Asian and Latino traditions, and the 1907 opening of Seattle's Pike Place Market, to such enterprising 1960s winemakers as Washington's Columbia Winery and Oregon's HillCrest. Restaurant game-changers include the Seattle area's Herbfarm (with its backyard produce) and Dahlia Lounge (the first creation from the restless imagination of Tom Douglas); Portland innovators at Genoa, Zefiro, and Heathman, its new stars like Gabriel Rucker (Le Pigeon and Little Bird), and its food truck nirvana. Nathan Myhrvold, an ex-Microsoft techie turned Seattle food geek, brought us the revolutionary 2011 cookbook *Modernist Cuisine*.

BAJA FISH TACOS

Baja fish tacos

A good fish taco, a cold Corona, and the beach—those equal summer up and down the coast of California. It all began when, somewhere in Baja California, someone concocted the prototypical modern fish taco: a lightly battered mild white fish deep-fried until crisp, then served in a corn tortilla or two with shredded cabbage, *crema*, salsa, and a spritz of lime. The batter on the fish is similar to that for tempura—and some speculate that the arrival of Japanese fishermen in Baja in the 1920s may have contributed to the birth of the fish taco.

The idea came north after Ralph Rubio and some friends from San Diego State went down to San Felipe, in Baja, in 1974. Rubio was fond of the fish tacos made by a vendor there named Carlos, and one night Rubio suggested Carlos open a stand north of the border. Carlos said he didn't want to leave Mexico. So Rubio asked him for the recipe, and in 1983, opened his first restaurant, in San Diego. Today, Rubio's Fresh Mexican Grill operates about 200 branches in the West.

MAKES 6 to 8 tacos | 45 minutes

1 cup *each* dark beer and flour
1 tsp. salt
Vegetable oil
1½ lbs. firm, white-fleshed fish fillets, such as Pacific
 cod or tilapia, cut into 1-in.-wide strips
12 to 16 corn tortillas (6 in. wide), warmed*
Cabbage and Cilantro Slaw (recipe follows)
Chipotle Tartar Sauce (recipe follows)
Lime wedges

1. Whisk beer, flour, and salt in a bowl until well blended.
2. Preheat oven to 200°. Pour about 1 in. of oil into a 10- to 12-in. nonstick frying pan (with sides at least 2 in. high); heat over medium-high heat until oil registers 360° on a deep-fry thermometer. With a fork, dip each piece of fish into beer batter, then lift out and let drain briefly. Slide fish into oil, a few pieces at a time, and cook until golden (adjust heat to maintain 360°), turning if necessary to brown on all sides, 2 to 4 minutes per batch. With a slotted spoon, transfer to a baking sheet lined with paper towels. Keep warm in oven while frying remaining fish.
3. To assemble each taco, stack 2 warm tortillas and top with a couple of pieces of fish, then a spoonful of slaw. Serve with tartar sauce and lime wedges on the side.
*To heat tortillas, wrap in a kitchen towel and microwave until warm and soft, about 1 minute.

PER TACO (NO SLAW OR SAUCE) 537 CAL., 57% (306 CAL.) FROM FAT; 20 G PROTEIN; 34 G FAT (18 G SAT.); 39 G CARBO (3.9 G FIBER); 573 MG SODIUM; 53 MG CHOL.

Cabbage and cilantro slaw Mix 1½ qts. finely shredded **cabbage** (about 10 oz.), ⅓ cup chopped **cilantro,** 3 tbsp. **lime juice,** 2 tbsp. **vegetable oil,** and ¼ tsp. **red chile flakes** in a large bowl. Add **salt** to taste. Makes 4¼ cups.

Chipotle tartar sauce Rinse 2 tbsp. **canned chipotle chiles in adobo sauce** and discard seeds and veins. In a blender, purée chiles with 1 cup **mayonnaise** and ¼ cup *each* **sweet pickle relish** and chopped **onion** until smooth. Makes 1⅓ cups.

Grilled sardines with cold bean salad

Plentiful in the Pacific, sardines have a rich, strong, slightly minerally flavor. They're an eco-friendly choice—and good for you too, full of omega-3 fatty acids and without pollutants concentrated in their flesh. A glass of sparkling wine would be ideal with these grilled sardines and the summery salad of creamy cannellini beans and grape tomatoes.

SERVES 4 | 30 minutes

1 tsp. minced garlic
¼ cup lemon juice
About ½ cup extra-virgin olive oil
1 tsp. kosher salt
½ tsp. pepper
8 whole fresh sardines (1¼ lbs. total), cleaned and
 backbones removed
2 cans (15 oz. each) cannellini beans, drained
1 cup halved grape tomatoes
1 cup curly parsley leaves

1. Prepare a grill for high heat (see "How-to: Grilling," page 83).
2. Whisk together garlic, lemon juice, oil, salt, and pepper in a bowl. Pour ¼ cup dressing over sardines in another bowl and let stand 10 minutes.
3. Meanwhile, add drained cannellini beans, grape tomatoes, and curly parsley leaves to remaining dressing and toss to coat.
4. Using a wad of oiled paper towels and tongs, oil cooking grate. Set sardines skin side down on oiled cooking grate. Grill, turning once, until dark grill marks appear, 5 minutes. Serve with bean salad.

PER SERVING 520 CAL., 49% (252 CAL.) FROM FAT; 22 G PROTEIN; 30 G FAT (12 G SAT.); 28 G CARBO (9.5 G FIBER); 1,019 MG SODIUM; 39 MG CHOL.

Crispy trout with capers

Unless you're lucky enough to catch a rainbow trout in one of the West's rivers or lakes, the trout you cook is probably farm-raised—and about 80 percent of trout sold in the United States come from Idaho, particularly the Snake River Valley. There, cold stream water is sent through contained ponds or raceways and the trout are raised with low environmental impact. They emerge with fresh, slightly earthy flavor.

SERVES 2 | 20 minutes

¼ cup *each* flour and cornmeal
About ½ tsp. salt
About ¼ tsp. pepper
1 whole trout (8 to 10 oz.), cleaned and boned
¼ cup butter
1 tbsp. drained capers
Lemon wedges and flat-leaf parsley sprigs

1. Combine flour, cornmeal, ½ tsp. salt, and ¼ tsp. pepper in a large, shallow dish. Rinse the trout and pat dry; set fish in flour mixture and turn to coat.
2. Bring butter to a simmer in a small pan over medium heat, then remove from heat. Skim off and discard the foam with

CRISPY TROUT
WITH CAPERS

a spoon, leaving clarified butter behind. Pour 1 tbsp. of clarified butter into a 10- to 12-in. frying pan over high heat. Place trout, skin side down, in pan and cook until browned on the bottom, 2 to 3 minutes. Turn with a wide spatula, reduce heat to medium, and cook until fish is barely opaque but still moist-looking in center of thickest part (cut to test), 2 to 4 minutes more.
3. Meanwhile, add capers to remaining clarified butter in small pan and shake pan often over medium heat until capers pop open, 1 to 2 minutes.
4. Transfer trout, skin down, to a plate. Spoon caper butter over fish and garnish with lemon wedges and parsley. Add salt and pepper to taste.

PER SERVING 428 CAL., 56% (238 CAL.) FROM FAT; 18 G PROTEIN; 27 G FAT (16 G SAT.); 28 G CARBO (1.4 G FIBER); 926 MG SODIUM; 135 MG CHOL.

Pan-fried trout with smoked salmon

Janie Hibler, author of *Dungeness Crabs & Blackberry Cobblers*, invented this dish about 25 years ago at her family's cabin in Washington's Cascade Range. The combination came about when she had smoked salmon in the fridge and her kids brought in trout they'd just caught at Swift Creek Reservoir.

SERVES 8 | 40 minutes

8 whole trout (4½ lbs. total), cleaned and boned, at room temperature
About 1 tsp. kosher salt, divided
8 thin slices smoked salmon* (4 to 5 oz. total)
½ cup cornmeal
5 to 7 tbsp. extra-virgin olive oil, divided
1 lb. (2 pts.) mini multicolored bell peppers, seeds and ribs removed and cut in half lengthwise*
2 limes, cut into wedges

1. Preheat oven to 150°. Sprinkle inside of each trout with a little salt (use about ½ tsp. total). Stuff each with a slice of smoked salmon. In a large, shallow dish, combine cornmeal and remaining ½ tsp. salt. Turn fish in cornmeal to coat.
2. Pour 2 tbsp. oil into each of two 12-in. frying pans and warm them over medium heat. (Or warm a large griddle over two burners.) Put 3 fish in each pan and cook, turning once, until golden brown outside and no longer translucent in the center, 8 to 9 minutes total; reduce heat if fish start to get too brown. Transfer fish to one or two platters and keep warm in oven. Repeat cooking in one pan with 1 to 2 more tbsp. oil and remaining fish.

3. If pan (or griddle) is dry, add 1 more tbsp. oil. Set pan over medium-high heat and quickly cook peppers, stirring, until they're softened and lightly browned, about 5 minutes. Sprinkle with salt to taste and scatter on top of fish. Serve with limes.

*Use soft, cold-smoked salmon, also called Nova-style salmon or Nova lox. Find mini bell peppers at Trader Joe's or farmers' markets, or use 1 lb. regular-size bell peppers, seeds and ribs removed and quartered.

PER SERVING 290 CAL., 53% (153 CAL.) FROM FAT; 23 G PROTEIN; 17 G FAT (2.7 G SAT.); 11 G CARBO (1.2 G FIBER); 512 MG SODIUM; 55 MG CHOL.

Grilled ahi citrus salad

Both yellowfin and bigeye tuna are called *ahi*, the Hawaiian word for those two tunas. In his terrific book, *Fish Forever*, Paul Johnson says that the best-quality bigeye comes from Hawaii during winter season—October through April.

SERVES 4 | 30 minutes

2 tbsp. *each* honey and Dijon mustard
4 ahi tuna* steaks (6 oz. each)

⅓ cup olive oil
2 tbsp. *each* Champagne vinegar and lime juice
¼ tsp. *each* kosher salt and pepper
6 oz. mixed baby greens
½ cup thinly sliced sweet onion, such as Maui or Walla Walla
2 large avocados, pitted, peeled, and sliced
2 navel oranges, peeled and segmented

1. Oil cooking grate and prepare a grill for medium heat (see "How-to: Grilling," page 83). Combine honey and mustard in a bowl. Rub over tuna steaks and let stand 10 minutes.

2. Meanwhile, whisk olive oil, vinegar, lime juice, salt, and pepper in a bowl. Combine greens, onion, avocados, and orange segments in another bowl and add two-thirds of vinaigrette.

3. Grill tuna until rare, 1 to 2 minutes per side. Slice across the grain ¼ in. thick. Set salad on plates and top with tuna. Drizzle with more vinaigrette.

*Look for troll- or pole-caught tuna, containing lower mercury levels and more sustainably fished than longline-caught.

PER SERVING 695 CAL., 58% (405 CAL.) FROM FAT; 44 G PROTEIN; 45 G FAT (7.6 G SAT.); 30 G CARBO (5 G FIBER); 339 MG SODIUM; 65 MG CHOL.

The Mountain states

In the 1800s, most inhabitants of the Rocky Mountains and Great Basin region ate, it seems, on the go. The Cheyenne and Arapaho were nomadic, following bison herds on horseback. Fur trappers roamed the area as well, living on elk and buffalo, beans and corn. In the mid-1800s, wagon trains began to wind through on the Oregon Trail, hauling flour, bacon, beans, coffee, molasses, and other staples, which the settlers cooked up in their dutch ovens.

Prospectors were migratory too: While some stayed in the gold and silver mining towns that sprang up after 1858—like Leadville, Colorado; and Helena, Montana—others moved on. Those who remained brought to the table flavors from their home countries, including Italy, Germany, and Croatia. Chinese workers opened noodle shops, while Cornish and Irish miners lunched on pasties—meat-filled turnovers. Struck-it-rich miners spent big at Denver's Brown Palace and Leadville's Clarendon (its chef plucked from Delmonico's in New York City).

Mormons arrived in the 1840s in Utah, where they lived (and continue to live) by the injunction toward self-sufficiency—including keeping a year's worth of beans, wheat, canned fruit, and other foodstuffs.

The irrigation of Colorado beginning in the 1870s allowed farmers to grow San Luis Valley's potatoes, Paonia's cherries, and Palisade's peaches. By the 1880s, the waves of bison were declining, replaced, especially in Montana and Wyoming, by cattle and ranchers. On the ranch, women cooked sourdough pancakes, beef stew, trout, and quail. Basque sheepherders passed platters of lamb and potatoes at boardinghouses in Idaho, Utah, Nevada, and Northern California.

Aspen installed its first ski lift in 1947, and serious money brought in serious restaurants there and at other resort towns in the Rockies. Today, breweries such as New Belgium in Fort Collins have put Colorado at the forefront of the American craft beer boom.

GRILLED BASS WITH
SALSA VERDE

Grilled bass with salsa verde

Tomatillos and fresh chiles give the salsa a bright, "green" flavor, and toasting them contributes a smoky element (and loosens the chiles' skins). Mexican cooks traditionally use a griddle or *comal* to toast salsa ingredients, but a broiler chars the chiles more evenly.

SERVES 2 | About 45 minutes

SALSA
¼ lb. tomatillos*, husked and rinsed
1 thick onion slice
1 small poblano chile*
1 serrano chile
1 tbsp. *each* chopped cilantro, basil, and mint leaves
1 small garlic clove
1 tbsp. lime juice
¾ tsp. kosher salt

FISH
2 whole small butterflied striped bass or trout with
    bones and heads removed
1 tbsp. olive oil
Salt and pepper
Chopped mint leaves

1. Make salsa: Preheat broiler. Line a rimmed baking pan with foil and set tomatillos, onion, poblano, and serrano in it.
2. Broil vegetables 3 in. from heat, turning as needed, until tomatillos and onion are speckled brown and chiles are black all over, 12 to 15 minutes; as vegetables are done, transfer to a bowl. Cover vegetables with a plate or foil and let stand about 5 minutes for chile skins to loosen.
3. Pull off stems and blackened skins from chiles; for best flavor, don't rinse chiles (a few blackened bits are okay to leave on). Open poblano and remove seeds.
4. Pulse vegetables and any juices, cilantro, basil, mint, and garlic in a food processor, until coarsely puréed. Scrape with a rubber spatula into a bowl and stir in 2 tbsp. water, the lime juice, and salt.
5. Prepare fish: Pat bass or trout dry, then rub all over with oil, salt, pepper, and mint. Set each fish, skin side down, on a double sheet of well-oiled heavy-duty foil.
6. Prepare a grill for direct medium-high heat (see "How-to: Grilling," page 83). Grill fish on foil, covered, until just opaque, about 3 minutes.
7. Spoon salsa onto plates. Carefully slide fish off foil and onto the salsa.

*Tart-tasting tomatillos look like green tomatoes with papery husks. Poblanos (sometimes mislabeled as pasillas) are large, meaty, deep green chiles with a fairly mild flavor; find them in the produce section.

PER SERVING 421 CAL., 33% (138 CAL.) FROM FAT; 58 G PROTEIN; 15 G FAT (2.7 G SAT.); 11 G CARBO (3.4 G FIBER); 944 MG SODIUM; 255 MG CHOL.

Pan-fried sardines with caramelized onions, pine nuts, and raisins

Based on the classic Venetian *sarde in saor* (sardines with sweet-sour flavors), this is a great introduction to the fish. Vinegar gives a mouthwatering acidity that balances the sardines' oiliness, nuts provide crunch, and raisins and onions add sweetness.

SERVES 4 to 6 | 50 minutes, plus 1 hour to marinate

⅓ cup pine nuts
2 medium yellow onions
1 cup red-wine vinegar
⅓ cup golden raisins
2 lbs. sardines, cleaned and filleted*, with heads removed
⅓ cup flour
⅓ cup olive oil, divided
1 tsp. kosher salt, divided
3 tbsp. coarsely chopped flat-leaf parsley

1. Preheat oven to 350°. Spread pine nuts out in a baking pan and toast in oven until golden, 5 to 7 minutes. Set aside. Cut onions lengthwise and slice into thin semicircles. Put vinegar in a measuring cup and add raisins.
2. Rinse sardines well inside and out, dry with paper towels, and roll in flour, shaking off excess.
3. Heat 3 tbsp. oil in a frying pan over medium heat until hot. Fry sardines in two batches, 1½ minutes per side. Transfer to a large shallow serving dish or platter and sprinkle with ½ tsp. salt.
4. Wipe out pan with paper towels, return to heat, and add remaining 7 tsp. oil. When oil is hot, add onions and remaining ½ tsp. salt. Cook, stirring often, until onions are very soft and browned, about 20 minutes.
5. Add vinegar and raisins and cook, stirring, 10 minutes.
6. Pour onion mixture over sardines and sprinkle with pine nuts. Cover with plastic wrap and let marinate at least 1 hour at room temperature. Serve at room temperature, sprinkled with parsley.
*Order the prepared sardines from your fishmonger.

PER SERVING 505 CAL., 56% (281 CAL.) FROM FAT; 35 G PROTEIN; 31 G FAT (5.7 G SAT.); 19 G CARBO (4.4 G FIBER); 1,596 MG SODIUM; 112 MG CHOL.

Cracked crab with herbed avocado sauce

With a beautiful color and a tarragon tang, this sauce is a standout with delicately flavored, sweet Dungeness crab. Buy the crab already cooked and cleaned or do it yourself.

SERVES 4 to 6 | 15 minutes, plus 30 minutes for sauce to rest

2 firm-ripe avocados, pitted and peeled
½ cup olive oil
¼ cup white-wine vinegar
About ½ tsp. salt
½ cup finely chopped chives (about 2 bunches)
2 tbsp. finely chopped tarragon
2 Dungeness crabs, cooked, cleaned, and cracked
   (by the fishmonger, or see "How-to: Dungeness Crab,"
   opposite page)

1. In a blender, purée avocados, oil, vinegar, ½ tsp. salt, and ½ cup water until smooth. Transfer to a bowl and stir in chives and tarragon. Cover and let stand 30 minutes at room temperature to let flavors blend.

2. Season sauce with salt to taste. Mound crab on a platter or on plates and serve with sauce.

PER SERVING 413 CAL., 76% (315 CAL.) FROM FAT; 19 G PROTEIN; 35 G FAT (5.1 G SAT.); 6.8 G CARBO (1.7 G FIBER); 482 MG SODIUM; 87 MG CHOL.

King crab on the half-shell

Alaska king crab is sorely misrepresented in the Lower 48 by imported Russian king crab, an often illegally caught species that's sometimes marketed as Alaska king crab. True Alaska king crab is pricier than Russian, but the meat is firmer, sweeter, and fresher tasting. (The Monterey Bay Aquarium's Seafood Watch recommends avoiding Russian king crab because of that industry's overfishing and illegal fishing. Ask for source information when you shop.)

You can buy the large Alaska king crab legs in the shell, already cooked and usually frozen (or thawed from frozen). (And if you ever have the chance to try the crab fresh, you're in for a treat.) The meat is wonderful simply butter-basted and broiled on the half-shell, as in this recipe.

SERVES 4 | 15 minutes

4 cooked Alaska king crab legs (about 3 lbs.),
   thawed if frozen*
¼ cup butter, melted
Kosher salt
Chopped flat-leaf parsley
1 lemon, cut into 8 wedges

1. Break crab legs at joints. (Wear thick, clean gloves—such as garden gloves—to protect yourself from the shell's many sharp points.) With scissors, cut along sides of shells and lift off the upper half of each. Arrange the crab legs, meat side up, on a baking pan and brush meat with melted butter. Sprinkle with salt to taste.

2. Broil crab 6 in. from heat until heated through, about 5 minutes. Serve several pieces (about 1 whole leg) to each person, sprinkled with parsley and served with a couple of lemon wedges.

*Plan to buy about ¾ lb. king crab per serving. Thaw frozen crab overnight in the refrigerator.

PER SERVING 292 CAL., 44% (129 CAL.) FROM FAT; 37 G PROTEIN; 15 G FAT (7.6 G SAT.); 1.4 G CARBO (0.4 G FIBER); 2,133 MG SODIUM; 132 MG CHOL.

CRACKED CRAB WITH HERBED AVOCADO SAUCE

How-to: Dungeness crab

Dungeness crabs are named after the town on Washington's Olympic Peninsula where they were first harvested for commercial sale in the mid-1800s. Today they're sustainably caught in traps along a huge stretch of Pacific Coast, from central California to Alaska, and are in season winter and spring—and in the northern stretch of their range, into summer. If you've never cooked live crabs, the prospect can seem a little daunting. But our paper-bag method for getting the critters in the water helps things go smoothly. Freshly cooked Dungeness crab is utterly delicious—one of the great culinary rewards of living in the West.

Cooking

1. BOIL THE WATER Keep live crabs chilled up to 12 hours in an open bowl or box, covered with damp paper towels. Fill a large pot with enough water to cover crabs by 2 to 3 in., leaving 3 to 4 in. of clearance below pot rim; bring to a boil.

2. TRANSFER THE CRABS Cut the handles off a sturdy paper bag. If the crabs are wrapped in newspaper or another material, gently unwrap them into the bag, putting in no more than two at a time. If the crabs are loose in a box, use tongs to lift each one up from the rear between the legs and put in the bag.

3. COOK Holding the bag near the bottom, gently upend it and let the crabs fall out into the water (avoid using tongs, which don't always give a steady grip if the crab starts to move); cover the pot. Cook, lowering the heat to a simmer once the water boils: 15 minutes for 1½- to 2½-lb. crabs, 20 minutes for bigger ones.

4. RINSE Lift out the crabs with tongs and rinse with cold running water until cool enough to handle.

Cleaning and Cracking

1. PUT a cooked crab, belly up, on a work surface. Pull off and discard the triangular flap and pointy appendages underneath it, plus the small paddles from the front of the crab.

2. PRY off the broad back shell from the rear end. Discard the liquid in the shell. Scoop out and save the soft, golden "butter" and white fat from the shell to eat with the crab, or discard with the back shell.

3. TURN the crab over. Pull off and discard any reddish membrane. Scoop out any remaining "butter." Pull off the long, spongy gills from sides of the body. Rinse the body well.

4. TWIST the legs and claws from the body. Using a nutcracker or wooden mallet, crack the shell of each leg and claw section. With a knife, cut the body into quarters.

California rolls

A quintessential fusion food, the California roll was probably invented in the early 1970s at Tokyo Kaikan, a long-gone restaurant in L.A.'s Little Tokyo. Whereas traditional sushi focused on one pristine, perfect ingredient, plus rice, the California roll was a combo: avocado, cucumber, and crab (cooked, to make it more accessible to a timid new audience). Instead of exotic nori seaweed wrapping the roll, familiar white rice encased the exterior, with the nori buried beneath, around the other fillings (we wrap our version, however, with the nori on the outside).

MAKES 6 rolls; 36 to 48 pieces | 1 hour

1½ cups short-grain white rice
¼ cup plus 1 tbsp. unseasoned rice vinegar
1 tbsp. sugar
¾ tsp. salt
6 sheets nori (dried seaweed; 7½ by 8 in.), toasted to soften*
2 tbsp. wasabi powder*, mixed with 2 tbsp. water
1 firm-ripe avocado (½ lb.), pitted, peeled, and cut
   into ¼-in.-thick slices
½ lb. shelled cooked crab
Soy sauce and pickled ginger*

1. In a fine-mesh strainer, rinse rice under cold running water until water runs clear, 5 to 10 minutes. Put rice in a 2- or 3-qt. pan and add 1½ cups water. Bring to a boil over high heat, then lower heat to maintain a simmer. Cover and cook until water is absorbed, 10 to 15 minutes.

2. Meanwhile, in a small bowl, combine ¼ cup vinegar, the sugar, and salt and stir until sugar and salt are dissolved.

3. Spread out rice in a shallow 12- by 16-in. baking pan and slowly pour vinegar mixture over it, turning rice gently and fanning it (with a handheld fan or a piece of paper) until it cools to warm room temperature, about 10 minutes.

4. Mix remaining 1 tbsp. vinegar with 1 cup water. Pour into a small bowl to moisten your hands so rice doesn't stick to them while you're rolling sushi.

5. Place a sheet of toasted nori, shiny side down, on a bamboo rolling mat* (with slats running horizontally) or on a piece of plastic wrap (about 10 by 12 in.). Align long side of nori with bottom edge of mat (the edge closest to you). Dip your hands in vinegar-water mixture and scatter ⅔ cup rice over nori; pat into an even layer, spreading out to sides and bottom of nori but leaving a 2-in.-wide strip bare along top edge.

6. With your finger, spread a thin stripe of wasabi paste (about 1 tsp.) horizontally across center of rice. Arrange 4 avocado slices along wasabi stripe (it's okay if slices overlap or if some ends stick out), then arrange about 2 tbsp. of crab on top of avocado.

7. Moisten top edge of nori with vinegar-water mixture. Holding fillings down with your fingers, lift bottom edge of mat with your thumbs (see photo 1, below) and roll to shape sushi into a cylinder, rolling over bare nori edge to seal. Briefly press mat around roll (photo 2).

8. Remove roll from mat. If desired, trim off any fillings sticking out. With a sharp knife, cut roll into 6 or 8 pieces, rinsing knife in water between cuts.

9. Repeat with remaining nori, rice, and fillings. Serve with soy sauce, pickled ginger, and remaining wasabi paste.

*To toast nori, use tongs to wave each sheet over a gas or electric burner on high heat. Within a few seconds, the nori will soften and turn green. You can find nori, wasabi powder, and pickled ginger in the Asian-foods aisle at most grocery stores and at Asian markets, and bamboo sushi mats at Japanese markets and well-stocked kitchenware stores.

PER PIECE (⅙ ROLL) 47 CAL., 17% (7.8 CAL.) FROM FAT; 2.1 G PROTEIN; 0.9 G FAT (0.1 G SAT.); 7.7 G CARBO (0.6 G FIBER); 74 MG SODIUM; 4.8 MG CHOL.

How-to: Sushi

For other sushi rolls, follow the steps for California Rolls (left), using different fillings in place of avocado and crab. A few ideas:
Sushi- or sashimi-grade ahi tuna (from a Japanese market or good fishmonger), cut into ¼-in. strips
Salmon roe, rinsed gently under cold running water
Japanese or English cucumber, cut into ¼-in. sticks
Enoki mushrooms, trimmed
Radish or broccoli sprouts, root ends trimmed
Spinach leaves, cooked in boiling water just until wilted, then drained and immersed in cold water; drained, put in kitchen towel, and squeezed until dry

Vietnamese calamari herb salad

In Vietnam, seafood and meats are often paired with lots of fresh herbs. Here, leafy mint, basil, dill, parsley, and cilantro make a clean-tasting counterpoint to rich, lightly crunchy calamari.

SERVES 4 to 6 | 1½ hours

¾ cup lime juice (6 to 8 large limes)
2 tbsp. sugar
¼ cup Thai or Vietnamese fish sauce
1 *each* red and green jalapeño chiles, seeds and ribs removed and minced
2 cups *each* loosely packed mint, basil, dill, flat-leaf parsley, and cilantro leaves
½ cup chopped red onion
½ cup sliced celery (¼-in.-thick slices)
1 cup salted whole cashews
4 cups vegetable oil
1 lb. cleaned fresh or thawed frozen squid tubes and tentacles*
½ cup *each* all-purpose flour and rice flour*
About 1 tsp. kosher salt
¼ tsp. cayenne

1. Combine lime juice, sugar, fish sauce, and chiles in a small bowl. Set dressing aside.
2. Combine fresh herbs, onion, celery, and cashews in a large serving bowl. Set aside.
3. Heat oil in a 4-qt. pot (about 10 in. diameter) until oil registers 360° on a deep-fry thermometer.
4. While oil is heating, slice squid tubes in half lengthwise with a sharp knife. Lay each half flat, inside up, and gently score three or four lines across it with the point of a knife; turn it 90° and score three or four lines across the first score marks to make a grid pattern (think tic-tac-toe). Put in a small bowl with tentacles. Set aside.
5. Combine all-purpose flour, rice flour, 1 tsp. salt, and the cayenne in another small bowl. Drop squid pieces into flour mixture, turning to coat well. Shake off any excess.
6. Working in three batches, fry squid 4 to 5 minutes per batch, until pieces are curled and light brown. Using a slotted spoon, transfer fried calamari to a large plate lined with several paper towels and sprinkle lightly with salt to taste. Allow oil temperature to return to 360° between batches.
7. Add warm calamari to herb mixture and pour half the dressing over it. Toss gently just until coated. Serve immediately, with remaining dressing on the side.

*If you discover any uncleaned squid tubes, just pull out and discard the long, clear quills and rinse out tubes. Rice flour can be found in the Asian-foods section of most supermarkets.

PER SERVING 469 CAL., 51% (240 CAL.) FROM FAT; 21 G PROTEIN; 27 G FAT (4.4 G SAT.); 39 G CARBO (6.5 G FIBER); 847 MG SODIUM; 176 MG CHOL.

Beer-battered razor clams

Succulent and mild when cooked, razor clams live in sandy beaches from Alaska's Aleutian Islands down to Pismo Beach, California; the commercial and recreational season runs from September to May.

SERVES 4 to 6 | 1½ hours

Vegetable oil for frying
1 large egg
1½ cups flour
Zest of 1 lemon
½ tsp. *each* paprika and cayenne
About 1 tsp. salt
½ tsp. pepper
1 bottle (12 oz.) lager beer, such as Rainier or Heineken, at room temperature
3 lbs. razor clams in the shell, cleaned*; or use 1½ lbs. cleaned razor clam meat or other clam meat, or squid tubes (cut into rings) and tentacles
Lemon wedges

1. Fill a large, deep pot with 1½ in. oil, insert a deep-fry thermometer, and bring to 375° over medium-high heat.
2. Preheat oven to 200°. Whisk egg in a large bowl to blend. Add flour, lemon zest, paprika, cayenne, 1 tsp. salt, and pepper, but don't mix. Add beer just before using (so batter retains bubbles; this will make coating light and crisp) and whisk until smooth.
3. Add clams to batter and stir to coat well. Using a slotted spoon or tongs, lift out a spoonful of clams, draining excess batter; lower into oil, shaking spoon a bit to separate clumps. Stand back (clams may spatter) and cook until golden all over, turning once, 1½ to 2 minutes; adjust heat as needed to keep oil at 375°.
4. Transfer clams to a baking sheet lined with paper towels. Sprinkle lightly with salt and keep warm in oven while you cook remaining clams. Serve immediately with lemon and salt to taste.
*For cleaning info, go to *sunset.com* and type in *razor clams*. In season, buy razor clams in the shell at specialty fish shops, and buy frozen year-round from *wildsalmonseafood.com*

PER SERVING 292 CAL., 28% (82 CAL.) FROM FAT; 31 G PROTEIN; 9.4 G FAT (1 G SAT.); 19 G CARBO (0.5 G FIBER); 327 MG SODIUM; 76 MG CHOL.

VIETNAMESE CALAMARI
HERB SALAD

Saffron steamed mussels

The briny sweetness of mussels comes to the fore in this easy Spanish-style dish. Mussel farms in Washington and British Columbia raise three varieties: blue (or Baltic), Mediterranean, and Pacific golden. The native California mussel isn't farmed, but can be foraged (contact state fish and game departments).

SERVES 4 | 1 hour

1 *each* red and yellow bell pepper, cut into ¼-in. dice
1 tbsp. olive oil
2 tbsp. minced garlic
½ tsp. *each* saffron threads and pepper
1 bottle (8 oz.) clam juice
1 cup aromatic white wine, such as Viognier
4 dozen mussels in the shell, scrubbed, beards pulled off
Finely chopped flat-leaf parsley
Lemon wedges

SAFFRON STEAMED MUSSELS

1. Sauté bell peppers in oil in a 5- to 6-qt. pan over medium-high heat until beginning to brown, 7 to 8 minutes. Add garlic, saffron, and pepper and cook, stirring, until garlic is softened, 1 to 2 minutes.

2. Pour in 1 cup water, the clam juice, and wine. Cover, bring to a boil over high heat, then reduce heat and simmer about 10 minutes to blend flavors.

3. Return broth to boiling and stir in mussels. Cook, covered, over medium heat until shells open, 8 to 10 minutes; discard any mussels that don't open. Ladle into bowls, sprinkle with parsley, and serve with lemon.

PER SERVING 290 CAL., 27% (77 CAL.) FROM FAT; 24 G PROTEIN; 8.6 G FAT (1.3 G SAT.); 15 G CARBO (1.1 G FIBER); 489 MG SODIUM; 56 MG CHOL.

Grilled marinated calamari

The key to grilled squid is speedy cooking; a few minutes too long and you've got rubber. Squid is abundant in California waters, supplying most of the world's catch.

SERVES 4 | 30 minutes, plus 1 hour to marinate

2 lbs. cleaned squid, tubes and tentacles separated but whole
1 tbsp. minced garlic
1½ tsp. red chile flakes
¼ cup chopped flat-leaf parsley
⅔ cup extra-virgin olive oil, divided
¼ cup lemon juice, divided
1 tsp. sea salt, divided
½ loaf crusty bread, such as ciabatta, cut in half horizontally

1. Combine squid, garlic, chile flakes, parsley, ⅓ cup oil, 2 tbsp. lemon juice, and ½ tsp. salt in a medium bowl. Chill, stirring often, 1 to 5 hours.

2. Put squid and marinade into a colander over a bowl. Brush marinade over cut sides of bread.

3. Prepare a grill for direct high heat (see "How-to: Grilling," page 83). Grill bread on each side until grill marks appear, 3 to 5 minutes. Cut into slices.

4. Set calamari tubes perpendicular to cooking grate, and grill, turning once, just until firm, about 3 minutes. Meanwhile, using tongs, drop tentacles in clumps onto grill just to firm up, then spread out to cook evenly, 4 minutes total.

5. Put squid in a dish and drizzle with remaining ⅓ cup oil, 2 tbsp. lemon juice, and ½ tsp. salt. Serve with bread.

PER SERVING 707 CAL., 57% (402 CAL.) FROM FAT; 39 G PROTEIN; 46 G FAT (7.4 G SAT.); 36 G CARBO (1 G FIBER); 998 MG SODIUM; 500 MG CHOL.

Pan-fried abalone

Eight species of the one-shelled mollusk live along the West Coast, where abalone has been commercially fished from the 1850s. Its harvest is now highly restricted, after years of overfishing, so your best bet is farm-raised (see "How-to: Abalone," right, for sources).

SERVES 2 or 3 | 25 minutes

1 cup flour
Salt and pepper
1 large egg
3/4 cup fine dried bread crumbs or *panko* (Japanese-style bread crumbs)
1 lb. abalone meat*, pounded and thinly sliced
2 tbsp. olive oil
Lemon wedges

1. Combine flour with salt and pepper to taste in a shallow bowl. In a separate shallow bowl, beat egg with 1 tsp. water. Put bread crumbs in a third shallow bowl. Dredge abalone in flour, shaking off excess. Dip in egg, then dredge in bread crumbs.
2. Heat oil in a large pan over high heat. Fry abalone 30 seconds to 1½ minutes per side. Serve with lemon wedges.
* See "How-to: Abalone," right. In slicing, cut parallel to the grain.

PER SERVING 456 CAL., 26% (117 CAL.) FROM FAT; 34 G PROTEIN; 13 G FAT (2.3 G SAT.); 48 G CARBO (1.8 G FIBER); 627 MG SODIUM; 199 MG CHOL.

Grilled abalone

For a luxurious summer meal, all you need are lemon-basted grilled abalone, a green salad, and a bottle of good white wine.

SERVES 2 or 3 | 25 minutes

1/2 cup butter
4 tsp. lemon juice
1 lb. abalone steaks*, pounded
Chopped fresh herbs or toasted sliced almonds

1. Prepare a grill for direct high heat (see "How-to: Grilling," page 83). Melt butter with lemon juice in a small saucepan over low heat.
2. Grill abalone steaks, brushing frequently with butter mixture, 2 to 3 minutes. Turn over and grill, brushing with more butter mixture, 2 to 3 minutes more.
3. Add herbs or nuts to remaining butter and serve with abalone.
* See "How-to: Abalone," right.

PER SERVING 366 CAL., 59% (217 CAL.) FROM FAT; 26 G PROTEIN; 25 G FAT (15 G SAT.); 10 G CARBO (0 G FIBER); 621 MG SODIUM; 190 MG CHOL.

How-to: Abalone

It used to be easy to find abalone off the California coast, and anyone could wade out at low tide and nab a couple of plate-size beauties without much effort. Now the mollusk is extremely scarce, collecting it is the sport of the brave, and the regulations are very strict—only a small area of the coast is open to sport divers. For most of us, the easiest way to taste this peerless sea creature is to order it from a farm. There, the mollusks dine on kelp and grow about an inch a year. The Abalone Farm in Cayucos, California, raises small (3 to 4 in.) red abalone and sells them as frozen tenderized steaks ready for the grill or pan, as well as live in the shell (find distributors at *abalonefarm.com*). Monterey Abalone Company farms red abalone beneath a pier in Monterey Bay (*monterey abalone.com*).

Preparation

If the abalone you buy is in the shell: Shuck the animal from the shell with a wide knife or large spoon (top photo). Trim off the black outer flesh and organs (middle). Slice the flesh (bottom). To tenderize, wrap loosely in plastic wrap. Pound very gently with the toothed side of a wooden mallet. Use a light, rhythmic motion and pound evenly until the piece is velvety and limp enough to drape over your fingers.

Cooking

Abalone cooks very quickly, and overcooking will make it tough, so keep close watch.

Grilled seafood and chorizo paella

Few dishes are as dramatic as an enormous paella. You can let your guests share the limelight and put them to work prepping and taking a turn at the grill. Or you can do it yourself; just complete the preliminary work before you head to the grill, so you get the timing right.

The range of the native Pacific littleneck clam extends from Baja California to the Aleutian Islands; the Manila clam, farmed on the West Coast, was introduced inadvertently in oyster shipments from Japan in the early 20th century. Both are delicious in the paella. You'll need a paella pan* for this recipe.

SERVES 12 | 2 hours

2 lbs. ripe tomatoes, cut in half
1 medium onion, chopped
1 *each* red and green bell pepper, seeds and ribs removed, chopped
2 tbsp. minced garlic
5 tsp. sweet Spanish paprika*
2 tsp. kosher salt
4 cups Spanish Valenciano* or Arborio rice
24 mussels in the shell, scrubbed, beards pulled off
24 small littleneck clams in the shell, scrubbed
24 medium shrimp (¾ lb.), shelled with tails left on and deveined
1¼ lbs. fully cured or semicured Spanish chorizo*, cut into thin diagonal slices
1 tsp. saffron threads
9 cups chicken broth, divided
2 cups dry white wine
7 tbsp. olive oil, divided
Coarsely chopped flat-leaf parsley
Allioli (recipe at right)

1. Coarsely grate tomatoes into a bowl and discard skins. Put onion and bell peppers in another bowl. Measure garlic, paprika, and salt into a small bowl. Put rice in a bowl, seafood in another, and chorizo in a third.

2. Prepare a grill for direct medium heat (see "How-to: Grilling," page 83). Toast saffron in a large saucepan over medium heat, stirring, until fragrant, about 2 minutes. Add 6 cups broth and the wine, cover, bring to a boil over high heat, and keep warm. In a small saucepan, bring remaining 3 cups broth to a boil; keep warm. Carry all ingredients, a long-handled wooden spoon, slotted spoon, and oven mitts to grill.

3. For charcoal, add 15 briquets to fire just before cooking and cook with lid off until step 7. For gas, keep lid closed as you cook.

Heat a 17- to 18-in. paella pan on grill. Add 3 tbsp. oil to pan, then chorizo, and brown, stirring occasionally, about 5 minutes. Using slotted spoon, transfer chorizo back to bowl.

4. Sauté onion and peppers in pan until onion softens, about 5 minutes. Stir in tomatoes and cook, stirring often, until liquid evaporates and paste turns a shade darker, 10 to 12 minutes. Stir in the remaining ¼ cup oil and the garlic mixture; cook, stirring, for 30 seconds. Stir in rice until evenly coated, then pat level.

5. Carefully pour hot saffron liquid over rice and scatter chorizo on top. Check to be sure grill and liquid in pan are level. If needed, reduce gas or airflow (for charcoal grill) to maintain a steady simmer. Cook for 12 minutes.

6. Pour enough hot plain broth over paella so rice is just covered in liquid (you may not use it all). Arrange mussels around rim of pan, almost touching, pushing them into liquid. Arrange any remaining mussels, the clams, and then the shrimp over paella in liquid.

7. Cover grill and cook until clams and mussels open and rice is *al punto* (al dente), another 6 to 10 minutes. (Discard any clams or mussels that don't open.) Carefully remove paella from grill, drape with paper towels, and let stand about 5 minutes. Sprinkle with parsley. Serve with allioli.

*Find sweet (unsmoked) Spanish paprika, Valenciano rice, Spanish chorizo, and a paella pan in a well-stocked supermarket, specialty-foods store, or at *spanishtable.com*

PER SERVING 692 CAL., 38% (262 CAL.) FROM FAT; 35 G PROTEIN; 29 G FAT (8.7 G SAT.); 63 G CARBO (3.6 G FIBER); 1,162 MG SODIUM; 123 MG CHOL.

Allioli

The Spanish version of aioli, with the same garlicky hit.

SERVES 12 or 13 (makes 1⅔ cups) | 5 minutes

1 cup extra-virgin olive oil
⅓ cup canola oil
4 large garlic cloves
1 egg plus 1 egg yolk
2 tbsp. lemon juice, plus more to taste
1 tsp. kosher salt, plus more to taste

Pour oils into a container with a spout. Blend remaining ingredients into a smooth paste in a food processor. With motor running, add oil in a slow stream until incorporated. Add more lemon juice and salt if you like.

Make ahead Up to 1 week, chilled.

PER 2-TBSP. SERVING 209 CAL., 98% (204 CAL.) FROM FAT; 0.8 G PROTEIN; 23 G FAT (3 G SAT.); 0.7 G CARBO (0 G FIBER); 32 MG CHOL.

Delfina's broccoli rabe pizza

In San Francisco, Pizzeria Delfina serves up a tasty slice of the Bay Area's inventive pizza-making. Fresh mozzarella, salty *caciocavallo* cheese from Italy's Campania, and peppery broccoli rabe make this one of our favorites. Drizzle on a bit of cream before shoving the pizza in the oven, to keep the cheese from burning.

MAKES 3 pizzas (12 in. each); 24 slices | 1 hour

10 oz. fresh mozzarella cheese packed in liquid
⅓ cup liquid from mozzarella container
¼ cup packed coarsely shredded *caciocavallo* or parmesan cheese
¼ cup *each* heavy whipping cream and buttermilk
½ tsp. kosher salt, divided
1 lb. (about 1 large bunch) broccoli rabe
2 garlic cloves, well smashed
About ¼ cup olive oil
About ¼ tsp. red chile flakes
Pepper
3 balls room-temperature Delfina's Pizza Dough (recipe on opposite page)
⅓ cup black olives (oil-cured or Gaeta, soaked in water and drained if very salty), pitted and torn in half

1. Preheat oven at 550° (or as high as oven will go). Heat a pizza stone or baking sheet on lowest rack for at least 30 minutes.
2. Meanwhile, with flat side of a chef's knife, mash a third of the mozzarella into a pulverized mass. Dice remaining mozzarella into ½-in. cubes. In a medium bowl, mix both mozzarellas with mozzarella liquid, caciocavallo, cream, and buttermilk. Add ¼ tsp. salt.
3. Cut broccoli rabe into 1-in. sections, discarding tough lower parts of stems.
4. In a large frying pan over very low heat, cook garlic in ¼ cup oil, stirring often, until garlic starts to turn transparent, about 5 minutes. Add ¼ tsp. chile flakes and toast for a second, then add broccoli rabe. Stir in remaining ¼ tsp. salt and several grinds of pepper.
5. Increase heat to medium-high and cook broccoli rabe, stirring, until liquid starts to evaporate and broccoli rabe is tender-crisp, 5 to 7 minutes (don't cook it to mush). If liquid is gone and broccoli rabe is still too crunchy, add ¼ cup water and cook until tender-crisp, repeating if necessary.
6. Working with one ball of dough at a time (keep remaining balls tightly covered), set dough on a well-floured pizza peel or rimless baking sheet and stretch it into a 12-in. circle (see

How-to: Stretch pizza dough

It's a hands-on procedure. Using a rolling pin to stretch dough will ruin the rim and flatten the air bubbles that give the crust its rise. Anthony Strong, of San Francisco's Locanda (and previously at Pizzeria Delfina), showed us how to stretch dough by hand. Start with dough at room temperature.

1. TAP DOWN the center of the dough ball with your fingertips to gently deflate it. Next, push dough outward from the center with your fingertips.

2. PICK UP the dough circle. With your fingers under the rim, turn it like a steering wheel.

3. DRAPE the dough over the backs of your hands and gently stretch outward.

"How-to: Stretch Pizza Dough," opposite page). Flop stretched-out dough onto peel.

7. Spread about ⅔ cup cheese mixture over dough. Top with ½ cup broccoli rabe, a generous pinch of chile flakes, and 2 tbsp. olives. Give peel a good shake every few seconds to keep dough from sticking.

8. Plant tip of pizza peel (or long edge of baking sheet) on pizza stone and shove pizza quickly onto it. Bake until pizza is puffy and browned, 5 to 6 minutes. Drizzle with oil.

9. Repeat with remaining two dough balls and topping.

Make ahead Cheese mixture and broccoli rabe topping, up to 1 day, chilled.

PER SLICE (⅛ PIZZA) 157 CAL., 43% (68 CAL.) FROM FAT; 5.5 G PROTEIN; 7.5 G FAT (3 G SAT.); 15 G CARBO (0.5 G FIBER); 540 MG SODIUM; 17 MG CHOL.

Delfina's pizza dough

From Pizzeria Delfina comes the best homemade pizza dough we've ever tried—smooth, supple, and easy to work with. You can use regular flour, but for a truly awesome, springy-yet-crunchy crust, go for high-gluten Italian "00" (finely milled) flour. Use this dough for Delfina's Broccoli Rabe Pizza or any other thin-crust pizza.

MAKES Enough dough for 6 pizzas (12 in. each) | 2 hours, plus 4 hours to rise

1 tsp. (slightly rounded) fresh yeast
1½ tsp. extra-virgin olive oil
1 lb., 14 oz. (about 6 cups) "00" flour, preferably Caputo*,
    or all-purpose flour
1½ tbsp. kosher salt*

1. Put yeast, oil, and 2 cups plus 1 tbsp. cold water in the bowl of a mixer. Mix, using dough hook, on lowest speed until yeast has completely dissolved, about 5 minutes. Add flour and mix another 8 minutes. If you mix by hand, stir ingredients together with a wooden spoon until blended; then turn dough out onto a lightly floured work surface and knead until it's smooth and stretchy, at least 15 minutes.

2. Cover bowl or dough loosely with a dampened kitchen towel and let dough rise 20 minutes in a warm (about 80°) place.

3. Add salt and mix on low speed until incorporated and dissolved, about 7 minutes; or, if mixing by hand, sprinkle dough with salt and knead 10 minutes.

4. Turn dough onto a lightly floured work surface and cut into six equal portions. Roll each into a tight ball. Set on a lightly floured baking sheet.

DELFINA'S BROCCOLI
RABE PIZZA

5. Cover tightly with plastic wrap and let rise at least 4 hours at warm room temperature. Dough balls have risen properly when they are soft, pillowy, and full of air.

*Find "00" flour in well-stocked supermarkets and Italian markets. For best results, measure flour by weight rather than volume. Though 1½ tbsp. may seem like a lot of salt, the dough won't taste too salty as long as you use coarse-grained kosher salt, not fine-grained table salt.

Make ahead Dough can be formed into balls and set on a lightly floured baking sheet (step 4), then tightly covered with plastic wrap and chilled overnight (dough will rise slowly in the refrigerator). After dough balls have risen, you can freeze them for up to 2 weeks. Let chilled or frozen dough come to room temperature before proceeding.

Lia's walnut burgers

Owner Lia Azgapetian closed the Mill Creek Station restaurant in Forest Falls, California, in 1986, but former customers still rave about these burgers.

MAKES 4 burgers | 30 minutes

2 eggs
²/₃ cup soft whole-wheat bread crumbs
½ cup *each* chopped walnuts, sliced green onions, toasted
  wheat germ, and small-curd cottage cheese
2 tbsp. chopped flat-leaf parsley
1 tsp. dried basil
½ tsp. *each* dried oregano and paprika
Garlic salt
4 slices (⅛ in. thick) jack cheese (3 oz.)
Toasted buns or bread
Thousand Island dressing, tomato and onion slices, and lettuce

1. Beat eggs in a large bowl. Stir in bread crumbs, walnuts, green onions, wheat germ, cottage cheese, parsley, basil, oregano, and paprika. Add garlic salt to taste.
2. On an oiled 12- by 15-in. baking sheet, shape mixture into four patties, each ½ in. thick. Broil 3 in. from heat until deep golden, turning once, about 6 minutes total. Top with jack cheese and broil until melted, about 30 seconds more.
3. Serve burgers on buns with toppings and condiments.

PER BURGER WITHOUT BUN 321 CAL., 59% (189 CAL.) FROM FAT; 19 G PROTEIN; 21 G FAT (6.4 G SAT.); 16 G CARBO; 301 MG SODIUM; 133 MG CHOL.

Grilled pizza

In the 1980s, a wave of wild new pizza rose up in California, epitomized by the anything-goes oeuvre of Ed LaDou and Wolfgang Puck at L.A.'s Spago. This is our tip of the hat—a template for which you can improvise toppings.

MAKES 6 individual-size pizzas | 1 hour, plus 2 hours to rise

1 package (2¼ tsp.) active dry yeast
6 tbsp. olive oil, divided
4 cups flour
1½ tsp. salt
Your choice of toppings (recipes at right)

1. Stir yeast into 1½ cups warm water (100° to 110°) in the bowl of a mixer. Let stand until yeast dissolves, about 5 minutes. Add ¼ cup oil, the flour, and salt. Mix with dough hook on low speed to blend, then mix on medium speed until dough is very smooth and stretchy, 8 to 10 minutes. If you mix by hand, mix in ¼ cup

oil, the flour, and salt with a wooden spoon, then turn out on a lightly floured work surface and knead vigorously for 8 to 10 minutes, until dough is very smooth and stretchy. Cover dough; let rise at room temperature until doubled in bulk, about 1½ hours.
2. Punch down dough and let rise again until doubled, 30 to 45 minutes. Meanwhile, cut six pieces of parchment paper, each about 12 in. long. Prepare a grill for direct medium heat (see "How-to: Grilling," page 83).
3. Turn dough out onto a work surface and cut into six portions. For each pizza, lay a sheet of parchment on work surface and rub with 1 tsp. oil. Using well-oiled hands, put each portion of dough on a parchment sheet. Flatten dough portions, then pat into 9- to 10-in. circles. If dough starts to shrink, let rest 5 minutes, then pat out again. Let dough stand until puffy, about 15 minutes.
4. Flip a circle of dough onto cooking grate, dough side down. Peel off parchment. Put on one or two more dough circles. Close lid and cook until dough has puffed and grill marks appear underneath, 3 minutes. Transfer circles, grilled side up, to baking sheets. Repeat with remaining dough. (Grilled crusts can stand at room temperature up to 2 hours; reheat grill to continue.)
5. Arrange pizza toppings on grilled side of dough. With a wide spatula, return pizzas, two or three at a time, to cooking grate and close lid on grill. Cook until browned and crisp underneath, rotating pizzas once for even cooking, 4 to 6 minutes.

Pizza bianca Scatter **onion** slices and **shredded mozzarella** over each half-grilled crust in step 5 of Grilled Pizza; sprinkle with chopped **rosemary leaves** and a little **salt.** Grill as directed.

PER PIZZA 587 CAL., 41% (243 CAL.) FROM FAT; 20 G PROTEIN; 27 G FAT (9.4 G SAT.); 66 G CARBO (2.6 G FIBER); 796 MG SODIUM; 44 MG CHOL.

Pizza margherita Spread each half-grilled crust in step 5 of Grilled Pizza with about 2 tbsp. **Ripe Tomato Pizza Sauce** (recipe below). Put 5 or 6 slices drained **water-packed fresh mozzarella** over sauce. Grill as directed, then top with **basil leaves.**

PER PIZZA 725 CAL., 45% (324 CAL.) FROM FAT; 27 G PROTEIN; 36 G FAT (14 G SAT.); 73 G CARBO (4.7 G FIBER); 1,001 MG SODIUM; 67 MG CHOL.

Ripe tomato pizza sauce Heat 1 tbsp. **olive oil** in a saucepan over medium heat. Add 1 tbsp. minced **garlic** and cook, stirring, until fragrant, about 1 minute. Stir in 4 large chopped **tomatoes,** 1 tsp. **sugar,** ¼ tsp. **red chile flakes,** and ½ tsp. *each* **kosher salt** and **pepper.** Bring to a boil, reduce heat to low, and simmer, stirring often, until very thick, about 1½ hours. Stir in 1 tbsp. chopped **oregano leaves.** Makes 1 cup.

PER 2-TBSP. SERVING 44 CAL., 43% (19 CAL.) FROM FAT; 1.1 G PROTEIN; 2.1 G FAT (0.3 G SAT.); 6.4 G CARBO (1.5 G FIBER); 83 MG SODIUM; 0 MG CHOL.

TAGLIATELLE WITH
NETTLE AND PINE NUT
SAUCE

Tagliatelle with nettle and pine nut sauce

At Delfina restaurant in San Francisco, chef Craig Stoll serves this fresh-tasting sauce over housemade nettle pasta. Nettles have small stinging hairs when raw; once cooked, they lose their sting and taste nutty and spinach-like. The plant grows throughout the country, thriving especially in the coastal Northwest woods.

SERVES 4 | 50 minutes

1 lb. stinging nettles* (or use 1½ qts. coarsely chopped
    mustard greens with stems and ribs removed, plus
    1 lb. baby spinach leaves)
12 oz. tagliatelle pasta
⅓ cup unsalted butter
1½ tsp. kosher salt
About ¾ cup grated parmesan cheese
⅔ cup toasted pine nuts

1. Bring a large pot of water to a boil over high heat. Meanwhile, fill the sink with water. Wearing rubber gloves, pull nettle leaves from stems into sink. Swish to rinse; drain. Add nettles to boiling water. Simmer until soft, 3 minutes. Drain, rinse with cool water, and squeeze out water. Blend in a food processor until smooth.

2. Cook pasta as package directs. Meanwhile, melt butter over medium heat in pot used for nettles. Whisk in nettle purée, salt, and 1 cup hot pasta water; keep warm over low heat.

3. Drain pasta, reserving about 2 cups water. Add pasta to pot of sauce and toss with ¾ cup parmesan, half of pine nuts, and some reserved water if needed so it's loose-textured. Transfer to a shallow bowl and sprinkle with remaining pine nuts and a little more parmesan if you like.

*Find nettles at farmers' markets. (They grow wild in many areas too.)

PER SERVING 610 CAL., 54% (327 CAL.) FROM FAT; 20 G PROTEIN; 37 G FAT (13 G SAT.); 52 G CARBO (10 G FIBER); 806 MG SODIUM; 54 MG CHOL.

Filipino-style stir-fried noodles with vegetables and tofu (Pancit)

Our version of the Filipino favorite is based on one at House of Sisig, in Daly City, California, a town where many restaurants and markets offer straight-out-of-Manila fare. And, though Los Angeles designated a historic Filipinotown near Echo Park in 2002, you hear more Tagalog elsewhere in the city, including in the Eagle Rock neighborhood, where Filipino Americans gather for familiar tastes and sounds.

SERVES 6 | 1 hour

3½ oz. rice vermicelli
½ lb. medium-thick fresh wheat noodles*
2 tbsp. plus ¼ cup vegetable oil, divided
2 tbsp. chopped garlic, divided
1 medium onion, thinly sliced
2 cups shredded green cabbage
1 carrot, finely shredded
1 package (12 oz.) firm tofu, patted dry and cut into ½-in. cubes
3 tbsp. soy sauce
1½ tsp. pepper
1 cup reduced-sodium chicken or vegetable broth
1 lemon, cut into wedges

1. In a medium bowl, cover vermicelli with boiling water. Let stand until tender, 5 to 8 minutes. Drain; rinse with cold water. Cut into 10-in. lengths and set aside.

2. Bring a 4-qt. pot of water to a boil. Add wheat noodles and cook until tender, 2 to 4 minutes; drain and set aside.

3. Heat 2 tbsp. oil in a large wok over medium heat. Fry 1 tbsp. garlic until light golden, 30 seconds. Strain oil into a bowl and put fried garlic in another bowl; set both aside.

4. Add remaining ¼ cup oil to hot wok and swirl to coat. Add remaining 1 tbsp. garlic and cook until fragrant, about 30 seconds. Add onion and cabbage; increase heat to medium-high. Cook, stirring occasionally, until vegetables begin to soften, about 3 minutes. Add carrot; cook, stirring, until it softens, about 1 minute.

5. Increase heat to high. Add tofu, reserved noodles, soy sauce, pepper, and broth to wok. Cook, stirring occasionally, until tofu is heated through and liquid has reduced by about half, about 5 minutes. Stir in reserved 2 tbsp. garlic oil. Sprinkle fried garlic on noodles and serve with lemon wedges on the side.

*Look for the words "pancit Canton" on the label.

PER SERVING 437 CAL., 51% (225 CAL.) FROM FAT; 12 G PROTEIN; 25 G FAT (10 G SAT.); 42 G CARBO (3.8 G FIBER); 829 MG SODIUM; 0 MG CHOL.

Chanterelle mushroom risotto

Golden, wavy-edged chanterelles show up on forest floors in the Northwest in autumn and in California in winter, drawing eager foragers. Hunt with an expert if you're new to mycology—or forage in your supermarket. Begin roasting the mushrooms for this savory risotto before you start the rest of the recipe.

SERVES 6 | 1 hour

4 oz. bacon, diced (optional)
About 2 tbsp. olive oil
1 onion (8 oz.) peeled, halved lengthwise, and thinly sliced
1 tbsp. minced garlic
About ¼ tsp. *each* **salt and pepper**
1 bunch (10 to 12 oz.) red chard
2 cups Arborio (short-grain white) rice
1 cup dry white wine
About 6 cups chicken or vegetable broth
¼ cup shredded parmesan cheese
2 tbsp. butter
Roasted Chanterelle Mushrooms* (recipe at right)

1. Cook bacon, if using, in a 12-in. frying pan with 2-in.-tall sides or in a 5-qt. pan over medium-high heat until browned and crisp, about 5 minutes. Transfer to paper towels to drain. Discard all but about ½ tbsp. bacon fat from pan.
2. Add 2 tbsp. olive oil to pan over medium-high heat (if not using bacon, add ½ tbsp. additional oil). When hot, add onion, garlic, salt, and pepper. Reduce heat to medium and stir frequently until onion is very soft and browned, 20 to 25 minutes (if onion starts to scorch, reduce heat further and stir in 2 tbsp. water).
3. Meanwhile, rinse chard. Trim and discard stem ends. Thinly slice stems crosswise and coarsely chop leaves. Bring about 3 qts. water to a boil in a 5- to 6-qt. pan over high heat. Add chard and cook, stirring occasionally, until stems are tender-crisp to bite, 3 to 4 minutes. Drain, place in a large bowl of ice water until cool, and drain again.
4. Add rice to onions and cook, stirring until opaque, about 3 minutes. Add wine and cook, stirring, over medium heat until absorbed, 1 to 2 minutes. Add 6 cups broth, a cup at a time, stirring after each addition until almost absorbed, 20 to 25 minutes total (rice should be tender to the bite).
5. Stir in cheese, butter, bacon, chard, and mushrooms. Add salt and pepper to taste. If risotto is thicker than desired, stir in a little more broth. Spoon risotto into wide, shallow bowls.

PER SERVING 457 CAL., 39% (180 CAL.) FROM FAT; 18 G PROTEIN; 20 G FAT (6.6 G SAT.); 52 G CARBO (5.8 G FIBER); 577 MG SODIUM; 23 MG CHOL.

Roasted chanterelle mushrooms Preheat oven to 400°. Mix 2 tbsp. **olive oil** in a 12- by 15-in. baking pan with 1 tsp. melted **butter,** 1 thinly sliced peeled **shallot,** 1 tsp. **thyme leaves,** ¼ tsp. *each* **salt** and **pepper,** and 8 oz. rinsed, trimmed **chanterelle mushrooms** (cut into 1-in. pieces). Bake, stirring occasionally, until tender and beginning to brown on edges, 12 to 15 minutes. Use immediately or let stand up to 4 hours.

Black rice salad with butternut squash and pomegranate seeds

Black (or "forbidden") rice, which has a mellow, sweet taste, comes from several places in the world, including China, Thailand, and Indonesia. Wild, brown, red, or Japonica black rice—which grows in the rice fields of California's Sacramento Valley—also works in the salad (cook according to package directions).

SERVES 3 as a main course, or 4 to 6 as a side | 1½ hours

⅔ cup black rice*
1 lb. butternut squash
½ tsp. sweet smoked Spanish paprika*
About ¼ tsp. kosher salt
3 tbsp. olive oil, divided
½ cup pecans, coarsely chopped
1½ tbsp. lemon juice
½ tbsp. maple syrup
Pepper
2 tbsp. sliced green onions
½ cup pomegranate seeds

1. Bring a large pot of salted water to a boil over high heat. Add the rice, adjust heat to maintain a lively simmer, and cook until rice is tender, about 30 minutes. Drain and rinse with cool water.
2. Preheat oven to 375°. Peel and seed squash and cut into 1-in. cubes. In a bowl, toss with paprika, ¼ tsp. salt, and 1 tbsp. oil. Spread on a baking sheet and roast, stirring occasionally, until browned and tender, 40 minutes. Let cool. Spread pecans on another baking sheet and toast until fragrant, stirring once, 6 to 8 minutes.
3. Whisk together remaining 2 tbsp. oil, the lemon juice, maple syrup, and pepper in a serving bowl. Toss with reserved rice, squash, green onions, and most of pecans and pomegranate seeds. Sprinkle with remaining pecans and pomegranate seeds.
*Find black rice (either fragrant "forbidden" black rice or chewy-tender black Japonica rice) and smoked Spanish paprika at Whole Foods Market or other well-stocked grocers.

PER 1-CUP SERVING 244 CAL., 53% (128 CAL.) FROM FAT; 3.8 G PROTEIN; 14 G FAT (1.7 G SAT.); 29 G CARBO (4.9 G FIBER); 69 MG SODIUM; 0 MG CHOL.

BLACK RICE SALAD WITH
BUTTERNUT SQUASH AND
POMEGRANATE SEEDS

GRILLED QUESADILLAS
WITH *NOPALES* AND
SALSA SLAW

Kimchi and avocado quesadillas

Spicy kimchi plays beautifully with buttery avocado. We took our cue from Roy Choi, who dreamed up the Korean taco and rolled out his Kogi Korean BBQ-to-Go truck in 2008 in Los Angeles, inspiring the faithful to track the truck's location via Twitter—and sparking a Korean-Mexican trend across the West, and beyond.

SERVES 4 | 30 minutes

8 flour tortillas (7 to 8 in. wide)
1 jar (14 oz.) kimchi, drained and chopped
2 cups shredded jack cheese
2 avocados, thinly sliced
1 tbsp. toasted sesame oil
2 tbsp. seasoned rice vinegar
1 tsp. toasted sesame seeds
Cilantro leaves

1. Top 4 tortillas with kimchi, then with cheese, avocados, and remaining tortillas.
2. Mix oil, vinegar, and sesame seeds in a small bowl; set aside.
3. Heat a 12-in. frying pan over medium-high heat. Toast each quesadilla until lightly browned and cheese has melted, 1 to 2 minutes per side. Slice each quesadilla into wedges, sprinkle with cilantro, and serve with sesame dipping sauce.

PER SERVING 731 CAL., 53% (390 CAL.) FROM FAT; 26 G PROTEIN; 43 G FAT (15 G SAT.); 58 G CARBO (11 G FIBER); 1,044 MG SODIUM; 50 MG CHOL.

Farro, green olive, and feta salad

An ancient form of wheat, farro has a sweet, nutty flavor. The grain (also known as emmer) is cultivated in only a few places in this country, including at Bluebird Grain Farms in Washington's Methow Valley. Our recipe, ridiculously easy to make, comes from Feel Good Foods Catering in Santa Cruz, California. Use the best green olives you can find—they really stand out here.

SERVES 2 or 3 (4 or 6 as a side dish) | 45 minutes

1 cup farro wheat*
2 tbsp. extra-virgin olive oil
3 tbsp. Meyer lemon juice
2 tbsp. finely chopped Meyer lemon zest (from about 4 lemons)
½ tsp. pepper
½ cup flat-leaf parsley leaves
½ cup crumbled sheep's-milk or other creamy feta cheese
⅔ cup mild green olives, such as Lucques, cut away from pit
**   in 3 pieces**

1. Bring 4 cups salted water to a boil and stir in farro. Reduce heat to a simmer and cook farro until just tender, about 20 minutes. Drain and spread out on a rimmed baking sheet to cool and dry a bit, about 5 minutes.
2. Whisk oil, lemon juice and zest, pepper, and parsley together in a medium bowl. Stir in feta, olives, and cooked farro.
*Find at well-stocked grocery stores or order online from *bluebirdgrainfarms.com*

PER SERVING 424 CAL., 43% (180 CAL.) FROM FAT; 12 G PROTEIN; 20 G FAT (6 G SAT.); 50 G CARBO (8.6 G FIBER); 726 MG SODIUM; 22 MG CHOL.

Grilled quesadillas with *nopales* and salsa slaw

Cactus pads, or *nopales*, from prickly pear, native to the Southwest and Mexico, are a popular ingredient in Mexican vegetarian cooking. Salsa slaw makes a vibrant, tart accompaniment.

SERVES 4 | 30 minutes

1 tbsp. vegetable oil
½ cup sliced onion
2 poblano chiles, seeded and sliced
1 cup cleaned and cubed *nopales* (cactus pads)*
About ½ tsp. kosher salt
8 corn or flour tortillas (8 in. wide)
1 cup shredded jack cheese
1 qt. shredded cabbage
1 cup salsa (any kind)
1 tbsp. lime juice
½ cup cilantro leaves

1. Prepare a grill for high heat (see "How-to: Grilling," page 83). Meanwhile, heat oil in a large frying pan over medium-high heat. Cook onion, chiles, and nopales until softened and starting to brown, about 5 minutes. Season with ½ tsp. salt and remove from heat.
2. Lay 4 tortillas on a baking sheet. Sprinkle each with ¼ cup cheese and ½ cup vegetable mixture. Top each with a second tortilla. Using a wad of oiled paper towels and tongs, oil cooking grate. Transfer quesadillas with a spatula to grill. Cook, turning once, until cheese melts. Remove from grill and quarter each.
3. Combine shredded cabbage, salsa, lime juice, cilantro, and a pinch of salt in a bowl. Serve quesadillas with slaw.
*Buy at a Latino market; many sell bags of cleaned and cubed nopales, which make this dish easy to toss together.

PER SERVING 494 CAL., 36% (179 CAL.) FROM FAT; 18 G PROTEIN; 20 G FAT (7.6 G SAT.); 63 G CARBO (8.3 G FIBER); 1,382 MG SODIUM; 25 MG CHOL.

Asparagus and morel quiche

Umami-delicious morels pop up in Western woods and orchards, and make plump, savory nuggets in this quiche. For neat slices, make in advance; cool, loosen from pan, and chill. Cut and reheat.

SERVES 6 to 8 | 1¼ hours, plus 30 minutes to cool

1½ cups whole-wheat pastry flour or all-purpose flour
10 tbsp. cold butter, cut into chunks
3 large eggs
½ oz. dried morel mushrooms
1 cup slender asparagus, cut in 2-in. pieces
1½ cups half-and-half
¾ tsp. salt
½ tsp. pepper
1 cup shredded gruyère cheese
1 green onion, finely chopped

1. Mix flour and butter in a food processor until mixture looks like cornmeal. Add 1 egg; pulse until dough holds together. Press over bottom and 1¼ in. up side of a 9-in. springform pan; chill.
2. Preheat oven to 375°. Soak mushrooms in a small bowl with 1 cup hot water until softened, 15 to 20 minutes, swishing around every so often. Squeeze out liquid. Cut in half lengthwise if large.
3. Blanch asparagus in a saucepan of boiling water until barely tender-crisp, about 45 seconds. Drain, transfer to a bowl of ice water, and cool. Drain and pat dry.
4. Whisk remaining 2 eggs in a bowl to blend. Whisk in half-and-half, salt, and pepper. Sprinkle cheese and onion in crust, then place asparagus and morels on top. Pour egg mixture over.
5. Bake on bottom rack until filling no longer jiggles when gently shaken, 40 to 45 minutes. Let cool in pan on a rack at least 30 minutes. Loosen from pan rim with a knife, remove rim, and slice.

PER SERVING 362 CAL., 65% (234 CAL.) FROM FAT; 11 G PROTEIN; 26 G FAT (15 G SAT.); 21 G CARBO (3.7 G FIBER); 411 MG SODIUM; 149 MG CHOL.

ASPARAGUS AND
MOREL QUICHE

Parsley ravioli with brown butter sauce

Flat-leaf parsley is more robust in flavor than the curly variety.

SERVES 4 | 1 hour

1 cup ricotta cheese
¼ cup grated parmesan cheese
1 cup finely chopped flat-leaf parsley, plus ½ cup leaves
1 large egg
About ½ tsp. kosher salt
¼ tsp. pepper
48 round won ton wrappers (about 9 oz.)
6 tbsp. butter
2 tsp. lemon juice

1. Combine cheeses, chopped parsley, egg, ½ tsp. salt, and pepper in a bowl. Bring a large pot of salted water to a boil.
2. Lay 8 wrappers on a flat surface and spoon 1 tbsp. cheese mixture onto center of each. Moisten edge of 1 wrapper with water; top with an empty wrapper, pressing to seal tightly. Transfer to a greased baking sheet, cover, and repeat to make more.
3. Preheat oven to 250°. Cook 4 or 5 ravioli at a time in boiling water until dough is tender, 3 minutes. Transfer to greased baking sheet in a single layer, cover with foil, and keep warm in oven.
4. Meanwhile, melt butter in a pan. Cook, swirling, until golden, 3 minutes. Remove from heat; stir in lemon and parsley leaves.

PER SERVING 499 CAL., 53% (264 CAL.) FROM FAT; 18 G PROTEIN; 29 G FAT (18 G SAT.); 41 G CARBO (1.9 G FIBER); 875 MG SODIUM; 135 MG CHOL.

Miso-glazed tofu with parsnips two ways

The West has taken avidly to tofu: The first U.S. manufacturer opened in San Francisco in 1878, and the nation's largest tofu producer today is House Foods of Garden Grove, California. Chef Douglas Keane often includes his own tofu on the tasting menu at Cyrus, a Michelin two-star restaurant in Healdsburg, California, and uses it in this uncommonly good creation. For her home rendition, San Francisco cookbook author Andrea Nguyen roasts the parsnips with sesame oil to amplify their sweet earthiness.

SERVES 4 | 1½ hours

3 tbsp. *each* white (*shiro*) miso and Dijon mustard
½ tsp. Sriracha chili sauce
¾ cup sake
½ cup plus 2½ tbsp. mirin (sweet sake), divided
2 tbsp. finely chopped fresh ginger
1½ tbsp. unseasoned rice vinegar
1½ tbsp. dried goji berries*
5 medium-small parsnips (1⅓ lbs. total), peeled
Salt
Ground white pepper
2 tbsp. toasted sesame oil
14 to 16 oz. firm tofu
4 oz. tatsoi, mizuna, or spinach, cut into bite-size pieces
    (4 lightly packed cups)

MISO-GLAZED
TOFU WITH PARNIPS
TWO WAYS

1. Whisk together miso, mustard, Sriracha, sake, and ½ cup plus 1 tbsp. mirin in a small saucepan. Add ginger. Bring to a boil, then lower heat and simmer 6 to 8 minutes, or until sauce is just thick enough to coat a spoon. Strain through a fine-mesh strainer, pushing against solids. Let glaze cool to room temperature.
2. Bring remaining 1½ tbsp. mirin and the vinegar to a boil in a very small saucepan. Add goji berries. Return to a boil and remove from heat. Let cool, uncovered.
3. Put rack in middle of oven, then preheat oven to 400°. Line a rimmed baking sheet with parchment paper.
4. Cut 1 parsnip lengthwise into 8 spears. Cut remaining parsnips into ¾-in. chunks. Transfer spears and chunks to baking sheet, season with salt and white pepper to taste, and toss with sesame oil. Spread in a single layer, with spears cut side down. Bake parsnips 20 minutes, turning 2 or 3 times.
5. Meanwhile, bring a saucepan of water to a boil. Cut tofu into 4 rectangular slabs, each the dimensions of a deck of cards, and put in a shallow bowl. Pour hot water over tofu and soak 15 minutes. Drain on a dish towel or a double layer of paper towels on a plate.
6. Remove parsnip spears from oven when tips begin to brown;

remove chunks when just fork-tender. Let chunks cool 5 minutes, then purée in a food processor with 2 tbsp. miso-mustard glaze and 1 cup hot water until smooth but able to hold a peak when spooned onto a plate (add up to ½ cup hot water if needed). Keep warm, covered.
7. Put tatsoi in a large saucepan with ¼ cup hot water and cook over low heat, covered, stirring occasionally, until wilted, 5 minutes; drain and return to pan. Stir in goji berries and some of their pickling liquid.
8. Pour remaining miso-mustard glaze into a medium frying pan. Blot moisture from tofu with paper towels and add tofu to glaze. Bring to a simmer and cook, spooning glaze over tofu, until glaze sticks to top of tofu and has reduced by one-half to two-thirds.
9. Spoon parsnip purée onto plates. With a spatula, set tofu on parsnip purée. Drizzle glaze over tofu and top with tatsoi and goji berries, then add parsnip spears.
*Find at Whole Foods Market, natural-foods stores, and Asian markets.
Make ahead Miso glaze and goji pickle, up to 3 days, chilled (bring pickle to room temperature before proceeding).

PER SERVING 464 CAL., 25% (115 CAL.) FROM FAT; 15 G PROTEIN; 13 G FAT (1.8 G SAT.); 53 G CARBO (8.1 G FIBER); 807 MG SODIUM; 0 MG CHOL.

AVOCADO FRIES
recipe on page 156

Side Dishes

Sometimes sides, like supporting actors, get the really interesting parts. If you simply grill meat or fish for the main course, let the sides provide the drama in the Western story: Choose avocado fries to show off the blissfully good California avocado, or grilled artichokes—from fields first planted here in the 1890s by Italian immigrants—or quinoa grown in the high altitudes of Colorado.

Grilled artichokes with green-olive dip

The char of fire-roasting adds an extra layer of flavor to the artichokes, as does the pungent, salty olive dip.

SERVES 6 | 1½ hours

6 artichokes
1 tbsp. plus ½ tsp. salt
Juice of 1 lemon, plus 2 tbsp. juice
3 garlic cloves, minced
3 tbsp. olive oil
¼ tsp. pepper
Green-Olive Dip (recipe at right)

1. Slice tops off artichokes, pull off small outer leaves, trim stems, and snip off thorny tips. In a large pot, bring 1 to 2 in. water to a boil. Add 1 tbsp. salt, juice of 1 lemon, and artichokes; cover and steam until artichoke bottoms pierce easily, 20 to 40 minutes, depending on their size. Drain artichokes. When cool enough to handle, cut each in half lengthwise and scrape out center choke.

2. In a small bowl, combine garlic, oil, remaining 2 tbsp. lemon juice and ½ tsp. salt, and the pepper. Brush artichokes with garlic mixture.

3. Prepare a grill for direct medium heat (see "How-to: Grilling," page 83). Grill artichokes, turning once, until lightly browned, 8 to 11 minutes.

4. Serve with olive dip.

PER SERVING WITHOUT DIP 126 CAL., 51% (64 CAL.) FROM FAT; 4.3 G PROTEIN; 7.3 G FAT (1.2 G SAT.); 14 G CARBO (7 G FIBER); 317 MG SODIUM; 0.9 MG CHOL.

Green-olive dip Purée ½ cup chopped **flat-leaf parsley,** 5 tbsp. **extra-virgin olive oil,** 2 tbsp. chopped **green olives,** 1 tbsp. drained **capers,** 1 tbsp. **lemon juice,** ½ tsp. **Dijon mustard,** ¼ tsp. **pepper,** and ⅛ tsp. **salt** in a blender until coarsely puréed.

PER TBSP. 54 CAL., 96% (52 CAL.) FROM FAT; 0.1 G PROTEIN; 6.1 G FAT (0.9 G SAT.); 0.4 G CARBO (0.2 G FIBER); 78 MG SODIUM; 0 MG CHOL.

From the field: Artichokes

For a vegetable, the artichoke has had its share of intrigue. The story starts quietly, with the first artichokes planted during the 1890s by immigrant Italian farmers in Half Moon Bay, about 30 miles south of San Francisco. A decade or so later, growers began shipping them to New York, where the business in baby artichokes became so profitable that it attracted the Mafia, which harassed distributors and shopkeepers and even destroyed artichokes in the fields. Finally, in the 1930s, New York City's mayor, Fiorello La Guardia, banned the possession of baby artichokes, declaring, "A racketeer in artichokes is no different than a racketeer in slot machines." (He lifted the ban after only a week, though.)

By 1922, artichokes had taken root farther down the California coast, in Castroville, where they thrived in the well-drained soil and fog. Castroville eventually grew 75 percent of the nation's artichokes. In honor of the crop, the town has held a festival every May since 1948, when a relatively unknown Marilyn Monroe was crowned its first Artichoke Queen.

Avocado fries

Crunchy on the outside, creamy and nutty inside, these fries are totally over the top. The recipe comes from chef Trey Foshee at George's at the Cove restaurant in La Jolla, California. (Photo on page 154.)

SERVES 6 | 30 minutes

Canola oil for frying
¼ cup flour
About ¼ tsp. kosher salt
2 eggs, beaten
1¼ cups *panko* (Japanese-style bread crumbs)
2 firm-ripe medium Hass avocados, pitted, peeled, and sliced into ½-in. wedges

1. Preheat oven to 200°. In a medium saucepan, heat 1½ in. oil until it registers 375° on a deep-fry thermometer.

2. Meanwhile, mix flour with salt in a shallow plate. Put eggs and panko in separate shallow plates. Dip avocado wedges in flour, shaking off excess. Dip in egg, then panko to coat. Set on two plates in a single layer.

3. Fry a quarter of the avocado wedges at a time until deep golden, 30 to 60 seconds. Transfer wedges to a plate lined with paper towels. Keep warm in oven while cooking the remainder. Sprinkle with salt to taste.

PER SERVING 271 CAL., 70% (189 CAL.) FROM FAT; 5.5 G PROTEIN; 21 G FAT (2.6 G SAT.); 16 G CARBO (2.1 G FIBER); 119 MG SODIUM; 71 MG CHOL.

ROASTED ROMANESCO
BROCCOLI

Roasted Romanesco broccoli

Romanesco broccoli is a beautiful lime green vegetable with a dense, heavy head covered in spiraling points. Widely grown in Italy, it has begun to show up in farmers' markets and backyard gardens here—part of our expanding vocabulary of vegetables in the West. Unlike its close cousin the cauliflower, Romanesco broccoli doesn't have a sulfurous taste; instead, its flavor is mild and gently sweet.

SERVES 4 | 25 minutes

1 head Romanesco broccoli, broken into large florets
2 tbsp. olive oil
½ tsp. kosher salt
½ tsp. pepper

Preheat oven to 450°. Toss Romanesco with oil, salt, and pepper on a rimmed baking sheet. Roast, turning halfway through, until golden and tender, about 20 minutes.

PER SERVING 112 CAL., 58% (65 CAL.) FROM FAT; 4.3 G PROTEIN; 7.3 G FAT (1 G SAT.); 10 G CARBO (4 G FIBER); 240 MG SODIUM; 0 MG CHOL.

Quick-cooked pea shoots

San Franciscan Niloufer Ichaporia King, author of *My Bombay Kitchen,* learned this method from a family in the Seychelles, where it's a popular way to cook greens. It works with all kinds of greens (amaranth greens, for instance, are excellent cooked like this). If the greens are tough, blanch them first.

SERVES 4 to 6 | 15 minutes

1 to 2 lbs. pea shoots* or watercress
2 tbsp. vegetable oil
1 tsp. kosher salt
1 fresh red or green arbol, Thai, or serrano chile, stem on
    and slit lengthwise; or 1 dried arbol or cayenne chile
6 quarter-size slices fresh ginger, cut into thin slivers

1. Trim any tough stems from pea shoots or watercress (for watercress, see note at end of Classic Cobb Salad, page 37).
2. Heat oil in a wok or large, heavy frying pan over high heat until hot. Throw in salt, whole chile, and ginger. When ginger starts to sear, immediately add pea shoots. Cook shoots, moving constantly with tongs, just until thoroughly wilted, 1 to 2 minutes. Serve immediately, with chile on top of greens or set aside.
*Sold at farmers' markets—generally from February through early June—and at Asian markets under their Chinese name, *dou miao.* Pea shoots are the sweet, leafy tips of the pea plant; pea sprouts are the whole baby pea plant, but are often labeled "pea shoots" by retailers. You can tell the difference, though, by looking: Pea sprouts are tiny and tender, whereas pea shoots have bigger leaves and tendrils. Either will work in this recipe.

PER SERVING 236 CAL., 22% (51 CAL.) FROM FAT; 13 G PROTEIN; 5.6 G FAT (0.8 G SAT.); 43 G CARBO (0.1 G FIBER); 357 MG SODIUM; 0 MG CHOL.

Chinese long beans with XO sauce

The Chinese diaspora that extends throughout the West includes Billy Ngo, who gave us this recipe. Chef at Kru in Sacramento, Ngo was born in Hong Kong to Chinese Vietnamese parents and came with them to California as a baby. Long beans, a common vegetable in China, are a staple in his American kitchen. With their slender, snakelike pods, the beans (also known as yard-long beans) look like regular green beans that just never quit. Cut the long beans for easy serving, or keep them whole to symbolize longevity.

SERVES 6 | 25 minutes

1 lb. Chinese long beans*, cut into 4-in. lengths if desired
2 tsp. XO sauce*, or prepared oyster sauce plus
    1 tsp. Asian chili oil
2 tbsp. hoisin sauce
1 tbsp. vegetable oil

1. Bring a medium pot of water to a boil. Cook beans in water until bright green and tender, about 5 minutes. Drain.
2. Mix XO sauce and hoisin in a small bowl.
3. Heat vegetable oil in a wok or large frying pan over high heat. Add beans and cook, stirring frequently, until starting to brown, about 4 minutes. Add sauce to beans, stirring to coat, and cook until sauce is fragrant and coats beans, about 3 minutes.
*Find long beans and XO sauce, a dried seafood-based condiment, at well-stocked grocery stores and Asian markets.
Make ahead Up to 1 day, chilled; microwave to rewarm.

PER SERVING 60 CAL., 50% (30 CAL.) FROM FAT; 1.4 G PROTEIN; 3.4 G FAT (0.4 G SAT.); 7.2 G CARBO (2 G FIBER); 145 MG SODIUM; 0.2 MG CHOL.

Indian spinach (Saag)

The Asian Indian communities of the West are thriving—especially in Silicon Valley, as well as in several rural areas in central California where Sikh farmers have settled. Every fall, a three-day festival in Yuba City, California, celebrates the Sikh sacred text with Indian food, dance, a parade, and other events, drawing tens of thousands of people.

Saag can be made using various greens—spinach is just one of the options. Serve the dish with steamed basmati rice and warm naan (Indian flatbread).

SERVES 4 | 30 minutes

1 medium onion, chopped
2 tbsp. olive oil
6 garlic cloves, chopped
2 tsp. minced fresh ginger

½ tsp. *each* ground coriander, turmeric, cayenne, and garam masala*
⅛ tsp. ground cardamom
2 lbs. spinach leaves, chopped
1 cup plain low-fat Greek yogurt
1 tsp. kosher salt

1. Cook onion in oil in a 6- to 8-qt. pot over medium heat until softened, 10 minutes. Add garlic and cook 2 minutes. Add ginger and spices and cook until fragrant, about 1 minute.
2. Working in batches, stir in spinach and cook until wilted, about 5 minutes. Remove from heat and stir in yogurt and salt.
***Garam masala is sold in the spice section of many supermarkets; if you can't find it, substitute 1 tsp. cinnamon, ½ tsp. *each* ground cumin and pepper, and ¼ tsp. *each* ground cardamom, nutmeg, cloves, and cayenne.

PER 1½-CUP SERVING 183 CAL., 43% (79 CAL.) FROM FAT; 12 G PROTEIN; 8.9 G FAT (1.9 G SAT.); 18 G CARBO (6.3 G FIBER); 682 MG SODIUM; 3.8 MG CHOL.

INDIAN SPINACH
(SAAG)

Green beans with crisp Meyer lemon bread crumbs

Sautéing bread crumbs with Meyer lemon zest gives this simple dish vivid flavor.

SERVES 10 | 45 minutes

2 cups coarse fresh ciabatta bread crumbs
¼ cup extra-virgin olive oil, divided
Finely shredded zest of 2 small Meyer lemons, plus 1 tsp. juice
About ⅛ tsp. *each* kosher salt and pepper
2½ lbs. green beans, trimmed

1. In a large frying pan over medium heat, cook crumbs in 2 tbsp. oil, stirring, 5 minutes. Stir in lemon zest and ⅛ tsp. *each* salt and pepper. Cook, stirring, until crumbs are golden, 5 minutes more. Pour into a bowl.
2. Steam beans over 1 in. boiling water in a large pot fitted with a steamer basket, stirring once, 7 minutes for very crisp beans and 10 minutes for tender-crisp.
3. Combine remaining 2 tbsp. oil with the lemon juice and salt and pepper to taste. Drain beans, toss with dressing, and pour into a shallow bowl. Top with crumbs.

PER SERVING 91 CAL., 54% (49 CAL.) FROM FAT; 2.1 G PROTEIN; 5.6 G FAT (0.8 G SAT.); 9.4 G CARBO (2.7 G FIBER); 94 MG SODIUM; 0 MG CHOL.

GREEN BEANS WITH
CRISP MEYER LEMON
BREAD CRUMBS

2. Pull back husk from each ear without detaching from bottom of cob. Remove as much silk as possible. Spread evenly with butter mixture. Fold husks back over ears and tie in place with kitchen string or strips torn from outer husks.

3. Prepare a grill for indirect medium heat (see "How-to: Grilling," page 83). Set corn over indirect-heat area and close lid on grill; cook corn until tender and charred, about 20 minutes. Serve with salt for sprinkling.

PER SERVING 112 CAL., 39% (44 CAL.) FROM FAT; 3 G PROTEIN; 4.9 G FAT (2.5 G SAT.); 17 G CARBO (2.5 G FIBER); 150 MG SODIUM; 10 MG CHOL.

The Southwest

For centuries, the Southwest nourished itself on corn. From 300 A.D., the Hohokam engineered hundreds of miles of canals to irrigate their flint corn in what is today southern Arizona. They also grew tepary beans and pumpkins and gathered pine nuts, prickly pears, and sweet mesquite pods. By 500 A.D., the Mogollan (in today's southeast New Mexico) and the Ancestral Puebloans (across northern New Mexico and Arizona) grew corn for flatbread, porridge, and stew.

In the 16th century, Spanish explorers and friars brought—along with their era's cruelties to Native Americans—wheat, melons, and cattle. A century later, Mexican Americans raised livestock on the region's ranchos, cooking wheat tortillas and chile-laced tamales, and by the 1840s, when New Mexico and Arizona were absorbed into the United States, Anglos and their recipes had moved in as well. Railroads and highways established wayside towns—especially Las Vegas—as refreshment stops, and in the 1910s, the Harvey House chain began to cater to travelers, including at El Tovar, beside the Grand Canyon. Resorts such as Tucson's Westward Look (1912) and Phoenix's Arizona Biltmore (1929) drew guests with fancy Continental menus.

New Southwestern cuisine arrived with Janos Wilder's Tucson restaurant, Janos, in 1983 and Vincent Guerithault's Vincent on Camelback in 1986 (both chefs applying French technique to regional foods); and Mark Miller's Coyote Cafe in Santa Fe in 1987.

CHILI-LIME CORN
ON THE COB

Chili-lime corn on the cob

Cooking corn on the cob in its de-silked husk keeps the kernels moist and adds a nice grassy flavor. You can also fully husk the corn and wrap it in foil. This recipe is from California restaurateur and Food Network personality Guy Fieri.

SERVES 6 | 35 minutes, plus 30 minutes to soak

¼ cup butter, softened
1 tsp. *each* finely shredded lime zest and chili powder
About ½ tsp. salt
½ tsp. pepper
¼ tsp. granulated garlic
6 ears unhusked corn

1. Combine butter, lime zest, chili powder, ½ tsp. salt, the pepper, and garlic in a small resealable plastic bag. Mush around to combine thoroughly.

Crispy grilled kale with creamy sesame dressing

Crispy-edged and a little smoky, grilled greens make a rustic side dish. A smooth sesame-mayo sauce counterpoints the kale's slightly bitter notes.

SERVES 4 | 25 minutes

1 tbsp. toasted sesame seeds*
1 tbsp. tahini (sesame paste)
2 tsp. soy sauce
2 tbsp. olive-oil mayonnaise or regular mayonnaise
1 tsp. honey
1 bunch Lacinato kale (about 10 oz.; often sold as "dinosaur kale" or "Tuscan kale")
1 tbsp. olive oil

1. Combine sesame seeds, tahini, soy sauce, mayonnaise, and honey in a medium bowl.
2. Prepare a grill for medium heat (see "How-to: Grilling," page 83). Separate kale bunch into leaves and rub with oil. Cook oil-rubbed greens directly on the grill, turning once, until slightly softened and streaked brown, 5 to 6 minutes total.
3. Cut kale into 1-in. slices, add to bowl, and toss to coat with dressing.
*Buy sesame seeds already toasted or toast them yourself: Put seeds in a small frying pan over high heat, and cook, frequently shaking pan, until lightly toasted, about 4 minutes.

PER SERVING 161 CAL., 67% (108 CAL.) FROM FAT; 1.4 G PROTEIN; 12 G FAT (1.2 G SAT.); 10 G CARBO (1.5 G FIBER); 236 MG SODIUM; 2.5 MG CHOL.

Slow-roasted tomatoes

Slow-roasted tomatoes add deep tomatoey flavor to pizza, fish or meat, and all kinds of salads. If you freeze them, they'll still offer up a taste of summer long after the season has gone. Any variety or size tomato will work. Roast tomatoes of the same size together so they cook evenly.

MAKES 8 cups | About 8 hours

10 lbs. tomatoes
½ cup extra-virgin olive oil
3 garlic cloves, finely chopped
2 tsp. fine sea salt
¼ cup chopped fresh oregano

1. Preheat oven to 250°. Core all tomatoes (except cherry tomatoes, if you're using). Cut small tomatoes in half, keep cherry tomatoes whole, and cut medium and large tomatoes into 1½-in.-thick wedges. Arrange tomatoes, cut side up and packed tightly together, on rimmed baking sheets (line with foil if you want).
2. Mix oil and garlic in a small bowl, then drizzle over tomatoes. Sprinkle with salt and oregano.
3. Roast tomatoes, switching pans among oven racks every 2 hours, until tomatoes have wrinkled and shrunk by more than half but are still slightly moist, 6 to 8 hours. If roasting cherry tomatoes, begin checking after 5 hours.
4. Let tomatoes cool completely, then transfer to a sturdy airtight container.
Make ahead Store in refrigerator up to 1 week or in freezer up to 5 months.

PER ¼-CUP SERVING 54 CAL., 59% (32 CAL.) FROM FAT; 1.2 G PROTEIN; 3.8 G FAT (0.54 G SAT.); 5.2 G CARBO (1.6 G FIBER); 147 MG SODIUM; 0 MG CHOL.

SLOW-ROASTED TOMATOES

Roasted cauliflower and shallots with chard and *dukkah*

The secret ingredient in the roasted cauliflower, inspired by a dish served by chef Matthew Dillon at the Corson Building in Seattle, is an easy-to-make Egyptian nut-and-spice blend called *dukkah*.

MAKES 8 cups; 8 to 10 servings | 1 hour

1 large cauliflower (2¾ lbs.), cored and cut into florets about 1½ in. wide
¾ lb. whole shallots, peeled and cut in half if large
5 tbsp. extra-virgin olive oil, divided
About ¾ tsp. kosher salt
½ lb. Swiss chard, stems and ribs sliced and leaves chopped separately
1 can (15 oz.) chickpeas, rinsed and drained
½ cup *Dukkah* (recipe at right)

1. Preheat oven to 425°. In a roasting pan, toss cauliflower and shallots with 3 tbsp. oil and ¾ tsp. salt. Roast, stirring occasionally, until light golden, about 20 minutes. Add chard stems and ribs, toss to coat, and roast until vegetables are very tender, 7 to 10 minutes more.
2. Stir in chard leaves, chickpeas, dukkah, and remaining 2 tbsp.

ROASTED CAULIFLOWER AND SHALLOTS WITH CHARD AND *DUKKAH*

oil. Roast until chard is wilted and tender, about 8 minutes. Stir; season to taste with more salt.

PER SERVING 162 CAL., 62% (101 CAL.) FROM FAT; 4.7 G PROTEIN; 12 G FAT (1.2 G SAT.); 12 G CARBO (2.5 G FIBER); 300 MG SODIUM; 0 MG CHOL.

Dukkah (Egyptian nut-and-spice blend) Toast 1½ tbsp. **coriander seeds** and 1½ tsp. **cumin seeds** in a small frying pan over medium-low heat until a shade darker, 5 to 7 minutes; let cool. Grind spices, ½ tsp. *each* **kosher salt** and **pepper,** and ¼ tsp. **dried thyme leaves** in a food processor until fairly finely ground. Add ¼ cup *each* **toasted hazelnuts** and **toasted sesame seeds** and pulse until coarsely ground. Makes about ½ cup.

La Super-Rica pinto beans

According to Isidoro Gonzalez, owner of La Super-Rica in Santa Barbara, California, these beans have been popular ever since they were added to the menu in 1981.

MAKES About 10 cups; 8 to 10 servings | 2 hours, plus at least 2 hours to soak beans

1 lb. dried pinto beans, sorted for debris and rinsed
About 1 tsp. salt
3 slices bacon, chopped
½ lb. Mexican chorizo*
1 poblano chile, seeds and ribs removed, finely chopped

1. Soak beans in a large pot of water overnight. Or bring beans to a boil, cover, boil for 2 minutes, and then let stand for 2 hours.
2. Put beans in a 5- to 6-qt. pan. Add 2½ qts. water. Cover and bring to a boil; reduce heat and simmer, stirring occasionally, until beans are tender to the bite, 1¼ to 1½ hours. Add 1 tsp. salt.
3. Meanwhile, cook bacon in an 8- to 10-in. frying pan over medium-high heat, stirring frequently, until browned, 8 to 10 minutes. With a slotted spoon, transfer bacon to a bowl.
4. Remove chorizo casings. Crumble sausage into frying pan. Cook, stirring frequently, until browned, 4 to 5 minutes. Add poblano and cook, stirring, until softened, 3 to 4 minutes.
5. Add bacon and ½ cup bean cooking liquid to sausage mixture; cook, stirring occasionally, 5 minutes. If beans seem very wet, drain off some liquid (keep in mind that they'll stiffen as they cool). Stir sausage-bacon mixture into beans and simmer to blend flavors, about 5 minutes. Add more salt to taste.
*Buy the best-quality chorizo you can find; avoid the soft kind in plastic casings. (Or substitute another spicy uncooked sausage.)

PER SERVING 300 CAL., 39% (117 CAL.) FROM FAT; 16 G PROTEIN; 13 G FAT (4.9 G SAT.); 30 G CARBO (5.6 G FIBER); 567 MG SODIUM; 25 MG CHOL.

Quinoa with toasted pine nuts

A mild, nutty taste and fluffy-but-chewy texture make quinoa ideal for pairing with spicy foods. A high-protein grainlike seed native to the South American Andes, quinoa is also being cultivated in the highlands of the Colorado Rockies these days. The seeds are naturally coated with saponin, a bitter resinlike substance, which is rinsed off before packaging—but it's a good idea to rinse them again prior to cooking.

SERVES 6 | 30 minutes

⅔ cup pine nuts
1 tbsp. canola oil
1 cup quinoa, thoroughly rinsed
1¾ cups chicken or vegetable broth
About ¼ tsp. kosher salt
½ cup chopped green onions
2 tbsp. chopped cilantro

1. Put pine nuts in a small pan and toast over medium heat, stirring, 3 to 5 minutes. Heat oil in a heavy-bottomed 4- to 5-qt. pot over medium-high heat. Add quinoa and cook, stirring, until it smells toasted, about 3 minutes. Add broth and ¼ tsp. salt. Bring to a boil over high heat, covered; reduce heat and simmer, stirring occasionally, until quinoa is tender and completely translucent, about 15 minutes.
2. Remove from heat and let stand 5 minutes. Stir in pine nuts, green onions, and cilantro; season with salt to taste.

PER SERVING 235 CAL., 55% (129 CAL.) FROM FAT; 7.8 G PROTEIN; 14 G FAT (1.1 G SAT.); 20 G CARBO (2.5 G FIBER); 195 MG SODIUM; 0 MG CHOL.

Grilled ratatouille

Grill vegetables on a baking sheet, and they won't fall through the cooking grate. Using a baking sheet also means you can glaze them with balsamic vinegar, which would scorch if applied to food directly on the grill. Serve the melt-in-your-mouth ratatouille in pita bread, over pasta, or alongside grilled meat.

SERVES 8 | 2 hours

⅓ cup toasted pine nuts
2 bell peppers (red or yellow), seeded, stemmed, and cut
　　into ¾-in.-wide wedges
2 red onions, cut into 1-in.-wide wedges
1 large eggplant, cut into 1-in. chunks
2 small yellow zucchini or crookneck squash, cut crosswise
　　into ¼-in.-thick slices
3 Roma tomatoes, quartered lengthwise
3 garlic cloves, chopped

QUINOA WITH
TOASTED PINE NUTS

1 tbsp. *each* finely chopped fresh oregano and flat-leaf parsley
5 tbsp. extra-virgin olive oil
1 tsp. pepper
About 2 tsp. kosher salt
3 tbsp. balsamic vinegar
½ cup crumbled ash-coated fresh goat cheese

1. Prepare a grill for indirect medium heat (see "How-to: Grilling," page 83). Put pine nuts in a small pan and toast over medium heat, stirring, 3 to 5 minutes.
2. Toss together all ingredients except pine nuts, vinegar, and cheese in a large bowl. Spread vegetables on a large rimmed baking sheet (not nonstick).
3. Cook vegetables over indirect heat, with lid closed on grill, until very tender, about 60 minutes (for charcoal, add 4 briquets to each side every 30 minutes and keep measuring heat), gently stirring every 15 minutes. Drizzle with vinegar, stir, and cook 15 minutes more. Let vegetables cool. Put in a medium bowl, toss with pine nuts and salt to taste, and sprinkle with cheese.

PER SERVING (ABOUT ¾ CUP) 295 CAL., 46% (135 CAL.) FROM FAT; 8.9 G PROTEIN; 15 G FAT (3.5 G SAT.); 35 G CARBO (3.5 G FIBER); 547 MG SODIUM; 6.7 MG CHOL.

Golden olive oil–roasted potatoes

Nothing more than good olive oil and crunchy sea salt turn potatoes into an irresistible side dish. Soaking the potatoes before cooking makes them crisper on the outside and creamier in the middle. The recipe comes from Maria Helm Sinskey, cookbook author and co-owner of Robert Sinskey Vineyards in Napa Valley.

SERVES 8 | 1¼ hours, plus overnight to chill

5 lbs. large Yukon Gold potatoes
3 tbsp. extra-virgin olive oil
About ½ tbsp. sea salt, such as fleur de sel

1. Peel potatoes and cut into 1½-in. cubes. Put in a large bowl, cover with cold water, and refrigerate overnight. Drain.
2. Preheat oven to 475°. Bring a large pot of lightly salted water to a boil over high heat. Add potatoes and cook until barely tender when pierced, about 10 minutes. Drain in a colander and let dry 10 minutes.
3. Set potatoes in a single layer in a large rimmed baking pan. Drizzle with oil and sprinkle with ½ tbsp. salt; stir gently to coat. Bake potatoes until golden brown, 25 to 30 minutes, turning halfway through baking.
4. Mound potatoes in a serving dish; season with salt.

PER SERVING 255 CAL., 18% (47 CAL.) FROM FAT; 6 G PROTEIN; 5.2 G FAT (0.8 G SAT.); 45 G CARBO (3 G FIBER); 383 MG SODIUM; 0 MG CHOL.

Makah Ozette potatoes with bacon cream

A dollop of cream with bacon and chives folded in melts over the potatoes, giving them a rich, salty glaze. A rare heirloom potato, the Ozette was until the 1980s known only to the Makah Nation on the Olympic Peninsula, who had been growing it ever since Spanish explorers brought the seeds from South America in 1791.

SERVES 8 | 1 hour

4 lbs. Makah Ozette* or fingerling potatoes, halved if large
12 oz. red pearl onions
2 tbsp. unsalted butter, melted
2 tbsp. extra-virgin olive oil
1¼ tsp. kosher salt, divided
½ tsp. plus ⅛ tsp. pepper, divided
¼ cup *each* crème fraîche and heavy cream
1 bunch (¼ cup) chives, chopped
4 oz. bacon, cooked until crisp, then finely chopped

1. Preheat oven to 400°. Put potatoes in a pot of salted water. Bring to a boil, then simmer until just tender, 10 to 15 minutes. Drain and put in a large bowl. Meanwhile, blanch onions in boiling water 2 minutes; rinse to cool, then peel.
2. Add onions, butter, oil, 1 tsp. salt, and ½ tsp. pepper to potatoes and stir. Divide between two rimmed baking sheets and bake, stirring occasionally, until potatoes are tender and golden brown with crisp edges, about 25 minutes. Transfer to a shallow serving dish.
3. Beat crème fraîche and cream in a bowl with a mixer until stiff peaks form. Stir in chives, bacon, ¼ tsp. salt, and ⅛ tsp. pepper. Top potatoes with bacon cream and gently stir to coat.
*Find Makah Ozette potatoes at Whole Foods Market in the Seattle area and at local farmers' markets.

PER SERVING 319 CAL., 39% (126 CAL.) FROM FAT; 7 G PROTEIN; 14 G FAT (6.6 G SAT.); 43 G CARBO (3.9 G FIBER); 370 MG SODIUM; 29 MG CHOL.

GOLDEN OLIVE OIL–ROASTED POTATOES

MAKAH OZETTE
POTATOES WITH
BACON CREAM

BUTTERNUT SQUASH
WITH GREEN CHILE
AND MUSTARD SEEDS

Butternut squash with green chile and mustard seeds

Butternut is one of the smoothest and creamiest of the squashes. This spicy side is a good accompaniment to meat—we particularly like it with roast chicken, crusty bread, and Greek-style yogurt on the side. Save time and effort by using a 2-lb. bag of cut-up butternut squash.

SERVES 8 | 30 minutes

2 tsp. vegetable oil
½ tsp. brown mustard seeds
3 garlic cloves, finely chopped
1 serrano chile, halved, seeds and ribs removed, and thinly sliced
1 medium butternut squash (about 2 lbs.), peeled, seeded, and cut into 1-in. cubes
Salt
Chopped cilantro (optional)

1. Combine oil and mustard seeds in a large frying pan. Cook over medium-high heat, covered, until seeds finish popping, about 1 minute. Add garlic and chile and cook, stirring, until garlic just starts to brown, about 1 minute.
2. Add squash and stir to coat with oil. Add ½ cup water, cover, and cook until squash is tender to the bite, 20 to 25 minutes. Sprinkle with salt to taste and garnish with cilantro if using.

PER SERVING 56 CAL., 21% (12 CAL.) FROM FAT; 1.1 G PROTEIN; 1.3 G FAT (0.2 G SAT.); 12 G CARBO (2 G FIBER); 4.1 MG SODIUM; 0 MG CHOL.

Caramelized shallots and walnuts

This side dish by chef Paul Canales is simultaneously sweet and savory, like a relish that's served warm. The crunchy walnuts and silky shallots work especially well with beef. Canales, who was the longtime chef at Oakland's Oliveto, now has another Oakland restaurant in the works—Duende.

SERVES 8 | 45 minutes

¼ cup butter
2 lbs. shallots, trimmed and peeled
½ tsp. salt
1 cup walnut halves
1 cup Vin Santo (Italian dessert wine)*
5 sprigs thyme

1. Melt butter in a large frying pan over medium-high heat. Add shallots and sprinkle with salt. Cook, stirring occasionally,

until shallots are well browned all over, about 20 minutes.
2. Add walnuts, Vin Santo, and thyme. Bring to a boil, then reduce heat to low, cover, and simmer until shallots are tender, about 5 minutes. Uncover, turn heat to medium-high, and cook until liquid is reduced and almost completely evaporated. Serve warm.
*Vin Santo is sold at liquor stores; substitute Madeira, Marsala, Port, or any other sweet wine, if you prefer.

PER SERVING 234 CAL., 58% (135 CAL.) FROM FAT; 4.8 G PROTEIN; 15 G FAT (4.4 G SAT.); 23 G CARBO (1.6 G FIBER); 220 MG SODIUM; 16 MG CHOL.

From the orchard: Nuts

Nut orchards with clouds of white and pale pink blooms are one of the pleasures of spring in the West, as is the crunchy, rich harvest.

ALMONDS Eighty percent of the world's almond crop grows in California's Central Valley. Franciscan missionaries introduced the tree in the 1700s; the nuts are now the state's most valuable crop after grapes, and farmers rent 1.6 million hives from beekeepers for grand-scale pollination in February.

HAZELNUTS French settlers brought hazelnuts (also called filberts) to Oregon in the mid-19th century, and these days the state grows nearly 100 percent of the U.S. crop.

PINE NUTS The tiny pine nut, or piñon, has been a significant part of the diet of the Hopi, Navajo, and other Native American peoples for thousands of years. Unlike most Western nuts, pine nuts are harvested from natural stands rather than farmed, and demand far exceeds supply. Piñon pines, widespread through the Colorado Plateau, stretch west to California's desert mountains and north to Wyoming.

WALNUTS Franciscan padres brought the English (also called Persian) walnut to California in the late 1700s, and the nuts thrived in the Mediterranean climate. (The black walnut, native to the Eastern United States, isn't often cultivated.) The first commercial planting was in 1867, and now California produces 99 percent of the country's crop.

Chinese rice stuffing

Some of the best Thanksgiving recipes *Sunset* has ever published have been cross-cultural creations. This one, from Rebecca Parker and Wei Chiu, of Palo Alto, California, is outstanding—savory, moist, and studded with bits of sweet-salty Chinese sausage and crunchy water chestnuts. It's a great side dish any time of the year—as well as an excellent stuffing for turkey, chicken, or Cornish hens.

SERVES 8 to 10 | 1 hour, plus 2 hours to soak rice

2 cups sweet rice
1 cup jasmine rice
½ tsp. salt
8 to 10 dried medium shiitake mushrooms
6 Chinese sausages (*lop chong*; about 9 oz. total)
1 can (8 oz.) sliced water chestnuts
6 tbsp. oyster sauce
1 tbsp. sugar
3 tbsp. vegetable oil
2 garlic cloves, minced
1 medium onion, diced
4 green onions, trimmed and thinly sliced, divided

1. In a large bowl, wash sweet rice well in several changes of water until water runs clear. Cover with plenty of cold water and soak at least 2 hours. Drain rice in a colander.***** Meanwhile, in a medium bowl, wash jasmine rice in a few changes of water until water runs clear. Put jasmine rice in a small saucepan with 1½ cups water and the salt and bring to a boil, covered, over high heat. Lower heat and simmer, covered, until water is absorbed, 10 to 15 minutes. Let stand 5 minutes.
2. Soak shiitakes in 1¾ cups warm water until softened, 15 to 30 minutes. Meanwhile, quarter sausages, then dice; put in a bowl. Dice water chestnuts and add to sausages. When shiitakes are softened, lift from water (reserve water) and remove and discard stems. Dice caps and add to bowl.
3. Pour 1¼ cups mushroom water into a measuring cup, leaving grit behind. Stir in oyster sauce and sugar.
4. Heat oil in a large frying pan or wok over medium heat. Add garlic and cook, stirring, until slightly browned, about 30 seconds. Add diced onion and cook, stirring, until translucent, about 5 minutes. Stir in sausage mixture and drained sweet rice. Cook, stirring often, until heated through, about 5 minutes.
5. Stir in oyster sauce mixture and cook, stirring, until bubbling, about 2 minutes. Stir in half the green onions, reduce heat to low, and simmer, covered and stirring occasionally, until rice is translucent and liquid is absorbed, about 20 minutes.
6. Gradually stir in cooked jasmine rice, 1 to 2 cups at a time, until thoroughly mixed; heat until hot, about 4 minutes. Transfer stuffing to a serving bowl and sprinkle with remaining green onions.
*If you have a rice cooker, you can cook the sweet and jasmine rices together after soaking the sweet rice (follow rice cooker instructions). Stir warm mixed rice into pan with other stuffing ingredients in step 6.
Make ahead Soak sweet rice up to 1 day at room temperature, covered. Cook jasmine rice 1 day ahead and chill.

PER SERVING (ABOUT ¾ CUP) 262 CAL., 38% (100 CAL.) FROM FAT; 6.1 G PROTEIN; 11 G FAT (3.1 G SAT.); 35 G CARBO; 451 MG SODIUM; 0 MG CHOL.

Spicy brussels sprouts with fried capers

Fields of brussels sprouts (and other cool-weather vegetables) lie along California's foggy Central Coast, where they've been cultivated since the 1920s; the small, bright green spheres reach their peak of flavor in late fall through early winter.

SERVES 8 | 25 minutes

2 lbs. brussels sprouts, trimmed and halved
½ cup drained brined capers
⅓ cup extra-virgin olive oil
2 garlic cloves, minced
3 oil-packed anchovy fillets, finely chopped
½ to ¾ tsp. red chile flakes
½ lemon

1. Bring a large pot of salted water to a boil. Add brussels sprouts and cook just until tender and bright green, about 5 minutes. Drain and set aside.
2. Meanwhile, blot capers on a paper towel. Heat oil in a large frying pan over high heat. Add capers and cook, stirring carefully (mixture will splatter), until capers start to open and are brown and crisp, about 5 minutes. With a slotted spoon, transfer capers to a paper towel to drain.
3. Add garlic and anchovies to pan and cook until fragrant, about 1 minute. Add brussels sprouts and chile flakes and stir to coat with oil. Cook, stirring occasionally, until starting to brown, about 5 minutes. Transfer to a serving plate and sprinkle with capers and a squeeze of lemon.

PER SERVING 161 CAL., 60% (97 CAL.) FROM FAT; 9 G PROTEIN; 11 G FAT (1.7 G SAT.); 9.9 G CARBO (3.9 G FIBER); 961 MG SODIUM; 14 MG CHOL.

CHINESE RICE
STUFFING

CORNBREAD-CHORIZO
DRESSING

and 2 cups broth and cook just until boiling. Remove from heat.

3. Preheat oven to 450°. In a large bowl, combine cornbread cubes and chorizo mixture. Stir until evenly moistened; season with salt and pepper. If mixture seems dry, moisten with about ½ cup additional broth. Spoon into a 9- by 13-in. baking dish.

4. Cover dressing and bake for 10 minutes; uncover and continue to bake until top is browned and dressing is heated through, 10 to 15 minutes more.

*Buy firm, fresh chorizo in natural casings at well-stocked grocery stores or Latino markets. Soft, bright red chorizo in plastic casings won't work well. For the cornbread, bake two 8-in. square pans of cornbread (your own recipe, or two batches Southwest Cornbread, at right), or a boxed mix (you'll have a little left over).
Make ahead Cornbread, up to 3 days, at room temperature. Through step 3, up to 2 days, chilled; bring to room temperature 3 hours before baking.

PER ¾-CUP SERVING 376 CAL., 53% (198 CAL.) FROM FAT; 12 G PROTEIN; 22 G FAT (9.3 G SAT.); 31 G CARBO (1.8 G FIBER); 959 MG SODIUM; 76 MG CHOL.

Cornbread-chorizo dressing

Sean Yontz, chef-owner of El Diablo restaurant in Denver, gave us this recipe, which has become one of our most requested.

MAKES 12 cups; 16 servings | 1 hour, plus time to make cornbread

1 lb. Mexican-style firm chorizo sausage*, casings removed
½ cup butter
1 red onion (½ lb.), chopped
½ cup *each* chopped celery and carrot
6 garlic cloves, minced
¼ cup chopped cilantro
1 tbsp. *each* chopped thyme, oregano, and sage leaves
2 to 2½ cups reduced-sodium chicken broth, divided
12 cups ¾-in. cubes cornbread*
Salt and pepper

1. Cook chorizo in a frying pan over medium heat, stirring, until it's crumbly and browned (leave some large chunks), about 5 minutes. Transfer to paper towels to drain.

2. Return pan to medium-high heat and melt butter. Add onion, celery, carrot, and garlic. Cook vegetables, stirring occasionally, until lightly browned, about 10 minutes. Add cilantro, thyme, oregano, and sage; cook until fragrant, 1 minute. Add chorizo

Artichoke parmesan sourdough stuffing

Every November, we're asked for this recipe, created by reader Leslie Jo Parsons of Sutter Creek, California (*Sunset* readers from all over the West have actually called Parsons to thank her for it).

MAKES 10 cups; 12 servings | 1½ hours

1 lb. mushrooms, trimmed and sliced
1 tbsp. butter
2 onions (¾ lb. total), chopped
1 cup chopped celery
2 tbsp. minced garlic
About 2 cups reduced-sodium chicken broth
1 loaf (1 lb.) sourdough bread, cut into ½-in. cubes
2 jars (6 oz. each) marinated artichoke hearts, drained and chopped
1 cup finely shredded parmesan cheese
1½ tsp. poultry seasoning
1½ tbsp. minced rosemary leaves or ¾ tsp. crumbled dried rosemary
Salt and pepper
1 large egg

1. Preheat oven to 325° to 350° (use the temperature your turkey requires). Cook mushrooms, butter, onions, celery, and garlic in a 12-in. frying pan over high heat, stirring often, until vegetables are lightly browned, about 15 minutes. Transfer to a large bowl. Add a bit of broth to pan and stir, scraping browned bits from the bottom of the pan. Add those to the bowl.

2. Pour 2 cups broth into bowl and add bread, chopped artichokes, parmesan, poultry seasoning, and rosemary; mix well. Add salt and pepper to taste. Make a well in stuffing. Drop egg in well and beat egg with a fork to blend; mix egg with stuffing. Spoon stuffing into a shallow 3-qt. (9- by 13-in.) baking dish.

3. For moist stuffing, cover baking dish with foil; for crusty stuffing, do not cover. Bake until hot (at least 150° in center; check with an instant-read thermometer) or lightly browned, about 50 minutes.

Make ahead Through step 2, up to 1 day, chilled. Allow about 1 hour to bake.

PER SERVING 195 CAL., 29% (56 CAL.) FROM FAT; 9 G PROTEIN; 6.2 G FAT (2.5 G SAT.); 26 G CARBO (2.7 G FIBER); 554 MG SODIUM; 27 MG CHOL.

Southwest cornbread

Corn was cultivated by Southwest Native Americans, beginning around 500 B.C. Celebrate the tradition with cornbread.

SERVES 9 to 12 | 30 minutes

1 cup *each* flour and yellow cornmeal
⅓ cup plus 1 tbsp. sugar
2½ tsp. baking powder
¾ tsp. salt
2 large eggs
1 cup buttermilk
¼ cup butter, melted and cooled
1 can (4 oz.) chopped green chiles, drained
¾ cup coarsely shredded jack cheese
1 tbsp. chili powder

1. Preheat oven to 400°. Butter an 8- or 9-in. square baking pan. Mix flour, cornmeal, ⅓ cup sugar, baking powder, and salt in a large bowl.

2. Beat eggs in a medium bowl; add buttermilk and butter and combine. Stir in chiles and cheese. Pour egg mixture into flour mixture and stir just until evenly moistened.

3. Scrape batter into pan with a rubber spatula; spread level. In a small bowl, mix remaining 1 tbsp. sugar and the chili powder. Sprinkle evenly over batter.

4. Bake until bread springs back when lightly pressed in center and begins to pull from pan sides, 20 to 25 minutes. Let cool slightly or completely and cut into pieces.

PER SERVING 192 CAL., 35% (68 CAL.) FROM FAT; 5.7 G PROTEIN; 7.5 G FAT (4.1 G SAT.); 26 G CARBO (1.2 G FIBER); 402 MG SODIUM; 54 MG CHOL.

From the oven: Sourdough

Because they relied on sourdough starters for breadmaking out in the undomesticated gold fields, Gold Rush prospectors were called "sourdoughs"—and ever since, sourdough has been a Western staple (though we can't claim to have invented the technique, an ancient art).

Sourdough starter is simply dough allowed to ferment: The bacteria in the flour, in the liquid, and even in the air break down natural sugars and produce carbon dioxide, making the bread rise. (Packaged yeast works similarly, but with a different, cultured organism.) As it ferments, the starter produces acidity—in the form of lactic acid and some acetic acid—creating the "sour" in sourdough.

Starters vary from place to place (because wild yeasts are different everywhere) and baker to baker. The ones that developed in the San Francisco area were uniquely sour; in fact, the bacterial strain was given the name *Lactobacillus sanfranciscensis*. Once established, a starter can be kept going for decades. Boudin Bakery, founded in San Francisco in 1849 and still operating, traces its sourdough starter to one begun more than 160 years ago by Isidore Boudin (borrowed, it's said, from a gold miner).

In the 1980s, sourdough helped fire up an artisanal breadmaking revolution when Steve Sullivan and his wife, Susie, founded Acme Bread Company in Berkeley; for their leavener, Steve created a starter inoculated with wild yeast from wine grapes.

Sourdough's been a standby at *Sunset* ever since we ran recipes using it in 1933. We found that capturing the right microorganisms can be hit or miss, but in 1973, staff writer Kandace Reeves, working with microbiologist George K. York from University of California, Davis, devised a dependable method (see recipe on page 175).

Sourdough French bread

When *Sunset* published this recipe in 1973, the baguette was the only shape sourdough bakers were interested in. Professional and home bakers have branched out to additional forms, but the baguette remains the classic. (See below for directions to making a round loaf.*)

MAKES 1 loaf (20 slices) | 50 minutes, plus up to 2½ hours to rise (and up to 24 hours for starter to ferment if you want a very sour dough)

1 cup sourdough starter*, at room temperature (see *Sunset's* Reliable Sourdough Starter, opposite page)
3 to 3½ cups bread flour, divided
1 package (2¼ tsp.) active dry yeast
1 tsp. *each* salt and sugar
Cornmeal

1. Stir together ½ cup warm (90°) water, the starter, and 1 cup flour in a large bowl until mixture is smooth. For sourest flavor, cover and let stand in a warm place until bubbly and sour-smelling, 12 to 24 hours, before proceeding. (The longer you let the mixture ferment, the more pronounced the sour flavor will be in the finished bread.) Soften yeast in ¼ cup warm (90°)

water; stir into sourdough mixture with salt and sugar.

2. Using your method of choice, mix remaining flour with sourdough-yeast mixture and knead:

By hand: Stir enough flour into sourdough-yeast mixture to form a kneadable dough, about 2 cups. Turn dough out onto a lightly floured work surface and knead until smooth and elastic, 12 to 15 minutes; add as little flour as possible to keep dough from sticking. Put dough in a greased bowl; turn over.

With a mixer fitted with a dough hook: Mix enough flour into sourdough-yeast mixture to form a somewhat stiff dough, about 2 cups. Beat on high speed until dough pulls cleanly from inside of bowl, about 8 minutes. If dough still sticks or feels sticky, add 1 tbsp. flour at a time until dough pulls free and isn't sticky. Leave in bowl.

In a food processor: Put 2¼ cups flour in processor with metal blade. With motor running, pour sourdough-yeast mixture into feed tube. Process until dough forms a ball and pulls from container, then process 45 seconds more. If dough feels sticky, add 1 tbsp. flour at a time and pulse. Put dough in a greased bowl; turn over.

3. Cover bowl with plastic wrap and let rise in a warm (about 80°) place until doubled in bulk, 1 to 2 hours.

4. Gently punch down dough. Turn out onto a lightly floured work surface and knead gently just until smooth. Roll with hands into a 3½- by 12-in. log. Generously sprinkle a piece of stiff cardboard with cornmeal; set dough on cornmeal. Cover lightly with plastic wrap and let rise in a warm place until puffy, 10 to 30 minutes.

5. Meanwhile, put a 12- by 15-in. baking sheet on lowest oven rack, then preheat oven to 400°.

6. With a flour-dusted razor blade or a sharp knife, cut several ¾-in.-deep diagonal slashes on loaf's top. Slip loaf off cardboard onto hot baking sheet, keeping slashed side up. Mist bread all over with water from a spray bottle.

7. Bake for 5 minutes, and then mist again with water. Repeat in 5 minutes, then bake until deep golden, 25 to 30 minutes more. Let cool completely on rack.

*Although it's gratifying to make your own sourdough starter, you can also order one online from *amazon.com*; we like Goldrush Sourdough starter. To form the dough into a round loaf, shape it after you have kneaded the dough in step 4, tucking the edges under and pushing them back up into the bottom of the dough (the top of the round should be slightly stretched). Put on a buttered baking sheet, cover, and let rise as directed, then bake as for a baguette.

PER SLICE 119 CAL., 4% (5.2 CAL.) FROM FAT; 4 G PROTEIN; 0.6 G FAT (0.1 G SAT.); 24 G CARBO (0.9 G FIBER); 123 MG SODIUM; 0.4 MG CHOL.

Sunset's Reliable Sourdough Starter

As with a classic starter, ours ferments flour and liquid—milk, in this case—with some yogurt, which is packed with helpful bacteria to get things off to a good beginning. Yogurt produces a very active, bubbly starter and gives a wonderful zesty flavor to the bread. After a few days' incubation in a warm place, the bacteria multiply, breaking down sugars in the flour and milk and giving the characteristic sour smell and tang—and the starter is ready to use. Despite their terrific souring qualities, yogurt-based starters don't always have a reliable yeast component (their high levels of acidity can inhibit yeast's gas production), so we add dry yeast when baking. For best results, buy milk (nonfat or low-fat for tangiest flavor) and yogurt that are as fresh as possible (check the sell-by date) and use right after they're opened. (See below for info on maintaining the starter.)

MAKES About 1⅓ cups starter | 1 week

1 cup nonfat or low-fat milk
3 tbsp. plain yogurt (any fat level; use a brand with
   live cultures and no gelatin)
1 cup all-purpose or bread flour

1. Heat milk to 90° to 100° in a 1-qt. pan over medium heat. Remove from heat and stir in yogurt. Pour into a warm 3- to 6-cup container with a tight lid.

2. Cover and let stand in a warm (80° to 90°) place until mixture has consistency of yogurt, a curd has formed, and the mixture doesn't flow readily when container is tilted. (It may also form smaller curds suspended in clear liquid.) The process takes 18 to 24 hours. If some clear liquid has risen to the top of the milk during this time, stir it back in. If liquid has turned light pink, discard batch and start again.

3. Once curd has formed, stir in flour until smooth. Cover tightly and let stand in a warm place until mixture is full of bubbles and has a good sour smell, 2 to 5 days. Again, if clear liquid forms during this time, stir it back into starter. If liquid turns pink, start over. To store, cover and refrigerate.

How-to: Sourdough

Care and Feeding

To keep the microorganisms healthy, yogurt starter (recipe above) must be nourished occasionally with flour and milk.

ENVIRONMENT When creating the starter, incubate it between 80° and 90°. Any hotter and the bacteria may die; any cooler and the starter could develop mold. Set it on top of your water heater, on a counter with a lamp warming it, or in an oven warmed with pans of boiling water. An established starter is stronger; after feeding, it can stand at room temperature.

FEEDING For best results, try to feed the starter at least once a month, even if you're not baking. To feed, add warm (90° to 100°) nonfat or low-fat milk and all-purpose flour to the starter, each in the quantity you'll be using in a recipe. For example, if the recipe calls for 1 cup starter, add 1 cup milk and 1 cup flour. (This is also the right amount for a monthly feeding even if you're not baking.) Cover tightly and let stand in a warm (80° to 90°) place until bubbly and sour-smelling and a clear liquid has formed on top, 12 to 24 hours. The clear liquid shows that the milk protein is starting to break down and the acid level has risen—which means sour flavor. Use at this point (just give it a stir first) or cover and chill.

GROWING To increase the starter supply (for gift-giving or quantity baking), you can add up to 10 cups *each* of milk and flour to 1 cup of starter (use a large container). The mixture may need to stand up to 2 days before the clear liquid forms on top.

Starter FAQs

WHAT IF I NEGLECT MY STARTER? Even with the best intentions, it's easy to forget to feed a starter, but they can be surprisingly resilient. If you rediscover yours in the back of the fridge, take its "pulse." An "old" smell, no bubbles at room temperature, a top layer of dark brown liquid, or slight mold growth indicates your starter isn't feeling its best. (If mold growth is heavy, begin a new starter.) Spoon off and discard any slight mold, then stir the starter. Feed it 1 cup *each* of flour and milk and let stand as directed in "Feeding" (at left). After 24 hours, discard half the starter and repeat feeding and standing. Repeat a third time, if needed, until the starter bubbles and has a "fresh" sour smell. If, after repeated feedings, your starter still smells "off" and won't bubble, throw it away.

CAN YOU USE A STARTER TOO OFTEN? If you bake several times a week or feed your starter a lot all at once (to increase quantity), it may take longer than usual to regain normal sourness. After feeding, let it stand as directed in "Feeding" (left).

WHY DO STARTERS "DIE"? The longer a starter stands without new food, the higher the acidity gets; too much acid, and the beneficial bacteria can't survive. Mold infestations may also kill off good bacteria.

CAN I FREEZE IT? Starters generally freeze successfully for up to a few months, but freezing does change the bacteria's cell structure. Longer freezing brings more changes and decreases the chance of success with the thawed starter.

Navajo fry bread

In the 16th century, the Spanish arrived in the Southwest and introduced their culture and foods to the region. One of the most significant of the imports was wheat, which Native Americans used to make a new version of their corn flatbread. A bonus of the wheat-flour iteration was that when fried, it turned into a golden, billowy pillow. In 1988, Navajo Maurice Begay of Midvale, Utah, gave us his mother's recipe, which is terrific topped with beans, salsa, and cheddar. Make the chili beans or use canned beans spiked with sautéed beef, chiles, and onions. We like spicy salsa here, because the rest of the ingredients are rather mild. Start the beans first and make the fry bread while they're soaking.

MAKES 6 pieces | 30 minutes (1½ hours if also making topping)

2 cups flour
½ cup instant nonfat dry milk
1 tbsp. baking powder
½ tsp. salt
2 tbsp. shortening or lard
Vegetable oil for frying

1. Mix flour, dry milk, baking powder, and salt in a medium bowl. Add shortening and rub mixture with your fingers until coarse crumbs form. Add ¾ cup water and stir with a fork until dough clings together.
2. Put dough on a lightly floured board. Knead until smooth, 2 to 3 minutes. Divide dough into 6 equal portions and keep covered with plastic wrap. Shape a portion of dough into a ball, then pat (or use a lightly floured rolling pin to roll) out to make a 6- to 7-in. circle. Cover with plastic wrap and repeat to make remaining portions.
3. Preheat oven to 200°. In a large pot, heat ¾ in. oil until it registers 375° on a deep-fry thermometer. Meanwhile, line two large baking sheets with several layers of paper towels.
4. Fry each circle of dough until puffy and golden brown, turning once, 1½ to 2 minutes. Transfer to baking sheet as done and keep warm in oven in a single layer.
Make ahead Let bread cool, then package airtight and chill up to 1 day. Warm in a single layer on baking sheets in a 375° oven until hot, about 5 minutes.

PER PIECE 275 CAL., 29% (81 CAL.) FROM FAT; 8.2 G PROTEIN; 9.2 G FAT (1.6 G SAT.); 40 G CARBO (1.2 G FIBER); 492 MG SODIUM; 2 MG CHOL.

Taco topping

SERVES 6 | 15 minutes

Navajo Fry Bread (recipe at left)
Chili Beans (recipe below)
½ lb. sharp cheddar, coarsely shredded (about 2 cups)
⅓ lb. iceberg lettuce, finely shredded (about 3 cups)
1¼ thinly sliced green onions
1 tomato, sliced thinly crosswise
About 1 cup tomato salsa
About 1 cup sour cream

Lay each piece of hot fry bread on a plate. Spoon chili beans onto bread, dividing evenly; then sprinkle with cheese, lettuce, and onions (it's okay if it's a little messy; this is a knife-and-fork taco). Top with a slice or two of tomato and serve with salsa and sour cream.

Chili beans

Three tablespoons of seasoning sounds like a lot, but beans need quite a bit to be flavorful. Make sure that your spices are fresh—chili powder in particular can start to taste dusty and faded if it's more than a year old.

MAKES About 7 cups | 1½ hours

1 cup dry pinto beans
2 tsp. salt, divided
1 tbsp. vegetable oil
1 medium onion, chopped
1 poblano chile, stemmed, seeded, and finely chopped
1 tbsp. *each* chili powder, cumin, and dried oregano, preferably Mexican
1 cup tomato sauce
3 garlic cloves, peeled and finely chopped
1 lb. ground beef or bulk pork sausage

1. Sort and discard debris from beans; rinse well. Put in a medium saucepan, cover with 2 in. water, and let soak overnight (or quick-soak by bringing to a boil, then letting sit, covered, 1 hour). Drain. Return to pan and cover with fresh water. Bring to a boil, reduce heat, and simmer, covered, until tender, 45 minutes to 1 hour, adding 1 tsp. salt about halfway through. Pour beans into a bowl along with about ½ cup liquid (save the rest for another use if you like).
2. Wipe pan dry. Add oil and heat over medium heat. Add onion, chile, chili powder, cumin, and oregano and cook, stirring occasionally, until onion is softened, about 5 minutes. Add tomato and garlic and cook another 5 minutes. Stir into beans.
3. Crumble beef or sausage into pan, add remaining 1 tsp.

salt (½ tsp. or none if using seasoned sausage), and cook over medium-high heat, stirring occasionally, until meat is well browned, about 10 minutes. Pour off and discard fat. Stir meat into beans.

PER TACO WITH ABOUT 3 TBSP. EACH SALSA AND SOUR CREAM 809 CAL., 43% (346 CAL.) FROM FAT; 41 G PROTEIN; 39 G FAT (18 G SAT.); 74 G CARBO (9.4 G FIBER); 1,933 MG SODIUM; 105 MG CHOL.

Sheepherder's bread

With this loaf, Anita Mitchell won the bread-baking contest at the National Basque Festival in Elko, Nevada, in 1975. The diaspora of Basques from northern Spain brought sheepherders to American grazing country from the Central Valley of California up through Idaho. They adapted traditional foods into a hearty cuisine, including cabbage soup, lamb stew, and this bread, which herders baked in a dutch oven over the campfire. Although it's tempting to cut into the bread while it's still warm, doing so will make the rest of the loaf gummy (as is true for most breads). Bake in a dutch oven or in a round loaf pan with sides at least 5 in. high.

MAKES 1 loaf (16 slices) | 3½ hours

½ cup *each* **room-temperature butter and sugar**
2½ tsp. salt
2 packages active dry yeast (not instant)
About 10 cups all-purpose flour, divided
Vegetable oil

1. In a large bowl, combine 3 cups very hot (120°) tap water with butter, sugar, and salt. Stir until butter melts; let cool until warm (110°). Stir in yeast, cover, and set in a warm place until bubbly, 10 to 15 minutes.

2. Add 5 cups flour. Beat with a heavy-duty mixer or spoon just until batter is stretchy, 5 to 8 minutes. Mix in enough of the remaining flour, about 3½ cups, to form a stiff dough.

3. To knead with a dough hook, beat on medium speed until dough pulls from side of bowl and no longer feels sticky, about 5 minutes. If required, add more flour, 1 tbsp. at a time. To knead by hand, scrape dough out onto a floured board and knead until smooth, about 10 minutes, adding flour as required to prevent sticking. Rinse bowl and rub with oil. Return dough to bowl and turn over to coat with oil.

4. Cover bowl with oiled plastic wrap and let dough rise in a warm place until doubled, 20 minutes to 1½ hours (it will rise faster in a warmer place).

5. Meanwhile, if using a 5-qt. cast-iron dutch oven, cut a circle of foil to fit bottom of pan; put foil in pan. Rub the foil and sides

SHEEPHERDER'S BREAD

of pan generously with oil. A nonstick pan that is not worn needs no preparation.

6. Knead dough with dough hook or on a floured board to expel air, then form into a smooth ball.

7. Place dough in baking pan. Cover loosely with oiled plastic wrap and let rise in a warm place until almost doubled again, 40 minutes to 1 hour; watch closely so it doesn't rise too much.

8. Preheat oven to 350°. Bake bread, uncovered, on lowest rack until loaf is golden brown and sounds hollow when tapped, 40 to 55 minutes.

9. Remove bread from oven and invert onto a rack (you'll need a helper); remove foil if necessary and turn loaf right side up. Cool completely, then cut into 12 wedges.

Make ahead Bake the loaf up to 1 day ahead and store, covered, at room temperature. Freeze to store longer.

PER SLICE 375 CAL., 17% (64 CAL.) FROM FAT; 9 G PROTEIN; 7.5 G FAT (3.8 G SAT.); 68 G CARBO (2.4 G FIBER); 407 MG SODIUM; 15 MG CHOL.

BLACKBERRY HAZELNUT
HONEY CRISP *recipe on page 189*

Desserts

Classic sweets get local flavor by way of Western orchards and fields—as with a sunny apricot tart and a deeply flavored berry crisp. Born-in-the-West desserts, meanwhile, tend toward the homespun: Hawaii's coconut *haupia* and the Southwest's *sopaipillas* are gloriously simple. What they all share is the distinctive taste of where we live.

APRICOT NUT TART

Apricot nut tart

Tangy dried apricots pair well with almonds (both thrive in California) and earthy hazelnuts (from Oregon) in a buttery crust. Dollop the tart with whipped cream if you like.

SERVES 12 | 1¼ hours

1 cup (6 oz.) dried apricots, preferably Blenheim
⅔ cup dessert wine, such as orange muscat (or orange juice), divided
½ tsp. finely shredded orange zest
⅔ cup honey, divided
1 cup *each* whole hazelnuts and blanched almonds
3 large eggs
1 tsp. vanilla extract
2 tbsp. butter, melted
Butter Pastry (recipe at right)

1. Simmer apricots, ⅓ cup wine, the orange zest, and 2 tbsp. honey in a saucepan over low heat, uncovered, stirring occasionally, until apricots are soft and liquid is absorbed, 10 to 25 minutes.

2. Meanwhile, preheat oven to 350°. Put whole hazelnuts and almonds in two separate shallow 9-in. pans. Bake until nuts are golden, shaking occasionally, about 10 minutes. Put hazelnuts in a clean kitchen towel and rub to remove as much of skins as possible; discard skins.

3. Whisk eggs, remaining wine and honey, vanilla, and butter in a bowl until blended. Stir in nuts.

From the orchard: Blenheim apricots

It's not a perfect-looking apricot, the Blenheim. Its thin skin sometimes has a greenish hue. Being unusually delicate, it's often also slightly bruised.

None of this really matters—because inside, the fruit is the deep orange of a setting sun, with a silky texture and a taste so rich and tangy-sweet, it makes ordinary apricots difficult to take seriously. This extraordinary flavor is what made the Blenheim (sometimes called the Royal) the dominant variety in California until the 1950s. That's when modern long-distance shipping began to require harder, more durable varieties, and

the Blenheim—so named because it was thought to have emerged from the gardens of England's Blenheim Palace—began to fade from the market shelves, replaced by bigger, tougher, rosy-cheeked apricots that look beautiful but often taste like Styrofoam.

Most of our remaining Blenheims are grown in Northern and central California, and you can still find them fresh there, mainly at farmers' markets, during their brief season in late June and early July. Dried, they're sturdier, and therefore more widely available.

4. Press pastry over bottom and up side of a 10- to 11-in. tart pan with removable rim. Distribute apricots evenly over pastry. Pour nut mixture over the fruit, arranging mixture evenly.

5. Bake tart on bottom rack of oven until golden brown, 50 to 55 minutes. Cool in pan on a rack, then remove pan rim. **Make ahead** Up to 1 day, covered and chilled.

PER SERVING 404 CAL., 53% (216 CAL.) FROM FAT; 7.6 G PROTEIN; 24 G FAT (7.5 G SAT.); 45 G CARBO (3.6 G FIBER); 121 MG SODIUM; 96 MG CHOL.

Butter pastry Blend 1⅓ cups **flour** and ¼ cup **sugar** in a food processor. Add ½ cup **butter,** cut in pieces; whirl until mixture forms fine crumbs. Add 1 large **egg yolk;** blend just until dough holds together. Makes one 10- to 11-in. tart crust.

Marionberry pie

Road food at its best: Anjou Bakery, in Washington's eastern Cascades, makes this amazing pie, which has a shortbread-like crust and a filling of marionberries—a particularly luscious strain of blackberry that grows well in the Northwest.

SERVES 8 | 1¾ hours, plus 3 hours to cool

2 cups flour
¼ tsp. salt
2½ tbsp. plus 1 cup granulated sugar
14 tbsp. (1¾ sticks) cold unsalted butter,
    cut into 2-tbsp. chunks
¼ cup cornstarch
1¾ lbs. (6½ cups) fresh or frozen marionberries
    or other blackberries (for frozen, measure, thaw
    until somewhat softened, and use all juices)
Coarse white sparkling sugar*

1. Combine flour, salt, and 2½ tbsp. granulated sugar in the bowl of a stand mixer. Add butter and beat with the paddle attachment on low speed, scraping bowl as needed, until pieces of dough are raisin-size. With mixer still on low speed, drizzle in 1 tbsp. ice water and beat until dough comes together, 1½ to 3 minutes. Form 1¼ cups dough into a disk and the rest into a smaller disk.

2. Preheat oven to 375° with a rack on lowest rung. On a lightly floured board, roll larger dough disk into a 12-in. circle. Loosen dough with a long metal spatula, gently roll around rolling pin, then unroll into a 9-in. pie pan (if dough cracks, press back together). Fold edge under, so it's flush with pan rim; then crimp. Chill 15 minutes.

3. Roll remaining dough into an 11-in. circle. With a cookie cutter, cut out enough shapes (such as squares) to cover most of pie. Set cutouts on a baking sheet and chill 15 minutes.

4. Stir together cornstarch and 1 cup granulated sugar in a large bowl. Add berries with their juices and toss to coat. Arrange evenly in pie shell. Lightly brush pastry cutouts with water and sprinkle with coarse sugar. Arrange cutouts over filling.

5. Bake pie until filling bubbles and pastry is golden in center, 55 to 60 minutes (up to 1½ hours if berries were frozen); if edge starts to get dark, cover with foil, and if pie starts to bubble over, put a rimmed pan underneath it.

6. Let cool on a rack to room temperature, at least 3 hours.
*Find in grocery markets with the baking supplies.

PER SERVING 487 CAL., 37% (182 CAL.) FROM FAT; 4.7 G PROTEIN; 21 G FAT (13 G SAT.); 72 G CARBO (5.7 G FIBER); 77 MG SODIUM; 53 MG CHOL.

MARIONBERRY PIE

SPICED BLUEBERRY PIE

Spiced blueberry pie

Black pepper, nutmeg, and cloves play up the underlying spicy note of blueberries in this pie. British Columbia harvests 20,000 acres of blueberries in fertile, mountain-edged Fraser Valley just north of Vancouver. Washington and Oregon (and, recently, California) also produce large blueberry crops.

SERVES 8 | 3 hours

2¾ cups flour, divided
1 tbsp. plus ¼ to ½ cup granulated sugar
2½ tsp. salt, divided
8 tbsp. very cold butter, cut into small pieces, divided
7 tbsp. very cold solid shortening, cut into pieces
¼ cup firmly packed light brown sugar
1 tbsp. quick-cooking tapioca
1 tsp. cinnamon
½ tsp. *each* pepper and freshly grated nutmeg
¼ tsp. ground cloves
2 pts. blueberries
1 tbsp. lemon juice

1. Mix 2½ cups flour, 1 tbsp. sugar, and 1½ tsp. salt in a large bowl. Drop in 7 tbsp. butter and the shortening. Using your hands, a fork, a pastry blender, or two knives, work butter and shortening into flour mixture until it resembles cornmeal with some pea-size pieces.

2. Using a fork, quickly stir in ½ cup very cold water. Turn dough and crumbs onto a work surface. Knead just until dough starts to hold together, 5 to 10 times. Divide dough in half and pat each half into a 6-in. disk. Wrap in plastic wrap or put in an airtight container and chill 15 minutes or up to overnight.

3. Preheat oven to 375° with a rack set on lowest rung. Put one disk of dough on a floured work surface. Roll into a 12-in. circle (about ⅛ in. thick), turning 90° after each pass of rolling pin to keep it from sticking. Transfer to a 9-in. pie pan, letting dough fall into place (if you push or stretch it into place, it will shrink back when baked). Trim dough edges to ¼ in. past rim of pie pan. Cover with plastic wrap and chill 15 minutes.

4. Roll second disk into an 11-in. circle. Cut into ten 1-in.-wide strips. Transfer to a baking sheet, cover with plastic wrap, and chill 15 minutes.

5. While crusts chill, mix remaining ¼ cup flour, ¼ cup granulated sugar, the brown sugar, tapioca, remaining 1 tsp. salt, the cinnamon, pepper, nutmeg, and cloves in a medium bowl. Add blueberries and lemon juice; toss. Taste and add more granulated sugar (up to ¼ cup) if you like. Pour berry mixture into crust and dot with remaining 1 tbsp. butter.

6. To weave a lattice crust, lay 5 strips of pie dough vertically across pie, spacing evenly. Take the far end of every other strip and fold it back halfway. Lay a strip horizontally across center of pie, next to folds of vertical strips. Unfold vertical strips back over horizontal strip. Fold back vertical strips that were left flat last time and repeat with a second horizontal strip, placing it parallel to the first strip. Repeat with a third horizontal strip next to second. Repeat this process, using remaining 2 strips of dough.

7. Fold bottom crust edge up over top crust and crimp edges together. Bake until crust is browned and filling is bubbling in center, 60 to 75 minutes. Cover edge with strips of foil if browning too quickly. Let cool until bottom of pie pan is room temperature.

PER SERVING 473 CAL., 46% (216 CAL.) FROM FAT; 5.1 G PROTEIN; 24 G FAT (10 G SAT.); 62 G CARBO (2.9 G FIBER); 859 MG SODIUM; 31 MG CHOL.

Plum almond-cream galette

For such a simple recipe, this free-form French-style tart has incredibly sophisticated flavor. California produces 95 percent of American plums, many of them descendants of hybrids bred by Luther Burbank from Asian plums at his farms in and around Santa Rosa, California.

SERVES 12 | 45 minutes

¼ cup almond paste
About 2 tbsp. firmly packed light brown sugar
¼ cup sour cream
9-in. single-crust pie pastry, store-bought or Best All-Purpose Pie Crust (page 192; use half the dough)
3 red plums, halved, pitted, and sliced
About 1 tbsp. whole milk

1. Preheat oven to 375°. Blend almond paste, 2 tbsp. brown sugar, and the sour cream in a food processor.

2. Roll out pie crust to a 13-in. circle and lay on a baking sheet.

3. Spread almond mixture evenly over dough, leaving a 2-in. border. Scatter plums evenly over top and fold dough edge over plums. Brush dough edge with milk and sprinkle more brown sugar on top of galette.

4. Bake until crust is golden, about 35 minutes.

PER SERVING 114 CAL., 46% (53 CAL.) FROM FAT; 1.6 G PROTEIN; 5.9 G FAT (1.8 G SAT.); 14 G CARBO (0.8 G FIBER); 64 MG SODIUM; 2.2 MG CHOL.

Brown sugar strawberry tart

Strawberry season is a rolling event in California, from San Diego County in January through Watsonville and Salinas in May and June, and the Oxnard and Santa Maria areas in the fall. The harvest's height, though, is April to June, when all the strawberry-growing regions are in full swing.

SERVES 8 | 30 minutes, plus 25 minutes to cool

1 cup flour
¼ cup packed dark brown sugar, divided
1 tbsp. cornstarch
⅛ tsp. salt
½ cup cold unsalted butter, cut into pieces
1 tsp. vanilla extract, divided
½ cup crème fraîche
½ cup whipping cream
12 oz. strawberries, hulled and sliced

BROWN SUGAR STRAWBERRY TART

1. Preheat oven to 350°. Blend flour, 2 tbsp. brown sugar, the cornstarch, and salt in a food processor until combined. Add butter and ½ tsp. vanilla and pulse until fine crumbs form and dough just begins to come together. Press evenly into bottom and up side of a 9-in. round tart pan with a removable rim.
2. Bake until edges are golden, 20 to 22 minutes. Let cool on a rack, then gently push tart crust from pan rim; set on a plate.
3. Beat crème fraîche, cream, remaining 2 tbsp. brown sugar, and remaining ½ tsp. vanilla in a bowl with a mixer on high speed until thick. Spread in cooled crust. Arrange strawberries in circles on top, alternating cut sides down and up.

PER SERVING 310 CAL., 66% (204 CAL.) FROM FAT; 2.8 G PROTEIN; 23 G FAT (14 G SAT.); 24 G CARBO (1.2 G FIBER); 48 MG SODIUM; 64 MG CHOL.

Macadamia nut tart

This buttery tart has just enough sweet filling to hold the nuts together. Serve with vanilla or ginger ice cream if you like.

SERVES 12 | 1 hour, plus 1 hour to cool

1¼ cups flour
2 tbsp. plus ½ cup packed dark brown sugar
½ tsp. salt, divided
¾ cup cold unsalted butter, cut into pieces, plus 2 tbsp. melted butter
1 large egg yolk, plus 1 large egg
¼ cup light corn syrup
2 tbsp. dark rum
1⅓ cups unsalted macadamia nuts, coarsely chopped

1. Preheat oven to 375°. Combine flour, 2 tbsp. brown sugar, and ¼ tsp. salt in a food processor. Add cold butter and pulse until mixture resembles coarse crumbs. Add egg yolk and pulse to combine. Add 2 to 3 tbsp. ice water, pulsing until mixture begins to come together in a ball.
2. Press dough into bottom and up side of a 9-in. round tart pan with 1-in. side. Prick bottom of tart with a fork and chill in freezer 15 minutes. Bake crust until medium golden brown, 15 to 25 minutes, and remove from oven (leave oven on).
3. Meanwhile, beat whole egg, remaining ½ cup brown sugar, and remaining ¼ tsp. salt with a mixer on high speed until pale and ribbony, 7 to 10 minutes. Beat in melted butter, corn syrup, and rum.
4. Pour sugar mixture into tart shell and sprinkle with macadamia nuts. Bake tart until a knife inserted in center comes out clean, about 25 minutes. Cool tart on a wire rack at least 1 hour.

PER SERVING 350 CAL., 64% (225 CAL.) FROM FAT; 3.5 G PROTEIN; 25 G FAT (10 G SAT.); 28 G CARBO (0.4 G FIBER); 118 MG SODIUM; 72 MG CHOL.

From Hawaii: Macadamia nuts

Native to Australia (and named after John Macadam, a friend of the botanist who first described the genus), the lush, buttery macadamia arrived in Hawaii around 1882. The nut thrived in the warm, moist climate, and Hawaii now supplies about 90 percent of the world's macadamias. To keep them fresh, refrigerate the nuts airtight for up to 6 months or freeze in an airtight container up to a year.

MACADAMIA NUT TART

BLACK MISSION
FIG TART

Black Mission fig tart

This rich, deep, spicy tart from Maria Hines, chef-owner of Tilth restaurant in Seattle, tastes like a nuanced Fig Newton. Although it isn't hard to make, the tart does take a while—so the make-ahead tips (at right) are useful to apply. As their name suggests, Mission figs—the first New World figs—were introduced here by Franciscan missionaries, who planted them in San Diego in 1759 and then in mission gardens up through what's now California.

SERVES 10 to 12 | 2 hours, plus 2½ hours to cook and cool

1 lb. dried black Mission figs
2 bottles (750 ml. each) light- or medium-bodied dry
    red wine (such as Pinot Noir)
1 cup plus 3 tbsp. sugar
¾ tsp. salt, divided
5 black peppercorns
1 cinnamon stick
3 whole allspice
2 whole cloves
1 tsp. vanilla extract
1½ cups flour
¾ cup very cold butter, cut into small pieces
8 oz. crème fraîche (about 1 cup)

1. Bring 6 cups water to a boil. Meanwhile, trim stems off figs, then cut into ⅛-in.-thick slices and put in a large heatproof bowl. Pour boiling water over figs and let stand 10 minutes. Drain. Put figs in a large pot over medium-high heat with wine, 1 cup sugar, and ½ tsp. salt. Bring to a boil. Meanwhile, tie up peppercorns, cinnamon, allspice, and cloves in a 6-in. square of cheesecloth and add to pot. Lower heat to maintain a simmer and cook until figs are soft and liquid is reduced to about ¾ cup, about 2 hours. Remove spices and discard. Stir in vanilla. Let figs and liquid cool to room temperature.

2. While figs are cooking, make and chill crust: Stir together flour and remaining 3 tbsp. sugar and ¼ tsp. salt in a large bowl. Drop in butter and work it into flour mixture with a pastry blender, your fingers, a fork, or two knives until it resembles coarse cornmeal with lots of pea-size chunks. Quickly stir in 2 tbsp. very cold water until dough starts to hold together (it will still be quite crumbly). Gently knead dough two or three times in bowl. Turn dough out onto a large piece of plastic wrap, shape into a 6-in. disk, and cover with wrap (or put disk in an airtight container). Chill at least 1 hour and up to 3 days.

3. Preheat oven to 350°. Put a 10-in. tart pan with a removable rim on a large baking sheet. Butter a large piece of foil. Put dough on a lightly floured work surface. With a lightly floured rolling pin, roll dough into a 13-in. circle, occasionally lifting and turning to keep it from sticking. Fold in half and ease into tart pan, allowing dough to fall into place (if you push or stretch it, it will shrink back when baked). Trim edges ½ in. past rim of pan and fold down to double the thickness of tart edge. Set foil, buttered side down, gently onto dough and top with pie weights or dried beans. Bake on lower rack 30 minutes. Remove weights and foil and bake until golden brown, about 15 minutes. Let cool completely, about 30 minutes.

4. Arrange cooled figs in cooled crust and pour fig-cooking liquid over them. Let stand at least 1 hour (at room temperature) and up to overnight (in refrigerator). Serve at room temperature, with crème fraîche to spoon on top.

Make ahead Figs through step 1, up to 1 day, chilled; dough through step 2, up to 3 days, chilled.

PER SERVING 418 CAL., 41% (171 CAL.) FROM FAT; 4 G PROTEIN; 19 G FAT (12 G SAT.); 60 G CARBO (4.2 G FIBER); 286 MG SODIUM; 48 MG CHOL.

Rhubarb cardamom galette

The stalks of rhubarb hold their shape as they bake, and look like brilliant ruby-colored columns laid in the crisp crust. Because rhubarb loves a cool climate, it's grown in Washington and Oregon (as well as Michigan).

SERVES 6 | 30 minutes

1 sheet (9 to 10 oz.) frozen puff pastry, thawed
3 tbsp. granulated sugar, divided
1 tbsp. firmly packed brown sugar
¼ tsp. ground cardamom
2 tbsp. flour
12 oz. rhubarb stalks (about 8 thin or 3 thick stalks),
    leaves trimmed and discarded
Sweetened whipped cream or ice cream

1. Preheat oven to 425° with a rack set on lowest rung. Unfold pastry onto a baking sheet lined with parchment paper. Mix 1 tbsp. granulated sugar, the brown sugar, cardamom, and flour in a small bowl. Sprinkle sugar mixture evenly over pastry.

2. Trim rhubarb stalks 1 in. shorter than pastry, then split lengthwise into ½-in.-wide pieces. Lay pieces parallel across pastry square, leaving ½-in. border of pastry. Sprinkle rhubarb with remaining 2 tbsp. granulated sugar.

3. Bake until edges are golden brown and puffed, 12 to 15 minutes. Serve with whipped cream or ice cream.

PER SERVING 233 CAL., 48% (113 CAL.) FROM FAT; 4.5 G PROTEIN; 13 G FAT (3.4 G SAT.); 28 G CARBO (1.6 G FIBER); 222 MG SODIUM; 0 MG CHOL.

Dark chocolate tart, cherries, and almond whipped cream

In the lush Okanagan Valley, in British Columbia, chef-caterers Cameron Smith and Dana Ewart serve summer feasts out in the valley's many vineyards. For this striking dessert, Ewart uses Balaton cherries, a tart variety that flourishes in the Okanagan, but any good fresh cherry will do—taste first and adjust the sugar accordingly. Pastry flour, sold at well-stocked grocery stores, produces a delicate but sturdy-enough crust; all-purpose flour works too.

SERVES 12 | 45 minutes, plus 5 hours to chill and cool

TART
1 large egg yolk plus 1 large whole egg
1½ tsp. milk
1 cup plus 2 tbsp. pastry or all-purpose flour
½ cup powdered sugar
¼ tsp. salt
7 tbsp. unsalted butter, cut into ½-in. cubes
1-in.-piece vanilla bean
7 oz. top-quality bittersweet chocolate, finely chopped
¾ cup whipping cream
⅓ cup half-and-half

TOPPING
¾ lb. pitted cherries, preferably tart
2 to 5 tbsp. organic granulated sugar, divided
½ cup whipping cream
¾ tsp. almond extract or 1½ tsp. amaretto

1. Make crust: Mix egg yolk with milk in a bowl. Pulse flour, powdered sugar, and salt in a food processor to blend. Add butter and pulse a few times until dough looks like cornmeal. Slit vanilla bean and carefully scrape out seeds with a spoon; add to dough. Drizzle in egg mixture and pulse until dough comes together.
2. Flatten dough into a disc and chill, wrapped in plastic wrap (or put in an airtight container), at least 1 hour and up to 2 days.
3. Roll dough on a lightly floured surface with a lightly floured rolling pin into a 10½-in. circle. Ease dough into a 9-in. tart pan and, using your thumb, press into side and bottom corner; fold edges over to form rim. Line shell with parchment paper; fill with pie weights or dried beans. Chill at least 1 hour and up to 1 day.
4. Preheat oven to 325°. Bake shell 15 to 25 minutes, or until lightly golden on the edge and set on the bottom (lift parchment to check). Carefully remove parchment and weights and bake shell until pale golden, 5 to 10 minutes more. Transfer tart shell to a rack, and lower oven temperature to 250°.
5. Make filling: Put chocolate in a medium heatproof bowl. Heat cream and half-and-half in a medium saucepan over medium heat until simmering, then pour over chocolate. Let sit a few minutes, then stir gently until smooth.
6. Beat whole egg in a small bowl, then pour into chocolate mixture, whisking constantly until incorporated (keep whisk in contact with bottom of bowl so as not to whip in air bubbles). Pour mixture into the tart shell and bake until just set (it no longer jiggles), 25 to 35 minutes. Let cool completely.
7. Make topping: Warm cherries in a saucepan over low heat with granulated sugar to taste until sugar melts. Whip cream with 2 tbsp. sugar and almond extract until soft peaks form.
8. Serve tart with cherries and a dollop of cream on top.
Make ahead Up to 2 days, chilled (bring to room temperature before serving).

PER SLICE, WITH CHERRIES AND CREAM 339 CAL., 65% (222 CAL.) FROM FAT; 4.2 G PROTEIN; 25 G FAT (14 G SAT.); 30 G CARBO (2 G FIBER); 69 MG SODIUM; 90 MG CHOL.

DARK CHOCOLATE TART, CHERRIES, AND ALMOND WHIPPED CREAM

Blackberry hazelnut honey crisp

Foods that grow in the same place tend to taste good together, as this pairing of blackberries and hazelnuts proves; Oregon is far and away the country's leading producer of both crops. (Photo on page 178.)

SERVES 8 | 2 hours, plus 30 minutes to cool

8 cups (36 oz.) fresh or frozen blackberries
3 tbsp. quick-cooking tapioca
¼ cup berry-blossom or wildflower honey
¼ cup lemon juice
¾ cup hazelnuts
¼ cup *each* flour and sugar
½ tsp. salt
½ cup *each* butter and quick-cooking rolled oats

1. Preheat oven to 350°. Toss berries with tapioca in a small bowl. Combine honey, lemon juice, and 1 tbsp. boiling water in a small bowl. Stir to dissolve honey. Add to berries and toss to combine. Put in an 8- by 8-in. baking pan and set aside.
2. Spread hazelnuts on a baking sheet and toast in oven until medium golden brown, 10 to 15 minutes. Rub nuts in a kitchen towel to remove skins; let nuts cool. Pulse nuts in a food processor until finely ground. Add flour, sugar, and salt and pulse to combine. Add butter and pulse until mixture forms a thick dough. Stir in oats. Drop in flattened 1-tsp. chunks over berries. Bake until topping is brown and berries are bubbling, about 1 hour. Let cool to set berry mixture, 30 minutes.

PER SERVING 341 CAL., 50% (171 CAL.) FROM FAT; 3.7 G PROTEIN; 19 G FAT (7.7 G SAT.); 43 G CARBO (7.3 G FIBER); 282 MG SODIUM; 31 MG CHOL.

Huckleberry skillet cobbler

This cobbler has just a hint of spices to pull out the complex, wine-rich flavor of the huckleberries. (The cobbler is also terrific with blueberries). Janie Hibler, author of *The Berry Bible* and other cookbooks, gave us this recipe—at her cabin in Washington's Cascade Range, she picks huckleberries to bake into cobblers, which, she says, taste even better at breakfast.

SERVES 8 to 10 | 1¾ hours, plus at least 45 minutes to cool

1½ cups plus 2 tbsp. sugar (if using blueberries, decrease
   to 1 cup plus 2 tbsp.)
⅓ cup quick-cooking tapioca
½ tsp. *each* cinnamon and ground cardamom
1 tbsp. lemon juice

2 qts. (2½ lbs.) fresh or frozen huckleberries* or blueberries
Buttery Pastry (recipe below)
½ tbsp. milk
1 cup crème fraîche

1. Preheat oven to 400°. Combine 1½ cups sugar (1 cup if using blueberries), tapioca, cinnamon, and cardamom in a 12-in. oven-proof frying pan or a 9- by 13-in. baking dish. Gently mix in lemon juice and berries. Let stand, stirring occasionally, for tapioca to soften slightly, 15 minutes (50 minutes for frozen berries; they'll start to look wet). Spread berries level.
2. On a floured surface with a floured rolling pin, roll out pastry to a 14-in. round or 10- by 14-in. rectangle, lifting up pastry and re-flouring underneath if needed to prevent sticking. Trim uneven edges with a knife. Slide a rimless baking sheet under pastry and ease it over berries. Fold edges of pastry under so they're flush with pan or dish, pressing any cracks together. Flute pastry edges with a finger and thumb to seal.
3. Brush crust (but not fluted edges) with milk and sprinkle with remaining 2 tbsp. sugar. Cut about six vents in crust to release steam. Bake until crust is golden brown and filling is bubbling through vents, 50 to 60 minutes; tent with foil if pastry starts to get too brown, and put a rimmed baking sheet underneath if cobbler starts to bubble over. Supporting cobbler underneath, transfer to a rack and let cool at least 45 minutes. Serve warm or cool, with crème fraîche to spoon on top.
***Buy huckleberries from specialty produce markets or pick your own, from your garden if you grow them, or from the wild. (If you pick in the Cascades, respect posted areas reserved for the Yakama Indian Nation. And, unless you have permission, don't pick on tribal land elsewhere.)

PER SERVING 499 CAL., 47% (234 CAL.) FROM FAT; 4.5 G PROTEIN; 26 G FAT (16 G SAT.); 64 G CARBO (3.3 G FIBER); 307 MG SODIUM; 68 MG CHOL.

Buttery pastry

MAKES 1 cobbler crust | 5 minutes

2 cups flour
¾ cup cold butter, cut into 1-in. pieces
1 tsp. *each* sugar and lemon juice
½ tsp. salt
¼ cup plus 1 tbsp. heavy whipping cream

Put all ingredients in a food processor and pulse just until dough comes together and is evenly moistened. Gather into a ball, then shape into a flat disk.

PINEAPPLE SATAYS WITH
COCONUT CARAMEL

Dutch-oven peach cobbler

Peach cobbler baked in a dutch oven—on a camping trip or just in the backyard—gets crusty and golden. (See "How-to: Dutch Oven," page 78.) Pancake mix makes an easy topping.

SERVES 6 | 30 minutes

2 lbs. frozen peaches, thawed
½ tsp. cinnamon
¾ cup sugar, divided
1 cup Hearty Whole-Grain Pancake Mix (recipe below)
    or other pancake mix
¼ cup butter, cut into ⅛-in. pieces
1 large egg
Sweetened whipped cream

1. Prepare fire as directed in "How-to: Dutch Oven," page 78, referring to top and bottom heat cooking. Mix peaches, cinnamon, and ½ cup sugar in a 4- to 6-qt. cast-iron camp dutch oven.
2. Stir pancake mix, butter, egg, remaining ¼ cup sugar, and ¼ cup water in a medium bowl to make a thick and chunky batter. Drop 4 evenly spaced heaping spoonfuls over peaches. Cover.
3. Arrange coals for top and bottom heat cooking and cook, checking every 10 minutes, until batter is puffed, firm, and starting to brown, 20 to 25 minutes. Serve with whipped cream.

PER SERVING 380 CAL., 21% (80 CAL.) FROM FAT; 4.8 G PROTEIN; 9 G FAT (5.3 G SAT.); 73 G CARBO (4.2 G FIBER); 286 MG SODIUM; 57 MG CHOL.

Hearty whole-grain pancake mix

Homemade pancakes (as well as cobbler crust) are just as fast as instant and a whole lot tastier.

MAKES 4 batches (each 8 to 10 pancakes) | 30 minutes

2½ cups all-purpose flour
3 cups whole-wheat flour
¼ cup wheat bran
¼ cup wheat germ
¼ cup packed light brown sugar
1 tbsp. baking powder
1 tbsp. kosher salt
1½ tsp. baking soda
1½ cups buttermilk powder*

1. Whisk together ingredients in a large bowl and transfer to an airtight container.
2. For cobbler, use 1 cup mix for recipe above. **For pancakes,** whisk 2 cups mix in a large bowl with 1¼ cups water, 2 large eggs, and 2 tbsp. oil until mostly smooth. Heat a large cast-iron skillet over medium heat and grease with ½ tbsp. oil. Ladle ⅓-cup portions of batter into skillet, working in batches and adding 1 tsp. oil to skillet between batches. Cook, turning once, until pancakes are golden brown on each side, about 5 minutes total.
***Find at well-stocked grocery stores.

PER 2-PANCAKE SERVING 390 CAL., 41% (162 CAL.) FROM FAT; 13 G PROTEIN; 18 G FAT (3.1 G SAT.); 42 G CARBO (4.5 G FIBER); 307 MG SODIUM; 101 MG CHOL.

Pineapple satays with coconut caramel

Hawaiian pineapples are the Smooth Cayenne variety, which is sweeter than Red Spanish from Central and South America, because picked when ripe. Identify Hawaiian pineapples by their large size, smooth-edged leaves, and deep yellow color. When grilling fruit, be sure to thoroughly clean the grill first so the fruit doesn't taste meaty. You'll need 16 skewers (4 to 6 in. each).

SERVES 4 | 35 minutes, plus 30 minutes to soak skewers if using wooden

1 ripe pineapple
1 cup sugar
¾ cup canned coconut milk
¼ cup unsweetened shredded coconut, toasted*

1. If using wooden skewers, soak skewers 30 minutes. Trim ends from pineapple, then stand it on one end and cut away peel. Halve pineapple lengthwise; reserve half for another use. Halve remaining pineapple lengthwise and cut out core. Cut each pineapple quarter into 4 lengthwise slices, then cut each slice in half crosswise to make 16 thin wedges. Skewer each wedge lengthwise.
2. Combine sugar with ½ cup water in a small saucepan. Bring to a boil, swirling to dissolve sugar; boil, swirling occasionally (do not stir), until just golden and honeylike. Remove from heat and slowly whisk in coconut milk (mixture will bubble furiously).
3. Prepare a charcoal or gas grill for direct high heat (see "How-to: Grilling," page 83). Using a pastry brush, coat pineapple pieces with caramel sauce (you'll have sauce left over). Grill just until grill marks appear, then turn to grill other side until marked, 4 to 5 minutes total. Put skewers on a platter, sprinkle with toasted coconut, and serve with remaining caramel sauce.
***To toast coconut, spread in a shallow layer in a rimmed baking pan and heat in a 300° oven, stirring occasionally, until golden, about 10 minutes.

PER 4-SKEWER SERVING 299 CAL., 30% (89 CAL.) FROM FAT; 1.4 G PROTEIN; 9.9 G FAT (8.3 G SAT.); 56 G CARBO (1.9 G FIBER); 7.3 MG SODIUM; 0 MG CHOL.

Ancho chile pumpkin pie

Denver chef and restaurateur Sean Yontz puts a Latin spin on pumpkin pie by adding a dose of warming ancho chile—which gives more spice than heat—to the traditional cinnamon and nutmeg. Serve with lightly sweetened whipped cream.

SERVES 8 to 10 | 1½ hours, plus 2 hours to cool

9-in. single-crust pie shell, store-bought or Best All-Purpose Pie Crust (at right; use half the dough)
1 can (15 oz.) pumpkin or 1½ cups Pumpkin Purée (at right)
1⅔ cups whipping cream
3 large eggs, beaten to blend
½ cup *each* granulated sugar and firmly packed brown sugar
1 tbsp. ground dried ancho chiles
1 tsp. cinnamon
½ tsp. *each* nutmeg and salt

1. Preheat oven to 375°. Top pie shell with foil and fill halfway with pie weights or dried beans. Bake pie shell on lower rack of oven until edges are dry and barely golden, about 15 minutes. Remove from oven and carefully remove pie weights and foil. Reduce oven temperature to 350°.

From the field: Pumpkins

Winter squashes—including pumpkin—are indigenous to the Americas and were cultivated by Native Americans as one of the "three sisters," the other two being corn and beans. Farmers' markets and U-pick farms have introduced us to a wide range of pumpkins, going far beyond the orange spheres of Halloween.

CINDERELLA Moist and delicate with red-orange skin.

FAIRYTALE Greenish gray outside, deep orange inside.

GOLDEN NUGGET Electric-orange flesh that tastes of carrots and melons.

JACK BE LITTLE Dense and candylike.

KABOCHA Orange, silky textured, and earthy.

LITTLE SUGAR PIE Mild and dryish—good for curries.

MARINA DI CHIOGGIA Knobby and gray-green, with burnt-sienna flesh and a deep, mellow flavor.

2. Meanwhile, in a large bowl, whisk pumpkin, cream, eggs, granulated and brown sugars, ground chiles, cinnamon, nutmeg, and salt until smooth.

3. Pour pumpkin mixture into hot crust and return pie to center rack of oven. Bake until center of pie barely jiggles when shaken, about 45 minutes. Let cool to room temperature on a rack, at least 2 hours.

Make ahead Up to 1 day, chilled.

PER SERVING 329 CAL., 52% (171 CAL.) FROM FAT; 3.3 G PROTEIN; 19 G FAT (11 G SAT.); 36 G CARBO (0.9 G FIBER); 232 MG SODIUM; 112 MG CHOL.

Best all-purpose pie crust

MAKES 1 double crust for a 9-in. pie (or 2 single-crust 9-in. pies), or 2 double crusts for 6-in. pies, or 4 double crusts for 4½-in. pies (measurements from inner rim to inner rim); dough can also be halved | 10 minutes, plus 20 minutes to chill

2 cups flour
1 tsp. salt
¾ cup cold vegetable shortening (or half shortening and half unsalted butter; or all butter; or fresh, unhomogenized lard)

1. Combine flour, salt, and shortening in a medium bowl. Cut shortening into flour with a pastry blender or two knives, one held in each hand and moved crosswise, until particles are the size of peas and mixture looks like fresh, shaggy bread crumbs.

2. Measure 6 tbsp. ice-cold water into a spouted measuring cup. Drizzle 4 tbsp. water over the flour mixture, stirring lightly and quickly with a fork until it just forms a dough. Gently squeeze a handful of dough into a ball; if it won't hold together, sprinkle dough with 1 to 2 more tbsp. water, then mix again until evenly moistened. Press into a ball with your hands and chill at least 20 minutes and up to 2 days.

Pumpkin purée Cut a **Sugar Pie pumpkin** or other deep orange–fleshed squash in half, using a large, heavy knife and a mallet to tap knife through flesh. Scoop out and discard seeds. Rub inside of pumpkin with **vegetable oil.** Set pumpkin cut side down on a rimmed baking sheet. Bake in a 375° oven until very soft when pierced, 45 to 75 minutes. Scoop flesh into a food processor; blend until smooth. If purée is watery, drain in a strainer 30 minutes. A 2-lb. pumpkin makes 1½ to 2 cups.

MEYER LEMON CAKE

Meyer lemon cake

Cooking the lemons before adding them to the cake mellows their flavor. We also like the sharper flavor of regular lemons, which may be substituted in equal amounts.

SERVES 10 | 2 hours

1 lb. Meyer lemons plus 1 tbsp. Meyer lemon juice and 10 thin Meyer lemon slices (or substitute regular lemons)
1½ cups whole almonds
½ cup flour
1 tsp. baking powder
½ tsp. salt
5 large eggs, separated
1¼ cups sugar
½ tsp. almond extract
¼ cup candied or crystallized ginger, finely diced
½ cup powdered sugar

1. Put whole lemons in a large pot over high heat, cover with cold water, and bring to a boil. Lower heat to medium and simmer until soft, about 30 minutes. Drain; transfer lemons to a bowl of ice water. Cut lemons into quarters when they have cooled and gently remove seeds, retaining as much juice as possible. Blend lemons in a food processor until they're a smooth, thick purée.
2. Meanwhile, preheat oven to 350°. Pulse almonds in a food processor until nuts resemble coarse cornmeal. Put in a large bowl and add flour, baking powder, and salt. Stir to combine.

From the orchard: Meyer lemons

Frank Meyer, a "plant explorer" for the U.S. Department of Agriculture, arrived in China in 1905. After battling heat, cold, and at least one assassin, he was traveling near Beijing when he encountered a dwarf lemon tree, most likely a hybrid between a lemon and an orange, with delicate, deep yellow, intensely fragrant fruit. He shipped it back to America.

Meyer's life was short: He drowned, mysteriously, on a return expedition to China. His namesake tree, however, won immortality. California growers deemed the lemons too soft for commercial use, but home

gardeners appreciated the Meyer's nearly year-round bounty, and cooks fell in love with its wonderful aroma and tart-sweet flavor.

For decades the Meyer was a Western gardening secret, but now Meyer sorbets and soufflés star on menus in Manhattan and Miami, and growers in the Central Valley of California are planting orchards to meet rising demand. Meyers (both fruit and zest) can replace standard Eureka lemons in recipes—just keep in mind that Meyers are more fragrant and their tartness is much subtler.

3. Butter and flour a 9-in. pan with a removable rim. Whisk together egg yolks and sugar in another large bowl until thick and pale yellow. Stir in lemon purée and almond extract. Add almond-flour mixture and stir to combine. Stir in candied ginger. Set aside.

4. Beat egg whites in another large bowl until they form firm peaks. Gently fold egg whites into lemon batter. Spread batter in prepared pan.

5. Bake until edge of cake begins to pull away from side of pan, about 1 hour. Cool on a rack for 15 minutes, then remove from pan and cool completely.

6. Combine powdered sugar and lemon juice in a small bowl. Spread glaze over cake. Garnish with lemon slices.

PER SERVING 333 CAL., 36% (119 CAL.) FROM FAT; 8.3 G PROTEIN; 13 G FAT (1.9 G SAT.); 51 G CARBO (4.7 G FIBER); 209 MG SODIUM; 106 MG CHOL.

Tangerine olive oil cake

A glass of Roussanne wine gives this citrusy cake a light floral note. Tangerines (grown in California and, to a lesser extent, Arizona) appear in markets from October through May. For this recipe, use fruit with tightly fitting skins (loose-skinned tangerines are more difficult to zest) and a good olive oil that's been crushed with tangerines, rather than infused after crushing.

SERVES 16 | 1¼ hours

4 large eggs
2 cups sugar, divided
1½ cups Roussanne, divided, or any other floral, fruity
    white wine, such as Viognier
¾ cup tangerine olive oil or very fresh, fruity unflavored
    extra-virgin olive oil
1 tsp. vanilla extract
5 tsp. tangerine zest (from about 4 tangerines),
    plus 1 whole tangerine
2½ cups flour
½ tsp. salt
2¼ tsp. baking powder
Lightly sweetened softly whipped cream (optional)

1. Preheat oven to 350°. Oil and flour a 12-cup Bundt pan.

2. Beat eggs and 1½ cups sugar in a large bowl with a mixer on medium speed until thoroughly combined, about 30 seconds. Add 1 cup Roussanne, the tangerine olive oil, vanilla, and tangerine zest. Beat on low until blended, about 30 seconds.

3. Whisk together flour, salt, and baking powder in another bowl. Add flour mixture to egg mixture and beat on low speed to incorporate. Increase speed to medium and beat 30 seconds, then scrape down side of bowl. Increase speed to medium-high; beat 30 seconds more to blend well. Pour into prepared pan.

4. Bake cake until a wooden skewer inserted in the center comes out clean, about 30 minutes. Let cake cool on rack, 5 minutes. Carefully run a thin knife between cake and pan to loosen, then invert cake onto rack.

5. Peel whole tangerine with a vegetable peeler. Bring remaining ½ cup sugar, ½ cup Roussanne, and the tangerine peel to a simmer in a small saucepan over medium heat and simmer until sugar has dissolved completely, about 5 minutes.

6. Poke deep holes in cake (about 50 holes spaced ½ in. apart) with a thin skewer. Remove peel from hot syrup and spoon syrup over the still-warm cake. Let cool completely and serve with whipped cream if you like.

PER SERVING 287 CAL., 37% (105 CAL.) FROM FAT; 3.7 G PROTEIN; 12 G FAT (1.9 G SAT.); 42 G CARBO (0.7 G FIBER); 161 MG SODIUM; 53 MG CHOL.

TANGERINE
OLIVE OIL CAKE

Tres leches cake with raspberries

The layer cake from Thomas Schnetz, chef-owner of Doña Tomás restaurant in Oakland, California, is his take on the moist, rich Mexican sponge cake of the same name. Like the traditional cake, it's soaked in "three milks" *(tres leches)*— evaporated milk, sweetened condensed milk, and cream. Those three milks come together in a sauce reminiscent of dulce de leche.

SERVES 10 to 12 | 1½ hours, plus 3 hours to cool and chill

CAKE

6 large eggs
1 cup *each* **granulated sugar and flour**
6 tbsp. butter, melted

TRES LECHES SAUCE

1 can (12 oz.) evaporated goat's milk*
6 tbsp. granulated sugar
2 tbsp. light corn syrup
1 cinnamon stick (about 2 in.)
⅛ tsp. baking soda mixed with 2 tsp. water
⅔ cup canned sweetened condensed milk
1¼ cups whipping cream

FILLING & FROSTING

1¾ cups raspberries
1½ tbsp. granulated sugar
2 cups whipping cream
2 tsp. vanilla extract
½ cup powdered sugar

1. Preheat oven to 350°. Butter and flour a 9-in. springform pan (with side at least 2 in. high). Put a medium bowl in the refrigerator to chill.

2. Make cake: Select a large stainless steel bowl (at least 10-cup capacity) that can nest comfortably in a large pot. Fill pot halfway with water and bring to a boil over high heat, then reduce heat to a gentle simmer. In the steel bowl, combine eggs and granulated sugar. Set bowl over water; beat eggs and sugar with a mixer on high speed, until pale and thick enough to fall from a spoon in a wide ribbon, about 10 minutes.

3. Remove bowl from heat. Shake flour through a sieve over egg mixture and fold in gently. Add melted butter and fold in gently until no streaks remain. Scrape batter into pan.

4. Bake until cake is evenly browned, just begins to pull from pan side, and springs back when lightly touched in center, about 40 minutes. Set pan on a rack and let cool at least 10 minutes.

Run a thin knife between cake and pan rim. Remove rim and let cake cool completely.

5. Make tres leches sauce: Combine goat's milk in a large pot (at least 6-qt. capacity) over high heat with granulated sugar, corn syrup, and cinnamon stick. Bring mixture to a boil. Stir in baking soda mixture (sauce will foam up), reduce heat, and simmer, stirring occasionally, until sauce turns a caramel color and has reduced to ¾ cup, 10 to 12 minutes.

6. Remove sauce from heat; discard cinnamon stick. Stir in condensed milk and cream. Use warm (see Make Ahead below).

7. Cut cake in half horizontally with a long, serrated knife. Leave bottom half on pan base. Lift off cake top and set, cut side down, on a flat plate.

8. Put cake bottom (with pan base) on a rack set on a rimmed baking sheet. Poke cake bottom all over with a toothpick, being careful not to poke all the way through. Slowly spoon enough warm tres leches sauce (about 1 cup) over cake bottom to saturate but not cause it to ooze. Let stand until cool, 10 minutes.

9. Make filling: Reserve several raspberries to go on top of cake, then put remaining fruit in a bowl and mix gently with granulated sugar. Set aside. Whip cream in the chilled bowl with a mixer on medium-high speed until cream holds soft peaks and is thick enough to spread. Add vanilla and powdered sugar; mix well.

10. Scoop about 1⅓ cups whipped cream onto cake bottom and spread level to edge. Dot with sugared raspberries, pushing them down into cream. Carefully set cake top, cut side down, onto cake bottom and neatly align. Poke top all over with a toothpick as before, then slowly spoon about 1 cup warm tres leches sauce evenly over cake top to saturate well. Smoothly frost top and side of cake with remaining whipped cream; transfer to a clean serving plate. Cover cake without touching (invert a large bowl over it) and chill at least 2 hours. Cover and chill raspberries if held longer than 2 hours. Cover and chill remaining tres leches sauce.

11. Uncover cake and decorate with reserved raspberries. Serve with remaining tres leches sauce.

*****Evaporated goat's milk (Meyenberg is a popular brand) is sold in most grocery stores. Look in the baking aisle, near the condensed milk.

Make ahead Cake and tres leches sauce, up to 1 day, chilled; reheat sauce before drizzling over cake. Completed cake, up to 1 day, chilled (garnish with raspberries just before serving).

PER SERVING 637 CAL., 55% (351 CAL.) FROM FAT; 10 G PROTEIN; 39 G FAT (24 G SAT.); 62 G CARBO (1.4 G FIBER); 203 MG SODIUM; 244 MG CHOL.

PEAR AND PECAN
UPSIDE-DOWN CAKE

Pear and pecan upside-down cake

When cooked, Bosc pears have an appealing density and graininess that bring the tender bourbon-infused crumb of the cake down to earth beautifully.

SERVES 8 | 2 hours

2 Bosc pears, cored, peeled, and cut into ¼-in.-thick slices
1¼ cups granulated sugar, divided
1 cup chopped pecans, divided
⅓ cup bourbon
1 tsp. salt, divided
¾ cup unsalted butter
½ cup firmly packed light brown sugar
3 large eggs
2 tsp. vanilla extract
1½ tsp. baking powder
½ tsp. baking soda
2 cups flour
¾ cup plain yogurt

1. Preheat oven to 350°. Generously butter a 9-in. round cake pan and arrange pear slices in a pattern on bottom.

2. Bring 1 cup granulated sugar and ½ cup water to a boil in a large frying pan over medium-high heat. Lower heat to maintain a steady simmer and cook, undisturbed, until mixture starts to brown (swirl pan to help mixture brown evenly). When mixture turns a medium amber color, add ½ cup pecans and cook until fragrant but not burning, about 30 seconds. Remove from heat and slowly stir in bourbon and ½ tsp. salt. Pour over pears in buttered pan.

3. Put butter, brown sugar, and remaining ¼ cup granulated sugar in a large bowl. Beat with a mixer on medium speed until smooth and a bit fluffy, about 3 minutes. Add eggs, one at a time, beating well after each addition. Beat in vanilla, baking powder and soda, and remaining ½ tsp. salt. Add half the flour and beat until combined. Beat in half the yogurt. Repeat with remaining flour and yogurt. Stir remaining ½ cup pecans into batter (it will be thick).

4. Drop spoonfuls of batter over pears and sauce in pan and spread evenly. Bake cake until golden and a toothpick inserted in center comes out clean, about 45 minutes.

5. Let cool on a rack 15 minutes. Run a knife between cake and pan sides and invert cake onto a plate or serving platter. Serve warm or at room temperature.

PER SERVING 602 CAL., 45% (270 CAL.) FROM FAT; 7.7 G PROTEIN; 30 G FAT (13 G SAT.); 79 G CARBO (2.7 G FIBER); 506 MG SODIUM; 130 MG CHOL.

Persimmon-currant bread

This delightfully old-fashioned quick bread is moist, firm, and fruit-filled; it keeps well in the refrigerator and the freezer. The recipe can also be adapted, with the addition of more fruits, to create a delicious dark fruitcake (for a boozy version, poke a few holes into the top and drizzle the fruitcake with ¼ cup brandy per week for 2 to 3 weeks).

MAKES 1 tube cake or 2 loaves (12 slices per loaf) | 1¾ hours

2 cups thawed frozen Hachiya persimmon purée*
    or 2 cups fresh persimmon purée mixed with 1 tbsp. lemon juice
2 tsp. baking soda
2 cups dried currants or raisins
2 cups chopped almonds
2 cups sugar
2 tbsp. canola or safflower oil
3 cups flour
2 tsp. cinnamon
1 tsp. salt
¼ tsp. ground cloves
1 cup milk

1. Preheat oven to 325°. Grease a 10-in. tube pan (also called angel food cake pan) or two 8½- by 4½-in. loaf pans. Mix persimmon purée with baking soda in a bowl. Mix currants, almonds, and sugar in a separate large bowl. Stir in oil and persimmon purée.

2. Sift flour in a medium bowl with cinnamon, salt, and cloves, then mix into persimmon mixture alternately with milk. Spoon batter into pan(s).

3. Bake until a toothpick inserted in center comes out clean, about 1½ hours for either cake or loaves. Cool in pan(s) 5 to 10 minutes. Turn out and cool on racks.

*To prepare persimmon purée, use fruit that is soft and almost jellylike throughout. Cut each persimmon in half and, with a spoon, scoop out the flesh. Discard skin, seeds, and stem. Purée a little at a time in a blender or press through a food mill. To freeze purée: Add 1 tbsp. lemon juice to every 2 cups purée. Pack in freezer containers to within 1 in. of top and cover tightly, or spoon into resealable plastic freezer bags. (See note in Persimmon Smoothies, page 29.)

Make ahead Up to 3 weeks, chilled; up to 2 months, frozen (wrap well in plastic and seal in a plastic freezer bag).

PER SLICE 323 CAL., 15% (49 CAL.) FROM FAT; 3.9 G PROTEIN; 5.5 G FAT (0.6 G SAT.); 67 G CARBO (2.2 G FIBER); 207 MG SODIUM; 1 MG CHOL.

Pasilla chile chocolate cake (Pastel de chocolate y chile pasilla)

This unusual recipe matches deep chocolate flavor with the spicy heat of dried chiles, an ancient Aztec pairing. Pasilla or ancho chiles give the chocolate cake a subtle fruit flavor with a hot finish. Agustín Gaytán, an Oakland chef who teaches classes on the cooking of his native Mexico, created the cake for a menu celebrating the holiday Día de los Muertos (Day of the Dead).

SERVES 12 | 1 hour, plus 4½ hours to cool and chill

2½ oz. dried pasilla chiles*, or 2½ oz. dried ancho chiles plus ¼ tsp. cayenne
1 lb. bittersweet or semisweet chocolate, chopped
¾ cup butter, cut into ½-in. chunks, at room temperature
5 large eggs, separated
2 tsp. vanilla extract
1½ tbsp. flour
½ cup firmly packed dark brown sugar or finely crushed piloncillo*
¼ tsp. cream of tartar
Powdered sugar
1 cup whipping cream
1 tsp. vanilla extract or 1 tbsp. coffee-flavored liqueur, such as Kahlúa

1. Heat a large cast-iron frying pan over medium-high heat. When hot, lay chiles in pan in a single layer and toast just until pliable, about 2 minutes (you may have to toast in batches). Wearing rubber gloves, break off stems, shake out seeds, and break chiles into small pieces, dropping into a small bowl; discard stems and seeds. Cover chiles with warm water and let soak until soft, 5 to 7 minutes. Drain chiles and put in a blender with ⅓ cup water; purée, adding up to 1 tbsp. more water as needed to make a thick paste. Push purée through a fine-mesh strainer; discard residue. You need ⅓ cup chile purée. If using ancho chiles, stir cayenne into chile purée.

2. Preheat oven to 425°. Line bottom of a 9-in. round cake pan (with side at least 1½ in. high) with parchment paper.

3. Combine chocolate and butter in a medium metal bowl set over a pan of simmering water. Stir occasionally, just until chocolate and butter are melted and mixture is smooth, about 8 minutes. Remove bowl from pan and whisk in the chile purée, egg yolks, vanilla, and flour until blended.

4. Put brown sugar in a small bowl and stir or whisk to loosen it and break up clumps. In a large bowl, with a mixer on high speed, beat egg whites and cream of tartar until mixture is very frothy and foamy. Gradually add brown sugar to egg whites, beating until stiff, moist peaks form. With a whisk, fold a third of beaten whites into chocolate mixture until well incorporated. Then fold in remaining whites just until blended. Scrape batter into cake pan.

5. Bake cake until it appears set and center barely jiggles when pan is gently shaken, about 15 minutes. Let cool in pan on a rack for about 15 minutes.

6. Run a knife between cake and pan side, then invert cake onto a serving platter. Lift off pan and peel off parchment. Let cake cool about 30 minutes, then reinvert and chill until firm and cold, at least 4 hours; cover cake with plastic wrap (or put in an airtight container) once completely chilled.

7. For best texture, let cake come to room temperature before serving, 45 minutes to 1 hour. Sift powdered sugar lightly over cake (lay a stencil made from light cardboard on cake before sifting the sugar, then carefully lift it off).

PASILLA CHILE CHOCOLATE CAKE (PASTEL DE CHOCOLATE Y CHILE PASILLA)

8. In a medium bowl, beat cream until soft peaks form. Stir in vanilla. Cut cake into wedges and serve each with a dollop of whipped cream.

*If the dried long, dark, skinny chiles labeled pasilla or chile negro are not available, use ancho chiles (dried poblanos), which are sweet and fruity with little heat, and add cayenne to boost the spiciness. Piloncillo, found in Latino markets, is a hard, unrefined Mexican brown sugar shaped into a cone. To use it, put piloncillo in a resealable plastic bag, cover with a kitchen towel, and pound it with a mallet or hammer until finely crushed. **Make ahead** Up to 2 days, chilled.

PER SERVING 434 CAL., 71% (306 CAL.) FROM FAT; 6.5 G PROTEIN; 34 G FAT (19 G SAT.); 35 G CARBO (2.2 G FIBER); 155 MG SODIUM; 142 MG CHOL.

Tart 'n' tangy fro-yo

If you have access to an ice cream maker, it's easy to turn out frozen yogurt that's every bit as good as the refreshing, not-too-sweet kind served at chains like Pinkberry (based in Los Angeles) and Red Mango (its first store opened in L.A.). We prefer a fairly tangy frozen yogurt—add more sugar to sweeten if you wish. And, if you like, top the fro-yo with nuts, fruit, or our sunshiny Apricot Sauce (recipe below).

MAKES About 4¾ cups | 25 minutes, plus 2 hours to freeze

1 container (32 oz.; about 4 cups) plain nonfat yogurt*
About ¾ cup sugar

1. Whisk together yogurt and sugar in a medium bowl until sugar dissolves. Taste and add more sugar if you like.
2. Spoon mixture into an ice cream maker (1½-qt. capacity). Freeze according to manufacturer's directions. Transfer yogurt to a freezer-safe container and freeze until firm, about 2 hours.
*The quality of the yogurt really matters; look for brands without unnecessary additives (we like Straus Family Creamery). **Make ahead** Up to 1 week, frozen. Let soften at room temperature several minutes until easy to scoop.

PER ½-CUP SERVING 121 CAL., 1% (1.8 CAL.) FROM FAT; 5.8 G PROTEIN; 0.2 G FAT (0.2 G SAT.); 24 G CARBO (0 G FIBER); 77 MG SODIUM; 2 MG CHOL.

Apricot sauce

In summer, when apricots are in season, we love cooking up a quick sweet-tart sauce to drizzle onto frozen or fresh yogurt, or ice cream. Depending on the sweetness of the apricots, you may need to adjust the amount of sugar called for in the recipe.

MAKES About 1 cup (8 servings) | 10 minutes

TART 'N' TANGY
FRO-YO WITH
APRICOT SAUCE

1 cup sugar, or more to taste
¾ lb. apricots, pitted and cut into chunks
1 tbsp. lemon juice

1. Bring sugar, ½ cup water, and the apricots to a simmer in a small saucepan. Cover and cook until apricots are completely tender, about 4 minutes.
2. Transfer apricot mixture and lemon juice to a food processor and pulse until sauce is blended but still slightly chunky. Taste and add more sugar if you like. Serve warm or chilled.

PER 2-TBSP. SERVING 31 CAL., 3% (0.9 CAL.) FROM FAT; 0.4 G PROTEIN; 0.1 G FAT (0 G SAT.); 7.8 G CARBO (0.4 G FIBER); 0.3 MG SODIUM; 0 MG CHOL.

Apricot almond swirl ice cream pie

A high-drama way to end an evening, apricot almond swirl ice cream pie is festive and easy. A crunchy, almondy crust of ground amaretti cookies holds vanilla ice cream layered with honey-simmered apricots. Apricot purée is curlicued across the top. We made the pie in an 8-in. cheesecake pan with a removable side, but you could also use a regular 9-in. pie pan and sprinkle the toasted almonds on top instead of pressing into the side. We like Blenheim dried apricots in the pie (see "From the Orchard: Blenheim Apricots," page 180) for their vibrant flavor.

SERVES 12 | 1 hour, plus 4½ hours to freeze

7 oz. amaretti cookies*
4 to 6 tbsp. butter, melted
1¾ cups dried apricot halves, preferably Blenheim

APRICOT ALMOND
SWIRL ICE CREAM
PIE

¾ cup honey
2 qts. vanilla ice cream, divided
1 cup toasted sliced almonds

1. Preheat oven to 325°. Grind cookies into fine crumbs in a food processor. Drizzle in 4 tbsp. melted butter and blend until crumbs start to come together, adding more melted butter as needed. Press crumb mixture firmly over bottom (not side) of an 8-in. cheesecake pan with removable rim. Bake until crust is set, about 10 minutes.

2. Let crust cool completely. Meanwhile, simmer apricots with 1½ cups water and the honey, covered, until apricots are very soft, 15 minutes; let cool. Take 1 qt. ice cream out of freezer to soften.

3. Arrange 1 cup apricots over cooled cookie crust. Blend remaining apricots and liquid in a blender into a thick, pourable purée (add more water if needed). Strain.

4. Stir softened ice cream until smooth. Spread over apricots in crust, set on a plate, and freeze until firm, about 1 hour. Spoon on all but 2 tbsp. apricot purée. Freeze until purée firms, about 1½ hours.

5. Let remaining 1 qt. ice cream soften; spread over purée. Top ice cream with small dollops of remaining purée, then swirl with a chopstick. Freeze 2 hours more.

6. Remove rim of pan and pat almonds firmly into side of pie. (If pie won't come out easily, set it over a bowl of hot water for a couple of minutes; slide a thin knife between the pan edge and crust. Pie should pop right out.) Serve immediately, though pie can be softened for 5 minutes at room temperature if necessary for easier slicing.

*Find crunchy Italian amaretti in well-stocked grocery stores. Alternatively, use almond biscotti and blend in 1 tsp. almond extract with the melted butter in step 1.

Make ahead Once the pie is made through step 5 and fully frozen, keeps up to 4 days, double-wrapped in plastic wrap. Add the almonds just before serving.

PER SERVING 452 CAL., 41% (185 CAL.) FROM FAT; 6.5 G PROTEIN; 21 G FAT (9.9 G SAT.); 63 G CARBO (3 G FIBER); 119 MG SODIUM; 54 MG CHOL.

Berry buttermilk sherbet

The berry flavors come through vividly, with buttermilk for a slight tang and an optional whiff of cardamom for spice.

MAKES 4½ cups | 40 minutes, plus 4 hours to freeze

1¼ cups (6 oz.) raspberries
1¼ cups (6 oz.) blackberries
1¼ cups (6 oz.) blueberries
¾ cup sugar
1 pt. low-fat buttermilk
1 tbsp. lemon juice
¼ tsp. ground cardamom (optional)

1. Purée berries in a food processor, then rub through a fine strainer into a medium bowl. Discard solids. Stir in sugar, buttermilk, lemon juice, and cardamom if you're using it.

2. Freeze mixture in an ice cream maker according to manufacturer's directions.

3. Transfer mixture to an airtight container and freeze until sherbet is firm enough to scoop, at least 4 hours and up to 2 weeks.

PER ½-CUP SERVING 116 CAL., 6% (6.8 CAL.) FROM FAT; 2.4 G PROTEIN; 0.8 G FAT (0.3 G SAT.); 26 G CARBO (2.6 G FIBER); 58 MG SODIUM; 2.2 MG CHOL.

BERRY BUTTERMILK SHERBET

From the field: Berries

Happiest in places that are not too hot and not too cold, berries like plenty of rain in winter, and in summer, warm days and cool nights. Much of the West supplies an ideal climate and soil—especially the California's Central Coast and Oregon's Willamette Valley, America's berry bowl.

BLACKBERRIES In addition to fruit simply labeled "blackberry," look for the following: Boysenberries, a fat, luscious cross between raspberry and wild blackberry, are grown in California and Oregon. Loganberries are another cross of raspberry and wild blackberry, red-black and richly flavored, with good acidity; nearly all are grown in Oregon. Marionberries are considered the queen of blackberries, with deep tangy-sweet flavor; buy frozen or, in Oregon (where they grow), fresh. Olallieberries are long and slender, sweet and full-flavored; cultivated mostly along California's Central Coast. (*Season: May–Sep*)

BLUEBERRIES Oregon is a big producer, third in the nation, after Michigan and New Jersey. With new low-chill varieties, California may be catching up. (*Apr–Sep*)

RASPBERRIES The fruit is more fragile than blackberries. Red raspberries (*May–Sep*) grow along the West Coast from British Columbia to California. Black (*Jul*) are drier and seedier than red; the North American native is a bit tart, with dusky, jammy flavor. Most grow in Oregon. Golden (*May–Sep*) are sweeter and more delicately flavored than red; Washington is the main source.

STRAWBERRIES California leads the world in commercial production, because of staggered planting cycles and varieties bred for shipping. Berries bought near where they're grown, however, have better flavor, as they're picked when riper. (*year-round; peak Apr–Jun*)

Pear sorbet

A light, refreshing way to end a fall or winter meal, this sorbet matches ripe pears with sparkling wine (or pear juice, if you prefer). If you serve sparkling wine alongside, choose one sweeter than that used in the sorbet.*

MAKES About 4 cups | 1 hour

2 lbs. ripe Bartlett or Anjou pears, cored, peeled, and chopped
1½ cups extra-dry or brut sparkling wine*, divided
¾ cup sugar
2 tbsp. light corn syrup

1. Put pears and ¾ cup sparkling wine in a medium pan over medium-high heat. Bring to a boil, then lower heat to maintain a steady simmer. Cook, stirring occasionally, until pears are tender, about 10 minutes. Blend pear mixture and sugar in a blender until smooth. Stir in corn syrup, cover, and chill.
2. When mixture is cold, stir in remaining ¾ cup sparkling wine and freeze in an ice cream maker according to manufacturer's instructions.
3. Serve immediately, or transfer sorbet to a freezer-safe container, cover, and freeze until ready to serve.
*Extra-dry sparkling wine is sweeter than brut. Pear juice may be substituted for the sparkling wine.

PER ½-CUP SERVING 179 CAL., 2% (3.6 CAL.) FROM FAT; 0.4 G PROTEIN; 0.4 G FAT (0 G SAT.); 39 G CARBO (2.5 G FIBER); 8.6 MG SODIUM; 0 MG CHOL.

Coconut avocado ice cream

An elegant celadon green, this ice cream is silky smooth, luscious, and surprisingly good with chocolate sauce. Make it with Hass avocados, which are buttery, with a slightly smoky note. To determine ripeness, squeeze the avocado with your whole hand; a ripe one should have the same give as chilled butter.

MAKES 1 qt. | 40 minutes, plus 2 hours to freeze

2 ripe medium avocados (about 1 lb. total), chilled
¼ cup sugar
1½ tbsp. lemon juice
1 can (14 oz.) sweetened condensed milk
1 can (13.5 oz.) coconut milk*, chilled

1. Put a metal bowl in freezer. Pit avocados. Scoop flesh into a food processor, add sugar and lemon juice, and blend until smooth. Add sweetened condensed and coconut milks and blend.
2. Pour avocado mixture into an ice cream maker and freeze according to manufacturer's instructions.

3. Scrape ice cream into the cold metal bowl. Cover and freeze until firm enough to scoop, about 2 hours.
*For a subtle flavor, buy real coconut milk. For a bigger coconut hit, buy a product made with coconut extract.

PER ½-CUP SERVING 354 CAL., 56% (198 CAL.) FROM FAT; 5.8 G PROTEIN; 22 G FAT (13 G SAT.); 38 G CARBO (1.2 G FIBER); 74 MG SODIUM; 17 MG CHOL.

From the orchard: Pears

Most domestic pears come from Oregon and Washington. Below, a guide to flavor and season.

ANJOU Sweet and juicy, with mild flavor and dense texture; either green or red. Good for eating raw or for cooking. (Season: green, Sep–Jul; red, Sep–May)

ASIAN Its crisp texture and delicate flavor make this pear great for eating raw. There are many varieties; most look like round, beige apples. (Jul–Nov)

BARTLETT The juiciest pear, it turns very soft and loses its shape when cooked. (Aug–Feb)

BOSC Crisp fruit with a soft, grainy texture, russet skin, long and tapered neck, and sweet aroma. Holds its shape when cooked, making it a good candidate for poaching. (Sep–Apr)

COMICE The plump Comice has a deeply indented blossom end, a finer texture than that of other pears, and a gentle sweetness. Juicy; excellent for eating raw. (Sep–Mar)

CONCORDE A slender, long-necked golden green pear. Floral, sweet, and very juicy, yet holds up well to cooking. (Sep–Feb)

FORELLE Small and chubby, with a freckled red blush over its green-gold skin. Crisp and slightly grainy, with a trace of tannin in the skin. (Oct–Mar)

SECKEL A golden, elf-size pear with green freckles. Highly perfumed pale gold flesh. (Sep–Feb)

STARKRIMSON Deep rose–colored skin with dark red freckles. Pale white, very juicy flesh with tingling acidity beneath the sweetness. (Aug–Jan)

Green apple Sauvignon Blanc sorbet

Sauvignon Blanc's characteristic green apple flavors blend seamlessly with the fruit itself. This recipe comes from Amy Traverso, a former *Sunset* food editor and author of *The Apple Lover's Cookbook.*

MAKES 3½ cups | 70 minutes

¾ **cup sugar**
1¼ **lbs. tart green apples, such as Granny Smith, cored and cut into 1-in. chunks (leave peels on), plus apple slices for garnish**
¾ **cup chilled Sauvignon Blanc**
¼ **tsp. kosher salt**
1 **tsp. lemon juice**

1. Heat 1 cup water, the sugar, and apple chunks in a medium saucepan over medium-high heat to a low boil, then reduce heat to low. Partially cover pan and gently simmer until apples are very tender, 10 to 15 minutes. Remove from heat and stir in wine, salt, and lemon juice.

2. Mash mixture through a fine-mesh strainer or a food mill into a bowl to remove skins. Whisk to blend evenly.

GREEN APPLE
SAUVIGNON
BLANC SORBET

3. Pour purée into a shallow 9- by 13-in. baking dish and put in freezer 20 minutes. Freeze in an ice cream maker according to manufacturer's directions. For a firmer texture, transfer to an airtight container and freeze another 8 hours before serving. Garnish with apple slices if you like.

PER ½-CUP SERVING 97 CAL., 0% FROM FAT; 0.1 G PROTEIN; 0 G FAT; 25 G CARBO (0.3 G FIBER); 70 MG SODIUM; 0 MG CHOL.

Mexican chocolate ice cream

When Jen Castle and Blake Spalding opened Hell's Backbone Grill, in Boulder, Utah, in 2000, they found the town was wary of them—especially since they are Buddhists, and Boulder is a traditional Mormon farming community. To warm things up, Castle and Spalding threw an ice cream social, with this recipe as part of the draw. Practically the entire town showed up, and the party has been held annually ever since. For an over-the-top ice cream experience, serve this with Hot Fudge Piñon Sauce and Spiced Piñon Brittle (recipes at right).

MAKES 1½ qts. | 1 hour, plus 6 hours to chill and freeze

½ **vanilla bean**
2 **cups** *each* **heavy whipping cream and whole milk**
9 **oz. Mexican chocolate (such as Ibarra*), coarsely chopped**
2 **oz. unsweetened chocolate, coarsely chopped**
2 **cinnamon sticks**
5 **large egg yolks**
½ **cup sugar**
¼ **tsp. salt**

1. Split vanilla bean lengthwise and scrape out seeds. Bring cream, milk, Mexican chocolate, unsweetened chocolate, cinnamon sticks, and vanilla seeds and pod to a simmer in a 4-qt. saucepan over medium heat. Remove cream mixture from heat and let steep 20 minutes.

2. Meanwhile, whisk egg yolks, sugar, and salt in a medium bowl with a mixer on medium-high speed, until mixture is thick and pale yellow, 2 to 3 minutes.

3. Return cream mixture to medium heat and bring just to a simmer. Remove from heat and pour through a fine-mesh strainer into a clean bowl; discard cinnamon sticks and vanilla pod. Pour ½ cup cream mixture into egg mixture with mixer running on medium speed. Slowly drizzle in remaining cream mixture, continuing to mix as you drizzle.

4. Pour this custard into saucepan. Return to stove and cook over low to medium-low heat, stirring with a wooden spoon, until custard thickens a bit and reaches 170° on an instant-read thermometer.

5. Pour custard into a bowl and set in a larger bowl of ice water. Let custard cool 10 minutes, stirring occasionally. Cover with plastic wrap and chill for at least 1 hour and up to 1 day.

6. Freeze the custard in an ice cream maker (2-qt. capacity) according to manufacturer's instructions. Transfer to a freezer-safe container, cover, and freeze until hardened, at least 5 hours.

*Mexican chocolate, often described on the package as "Mexican chocolate drink mix," is a spiced chocolate bar melted for hot chocolate. It gives the ice cream a pudding-like texture. Look for it (sold in boxes of 5 or 6 disk-shaped bars) at Latino markets or in the Latino-foods aisle of large supermarkets.

Make ahead Up to 2 weeks, frozen airtight (although it's best when fresh).

PER 1/2-CUP SERVING 346 CAL., 62% (216 CAL.) FROM FAT; 3.8 G PROTEIN; 24 G FAT (13 G SAT.); 30 G CARBO (0.7 G FIBER); 86 MG SODIUM; 149 MG CHOL.

Hot fudge piñon sauce

Piñon nuts, grown in the Southwest's high desert, are the intensely flavored cousins of the more common Italian pine nut.

MAKES 4 cups | 35 minutes

1½ cups shelled piñon or pine nuts*
½ cup sugar
¼ cup unsweetened cocoa powder (not Dutch-processed)
¼ tsp. salt
1¼ cups heavy whipping cream
1 cup light corn syrup
1 tbsp. distilled white vinegar
⅓ cup semisweet chocolate chips
2 oz. unsweetened chocolate, coarsely chopped
¼ cup butter
1 tbsp. vanilla extract

1. Pulse nuts in a food processor until coarsely ground (like the texture of couscous).

2. Sift sugar, cocoa, and salt into a medium saucepan. Add ¾ cup warm water and stir to combine. Bring to a simmer over medium heat, stirring until smooth.

3. Add cream, corn syrup, vinegar, and chocolate chips. Raise heat to medium-high and boil, swirling occasionally, until slightly reduced (mixture will be thin and sticky), 8 to 10 minutes; remove from heat. Stir in unsweetened chocolate, butter, vanilla, and ground pine nuts. Serve warm.

*Either Southwest piñons or Italian pine nuts work well.

Make ahead Up to 1 week ahead, chilled. Warm over medium-low heat.

PER 2-TBSP. SERVING 142 CAL., 61% (86 CAL.) FROM FAT; 2 G PROTEIN; 9.6 G FAT (4.4 G SAT.); 14 G CARBO (0.8 G FIBER); 50 MG SODIUM; 17 MG CHOL.

MEXICAN CHOCOLATE ICE CREAM WITH HOT FUDGE PIÑON SAUCE AND SPICED PIÑON BRITTLE

Spiced piñon brittle

Chili powder and cloves give the brittle its subtle spiciness.

MAKES 3 cups | 30 minutes

¾ cup shelled piñon or pine nuts*
1½ cups sugar
1 tsp. chili powder
½ tsp. *each* ground cloves and salt

1. Line a baking sheet with parchment paper and grease paper well. Toast nuts in a small frying pan over low heat until light golden brown, 7 to 10 minutes.

2. In a nonstick frying pan over medium heat, combine sugar, chili powder, cloves, and salt. Cook, stirring constantly, until mixture is smooth and dark brown. Be vigilant, as cooking sugar can burn easily. If it darkens too quickly, remove from heat, stir well, then return to heat. When sugar has entirely melted, stir in nuts.

3. Quickly pour mixture onto parchment and spread ⅛ to ¼ in. thick. Let cool until hard, then break into pieces.

*Either Southwest piñons or Italian pine nuts.

Make ahead Up to 2 weeks; store airtight at room temperature.

PER 1/4-CUP SERVING 147 CAL., 28% (41 CAL.) FROM FAT; 2.1 G PROTEIN; 4.5 G FAT (0.7 G SAT.); 26 G CARBO (0.5 G FIBER); 99 MG SODIUM; 0 MG CHOL.

TRIPLE-BERRY
POPSICLES

BLUEBERRIES IN
BLACK PEPPER–SYRAH
SYRUP

Triple-berry popsicles

One night in 1905, Frank Epperson, an 11-year-old San Francis-can, left a soda-water mix outside with a stick in it. Unusually cold weather froze his drink, creating the first popsicle. Eighteen years later, he decided to market the inadvertent invention, calling it the Epsicle (later renaming it Popsicle). Summer's been better ever since. In our fresh berry version, the seeds remain—we like the texture—but strain them out if you prefer. Pitted cherries or other fruit can be substituted in the recipe. You'll need 10 (4-oz.) popsicle molds and 10 popsicle sticks.

MAKES 10 popsicles | 20 minutes, plus at least 8 hours to freeze

⅔ **cup sugar***
1 cup blueberries
1 cup strawberries, hulled and sliced

1 cup raspberries
¼ cup lemon juice

1. Put sugar and ⅓ cup water in a small saucepan and bring to boil over high heat, stirring until sugar is dissolved. Set this simple syrup aside.
2. Combine blueberries, strawberries, raspberries, and lemon juice in a blender and purée until smooth, about 30 seconds. Add ⅓ cup simple syrup and blend just until combined. (Save remaining syrup for another use, such as sweetening iced tea.)
3. Transfer purée to popsicle molds and freeze 4 hours. Insert popsicle sticks and freeze an additional 4 to 6 hours, or until frozen solid.

***Simple syrup makes the popsicles velvety; if you don't have time to make it, add ⅓ cup undissolved sugar to the purée in step 2.

PER POPSICLE 44 CAL., 4% (1.8 CAL.) FROM FAT; 0.3 G PROTEIN; 0.2 G FAT (0 G SAT.); 11 G CARBO (1.3 G FIBER); 6.4 MG SODIUM; 0 MG CHOL.

Blueberries in black pepper–Syrah syrup

Instead of pairing wine with dessert, why not just put it right in? Syrah often has blueberry flavors among its notes of dark fruit; add a little black pepper to the real berries to clinch the match. Chocolate truffles are terrific alongside.

SERVES 6 | 15 minutes, plus 2 hours to chill

1 bottle (750 ml.) Syrah
¼ cup sugar
1 tsp. vanilla
½ tsp. pepper
3 cartons (6 oz. each) blueberries
Twists of lemon peel

1. In a small pan, combine Syrah and sugar. Boil over medium-high heat (watch to make sure mixture doesn't boil over), stirring often, until reduced by about half, about 15 minutes. Stir in vanilla and pepper and let cool.
2. Put blueberries in a bowl and pour Syrah mixture over them. Chill airtight for at least 2 hours or up to 1 day.
3. Serve in dessert bowls or glasses garnished with lemon twists.

PER SERVING 132 CAL., 2% (2.7 CAL.) FROM FAT; 0.8 G PROTEIN; 0.3 G FAT (0 G SAT.); 23 G CARBO (2 G FIBER); 12 MG SODIUM; 0 MG CHOL.

Coconut triangles (Haupia)

The delicious firm coconut pudding called *haupia* is a traditional Hawaiian sweet that's usually cut into small squares. It shows up at just about every potluck on the Islands.

MAKES 22 to 24 triangles; 12 servings | 10 minutes, plus 1 hour to chill

½ cup sweetened flaked coconut
1 can (14 oz.) coconut milk*, divided
6 tbsp. cornstarch
⅓ cup sugar
½ tsp. vanilla
⅛ tsp. salt

1. Preheat oven to 325°. Spread flaked coconut on a baking sheet and bake until golden brown, 6 to 8 minutes.
2. Grease an 8-in. square baking dish with vegetable oil. Stir ½ cup coconut milk in a small bowl with cornstarch until smooth.
3. Combine sugar in a medium saucepan with 1½ cups coconut milk (if you don't have enough, augment with water). Stir over medium heat until sugar has dissolved. Drizzle cornstarch

COCONUT TRIANGLES
(*HAUPIA*)

mixture slowly into saucepan, whisking, and whisk in vanilla and salt. Cook, whisking vigorously (do not allow to boil), until mixture is very thick, pulling away from pan, and no longer tastes floury, 4 to 6 minutes. Pour into prepared dish and spread evenly. Let cool briefly, then cover with plastic wrap and chill until set, at least 1 hour.
4. Cut haupia into 22 to 24 triangles and sprinkle each with a pinch of toasted coconut.
*Coconut milk is fun to make from scratch and has a more delicate flavor than canned, though it's time-consuming. For a method, go to *sunset.com* and type in *fresh coconut milk*.

PER SERVING 188 CAL., 62% (117 CAL.) FROM FAT; 1.3 G PROTEIN; 13 G FAT (11 G SAT.); 19 G CARBO (0.3 G FIBER); 58 MG SODIUM; 0 MG CHOL.

Chocolate liliko'i parfaits

The tart liliko'i (as the Hawaiians call passion fruit) creates a rich but surprisingly refreshing dessert when it's mixed into a custardy cream and paired with brownies. A native of the Amazon Basin, purple passion fruit arrived on Maui in 1880 and the yellow variety came in 1923. (Find the purée in the freezer section of supermarkets, and in Hawaii, buy fresh fruit at farmers' markets.)

SERVES 12 | 1 hour, plus time to chill

¾ cup *each* **passion fruit purée* and butter**
1 cup sugar
12 large egg yolks
1½ cups whipping cream
2 lbs. brownies*, cut into about 60 cubes (¾ in.)
Chocolate sauce*

1. In a medium, heavy-bottomed saucepan, heat passion fruit purée and butter over medium heat, stirring occasionally, until simmering. In a medium bowl, whisk sugar and yolks together to form a paste. Slowly add passion fruit mixture, whisking constantly, until combined. Pour mixture into pan and cook, whisking constantly, until it just reaches a simmer around the edges, about 4 minutes. Transfer to a glass or ceramic bowl, cover with a piece of waxed paper or plastic wrap pressed against the curd's surface to prevent a skin from forming, and chill until cold and firm, about 1½ hours.
2. Whisk cream with a mixer until soft peaks form. Whisk in one-third of the cold curd; then, using a rubber spatula, fold in the remaining curd. Put 3 or 4 brownie chunks into the bottom of a small glass or dish. Top brownies with about ¼ cup passion fruit cream, another 3 or 4 brownie chunks, then another ¼ cup cream. Repeat with 11 more glasses. Chill until ready to serve.
3. Heat chocolate sauce in a microwave until it is warm and easily drizzles off the back of a spoon. Spoon about 1 tbsp. chocolate sauce over each parfait and serve.

*Find passion fruit purée in the freezer section of most well-stocked grocery stores. Buy brownies and chocolate sauce or make them yourself (see Dark Chocolate–Chunk Brownies and Chocolate Sauce, right).
Make ahead Passion fruit cream 1 day ahead; assemble parfaits 1 day ahead. Add chocolate sauce at the last minute.

PER SERVING 713 CAL., 54% (387 CAL.) FROM FAT; 8.4 G PROTEIN; 43 G FAT (20 G SAT.); 79 G CARBO (1.6 G FIBER); 400 MG SODIUM; 297 MG CHOL.

Dark chocolate–chunk brownies

The sweet half of the sweet-tart chocolate liliko'i parfait can be any brownie, but we love these from Michael Recchiuti, a San Francisco chocolatemaker. The key is to use a distinctive, high-quality bittersweet chocolate. Add walnuts if you like.

MAKES 16 small brownies | 40 minutes, plus 1 hour to cool

10 oz. bittersweet chocolate*
½ cup (¼ lb.) butter, cut into ½-in. chunks
3 large eggs
1 cup sugar
¼ tsp. salt
½ tsp. vanilla
¾ cup flour

1. Chop chocolate into about ½-in. chunks; you should have about 2 cups. Combine half the chocolate and the butter in a microwave-safe bowl. Heat in a microwave oven just until chocolate is soft and butter is melted, 1 to 1½ minutes. Stir until mixture is smooth. Let stand until just warm to touch.
2. Preheat oven to 325°. Beat eggs, sugar, salt, and vanilla in a bowl with a wooden spoon until mixture is smooth. Add chocolate mixture and stir until well blended. Add flour, about a third at a time, stirring after each addition just until blended. Add remaining chopped chocolate and mix just until chunks are evenly distributed.
3. Line bottom and sides of a 9-in. square baking pan with parchment paper, draping it over rim a little. Scrape batter into pan; spread level.
4. Bake just until surface develops a thin crust (like the delicate layer of ice that forms on freezing water) and a fingertip pressed very gently in the center leaves a soft impression, 20 to 25 minutes; take care not to overbake.
5. Cool completely in pan on a rack, at least 1 hour. Lift out brownie on parchment, peel off parchment, and set on a board. Cut into 16 squares (or, for Chocolate Liliko'i Parfaits, left, into ¾-in. cubes).

*Use high-quality bittersweet chocolate such as L'Harmonie, a 64 percent dark chocolate blend from E. Guittard.

PER 2¼-IN. BROWNIE 222 CAL., 53% (117 CAL.) FROM FAT; 4 G PROTEIN; 13 G FAT (7 G SAT.); 27 G CARBO (0.6 G FIBER); 107 MG SODIUM; 56 MG CHOL.

Chocolate sauce In a 2-cup glass measure, combine 1½ cups **semisweet chocolate chips,** ⅔ cup **whipping cream,** and 1 tsp. **vanilla.** Heat in a microwave oven, stirring every 60 seconds, until smooth, 2 to 3 minutes total. If sauce is too thick, stir in a little more cream.

HOMEMADE FORTUNE
COOKIES

Homemade fortune cookies

Watching skilled workers in a fortune cookie factory in San Francisco convinced us that these cookies could be made at home. If you can shape the cookie in less than 15 seconds, you can make fortune cookies. That's about how long it takes the cookie—warm and pliable from the oven—to cool a little and become rigid. It's a little tricky, but you get the hang of it after a while. You'll need cotton gloves from a hardware store or garden shop (to handle the hot cookie quickly) and a muffin pan (to hold the folded cookie in shape for the few minutes it takes to cool).

For the fortunes, rely on your sense of humor or go with poetry or proverbs. Original messages are entertaining, since fate has a curious way of matching fortunes and people. Write the fortunes on 3- by ½-in. slips of paper, then set them near the oven so they're ready to go into the hearts of the cookies.

Fortune cookies were probably a variation on the Japanese *tsujiura senbei,* a fortune-stuffed cracker made of sesame-miso batter. The fortune cookie as we know it came into being in California around 1900—and at least three Asian Americans have claimed its invention: the designer of the Japanese Tea Garden in San Francisco's Golden Gate Park; the founder of the Hong Kong Noodle Company, in Los Angeles; and an owner of the L.A. Japanese pastry shop Fugetsu-Do. The association with Chinese food in America began in the terrible period during World War II when most Japanese Americans were interned. In their absence, Chinese Americans entered the fortune cookie business. Until recently, the cookie was unknown in China.

MAKES About 20 cookies | 1½ hours

1 cup flour, sifted
¼ tsp. salt
2 tbsp. cornstarch
6 tbsp. sugar
7 tbsp. canola oil
⅓ cup egg whites (from 2 or 3 large eggs)

1. Preheat oven to 300°. Line a baking sheet with parchment paper or a silicone baking mat. In a medium bowl, whisk together flour, salt, cornstarch, and sugar. Stir in oil and egg whites; continue stirring until smooth. Gradually blend in 3 tbsp. water.
2. Drop four level 1-tbsp. portions of batter on baking sheet, spacing at least 5 in. apart. With the back of a small offset spatula or a butter knife, spread each evenly into a 4-in. circle. Bake until dark golden brown, about 25 minutes. (Homemade fortune cookies need to be a bit dark in order to bend properly, and will be a little speckled rather than uniformly gold in color.) Meanwhile, set a muffin pan (with cups 2¾ in. wide) next to the oven.
3. Using a wide spatula and wearing cotton gloves, remove a cookie from the oven and flip it onto one gloved hand. Place a fortune in center of cookie while bringing edges together to enclose (don't fold it too firmly in half). Grasp ends of cookie and bend corners down to form a crescent. If cookie hardens too fast or starts to crack, return it to oven for about 1 minute before continuing the fold. Once it's shaped, fit it, ends down, into a muffin cup to fix the shape as it cools. Shape other cookies the same way. Let cool completely. Repeat to bake and shape remaining cookies.

PER COOKIE 84 CAL., 52% (44 CAL.) FROM FAT; 1 G PROTEIN; 5 G FAT (0.4 G SAT.); 8.9 G CARBO (0.2 G FIBER); 36 MG SODIUM; 0 MG CHOL.

Honey caramel nut bars

We paved buttery shortbread with toasted nuts and chewy caramel for a dreamy bar cookie.

MAKES 16 cookies | 1¼ hours

SHORTBREAD
2 cups flour
1 cup cold unsalted butter, cubed
½ cup sugar
¼ tsp. salt

NUT TOPPING
3 tbsp. butter
⅓ cup honey
⅓ cup sugar
¾ cup *each* toasted whole almonds, pecan halves, salted cashews, and salted pistachios

1. Preheat oven to 325°. Make shortbread: Mix flour, butter, sugar, and the salt in the bowl of a mixer on low speed until just blended. Increase speed to medium and mix until dough is no longer crumbly and just comes together.
2. Press dough evenly into a greased 9- by 9-in. baking pan. Bake 10 minutes.
3. Meanwhile, make nut topping: Bring butter, honey, and sugar to a boil in a small saucepan. Remove from heat. Stir in nuts. Carefully spoon mixture over shortbread and continue to bake until nuts are toasted and liquid is bubbling, about 30 minutes. Let cool. Use a serrated knife to cut into 16 squares; cut each square diagonally to make 32 triangles.
Make ahead Store airtight up to 1 week.

PER COOKIE 185 CAL., 63% (117 CAL.) FROM FAT; 2.9 G PROTEIN; 12 G FAT (7.3 G SAT.); 20 G CARBO (0.4 G FIBER); 38 MG SODIUM; 31 MG CHOL.

Nanaimo bars

Bliss in a bar, these have a nutty layer, a creamy layer, and a dark chocolate layer. Near Nanaimo, on Vancouver Island, British Columbia, Mabel Jenkins devised the recipe in the early 1950s.

MAKES 16 bars | 30 minutes, plus at least 2 hours to chill

10 graham crackers (5- by 2¼-in. each)
⅔ cup toasted slivered almonds
1 cup plus 2 tbsp. unsalted butter, divided
¼ cup granulated sugar
5 tbsp. Dutch-process unsweetened cocoa powder
1 large egg, beaten
1 cup sweetened shredded dried coconut
2 tbsp. plus 2 tsp. heavy whipping cream
2 tbsp. vanilla custard powder, such as Bird's
2 cups powdered sugar
2 oz. *each* semisweet and bittersweet chocolate

1. Put graham crackers and almonds in a food processor and grind into fine crumbs. Bring ½ in. water to a simmer in a medium saucepan or bottom of double boiler. Nest bowl or top of double boiler over, but not touching, the water; then add ½ cup butter, granulated sugar, and cocoa. When butter

NANAIMO BARS

is melted, whisk in egg and cook, whisking, until mixture thickens. Remove from heat. Stir in graham cracker mixture and coconut. Press very firmly into an ungreased 8-in. square baking pan.
2. Make middle layer: With a mixer on medium speed, beat ½ cup butter with the cream, custard powder, and powdered sugar in a medium bowl until light and fluffy. Spread over bottom layer.
3. Make top layer: With the double-boiler setup used in step 1, melt chocolate with remaining 2 tbsp. butter over simmering water. Let cool until warm but still liquid, then pour over middle layer. Chill bars until cold, then cut into 16 bars.

PER BAR COOKIE 305 CAL., 61% (186 CAL.) FROM FAT; 2.7 G PROTEIN; 21 G FAT (12 G SAT.); 30 G CARBO (1.9 G FIBER); 35 MG SODIUM; 51 MG CHOL.

Bizcochitos

New Mexico's official state cookie, the bizcochito, or at least its forebear, arrived in the 16th century with the Spanish. The cookie—often made with lard, though we opted for butter—is traditional at New Mexican Christmas and wedding celebrations.

MAKES 55 2¾-in. cookies | 2 hours

1 cup (½ lb.) butter, at room temperature
1 cup sugar, divided
1 large egg, beaten
2 tbsp. brandy
1½ tsp. anise seeds
3 cups flour
1 tsp. *each* baking powder and cinnamon

1. Beat butter and ¾ cup sugar with a mixer on medium speed until smooth. Beat in egg, brandy, and anise seeds. Stir or beat in flour and baking powder until well blended.
2. Divide dough in half. Flatten each portion into a 1-in.-thick circle. Put in airtight containers; freeze until firm, 30 minutes.
3. Preheat oven to 300°. Unwrap dough. On a lightly floured surface, with a floured rolling pin, roll a portion of dough at a time to ⅛ in. thick. Cut dough with floured 2¾-in. cookie cutters.
4. Transfer cookies to buttered or parchment paper–lined baking sheets, spacing cookies about 1 in. apart. Pat scraps into a ball; repeat rolling and cutting. Mix remaining ¼ cup sugar and the cinnamon in a bowl. Sprinkle cinnamon sugar over cutouts.
5. Bake until golden, about 15 minutes. Transfer cookies with a spatula to racks to cool. If hot cookies start to break, slide a thin spatula underneath to release, let rest on sheets to firm up, 5 minutes, then transfer to racks to cool completely.

PER COOKIE 75 CAL., 43% (32 CAL.) FROM FAT; 0.9 G PROTEIN; 3.7 G FAT (2.3 G SAT.); 9.4 G CARBO (0.2 G FIBER); 35 MG SODIUM; 13 MG CHOL.

Sopaipillas

Light, airy pillows of fried dough, drizzled with honey or sprinkled with powdered sugar, *sopaipillas* are one of the Southwest's great treats. They're rewarding to make because the process seems magical: When you push the pieces of dough into the hot oil, they puff up like balloons.*

MAKES 2 dozen sopaipillas | 1 hour, plus 1 hour to rise

1 package (2¼ tsp.) active dry yeast
1½ cups milk
3 tbsp. fresh lard or vegetable shortening
2 tbsp. granulated sugar
1 tsp. salt
4½ to 5 cups all-purpose flour, divided
1 cup whole-wheat flour
Vegetable oil
Powdered sugar and/or honey

SOPAIPILLAS

1. Dissolve yeast in ¼ cup warm (100° to 110°) water in a large bowl for 5 minutes. Combine milk in a small saucepan with lard, sugar, and salt; heat to 110° and add to dissolved yeast. With a wooden spoon or mixer fitted with a dough hook, stir 3 cups all-purpose flour and all the whole-wheat flour into the yeast mixture; beat until dough is stretchy. Stir in another 1 cup all-purpose flour to form a stiff dough.

2. Beat on medium speed until dough pulls cleanly from side of bowl and is no longer sticky (or knead until no longer sticky). If it's still sticky, add more all-purpose flour, 1 tbsp. at a time, and beat or knead until dough is smooth. Put dough in an oiled bowl and turn over to coat top.

3. Cover dough with plastic wrap (or a clean towel topped by a plate) and let stand in a warm (about 80°) place until doubled in bulk, about 1 hour. Punch down dough. If you're not ready to cut and fry dough, cover again and chill up to 1 day.

4. Knead dough on a lightly floured work surface to expel air. Cut into four equal portions. Working with a portion at a time, roll into a circle about ⅛ in. thick; with a floured knife, cut into six equal wedges and lay in a single layer on a floured rimmed baking sheet. Cover with plastic wrap and chill while you roll and cut remaining dough.

5. Pour enough oil into a 5- to 6-qt. pan to come 1½ to 2 in. up side of pan. Heat over medium-high heat until a deep-fry or candy thermometer registers 350°, then adjust heat to maintain temperature. Drop one or two pieces of dough into oil. With a slotted spoon, push them down into oil until they begin to puff. Fry until pale gold on both sides, turning over as needed to brown evenly, 2 to 3 minutes total. Drain in paper towel–lined pans. Fry remaining sopaipillas the same way.

6. Serve immediately, or keep first ones warm in a 200° oven until all are fried. Serve plain or dusted with powdered sugar, and set out honey for drizzling.

*For a shortcut, replace the homemade dough with two 1-lb. loaves of thawed frozen white or wheat dough; then, in step 4, cut each loaf in half and roll out thinly. The sopaipillas are quite large, so feel free to halve the recipe.

Make ahead Through step 3, up to 1 day, chilled; cut and fry dough the next day. Fried sopaipillas, up to 1 day, stored at room temperature; up to 2 months, frozen in resealable plastic freezer bags. To reheat fried sopaipillas, thaw (if frozen) and bake, uncovered, in a single layer on baking sheets in a 300° oven, turning once, just until warm, 5 to 8 minutes. Do not overheat or they'll harden.

PER SOPAIPILLA 197 CAL., 55% (108 CAL.) FROM FAT; 3.3 G PROTEIN; 11 G FAT (2.1 G SAT.); 20 G CARBO (1.2 G FIBER); 105 MG SODIUM; 3.7 MG CHOL.

Candied orange peels

Citrus fruit is winter's gift, and candying the peels is an old Christmas tradition—especially in the Western citrus-growing states of California and Arizona.

MAKES 6 cups peel | 5 hours, plus 8 hours to dry

5 lbs. oranges (or grapefruits, lemons, limes, or any other kind of citrus), washed and dried
8 cups sugar, divided

1. Halve and juice fruit; reserve juice for another use. Put peels in a large pot and cover with cold water. Bring to a boil and cook 3 minutes. Drain. Return peels to pot, cover with cold water, bring to a boil, cook 3 minutes, and drain. Repeat once more.
2. Spread peels on baking sheets and let stand until cool enough to handle, 20 minutes. With a soup spoon, scrape inner membranes from peels; discard. Cut peels into ¼-in. strips; set aside.
3. In a large, heavy-bottomed pot over high heat, bring 8 cups water and 6 cups sugar to a boil. Add peels, then reduce heat to maintain a steady, gentle simmer; cook, stirring occasionally, until peels are tender, sweet, and translucent, about 3 hours. (Don't let sugar brown or caramelize.)
4. Drain peels and spread on racks set over baking sheets. Let stand until dry, at least 8 hours.
5. Toss a handful of peels at a time with remaining 2 cups sugar. Shake off excess sugar and put peels in an airtight container.

PER ¼-CUP PEEL 126 CAL., 1% (0.9 CAL.) FROM FAT; 0.2 G PROTEIN; 0.1 G FAT (0 G SAT.); 32 G CARBO (0 G FIBER); 0 MG SODIUM; 0 MG CHOL.

Almond toffee

Our homage to Almond Roca (inspired by English toffee and made in Tacoma, Washington, since 1923) is a fresh, buttery, super-nutty interpretation. A candy thermometer is useful to gauge doneness, but you can also go by color; look for a rich caramel shade in step 2.

MAKES 3 lbs. | 45 minutes, plus 1½ hours to cool

1½ cups whole raw almonds
3¾ cups sugar
1½ cups (¾ lb.) butter
¼ cup light corn syrup
½ tsp. salt
1 tbsp. vanilla
12 oz. bittersweet or semisweet chocolate, finely chopped

1. Preheat oven to 350°. Put almonds in a baking pan and bake, shaking pan occasionally, until golden beneath skins, 10 to

CANDIED ORANGE
PEELS

12 minutes. When cool enough to handle, finely chop nuts.
2. Insert a candy thermometer in a large, heavy-bottomed stainless steel pan over medium-low heat. Add sugar, butter, corn syrup, salt, and ¾ cup water and cook, stirring, until butter is melted and sugar is dissolved. Increase heat to medium-high and cook, stirring occasionally, until mixture is deep golden brown (300° on thermometer), 10 to 15 minutes. Remove from heat and carefully stir in vanilla and half the almonds (mixture may bubble up). Immediately pour into a 10- by 15-in. baking pan with 1-in.-high sides. Let cool at room temperature until set, at least 30 minutes.
3. Meanwhile, put chocolate in the top of a double boiler or in a heatproof bowl. Bring a few inches of water to a simmer in bottom of double boiler or a pan that the bowl can nest in; remove pan from heat. Place chocolate over water and let stand, stirring occasionally, until melted, 10 minutes.
4. Pour chocolate over cooled toffee; spread level. Sprinkle remaining almonds over chocolate. Let cool at room temperature until set, 1 hour (or chill 30 minutes).
5. Gently twist pan to release toffee; chop or break into chunks.

PER OZ. 158 CAL., 54% (85 CAL.) FROM FAT; 1 G PROTEIN; 9.4 G FAT (5 G SAT.); 20 G CARBO (0.4 G FIBER); 85 MG SODIUM; 16 MG CHOL.

CHERRY DUTCH BABY
recipe on page 233

Breakfast & Brunch

Reinventing tradition comes naturally to us Westerners, even in the morning. We freshen up streusel coffee cake with ripe, juicy local figs, add hunks of Dungeness crab to eggs Benedict, and bake chiles rellenos in rich, custardy eggs rather than frying them. Some icons we leave untouched, though—like huevos rancheros or the fruit-studded Dutch baby. Why mess with perfection?

Fresh fig coffee cake

This moist, seriously scrumptious coffee cake modernizes its retro roots (it calls for cornflakes!) with a basketful of ripe figs. Dozens of fig tree varieties grow in California, most bearing fruit twice a year—look for figs in the market briefly in early summer and again in late summer to early fall.

SERVES 12 | 1¼ hours

1 lb. (about 15 large) fully ripe figs
2 tbsp. lemon juice
¼ cup granulated sugar
1 tbsp. finely shredded lemon zest
½ cup raisins
1 large egg
¾ cup firmly packed brown sugar, divided
½ cup canola or safflower oil
½ tsp. vanilla extract
2 cups flour
1 tbsp. baking powder
¾ tsp. cinnamon, divided
½ tsp. salt
¼ tsp. *each* ground cloves and ground ginger
¾ cup milk
1 cup lightly crushed cornflakes
½ cup chopped walnuts
3 tbsp. butter, melted

1. Preheat oven to 350°. Grease an 8-in. square baking pan. Cut stems and blossom ends off figs. Coarsely chop (you should have about 3½ cups). Combine figs in a medium saucepan with lemon juice, granulated sugar, lemon zest, raisins, and ¼ cup water. Cook over medium heat, stirring often, until thick and reduced to 3 cups, about 30 minutes (as mixture thickens, reduce heat to prevent scorching). Let cool.
2. Beat egg, ½ cup brown sugar, the oil, and vanilla in a large bowl until smooth.
3. Stir together flour, baking powder, ½ tsp. cinnamon, the salt, cloves, and ginger in a medium bowl. Add flour mixture and milk alternately to egg mixture, blending well after each addition.
4. Combine cornflakes in a small bowl with walnuts, butter, and remaining ¼ cup brown sugar and ¼ tsp. cinnamon.
5. Spoon half the batter into pan. Spread fig mixture over top, then spoon remaining batter evenly over fig layer. Sprinkle cornflake mixture over top. Bake until a toothpick inserted in center comes out clean, 45 to 50 minutes. Cool slightly or completely. Cut into squares and serve warm or cool.

PER SERVING 433 CAL., 35% (152 CAL.) FROM FAT; 5.4 G PROTEIN; 17 G FAT (3.4 G SAT.); 68 G CARBO (3.8 G FIBER); 326 MG SODIUM; 27 MG CHOL.

Hazelnut-butter muffins

Oregon produces 99 percent of American hazelnuts. Celebrate the crop—and your health—with a tender, tasty muffin in which hazelnut butter is swapped in for regular butter, boosting monounsaturated fat and decreasing the saturated fat. Buy nuts that are stored airtight, as they'll be fresher-tasting, and keep them airtight in your freezer.

MAKES 18 muffins | 45 minutes

1 cup hazelnut flour* (also called hazelnut meal)
1 cup whole-wheat flour
1 cup all-purpose flour
1 tbsp. baking powder
¾ tsp. salt
½ cup hazelnut butter*
1 cup hazelnut milk*
2 large eggs
¼ cup vegetable oil
1 tsp. cinnamon
1 tsp. vanilla extract
½ cup packed light brown sugar
¼ cup honey
6 tbsp. roughly chopped toasted hazelnuts

1. Preheat oven to 375°. Whisk together flours, baking powder, and salt in a medium bowl.
2. Whisk together hazelnut butter, hazelnut milk, eggs, oil, cinnamon, vanilla, brown sugar, and honey in a large bowl until blended.
3. Gently fold flour mixture into wet ingredients until just combined. Divide mixture evenly among 18 paper-lined muffin cups and sprinkle 1 tsp. chopped hazelnuts over each muffin. Bake until golden and a toothpick inserted in the center of a muffin comes out clean, about 20 minutes. Cool on a wire rack.
*Hazelnut flour, milk, and butter are sold at Whole Foods Market and some natural-foods stores. Other nut flours, milks, and butters, such as almond, can be substituted.

PER MUFFIN 222 CAL., 52% (117 CAL.) FROM FAT; 4.8 G PROTEIN; 13 G FAT (1.24 G SAT.); 24 G CARBO (2.9 G FIBER); 130 MG SODIUM; 24 MG CHOL.

HAZELNUT-BUTTER
MUFFINS

BLUE CORN PANCAKES

Blue corn pancakes

The Arizona Inn in Tucson serves its thin, slightly crunchy blue corn pancakes with prickly pear syrup; they're delicious with maple syrup too.

MAKES 10 pancakes; 4 to 5 servings | 25 minutes

1 cup blue or yellow cornmeal
1 cup flour
1 tbsp. baking powder
1/2 tsp. salt
1 1/2 cups milk
2 large eggs, beaten to blend
6 tbsp. butter or margarine, melted
Vegetable oil

1. In a bowl, mix cornmeal, flour, baking powder, and salt. Whisk in milk and eggs just until blended, then whisk in melted butter.
2. Preheat oven to 200° if you plan to keep pancakes warm while cooking batches. Heat a griddle or large frying pan over medium heat; when hot, oil lightly. Adjust heat if necessary to maintain temperature. Pour batter in 1/3-cup portions onto griddle and cook until pancakes are browned on the bottom and edges begin to look dry, about 2 minutes. Turn with a wide spatula and cook until brown on bottom, 1 1/2 to 2 minutes more. Coat pan with more oil as necessary to cook remaining pancakes.
3. Serve pancakes as cooked or keep warm in a single layer on baking sheets in oven for up to 15 minutes.

PER SERVING 410 CAL., 46% (189 CAL.) FROM FAT; 10 G PROTEIN; 21 G FAT (11 G SAT.); 45 G CARBO (2.1 G FIBER); 727 MG SODIUM; 132 MG CHOL.

From the field: Blue corn

Native Americans cultivated blue corn in the Southwest for centuries, and today it appears there in everything from breads to stews to drinks. One of the more spectacular dishes comes from the Hopi, who use finely ground blue cornmeal to make *piki*, a crisp, tissue-paper-thin bread rolled up like a scroll.

Blue corn can be found as flour and cornmeal, in hues ranging from pale lilac to deep purple, and has a sweet, nutty flavor. It's higher in protein than either white or yellow dent corn (the kind we eat most often), and the blue pigment—called anthocyanin—is thought to be a potent antioxidant.

Sourdough pancakes

Tender pancakes with a pleasant, mild tang borrow from the Northern California sourdough tradition. The recipe comes from reader Jennifer Roeser, of Mammoth Lakes, California.

MAKES 10 or 11 pancakes; 4 servings | 15 minutes

2 tbsp. sugar
1 tsp. *each* salt and baking powder
About 3 tbsp. canola or safflower oil
Overnight Starter (recipe below)
2 large eggs
1/2 tsp. baking soda
Butter
Maple syrup or powdered sugar

1. Add sugar, salt, baking powder, and 3 tbsp. oil to overnight starter; mix well. Add eggs and beat to blend. Mix baking soda with 1 tsp. water; stir into batter. (Batter will be thin.)
2. Heat a griddle or large frying pan over medium heat; when hot, oil lightly. Pour batter in 1/3-cup portions onto griddle, spacing about 1 1/2 in. apart. Cook until bubbles form on top of pancakes and bottoms are browned, about 1 minute. Turn with a wide spatula and cook until brown on bottom, about 1 minute more. Coat pan with more oil as necessary to cook remaining pancakes. Serve hot with butter and syrup or powdered sugar.

PER SERVING 439 CAL., 28% (123 CAL.) FROM FAT; 11.8 G PROTEIN; 13.9 G FAT (1.8 G SAT.); 65 G CARBO (2 G FIBER); 927 MG SODIUM; 107 MG CHOL.

Overnight starter In a large bowl, mix 2 cups **flour,** 1 1/4 cups warm (100° to 110°) water, and 1/2 cup **Sunset's Reliable Sourdough Starter** (recipe, on page 175, requires 1 week to make; or use 1/2 cup store-bought starter*). Cover with plastic wrap and let stand in a warm place (about 80°) at least 8 and up to 24 hours. Mix 1/2 cup overnight starter into reliable sourdough starter to replenish it for future use. Use remaining overnight starter to make pancakes; cover reliable sourdough starter and store it in refrigerator.
*Although it's gratifying to make your own sourdough starter, you can also order starter through *amazon.com* or from Goldrush (*goldrushproducts.com*).

EGGS BENEDICT
WITH CRAB

Eggs Benedict with crab

The quintessential brunch dish gets a West Coast twist with Dungeness crab. Creamy, and bright with lemon, this dish also makes an elegant supper when paired with a green salad.

SERVES 6 | 45 minutes

6 large egg yolks
¼ cup lemon juice
2 tbsp. Dijon mustard
1½ cups unsalted butter, melted
½ tsp. salt
⅛ tsp. pepper
⅛ tsp. cayenne
6 English muffins
3 cups Dungeness crab, picked over and at room
    temperature
12 large eggs

1. Make hollandaise sauce: In the bottom of a double boiler or in a medium saucepan, bring 1 in. of water to a simmer over high heat and adjust heat to maintain simmer. Put egg yolks, lemon juice, and mustard in top of a double boiler or in a round-bottomed medium bowl, and set over simmering water. Whisk yolk mixture to blend.
2. Whisking constantly, add melted butter in a slow, steady stream (it should take about 90 seconds). Cook sauce, whisking, until it reaches 140°, then adjust heat to maintain temperature (remove from simmering water if necessary). Add salt, pepper, and cayenne and continue whisking until thick, about 3 minutes. Adjust seasonings to taste. Remove from stove and set aside.
3. Preheat oven to 450°. Split English muffins and arrange on a baking sheet in a single layer. Bake muffins until toasted, about 5 minutes.
4. Put 2 muffin halves on each plate and top each with crab.
5. Poach eggs: Bring 1 in. water to a boil in a large pan. Lower heat so that small bubbles form on the bottom of the pan and break to the surface only occasionally. Crack eggs into water 1 at a time, holding shells close to the water's surface and letting eggs slide out gently. Poach eggs, in two batches to keep them from crowding, 3 to 4 minutes for soft-cooked. Lift eggs out with a slotted spoon, pat dry with a paper towel, and place an egg on each crab-topped muffin half.
6. Top each egg with 2 to 3 tbsp. reserved hollandaise sauce and serve hot.

PER SERVING 833 CAL., 68% (567 CAL.) FROM FAT; 36 G PROTEIN; 63 G FAT (34 G SAT.); 28 G CARBO (1 G FIBER); 949 MG SODIUM; 837 MG CHOL.

ASPARAGUS AND EGG TOASTS

Asparagus and egg toasts

The green spears of asparagus, a big California crop, spell spring.

SERVES 2 | 30 minutes

2 tbsp. extra-virgin olive oil, divided
8 asparagus spears, ends trimmed
1 rosemary sprig (about 3 in. long)
2 slices crusty bread, such as ciabatta, sliced 1 in. thick
¼ cup grated parmesan cheese
2 large eggs
4 thin slices (2 oz.) prosciutto
¼ tsp. *each* salt and pepper

1. Heat 1 tbsp. oil in a frying pan over high heat. Add asparagus; sauté until tender, about 5 minutes. Set aside. Add rosemary and remaining oil to pan and cook, 2 minutes; discard rosemary. Toast bread in oil in pan, turning once, 1 minute. Sprinkle parmesan on bread; cook until bread browns slightly, 2 minutes. Set aside.
2. Reduce heat to medium and in the same pan, gently fry eggs to your liking. Top each toast with 2 slices prosciutto and 4 asparagus spears. Set an egg on each; sprinkle with salt and pepper.

PER SERVING 456 CAL., 51% (232 CAL.) FROM FAT; 27 G PROTEIN; 26 G FAT (6.7 G SAT.); 30 G CARBO (2.1 G FIBER); 1,661 MG SODIUM; 237 MG CHOL.

Speedy huevos rancheros with the works

Westerners have enthusiastically adopted (and adapted) a handful of Mexican foods as our own, including huevos rancheros. It's little wonder that we love our eggs with salsa, beans, and rice—before being handed over to the United States in 1848, an enormous sweep of land that included California and the Southwest was simply the northern reaches of Nueva España and then Mexico. And today, 31 percent of California's inhabitants are Mexican American or Mexican (as are 26 percent of Arizonans and 29 percent of New Mexicans). Make the salsa, beans, and rice for this recipe ahead of time, and you can put together a restaurant-style bonanza in less than half an hour.

SERVES 4 | 25 minutes, plus 1 hour for salsa, beans, and rice

2 cups Salsa Ranchera (recipe at right) or store-bought
  hot red salsa
Vegetable oil for frying
8 corn tortillas (5 to 6 in. wide)
8 large eggs
About 1 cup coarsely shredded jack cheese
¼ cup chopped green onions
3 tbsp. shredded *cotija* or parmesan cheese
2 tsp. dried Mexican oregano or 2 tbsp. chopped cilantro
Chorizo Refried Beans (recipe at right)
Mexican Red Rice (recipe on page 229)

1. Put four heavy plates in oven and preheat to 200°. Heat salsa in a small saucepan over low heat, covered.
2. Fill a large frying pan with ½ in. oil and heat over medium heat until handle of a wooden spoon bubbles when you stand it in oil. Remove plates from oven. Using tongs, fry each tortilla 2 seconds per side. Drain against side of pan, then overlap 2 tortillas on each warm plate. Pop in oven to keep warm.
3. Reduce heat to medium low. Cook 4 eggs, spooning oil over yolks to set them, 2 minutes for firm whites and runny yolks.
4. Spoon about 3 tbsp. warm salsa onto each plate of tortillas. Using a slotted spatula or spoon, transfer 2 eggs to each of two warm plates, draining eggs against side of pan first; top each pair of eggs with another 3 tbsp. salsa. Keep warm in oven while frying and plating remaining 4 eggs. (You may have to increase the heat a little for second batch.)
5. Sprinkle eggs with jack cheese, onions, cotija, and oregano. Add beans and rice alongside; top beans with jack cheese.

PER SERVING 661 CAL., 36% (238 CAL.) FROM FAT; 36 G PROTEIN; 26 G FAT (11 G SAT.); 71 G CARBO (16 G FIBER); 458 MG CHOL.

Salsa ranchera

An all-purpose salsa that's good even when tomatoes aren't in season.

MAKES 2 cups | 15 minutes

2 serrano chiles
2 tbsp. canola oil
½ white onion, finely chopped
2 cups canned fire-roasted tomatoes (such as
  Muir Glen brand)
2 garlic cloves, minced
Mexican-style hot sauce (optional)

1. Toast serrano chiles in a dry frying pan until brown spots appear all over. Stem and finely chop chiles.
2. Put oil and onion in a medium pan over medium heat and cook until onion softens, about 5 minutes. Meanwhile, put tomatoes, garlic, and chiles in a blender and pulse a few times (leave mixture a bit chunky).
3. Pour tomato mixture into pan with onions and cook 5 minutes over high heat to thicken. Taste and add hot sauce if you like.

PER ¼ CUP 48 CAL., 66% (32 CAL.) FROM FAT; 0.7 G PROTEIN; 3.5 G FAT (0.3 G SAT.); 3.5 G CARBO (0.7 G FIBER); 146 MG SODIUM; 0 MG CHOL.

Chorizo refried beans

Chorizo makes these velvety beans rich and spicy. If you don't want chorizo—or you're in a rush—just microwave the beans, thinned with a bit of water, while you're making the huevos.

SERVES 4 to 6 | 15 minutes

6 oz. Mexican chorizo*, squished out of casing and crumbled
¼ cup canola oil
2 cans (15 oz. each) refried pinto beans
¼ cup coarsely shredded jack cheese (optional)

Cook chorizo in oil in a large nonstick frying pan over low heat, mashing, until it starts to brown, about 5 minutes. Add beans and a few tbsp. of water to thin them if necessary. Heat for a few minutes, stirring occasionally. Spoon onto warm plates and top with cheese if you like.

*Good Mexican chorizo is available at butcher shops or Latino markets. Avoid the very soft chorizo sold in plastic casings; it tends to break down in cooking and can have an unpleasant flavor.

PER SERVING 310 CAL., 61% (189 CAL.) FROM FAT; 13 G PROTEIN; 21 G FAT (4.8 G SAT.); 21 G CARBO (7.6 G FIBER); 546 MG SODIUM; 25 MG CHOL.

New Mexican red chile breakfast burritos

Smothered in an earthy, medium-hot red chile sauce, these morning marvels are stuffed with scrambled eggs, country-style hash browns, and chorizo. Try them for dinner too.

MAKES 6 burritos | 1¼ hours

1 tsp. corn oil
1 cup chopped yellow onion
2 garlic cloves, minced
2 tbsp. flour
⅔ cup ground New Mexico or California chiles*
1½ cups chicken broth
Salt
1½ lbs. thin-skinned potatoes
¾ lb. Mexican chorizo* or 10 slices bacon
6 flour tortillas (10 in. wide)
Pepper
8 large eggs
1 cup shredded sharp cheddar cheese
½ cup sour cream (optional)
⅓ cup sliced green onions

1. In a small pan over medium heat, heat oil; add yellow onion and garlic and cook, stirring, until onion is limp, 6 to 8 minutes. Add flour and ground chiles; toast, stirring, 1 to 2 minutes, until fragrant. Add broth and 1½ cups water and cook, stirring, until sauce is smooth and bubbling, about 8 minutes. Reduce heat to low and simmer, stirring occasionally, 10 minutes. Season to taste with salt. Set aside and keep warm.

2. Peel potatoes, halve lengthwise, and cut crosswise into ⅓-in.-thick slices. Put in a medium pan with water to cover and bring to a boil over high heat. Reduce heat and simmer, covered, until tender when pierced, about 6 minutes. Drain.

3. Meanwhile, remove casings from chorizo and crumble into a large frying pan (or cut bacon into 1½-in. pieces and put in pan). Cook over medium-high heat, stirring often, until meat is brown and crisp, 8 to 10 minutes. With a slotted spoon, lift meat to paper towels; drain fat from pan, reserving 4 tbsp. (If chorizo is very finely crumbled, drain fat through a strainer.) If necessary, add vegetable oil to equal 4 tbsp.

4. Preheat oven to 350°. Seal tortillas in foil and warm in the oven until hot, about 10 minutes. Meanwhile, return 2 tbsp. reserved fat to frying pan. Add potatoes and cook over medium-high heat, turning occasionally, until well browned, about 10 minutes (you may need to add another 1 tbsp. fat to pan). Season with salt and pepper, remove from pan, and keep warm.

5. In a medium bowl, beat eggs to blend. Coat pan with 1 tbsp. reserved fat. Add eggs; cook, stirring, over medium heat until softly set, about 2 minutes. Add salt and pepper to taste.

6. Lay tortillas flat. Toward one edge of each, fill with potatoes, eggs, and chorizo. Fold over sides and roll up tightly to enclose. Put each on an ovenproof plate and ladle chile sauce on top. Sprinkle with cheddar; bake until cheese melts, 2 to 3 minutes.

7. Dollop sour cream on burritos, if you like, and sprinkle with green onions.

*It's crucial to use fresh chile powder in this recipe—anything more than a year old will taste dusty and flat. For especially rich chile flavor, buy ground Dixon or Chimayo chiles, available from *peppahead.com* (see "From the Field: New Mexico Chiles," page 104). Find good Mexican chorizo at butcher shops or Latino markets. Avoid the very soft chorizo in plastic casings; it tends to break down in cooking and can have an unpleasant flavor.

PER BURRITO 618 CAL., 44% (270 CAL.) FROM FAT; 26 G PROTEIN; 30 G FAT (10 G SAT.); 62 G CARBO; 926 MG SODIUM; 317 MG CHOL.

Mexican red rice (*Arroz rojo*)

This is exactly the kind of red rice you find in Mexican restaurants: slightly sweet, slightly sticky, and lip-smacking good.

MAKES 4 cups; 4 to 6 servings | 1 hour

1 cup long-grain rice
2 tbsp. vegetable oil
1 white onion, chopped
1 garlic clove, minced
1 small serrano chile, stemmed and finely chopped
1 can (about 15 oz.) diced or chopped tomatoes, drained
1½ cups reduced-sodium chicken broth
¾ tsp. kosher salt

1. Put rice in a pot and cover with 1 in. cold water. Swish around until water is milky; pour off water. Repeat rinsing twice. Drain rice well in a colander and let dry 15 minutes.

2. Heat oil in a medium saucepan over medium-low heat. Add rice and cook, stirring, 2 minutes; increase heat to medium and cook until rice starts to turn golden, 6 to 8 minutes, stirring often.

3. Meanwhile, in a blender, purée onion, garlic, chile, and tomatoes. Add purée to rice, increase heat to high, and cook, stirring, until purée has been more or less absorbed, about 3 minutes (it will bubble and spatter). Stir in broth and salt and bring to a boil. Reduce heat to low, cover, and simmer until liquid has been absorbed, 15 to 20 minutes. Let stand 10 minutes.

PER SERVING 186 CAL., 24% (45 CAL.) FROM FAT; 4.2 G PROTEIN; 5.3 G FAT (0.9 G SAT.); 30 G CARBO (1.3 G FIBER); 433 MG SODIUM; 6.3 MG CHOL.

Chilaquiles

Made with torn-up leftover tortillas fried in oil and then simmered in spicy tomato or tomatillo sauce, soft, luscious chilaquiles are a breakfast staple in Northern Mexico, Southern California, and the Southwest—and are usually eaten with eggs. The name comes from the Aztecan Nahuatl phrase *chila-quilitl* ("chile and herb").

SERVES 4 | 1 hour

12 dried California or New Mexico chiles (5 to 6 in. each, about 2½ oz. total)
2 cups chicken broth
1 onion (½ lb.), peeled
½ lb. firm-ripe Roma tomatoes
3 garlic cloves, unpeeled
½ tsp. *each* ground cumin and dried oregano
12 corn tortillas (6 in. wide)
Vegetable oil
6 oz. thinly sliced *asadero** or jack cheese
1 tbsp. minced cilantro
Salt

1. Preheat oven to 250°. Wipe chiles with a damp cloth. Discard stems and seeds. Lay chiles in a 10- by 15-in. baking pan. Bake until fragrant, about 3 minutes.
2. Combine chiles and broth in a bowl. Heat in a microwave until boiling, about 3 minutes. Let stand until chiles are soft, 10 to 15 minutes.
3. Meanwhile, cut onion crosswise into ½-in.-thick slices. Core tomatoes and cut in half lengthwise. Lay onion, tomatoes (cut sides up), and garlic cloves, slightly separated, in a 10- by 15-in. pan. Broil 4 to 6 in. from heat until vegetables are browned, 8 to 10 minutes; remove from pan as they are browned. Peel garlic.
4. Purée chiles and broth in a blender until smooth (or purée chiles in a food processor, then gradually process in broth). Rub mixture through a fine-mesh strainer back into bowl; discard chile residue.
5. Return chile purée to blender or food processor; add onion, tomatoes, garlic, cumin, and oregano and process until smooth; return mixture to bowl.
6. Stack tortillas and cut into ½-in.-wide strips. Heat ½ in. oil in a large frying pan over high heat until hot. Add about one-third of tortilla strips. Cook, stirring often, until strips are golden and crisp, about 2 minutes. With a slotted spoon, transfer strips to paper towels to drain. Repeat to cook remaining tortillas. Add tortilla strips to sauce in bowl and mix.

7. Preheat oven to 400°. Scrape mixture into a shallow 2-qt. baking dish. Cover with cheese. Bake until cheese has melted and chilaquiles are hot in the center, 8 to 10 minutes. If desired, broil 4 to 6 in. from heat until cheese is lightly browned, about 4 minutes more.
8. Sprinkle chilaquiles with cilantro. Add salt to taste.
*Asadero (grilling) cheese is a dryish fresh Mexican cheese that melts nicely when heated. Find it at Mexican markets.
Make ahead Sauce, through step 5, up to 1 day, chilled. Fry tortillas up to 1 day ahead; store airtight at room temperature.

PER SERVING 581 CAL., 56% (324 CAL.) FROM FAT; 22 G PROTEIN; 36 G FAT (10 G SAT.); 51 G CARBO (9.4 G FIBER); 470 MG SODIUM; 37 MG CHOL.

Hangtown fry

Placerville, California, in the Sierra Nevada foothills, saw three famous hangings during the Gold Rush, giving it the name Hangtown. The most-oft-told story about the origin of Hangtown fry describes a prospector rushing into the town's El Dorado Hotel, plunking his nuggets on the bar, and ordering the priciest dish in the place. The cook came up with a concoction using the most expensive items in his larder: oysters, bacon, and eggs.

SERVES 1 | 20 minutes

2 slices bacon
2 large eggs
1 tbsp. milk
Salt and pepper to taste
1 tbsp. chopped flat-leaf parsley (optional)
Dash or 2 of Worcestershire
5 oz. shucked medium oysters (at least 6 oysters)
Toast and lemon wedges

1. In a frying pan over medium-high heat, cook bacon until brown and crisp; transfer to paper towels to drain.
2. Meanwhile, whisk together eggs, milk, salt, pepper, parsley if using, and Worcestershire. Chop oysters into ¾-in. pieces, add to bacon drippings, and cook 1 minute; transfer to bowl of eggs.
3. Return bacon to pan, spacing slices about 3 in. apart. Pour egg mixture over top and, using 1 or 2 wide spatulas, keep the egg mixture pulled in toward the center of pan as it cooks. When omelet is set on bottom, turn it over, trying to keep it as intact as possible. This should expose the bacon on top. Cook about 1½ minutes more. Transfer bacon-topped omelet to a warm plate and serve with toast and lemon wedges.

PER SERVING 475 CAL., 65% (307 CAL.) FROM FAT; 32 G PROTEIN; 34 G FAT (11 G SAT.); 8.9 G CARBO (0 G FIBER); 681 MG SODIUM; 526 MG CHOL.

CHILAQUILES

BAKED CHILES
RELLENOS

Baked chiles rellenos

We reimagined fried chiles rellenos by baking the stuffed chiles in rich, cheesy eggs. Bonus: You can make the dish a day ahead.

SERVES 8 | 1¼ hours

8 poblano chiles
¾ lb. Mexican chorizo*
1 cup crumbled *cotija* cheese*
1 tsp. minced oregano leaves
12 large eggs
⅓ cup flour
1 tsp. baking powder
½ tsp. salt
1 cup finely shredded jack cheese, divided

1. Preheat broiler. Lay chiles in a single layer on a baking sheet. Broil about 4 in. from heat until chiles are blistering and black, about 5 minutes. Turn chiles over and broil until blistering and black all over, about 5 minutes. Put chiles in a large metal bowl and cover with foil or plastic wrap. Let stand 15 minutes.

2. Peel chiles and discard skins. Cut off stem ends and discard; remove seeds and ribs. Set chiles aside on layers of paper towels to dry.

3. Meanwhile, remove chorizo from casings. In a large frying pan over medium-high heat, cook chorizo, stirring occasionally to break up meat, until cooked through, about 4 minutes.

4. Preheat oven to 375°. In a large bowl, mix chorizo, cotija, and oregano. Stuff chiles with chorizo mixture and set them in an 8- by 12-in. baking dish.

5. In a large bowl, whisk eggs until uniform in color and texture. Whisk in flour, baking powder, and salt. Sprinkle chiles with half the jack cheese. Pour egg mixture over chiles and sprinkle with remaining jack.

6. Bake until top starts to brown and eggs are set but still soft, about 30 minutes.

*Good Mexican chorizo is available at butcher shops or Latino markets. Avoid the very soft chorizo sold in plastic casings; it tends to break down in cooking and can have an unpleasant flavor. Find cotija, an aged, crumbly white Mexican cheese, at Latino markets and well-stocked grocery stores. If you can't find it, substitute finely shredded parmesan.

Make ahead Through step 5, up to 1 day, chilled (bake an extra 5 to 10 minutes).

PER SERVING 444 CAL., 63% (279 CAL.) FROM FAT; 28 G PROTEIN; 31 G FAT (13 G SAT.); 14 G CARBO (1.4 G FIBER); 1,093 MG SODIUM; 378 MG CHOL.

Cherry Dutch baby

Most likely based on the German pancake *Apfelpfannkuchen*, the Dutch (a mispronunciation of *Deutsch*, meaning German) baby is said to have been dreamed up at Manca's Café, in Seattle, in the early 1900s. Until Manca's closed, in 1988, the Dutch baby remained a signature dish. The recipe is also good with other fruits if cherries aren't in season. (Photo on page 218.)

SERVES 4 | 30 minutes

¾ cup flour
2 tbsp. granulated sugar
¾ cup milk
3 large eggs
¼ tsp. salt
¼ cup butter
2 cups pitted sweet cherries
Powdered sugar
Lemon wedges

1. Preheat oven to 425°. In a blender, blend flour, granulated sugar, milk, eggs, and salt until smooth.

2. Melt butter in a 12-in. ovenproof frying pan over high heat. Add cherries; cook until warm, about 2 minutes. Pour in batter. Bake until golden brown and puffed, about 20 minutes. Serve with a dusting of powdered sugar and a squeeze of lemon juice.

PER SERVING 348 CAL., 44% (152 CAL.) FROM FAT; 9.6 G PROTEIN; 17 G FAT (9.4 G SAT.); 41 G CARBO (2.3 G FIBER); 298 MG SODIUM; 194 MG CHOL.

From the farm: Better eggs

A fresh egg from a hen that spends most of its time pecking in open pasture is a wonderful thing: deeply flavorful, with a bright yellow (sometimes almost orange) yolk. Studies suggest that pasture-raised eggs are better for you too, higher in omega-3s and vitamins, lower in fat and cholesterol. Though "pasture-raised" isn't a government-approved definition, it's accepted to mean that the chicken got most of its nutrition from foraging on grass and insects, with some grain to supplement. The label "cage-free" doesn't specify feed and doesn't necessarily mean that the bird spent time outside. Pick up a dozen pasture-raised eggs and treat yourself.

Pork and shrimp dumplings (Shu mai)

Shu mai are one of the mainstays of a dim sum feast. Cantonese-style dim sum—savory and sweet snacks, eaten with tea—arrived in America in the 1840s with the wave of Chinese immigrants seeking fortune in the California Gold Rush. San Francisco's Chinatown, the first in the country, probably opened teahouses not long after, according to Chinatown historian Shirley Fong-Torres. And from those small beginnings grew the great urban dim sum palaces we know today, where waiters push steaming carts past diners eager to snag a dumpling or fried tidbit. We're used to thinking of dim sum as a restaurant experience, but it's possible—and fun—to make dumplings yourself.

MAKES 24 dumplings | 45 minutes

½ lb. ground pork
¼ lb. peeled deveined shrimp, chopped
3 green onions, finely chopped
One 2-in.-piece ginger, peeled and finely shredded
     (about 2 tbsp.)
1 tbsp. rice wine, sake, or fino sherry
1 tbsp. soy sauce
24 gyoza (round Japanese potsticker) wrappers
1 large egg, beaten

1. Mix pork, shrimp, green onions, ginger, rice wine, and soy sauce in a bowl.
2. Lay out gyoza wrappers on a flat, clean surface. Top each with 1 tbsp. pork-shrimp mixture. Brush edges of wrapper with beaten egg. Pull each wrapper up around filling like a bowl; pinch pleats around filling (see photo at right). Put shu mai in parchment-lined steamers (see "How-to: Steam Dim Sum," below).
3. Steam dumplings until cooked through, about 10 minutes. Serve immediately.

PER DUMPLING 49 CAL., 43% (21 CAL.) FROM FAT; 2.7 G PROTEIN; 2.3 G FAT (0.8 G SAT.); 3.3 G CARBO (0.1 G FIBER); 82 MG SODIUM; 21 MG CHOL.

How-to: Steam dim sum

Measure your steamer basket and choose a pot with a diameter at least 2 in. wider. To keep dumplings from sticking, cut a circle of parchment paper 1 in. smaller in diameter than the basket (so steam can flow up around the edges) and fit it in. Pour water into the pot to a depth of 1 in. and bring to a boil over high heat. Fill the basket with dim sum, then set it in the pot. Cover and cook, adding hot water as needed.

Spicy rice balls

Often known as "porcupine balls," these dumplings aren't common on dim sum carts, but their intense flavor and easy preparation made them a hit in our test kitchen.

MAKES About 32 dumplings | 40 minutes, plus 2 hours to soak rice

½ cup short-grain, sweet, or sticky rice
½ lb. ground pork
1 large egg
2 tbsp. soy sauce
½ tsp. sugar
5 green onions, finely chopped
One 1-in.-piece ginger, peeled and finely shredded
     (about 1 tbsp.)
1 bird's eye or serrano chile, seeded and minced

1. Soak rice in 2 cups water in a medium bowl for 2 hours. Drain; spread rice on a plate.
2. Combine pork, egg, soy sauce, sugar, green onions, ginger, and chile in a bowl. Cover and chill until rice is ready.
3. Divide pork mixture into 32 pieces. Roll into balls, then roll balls in rice. Put balls in parchment-lined steamers (see "How-to: Steam Dim Sum," below left). Cook until rice is tender and pork is cooked, about 10 minutes. Serve immediately.

PER BALL 29 CAL., 38% (11 CAL.) FROM FAT; 1.7 G PROTEIN; 1.2 G FAT (0.4 G SAT.); 2.7 G CARBO (0.1 G FIBER); 70 MG SODIUM; 11 MG CHOL.

Naked shrimp and chive dumplings

These dumplings are just the filling, no wrapper. Serve with soy sauce, ponzu (Japanese citrus sauce), or other dipping sauce.

MAKES 24 dumplings | 30 minutes

½ lb. peeled deveined shrimp, divided
1 bunch chives, minced (about ⅓ cup)

In a food processor, chop ¼ lb. shrimp until not quite a smooth paste. Add remaining ¼ lb. shrimp and pulse to chop coarsely. Pulse in chives. Divide mixture into 24 pieces. Roll each piece into a ball and place in parchment-lined steamers (see "How-to: Steam Dim Sum," left). Steam dumplings until cooked through, about 10 minutes. Serve immediately.

PER DUMPLING 20 CAL., 15% (3 CAL.) FROM FAT; 3.9 G PROTEIN; 0.3 G FAT (0.1 G SAT.); 0.2 G CARBO (0 G FIBER); 28 MG SODIUM; 29 MG CHOL.

NAKED SHRIMP AND
CHIVE DUMPLINGS

PORK AND SHRIMP
DUMPLINGS (*SHU MAI*)

SPICY RICE BALLS

FIG-BLACKBERRY-
ORANGE QUICK JAM
recipe on page 241

PEACH-RASPBERRY-
LAVENDER QUICK
JAM *recipe on page 241*

Preserves & Pantry

Westerners are rediscovering the satisfaction of a pantry stocked with their own jewel-like jams, as well as a fridge full of luscious homemade yogurt and cheese. We draw on the DIY history of resourceful Native Americans, Oregon Trail pioneers, World War II families, and '60s back-to-the-land homesteaders.

Cherry-rhubarb quick jam

The rhubarb gives the cherries a slightly savory depth. Ah Bing, a Chinese American orchardist, helped breed the Bing cherry in Oregon in 1875.

MAKES 4 jars (8 oz. each) | 35 minutes

2½ tbsp. (half a 1¾-oz. package) Sure-Jell pectin
    labeled "For less or no sugar needed recipes"
1½ cups sugar, divided
2½ cups coarsely chopped Bing cherries (from about 1 lb. fruit)
1 cup chopped rhubarb stalks
1¼ cups unsweetened cherry juice
1½ tbsp. lemon juice
¼ tsp. butter (prevents foaming)

1. Combine pectin and ¼ cup sugar in a 5- to 6-qt. pot. Stir in cherries and rhubarb, then cherry and lemon juices and butter. Bring mixture to a brisk boil over high heat, stirring often.
2. Add remaining 1¼ cups sugar. Return jam to a brisk boil, stirring. Cook, stirring constantly, 1 minute. Remove from heat.
3. Ladle jam into heatproof jars and close with lids. Let cool to room temperature, inverting jars occasionally to distribute fruit.
Make ahead Up to 1 month, chilled.

PER TBSP. 26 CAL., 1% (0.3 CAL.) FROM FAT; 0.1 G PROTEIN; 0 G FAT; 6.5 G CARBO (0.2 G FIBER); 4.4 MG SODIUM; 0 MG CHOL.

Spiced plum quick jam

Peppercorns and other spices play up the plums' natural spiciness. To keep this and Cherry-Rhubarb Quick Jam (above) longer than a month, follow steps in "How-to: Canning," page 242.

MAKES 4 jars (8 oz. each) | 40 minutes

About 1¾ cups apricot nectar, preferably unsweetened
1 tsp. whole allspice
2 cinnamon sticks
4 green cardamom pods, cracked
1 tsp. peppercorns
2½ tbsp. (half a 1¾-oz. package) Sure-Jell pectin
    labeled "For less or no sugar needed recipes"
1½ cups sugar, divided
3½ cups chopped ripe plums (from about 1¼ lbs. fruit)
1 tbsp. lemon juice
¼ tsp. butter (prevents foaming)

1. Bring 1¾ cups apricot nectar and spices to a boil in a small saucepan over high heat, covered. Reduce heat; simmer 10 minutes. Strain. Measure 1¼ cups, adding more juice if needed.
2. Combine pectin and ¼ cup sugar in a 5- to 6-qt. pot. Stir in

plums, then spiced nectar, lemon juice, and butter. Bring mixture to a brisk boil over high heat, stirring often.
3. Add remaining 1¼ cups sugar. Return jam to a brisk boil, stirring. Cook, stirring constantly, 1 minute. Remove from heat.
4. Ladle jam into heatproof jars, distributing fruit evenly, and close with lids. Let cool to room temperature, inverting jars occasionally to distribute fruit.
Make ahead Up to 1 month, chilled.

PER TBSP. 26 CAL., 2% (0.4 CAL.) FROM FAT; 0.1 G PROTEIN; 0.1 G FAT (0 G SAT.); 6.7 G CARBO (0.2 G FIBER); 4.5 MG SODIUM; 0 MG CHOL.

Pear chutney

Margaret Freed of Merced, California, makes hundreds of jars of preserves for her church's bazaar every year. She gave us this recipe, which she got from her friend Phyllis Warford.

MAKES 6 to 7 pts. | 2¾ hours

1 cup blanched almonds
6 lbs. ripe pears
1¾ cups coarsely chopped red bell pepper (about 14 oz.)
4 cups sugar
1½ cups cider vinegar
2⅓ cups golden raisins (15 oz.)
2⅔ cups chopped dried apricots (15 oz.)
1⅔ cups chopped red onions (about 14 oz.)
2 tbsp. chopped crystallized ginger
1 tsp. *each* ground cinnamon and ground allspice
½ tsp. *each* ground cloves and garlic salt
¼ tsp. cayenne

1. Follow "Get Ready" directions in "How-to: Canning" (page 242), using 7 pint-size jars, with rings and lids.
2. Preheat oven to 350°. Put almonds in a baking pan and bake until golden, shaking pan occasionally, 8 to 10 minutes.
3. Peel, core, and chop pears (you should have 10½ cups).
4. Combine all ingredients in a large pan. Measure volume: Insert a clean wood ruler into pan and measure mixture height; remove ruler. Bring mixture to a boil over high heat, stirring occasionally. Reduce heat to medium-high and cook, stirring often, until reduced by a third (measure with ruler), about 1¼ hours.
5. Follow steps in "Fill and Seal Jars" (page 242), leaving ½-in. headspace in each jar. Follow steps in "Process Jars" (page 243), processing 10 minutes (at altitudes of 1,000 to 6,000 ft., 15 minutes; above 6,000 ft., 20 minutes).
Make ahead Store up to 1 year.

PER TBSP. 36 CAL., 10% (3.6 CAL.) FROM FAT; 0.3 G PROTEIN; 0.4 G FAT (0 G SAT.); 8.4 G CARBO (0.6 G FIBER); 4 MG SODIUM; 0 MG CHOL.

SPICED PLUM
QUICK JAM

CANNED HEIRLOOM
TOMATOES

Peach-raspberry-lavender quick jam

Lavender contributes a floral note; omit if you like. To keep longer, follow "How-to: Canning," page 242. (Photo on page 236.)

MAKES About 3 cups | 45 minutes, plus 2 hours to chill

2 tsp. dried culinary lavender buds
1 lb. ripe peaches (about 5), peeled*, pitted, and
    chopped into 1-in. pieces
3 oz. red raspberries
1½ cups sugar
3 tbsp. lemon juice

1. Put lavender in a bowl. Pour ¼ cup boiling water over buds; steep 10 minutes. Strain into a bowl and set aside; discard buds.
2. Combine fruit, sugar, and lemon juice in a 4-qt. pan over medium-high heat. Bring to a boil and cook, stirring often, until liquid has the consistency of thick maple syrup, about 14 minutes. Stir in lavender water and boil, stirring often, until mixture reaches desired thickness*, about another 2 minutes.
3. Remove jam from heat and let cool at room temperature 15 minutes. Chill, covered, at least 2 hours before eating.
*To peel peaches, immerse in boiling water for about 30 seconds. Lift out with a slotted spoon, let cool, then pull off skin. To determine whether jam has cooked long enough to thicken to your taste, put a tablespoonful onto a plate you've chilled for 20 minutes in the freezer. The jam will cool and thicken to its final consistency.
Make ahead Up to 1 month, chilled.

PER TBSP. 28 CAL., 0% FROM FAT; 0.1 G PROTEIN; 7.3 G CARBO (0.2 G FIBER); 0.1 MG SODIUM; 0 MG CHOL.

Fig-blackberry-orange quick jam

An intensely fruity jam that's delicious in yogurt. To keep longer, follow "How-to: Canning," page 242. (Photo on page 236.)

MAKES About 3 cups | 25 minutes, plus 2 hours to chill

2 lbs. (about 2 pts.) ripe figs, stems trimmed and fruit quartered
6 oz. (½ pt.) blackberries
¾ cup sugar
½ cup fresh orange juice
1½ tsp. finely shredded orange zest

1. In a 4-qt. pan over medium-high heat, combine figs, blackberries, sugar, and orange juice. Bring to a boil and cook, stirring

often, until liquid has consistency of thick maple syrup, about 12 minutes. Stir in orange zest. Boil, stirring often, until mixture reaches desired thickness (test a tablespoonful on a plate you've chilled 20 minutes in the freezer), about another 2 minutes.
2. Remove jam from heat; cool at room temperature 15 minutes. Chill, covered, at least 2 hours in refrigerator before eating.
Make ahead Up to 1 month, chilled.

PER TBSP. 29 CAL., 3% (0.9 CAL.) FROM FAT; 0.2 G PROTEIN; 0.1 G FAT (0 G SAT.); 7.4 G CARBO (0.8 G FIBER); 0.2 MG SODIUM; 0 MG CHOL.

Canned heirloom tomatoes

Use vine-ripened tomatoes and you'll have summer in a jar. **Important note** It's essential that you acidify the tomatoes with bottled (not fresh) lemon juice or citric acid (each has a standardized acidity), and that you not increase the amount of herbs or add other ingredients. Buy citric acid in the baking aisle.

MAKES 6 to 7 qts. | 3 hours

17 lbs. ripe yellow or red heirloom tomatoes
14 tbsp. bottled ReaLemon lemon juice or 3½ tsp. citric acid,
    such as Fruit Fresh (see note, above)
7 tsp. salt (optional)
7 thyme sprigs (3 to 4 in. long; optional)

1. Follow "Get Ready" directions in "How-to: Canning" (page 242), using 7 wide-mouthed quart-size jars, with rings and lids.
2. Meanwhile, peel tomatoes: Fill a large saucepan three-quarters full of water and bring to a boil. Cook one layer of tomatoes at a time in water, until skins split or peel easily with a knife, 20 to 40 seconds. Remove from water with a slotted spoon; let cool, then core, pull off skins, and trim any brown areas, working over a bowl to catch juice.
3. Put 2 tbsp. lemon juice or ½ tsp. citric acid in each jar. Add 1 tsp. salt if you like. Follow steps under "Fill and Seal Jars" (page 242), cutting tomatoes to fit into jars if needed, and pushing them into jars to fill compactly; leave ½-in. headspace. Pushing will create juice; if needed, add more juice from bowl so tomatoes are covered. Using a fork handle, poke 1 thyme sprig into each jar if you like. Release air, wipe rims, and seal as directed.
4. Process as directed in "Process Jars" (page 243), boiling 1 hour and 25 minutes (add 5 minutes for every 3,000 ft. in altitude above sea level). It's okay if jars leak a little.
5. Turn off heat and let jars stand in water in canner 5 minutes.
Make ahead Store up to 1 year.

PER ½-CUP SERVING 28 CAL., 13% (3.6 CAL.) FROM FAT; 1.1 G PROTEIN; 0.4 G FAT (0.1 G SAT.); 6.3 G CARBO (1.6 G FIBER); 14 MG SODIUM; 0 MG CHOL.

How-to: Canning

Canning is the best way to make summer's fresh produce last through the year. With a few tools and some basic techniques under your belt, you'll be on your way to a pantry and refrigerator filled with glowing jams, rich red tomatoes, and piquant pickles to enjoy and share.

Get Ready

1. GATHER EQUIPMENT. Canning jars with matching metal lids and rings, a 20-qt. boiling-water canner with rack, a wide-mouthed funnel, tongs, and a jar lifter. Most hardware stores carry all these items.

2. FILL CANNER WITH WATER AND HEAT IT UP. The canner should be two-thirds full for pint and half-pint jars; half-full for quart jars. Set rack on pan rim and cover pan. Over high heat, bring water to a boil (or to 180° to 185° for pickles); this takes 30 to 45 minutes.

3. MEANWHILE, WASH canning jars and rings in a dishwasher and hand-wash lids; drain. For jam (and jelly, if you make it), sterilize the washed jars too: When water in canner boils, place jars on rack, lower into water, and boil for 10 minutes (at elevations of 1,000 ft. or higher, add 1 minute for each 1,000-ft. increase above sea level). Reduce heat to a simmer and keep jars in water until needed. Nest lids inside rings in a saucepan and cover with water. Heat until small bubbles form (about 180°; do not boil). Remove pan from heat and cover.

4. RINSE OR WIPE produce clean, then prepare as recipe directs.

Fill and Seal Jars

1. PUT FOODS INTO JARS through a wide funnel or arrange with fingers, leaving the headspace (the distance between jar rim and food) specified by the recipe. If the last jar isn't completely full, let cool, then serve or chill; do not process.

2. RELEASE AIR BUBBLES in chunky mixtures: Gently run a knife around inside of jars. Wipe jar rims and threads with a clean, damp cloth so that lids will seal.

3. CENTER THE CLEAN LIDS ON JARS so sealing compound on lids touches jar rims. Screw metal rings on firmly, but don't force.

Before getting started, assemble all your equipment.

Arrange the fruit or vegetables in the canning jar.

Run a knife around the inside of the jar to release any air bubbles. Use a plastic knife, if possible, to avoid nicking glass.

Process Jars

1. LOWER JARS ON RACK INTO WATER. The water should cover jars by at least 1 in.; add hot water as needed during processing. Cover canner and return water to a boil (or to 180° to 185° for pickles). Cook for time specified in recipe.

2. LIFT RACK WITH JARS onto edge of canner, using tongs and a hot pad. Using jar lifter, transfer jars to kitchen towels on a work surface. Don't tighten rings. Cool completely at room temperature. You may hear a "ping" as jars form a seal.

3. PRESS ON THE CENTER OF EACH LID. If it stays down, the jar is sealed. If it pops up, it isn't (you can still eat the food—chill it as you would leftovers). Label jars and store in a cool, dark place up to 1 year. Once opened, refrigerate; eat jams and chutneys within 3 weeks, pickles within 2 months.

Can Safely

Home canning is not complicated, but for success and safety, you must follow the recipes and certain guidelines precisely.

» Do not double recipes. If you want to make more, cook successive batches.

» Always use the processing method the recipe calls for.

» Maintain safe levels of vinegar and sugar. Use the recommended amount of commercial vinegar or citric acid to prevent the growth of harmful bacteria. Using the full amount of sugar called for is also vital for safe preservation, and it ensures the correct consistency.

» For more details on canning safety: Go to the National Center for Home Food Preservation (*uga.edu/nchfp*) for USDA canning guidelines.

Remove a sterilized lid from the hot water and screw it onto the filled jar, firmly but without forcing it.

When the jars are filled, set them into the rack, lower it into the boiling water, and cover the canner.

After processing, remove the jars from the canner using a jar lifter.

Quick pickled green beans with lemon

Kombu, a kind of kelp, gives this pickle a velvety umami character, especially when it's allowed to sit for a few days. The pickle gets spicier with time.

MAKES 8 cups | 45 minutes, plus overnight to chill

1 lb. green beans, ends trimmed
2 cups unseasoned rice vinegar
¼ cup sugar
2 tbsp. kosher salt
6 small dried red chiles, such as Thai or arbol
1 tsp. pink peppercorns
3-in.-long piece *kombu* (dried kelp)*
1 lemon, ends removed, halved lengthwise, cut into
⅓-in.-thick slices, and seeds removed

1. Bring a medium pot of water to a boil and blanch green beans until tender-crisp, 2 to 3 minutes. Drain and put in a large heat-proof bowl.
2. Bring 2½ cups water to a boil in another medium pot with vinegar, sugar, salt, chiles, peppercorns, and kombu. As soon as liquid boils, pour vinegar mixture over beans and add lemon. Let cool to room temperature.
3. Slit 3 chiles to let seeds spill into liquid. Chill, covered, overnight to let flavors develop. Serve cold.
*Look for kombu in the grocery store's Asian-foods aisle.
Make ahead Up to 1 week, chilled.

PER ¼-CUP SERVING 5.4 CAL., 6% (0.3 CAL.) FROM FAT; 0.2 G PROTEIN; 0 G FAT; 1.3 G CARBO (0.4 G FIBER); 73 MG SODIUM; 0 MG CHOL.

QUICK PICKLED GREEN
BEANS WITH LEMON

Pickled jalapeños
(Jalapeños en escabeche)

Elena Cota, a San Diego native and cooking teacher, serves this classic tangy-hot Mexican pickle as part of a buffet with tacos of all kinds, skirt steak, grilled shrimp, pinto beans, and salads.

MAKES 8 to 10 servings | 30 minutes, plus overnight to chill

1 lb. jalapeño chiles
2 carrots (6 oz. total)
1 onion (6 oz.)
2 cups distilled white vinegar
½ cup vegetable oil
3 or 4 garlic cloves, peeled
1 tsp. dried oregano, crumbled
1 bay leaf
Salt and pepper

1. Pierce each jalapeño with a fork. Peel carrots and cut crosswise into ¼-in.-thick slices. Peel onion and cut vertically into ¼-in.-wide slivers.
2. In a 3- to 4-qt. pan over high heat, combine jalapeños, carrots, onion, 2 cups water, vinegar, oil, garlic, oregano, and bay leaf. Bring to a boil. Reduce heat and simmer just until carrots are tender-crisp when pierced, 5 to 8 minutes. Add salt and pepper to taste.
3. Pour into jars, cover, and chill at least overnight. Use a slotted spoon to serve.
Make ahead Up to 2 months, chilled.

PER SERVING 130 CAL., 76% (99 CAL.) FROM FAT; 1 G PROTEIN; 11 G FAT (1.4 G SAT.); 8.8 G CARBO (1.2 G FIBER); 8.7 MG SODIUM; 0 MG CHOL.

PICKLED JALAPEÑOS
(*JALAPEÑOS EN ESCABECHE*)

CLASSIC BASIL PESTO
(ON FRESH MOZZARELLA)

LEMON, BASIL, AND
WALNUT PESTO

Classic basil pesto

In 1946, when authentic Italian food was exotic in this country, *Sunset* ran a pesto recipe, likely the first in a major U.S. publication. Its source was Angelo Pellegrini, a Tuscan-born English professor, writer, and Renaissance man who lived in Seattle. In this update, we've used less oil, but the flavor remains true.

MAKES About ⅓ cup | 10 minutes

½ cup loosely packed basil leaves
4 large or 6 medium garlic cloves
⅓ cup shredded romano cheese
3 tbsp. pine nuts
2 tbsp. minced flat-leaf parsley
½ tsp. salt
5 tbsp. extra-virgin olive oil

Put basil in a mortar with garlic, cheese, pine nuts, parsley, and salt. Pound until smooth, then add oil and mix until smooth. Or blend all ingredients in a blender until smooth.

PER TBSP. 76 CAL., 78% (59 CAL.) FROM FAT; 3.1 G PROTEIN; 6.5 G FAT (1.6 G SAT.); 2.3 G CARBO (0.6 G FIBER); 278 MG SODIUM; 5.2 MG CHOL.

Lemon, basil, and walnut pesto

We developed this lemony, herb-rich pesto as a way to use summer's bounty of basil. To serve on pasta, toss the pesto with cooked pasta and a little pasta water. At the table, add more pepper and parmesan to taste.

MAKES About 1 cup | 5 minutes

2 cups packed basil leaves
1 garlic clove
¼ cup extra-virgin olive oil
Juice and zest of ½ lemon
½ cup grated parmesan cheese
⅓ cup toasted walnuts
Salt and pepper

Blend basil, garlic, oil, lemon juice and zest, parmesan, and walnuts in a food processor until smooth. Add salt and pepper to taste.

PER TBSP. 64 CAL., 83% (53 CAL.) FROM FAT; 2.5 G PROTEIN; 6 G FAT (1.1 G SAT.); 0.8 G CARBO (0.4 G FIBER); 63 MG SODIUM; 2.5 MG CHOL.

Fresh homemade yogurt

Making your own yogurt is surprisingly easy. It's just milk with a bit of yogurt stirred in, which, after several hours, turns all the milk into yogurt. It'll have a softer texture than store-bought; if you want it firmer, boil the milk for 10 to 15 minutes before cooling it, to evaporate liquid (yogurt will have a slightly "cooked" taste). Or drain yogurt to release water. Swirl in jam if you like.

MAKES 3 cups | 30 minutes, plus at least 8 hours to set

1 qt. milk (full-fat, low-fat, or nonfat)
2 tbsp. very fresh plain regular or Greek-style live-culture
    yogurt (full-fat, low-fat, or nonfat)

1. Pour milk into a large, heavy pot and bring to a boil over medium-high heat, stirring often. When milk foams up, pour into a bowl and put bowl in a sink of cold water. Cool milk to 110°.
2. Whisk ¼ cup 110° milk with yogurt in a bowl, then whisk into milk. Pour into 2 large glass jars, cover, wrap jars in towels, and put in a cooler. Add a few more jars filled with hot water to cooler to keep milk warm, and cover cooler. Let milk sit 8 to 12 hours to set (it will look and taste like yogurt when it's done). The longer it sits, the tangier it gets; chilling stops the process. **Make ahead** 1 week, chilled.

PER ¾-CUP SERVING (MADE WITH WHOLE MILK) 154 CAL., 48% (74 CAL.) FROM FAT; 8 G PROTEIN; 8.2 G FAT (4.7 G SAT.); 12 G CARBO (0 G FIBER); 108 MG SODIUM; 25 MG CHOL.

FRESH HOMEMADE YOGURT (WITH BLACKBERRY JAM)

Golden tomato ketchup

Homemade ketchup is a revelation and is entirely worth making. You can substitute red tomatoes for yellow.

MAKES 4 pts. | 3 hours

11 lbs. ripe yellow tomatoes
1 tbsp. *each* **whole cloves, black peppercorns, whole allspice,**
    and celery seeds
2 tsp. mustard seeds
1 dried bay leaf
1 lb. red bell peppers (about 2), cored, seeded, and quartered
1⅓ lbs. onions (about 2), peeled
1 garlic clove, peeled
1 tbsp. salt
¾ cup firmly packed brown sugar
2 cups cider vinegar

1. Follow "Get Ready" directions in "How-to: Canning" (page 242), using 4 pint-size jars, with rings and lids.
2. Meanwhile, immerse tomatoes in a pot of boiling water until skins crack, 15 seconds. Lift out with a slotted spoon. Cool, then peel. Enclose cloves, peppercorns, allspice, celery and mustard seeds, and bay leaf in two layers of cheesecloth; tie with string.
3. Blend tomatoes, bell peppers, onions, and garlic, in batches, in a blender or food processor until smooth. Pour purée into a 10- to 12-qt. pan. Add spice bag, salt, sugar, and vinegar.
4. Bring mixture to a boil over high heat, stirring occasionally. Reduce heat to medium-high and cook, stirring often, until reduced by half and liquid doesn't separate from solids (spoon some into a bowl to check), about 1¾ hours. Remove spice bag. If desired, blend ketchup, in batches, in a blender until smooth.
5. Follow steps under "Fill and Seal Jars" and "Process Jars" (page 242), leaving ⅛-in. headspace in jars and processing 15 minutes (at altitudes of 1,000 to 6,000 ft., process 20 minutes; above 6,000 ft., 25 minutes).
Make ahead Store up to 1 year.

PER TBSP. 17 CAL., 5.3% (0.9 CAL.) FROM FAT; 0.5 G PROTEIN; 0.1 G FAT (0 G SAT.); 4 G CARBO (0.1 G FIBER); 60 MG SODIUM; 0 MG CHOL.

HOMEMADE
FROMAGE BLANC

HOMEMADE
RICOTTA

Homemade fromage blanc

Some fancy (and pricey) cheeses are astonishingly easy to make, even for beginners. We asked the staff at Cowgirl Creamery, in Northern California, to show us how to create fromage blanc, a French-style soft cheese. Below is our adaptation for the home kitchen. The supplies may seem a bit mad-scientist, but they're simple to use. Note: Before starting, scrub work surface with antibacterial soap, and boil utensils for 20 minutes before using. You'll need a dairy thermometer* or candy thermometer for this recipe, plus cheesecloth.

MAKES 4 cups (plus 10 cups whey) | 1 hour, plus overnight to culture and 6 to 8 hours to drain (stirring hourly)

1 gal. pasteurized whole milk
⅛ tsp. fromage blanc culture*
1 drop (0.1 ml.) vegetarian rennet*
2 drops (0.2 ml.) calcium chloride*
½ cup crème fraîche
¾ to 1 tsp. fine sea salt

1. "Ripen" the milk: Pour milk into an 8- to 10-qt. heavy-bottomed pot and insert dairy thermometer. Heat milk over medium-high heat to 85°, stirring often to prevent scorching.
2. Remove from heat, remove thermometer, and sprinkle culture as evenly as possible over milk; let rest 10 minutes, then gently stir 1 minute in one direction. Dilute rennet in 2 tbsp. cool water and pour in evenly all over the milk; stir the same way. Dilute calcium chloride in 2 tbsp. cool water; pour and stir as you did the culture and rennet. Stir once in opposite direction to stop movement of milk. Cover with cheesecloth; let rest overnight on counter.
3. Drain curds: Ladle curds from the pot into a large colander, lined with a double thickness of cheesecloth and set over a clean bucket. About 10 cups of whey will drain into the bucket. (Use for Homemade Ricotta; see recipe at right. Transfer whey to a bowl in the fridge whenever there's enough to collect.) Drain curds 6 to 8 hours at room temperature, until the cheese resembles thick sour cream, scooping and turning with a soup spoon every hour or so in order to let the curds dry evenly.
4. Dress curds: Turn fromage blanc into a large bowl and stir in crème fraîche and salt to taste. Cheese is now ready to eat. It keeps, chilled in an airtight container, up to 1 week.
*Find dairy thermometer, fromage blanc culture, vegetarian rennet, and calcium chloride at *thebeveragepeople.com*
Make ahead Up to 1 week, chilled airtight.

PER OZ. 45 CAL., 60% (27 CAL.) FROM FAT; 2 G PROTEIN; 3 G FAT (2 G SAT.); 2 G CARBO (0 G FIBER); 40 MG SODIUM; 15 MG CHOL.

Homemade ricotta

Make luscious ricotta from tips we learned at Bellwether Farms, in Sonoma County, California. Before starting, scrub work surfaces with antibacterial soap, and boil utensils for 20 minutes. You'll need a 20-qt. boiling-water canner, a dairy thermometer*, a ricotta mold (4½ in. wide)* or a colander, and cheesecloth.

MAKES 1¼ to 1½ cups (3½ cups if you use all milk) | 2 hours

10 cups fresh whey (from Homemade Fromage Blanc, recipe at left; optional)
6 cups whole milk (or use 1 gal. whole milk instead of a whey-milk combination; it will taste similar to ricotta but less delicate)
2 tsp. fine sea salt
3½ tbsp. distilled white vinegar (4½ tbsp. if you're usin g all milk and no whey)

1. Set the canner on the stovetop and insert canning rack upside down (handles down). Fill canner with water to 1 in. below top ring. Bring to a boil, covered. Fill a sink with cold water.
2. Set an empty 8-qt. pot on upturned rack in canner. Pour whey if using, milk, and salt into pot and insert dairy thermometer into milk. With a slotted spoon, stir milk 20 times with a gentle surface-to-bottom circular motion to distribute heat. Let milk heat over high heat, covered and undisturbed, until 192° to 194° (water will be boiling), 30 to 40 minutes; adjust heat to maintain temperature. If milk starts to get too hot, cool it in sink of water.
3. Slowly pour vinegar over the warm milk. With a slotted spoon, stir milk 20 times with a gentle surface-to-bottom circular motion. Small curds will begin to form (they may have already).
4. Cover pot with canner lid and let mixture stand, undisturbed, over high heat 25 minutes for curds to finish forming (temperature should remain between 192° and 194°; check occasionally and adjust heat as needed). Meanwhile, line mold or colander with two layers of cheesecloth, trimmed to hang slightly over rim. Drain sink and set mold in sink.
5. Ladle curds and whey into mold, occasionally pouring out liquid from bowl, until draining slows to a trickle. Smooth cheese level in mold. Cover with plastic wrap, set in a bowl, and chill.
6. Let curds drain in refrigerator until visible pockets of liquid are gone (curds should be moist), a few minutes to about 30 minutes more. To serve, invert mold onto a plate or, if using a colander, spoon into a bowl.
*Find thermometer and ricotta mold at *thebeveragepeople.com*
Make ahead Up to 4 days, chilled (wrap mold airtight or transfer cheese to an airtight container).

PER ¼ CUP 108 CAL., 66% (71 CAL.) FROM FAT; 7 G PROTEIN; 8.1 G FAT (5.2 G SAT.); 2 G CARBO (0 G FIBER); 52 MG SODIUM; 32 MG CHOL.

Measurement Equivalents

Refer to the following charts for metric conversions as well as common cooking equivalents. All equivalents are approximate.

Cooking/Oven Temperatures

	Fahrenheit	Celsius	Gas Mark
Freeze Water	32°F	0°C	
Room Temp.	68°F	20°C	
Boil Water	212°F	100°C	
Bake	325°F	160°C	3
	350°F	180°C	4
	375°F	190°C	5
	400°F	200°C	6
	425°F	220°C	7
	450°F	230°C	8
Broil			Grill

Liquid Ingredients by Volume

¼ tsp.	=							1 ml.	
½ tsp.	=							2 ml.	
1 tsp.	=							5 ml.	
3 tsp.	=	1 tbsp.	=	½ fl. oz.	=	15 ml.			
2 tbsp.	=	⅛ cup	=	1 fl. oz.	=	30 ml.			
4 tbsp.	=	¼ cup	=	2 fl. oz.	=	60 ml.			
5⅓ tbsp.	=	⅓ cup	=	3 fl. oz.	=	80 ml.			
8 tbsp.	=	½ cup	=	4 fl. oz.	=	120 ml.			
10⅔ tbsp.	=	⅔ cup	=	5 fl. oz.	=	160 ml.			
12 tbsp.	=	¾ cup	=	6 fl. oz.	=	180 ml.			
16 tbsp.	=	1 cup	=	8 fl. oz.	=	240 ml.			
1 pt.	=	2 cups	=	16 fl. oz.	=	480 ml.			
1 qt.	=	4 cups	=	32 fl. oz.	=	960 ml.			
				33 fl. oz.	=	1,000 ml.	=	1 l.	

Dry Ingredients by Weight
(To convert ounces to grams, multiply the number of ounces by 30.)

1 oz.	=	¹⁄₁₆ lb.	=	30 g.
4 oz.	=	¼ lb.	=	120 g.
8 oz.	=	½ lb.	=	240 g.
12 oz.	=	¾ lb.	=	360 g.
16 oz.	=	1 lb.	=	480 g.

Equivalents for Different Types of Ingredients

Standard Cup	Fine Powder (e.g., flour)	Grain (e.g., rice)	Granular (e.g., sugar)	Liquid Solids (e.g., butter)	Liquid (e.g., milk)
1	140 g.	150 g.	190 g.	200 g.	240 ml.
¾	105 g.	113 g.	143 g.	150 g.	180 ml.
⅔	93 g.	100 g.	125 g.	133 g.	160 ml.
½	70 g.	75 g.	95 g.	100 g.	120 ml.
⅓	47 g.	50 g.	63 g.	67 g.	80 ml.
¼	35 g.	38 g.	48 g.	50 g.	60 ml.
⅛	18 g.	19 g.	24 g.	25 g.	30 ml.

Length
(To convert inches to centimeters, multiply the number of inches by 2.5.)

1 in.	=			2.5 cm.
6 in.	=	½ ft.	=	15 cm.
12 in.	=	1 ft.	=	30 cm.
36 in.	=	3 ft. = 1 yd.	=	90 cm.
40 in.	=			100 cm. = 1 m.

Index

A

Abalone, 139
  grilled, 139
  pan-fried, 139
Adobo, easy chicken, 106
Aguas frescas, melon-berry, 26
Ahi tuna
  citrus salad, grilled, 129
  poke, sesame, 18
Aioli, tarragon, 14
Allioli, 140
Almonds, 169
  apricot nut tart, 180
  -cream galette, plum, 183
  green chiles stuffed with
      beef, raisins, and, 81
  honey caramel nut bars, 213
  Meyer lemon cake, 194
  Nanaimo bars, 214
  pear chutney, 238
  swirl ice cream pie, apricot, 202
  toffee, 217
Anchovy fries with smoked
    paprika mayo, 18
Apples, 47
  endive salad, 47
  Sauvignon Blanc sorbet,
      green, 206
Apricots
  almond swirl ice cream pie, 202
  Blenheim, 180
  nut tart, 180
  pear chutney, 238
  salsa, fresh, 123
  sauce, 201
  -stuffed leg of lamb, grilled, 96
Arracheras (grilled skirt steak), 77
Artichokes, 156
  dip, hot, 13
  Green Goddess salad, 46
  grilled, with green-olive dip, 156
  parmesan sourdough
      stuffing, 172
  roasted baby, with spring
      salsa, 11
  soup, creamy, 54
Arugula, marionberry, and
    blue cheese salad, 45

Asparagus
  chicken salad, best-ever
      Chinese, 109
  and egg toasts, 225
  herb salad, 46
  and morel quiche, 152
  salmon, grilled king, with
      morels, leeks, and, 119
Avocados, 13
  California rolls, 135
  Cobb salad, classic, 37
  and corn salad, fresh, 45
  fries, 156
  green salad with papaya-seed
      dressing, 40
  guacamole
    basic, 88
    Gabriel's, 13
  ice cream, coconut, 205
  -poblano salad, spicy, 42
  quesadillas, kimchi and, 151
  salad, ruby grapefruit, spinach,
      and, 50
  sauce, herbed, cracked crab
      with, 132
  tomato soup, tiered, 54
  with warm bacon parsley
      vinaigrette, 10

B

Bacon
  -and-beef chili, smoky, 62
  burritos, New Mexican red chile
      breakfast, 229
  Cobb salad, classic, 37
  cream, Makah Ozette potatoes
      with, 166
  Hangtown fry, 230
  pinquito beans, Santa Maria–
      style, 74
  vinaigrettes, 10, 49
Baja fish tacos, 127
Bánh mì thit Hoi An (Hoi An–
    style oven-crisped pork
    sandwiches), 91
Bánh xèo (sizzling Saigon
    crêpes), 89

Bars
  honey caramel nut, 213
  Nanaimo, 214
Basil pesto
  classic, 246
  lemon, walnut, and, 246
Bass, grilled, with salsa
    verde, 131
Beans
  black
    and chicken taquitos, 10
    Frito pie, 61
    nachos, chorizo-beef
        dinner, 85
  cannellini
    salad, cold, grilled sardines
        with, 127
  chickpeas
    and broccolini dal, 66
    cauliflower and shallots,
        roasted, with chard
        and *dukkah*, 164
  Chinese long, with XO
      sauce, 159
  fava
    spring salsa, roasted baby
        artichokes with, 11
  green
    beef, dutch oven–braised,
        and summer
        vegetables, 78
    Caesar salad with baby
        romaine lettuces, 40
    Chinese long, with XO
        sauce, 159
    with crisp Meyer lemon
        bread crumbs, 160
    pickled, with lemon, 244
  heirloom, 57
  pinquito, Santa Maria–style, 74
  pinto
    beef-and-bacon chili,
        smoky, 62
    burritos grandes, *Sunset's*, 88
    chili, 176
    La Super-Rica, 164
    refried, chorizo, 226
  tepary, and fennel ragout, 56

Bars
  honey caramel nut, 213
  Nanaimo, 214
Beef
  -and-bacon chili, smoky, 62
  burgers
    grass-fed, with chipotle
        barbecue sauce, 82
    Korean kimchi, 82
  -chorizo dinner nachos, 85
  dutch oven–braised, and
      summer vegetables, 78
  Frito pie, 61
  green chiles stuffed with
      almonds, raisins, and, 81
  noodle soup, Vietnamese
      (*pho bo*), 69
  rib-eye steaks, grilled, with miso
      butter and sweet onions, 77
  skirt steak, grilled (*arracheras*), 77
  steak salad, Vietnamese-style,
      84
  tacos, cola shredded-, 81
  tri-tip, Santa Maria–style
      grilled, 74
Beer, 22
  -battered razor clams, 136
  lime-chile, 22
  pork stew, shot-and-, 95
Belgian endive
  apple salad, 47
  crab Louis, deviled, 38
Bell peppers
  pear chutney, 238
  ratatouille, grilled, 165
  roasted, lamb stew with, 99
Berries, 203. *See also individual
    berries*
  buttermilk sherbet, 203
  popsicles, triple-berry, 208
Bison, 100
  and beer burgers with pub
      cheese, 101
  roast, with velvety pan
      gravy, 100
Bizcochitos, 214
Blackberries, 203. *See also
    Marionberries*
  crisp, hazelnut honey, 189
  jam, fig-orange-, 241
  sauce, orange-, 101
  sherbet, berry buttermilk, 203

Bloody Mary, fresh, 26
Blueberries, 203
    in black pepper–Syrah
        syrup, 209
    pie, spiced, 183
    popsicles, triple-berry, 208
    sherbet, berry buttermilk, 203
Brandy
    Keoke coffee, 30
    -peppercorn sauce, 101
    watermelon sidecar, 26
Bread. See also Cornbread
    grilled, halibut kebabs with
        pancetta and, 123
    Navajo fry, 176
    persimmon-currant, 199
    sheepherder's, 177
    sourdough
        French, 174
        starters, 173, 175, 223
        stuffing, artichoke
            parmesan, 172
    toasts, asparagus and egg, 225
Brittle, spiced piñon, 207
Broccolini and chickpea dal, 66
Broccoli rabe pizza, Delfina's, 142
Brownies
    chocolate liliko'i parfaits, 210
    dark chocolate–chunk, 210
Brussels sprouts, spicy, with
    fried capers, 170
Bubble tea
    mango-coconut, 30
    rhubarb-rose, 30
Bun (cooked rice noodles), 69
Burgers
    bison and beer, with pub
        cheese, 101
    grass-fed, with chipotle
        barbecue sauce, 82
    Korean kimchi, 82
    walnut, Lia's, 144
Burritos
    grandes, Sunset's, 88
    New Mexican red chile
        breakfast, 229

C

Cabbage. See also Kimchi
    chicken salad, best-ever
        Chinese, 109
    salad, Champagne, 14
    slaw, salsa, 151
    steak salad, Vietnamese-style, 84

Caesar salad, green bean, with
    baby romaine lettuces, 40
Cakes
    fig coffee, 220
    Meyer lemon, 194
    pasilla chile chocolate (pastel de
        chocolate y chile pasilla), 200
    pear and pecan upside-
        down, 199
    tangerine olive oil, 195
    tres leches, with raspberries, 196
Calamari
    grilled marinated, 138
    herb salad, Vietnamese, 136
California, cuisine of, 45
California rolls, 135
Canning, 242
Cantaloupe and prosciutto
    salad, 42
Carne adovada (red chile and
    pork stew), 71
Carrot soup with Dungeness
    crab, 57
Cashews
    calamari herb salad,
        Vietnamese, 136
    honey caramel nut bars, 213
    persimmon salad with dates,
        honey, and, 50
Cauliflower and shallots, roasted,
    with chard and dukkah, 164
Celery Victor with watercress and
    capers, 38
Chard
    cauliflower and shallots, roasted,
        with dukkah and, 164
    sablefish, sake and birch syrup–
        roasted, with fresh peas
        and, 124
Cheese
    fromage blanc, homemade, 249
    goat, baked, with spring lettuce
        salad, Chez Panisse's, 34
    manchego, grilled lettuces
        with, 48
    quesadillas
        grilled, with nopales and
            salsa slaw, 151
        kimchi and avocado, 151
    ricotta, homemade, 249
    turkey and, Golden Gate
        grilled, 117

Cherries
    chocolate tart, dark, with
        almond whipped cream
        and, 188
    Dutch baby, 233
    jam, -rhubarb, 238
Chicken
    adobo, easy, 106
    and bean taquitos, 10
    Bengali five-spice roasted, and
        vegetables, 102
    Cobb salad, classic, 37
    enchiladas, green chile, 102
    laksa, 58
    posole, speedy, with avocado
        and lime, 65
    roast, with Meyer lemon–shallot
        sauce, 106
    salad, best-ever Chinese, 109
    tortilla soup, 61
Chickpeas
    and broccolini dal, 66
    cauliflower and shallots,
        roasted, with chard and
        dukkah, 164
Chilaquiles, 230
Chiles
    chipotle barbecue sauce, 82
    green
        chicken enchiladas, 102
        cornbread, Southwest, 173
        pork stew, 70
        sauce (chile verde), 105
        stuffed with beef, almonds,
            and raisins, 81
    jalapeños, pickled (jalapeños
        en escabeche), 244
    New Mexico, 104
    pasilla, and chocolate cake
        (pastel de chocolate y chile
        pasilla), 200
    poblano
        -avocado salad, spicy, 42
        chicken posole, speedy, with
            avocado and lime, 65
        chipotle salsa, roasted, 14
        rellenos, baked, 233
        salsa, Santa Maria, 74
    red
        burritos, breakfast, 229
        chilaquiles, 230
        and pork stew (carne
            adovada), 71
        sauce (chile colorado), 105

Chili
    beans, 176
    beef-and-bacon, smoky, 62
    Frito pie, 61
Chocolate
    brownies, dark, 210
    hot fudge piñon sauce, 207
    ice cream, Mexican, 206
    liliko'i parfaits, 210
    Nanaimo bars, 214
    pasilla chile cake (pastel de
        chocolate y chile pasilla), 200
    sauce, 210
    tart, dark, with cherries
        and almond whipped
        cream, 188
    toffee, almond, 217
Chutney, pear, 238
Cioppino, 62
Citrus
    peels, candied, 217
    salad, grilled ahi, 129
    smoothies, 29
Clams
    cioppino, 62
    paella, grilled seafood and
        chorizo, 140
    razor, beer-battered, 136
Cobblers
    buttery pastry for, 189
    huckleberry skillet, 189
    peach, dutch-oven, 191
Coconut
    avocado ice cream, 205
    caramel, pineapple satays
        with, 191
    -mango bubble tea, 30
    Nanaimo bars, 214
    triangles (haupia), 209
Coffee, Keoke, 30
Coffee cake, fig, 220
Cola shredded-beef tacos, 81
Cookies. See also Bars
    bizcochitos, 214
    fortune, homemade, 213
Corn. See also Cornbread
    and avocado salad, fresh, 45
    beef, dutch oven–braised, and
        summer vegetables, 78
    blue, 223
    chicken posole, speedy, with
        avocado and lime, 65
    on the cob, chili-lime, 162

pancakes, blue, 223
soup, chilled, 58
Cornbread
-chorizo dressing, 172
Southwest, 173
Cosmo, pineapple, 22
Crab
cooked
-cakes, classic, 14
California rolls, 135
Louis, deviled, 38
Dungeness, 133
carrot soup with, 57
cioppino, 62
cracked, with herbed avocado
sauce, 132
eggs Benedict with, 225
king, on the half-shell, 132
Crème de cacao
Keoke coffee, 30
Crêpes, sizzling Saigon
(bánh xèo), 89
Crisp, blackberry hazelnut
honey, 189
Cucumber salad, grilled salmon
with, 120
Curry, herb and tofu, 66

D

Dal, broccolini and chickpea, 66
Dates, 29
persimmon salad with cashews,
honey, and, 50
shake, California, 29
Desserts
bars
honey caramel nut, 213
Nanaimo, 214
blueberries in black pepper–
Syrah syrup, 209
bread, persimmon-currant, 199
cakes
Meyer lemon, 194
pasilla chile chocolate (pastel
de chocolate y chile
pasilla), 200
pear and pecan upside-
down, 199
tangerine olive oil, 195
tres leches, with raspberries,
196
cobblers
huckleberry skillet, 189
peach, dutch-oven, 191

coconut triangles (haupia), 209
cookies
bizcochitos, 214
fortune, homemade, 213
crisp, blackberry hazelnut
honey, 189
fro-yo, tart 'n' tangy, 201
galettes
plum almond-cream, 183
rhubarb cardamom, 187
ice cream
chocolate, Mexican, 206
coconut avocado, 205
pie, apricot almond swirl, 202
orange peels, candied, 217
parfaits, chocolate liliko'i, 210
pies
apricot almond swirl ice
cream, 202
blueberry, spiced, 183
marionberry, 181
pumpkin, ancho chile, 192
popsicles, triple-berry, 208
satays, pineapple, with coconut
caramel, 191
sherbet, berry buttermilk, 203
sopaipillas, 216
sorbets
green apple Sauvignon
Blanc, 206
pear, 205
tarts
apricot nut, 180
chocolate, dark, with cherries
and almond whipped
cream, 188
fig, Black Mission, 187
macadamia nut, 184
strawberry, brown sugar, 184
toffee, almond, 217
Dim sum, 234
Dips. See also Guacamole
artichoke, hot, 13
green-olive, 156
onion, caramelized Maui, 13
Dressings. See Salad dressings;
Stuffings and dressings
Drinks
aguas frescas, melon-berry, 26
beer, lime-chile, 22
Bloody Mary, fresh, 26
bubble tea
mango-coconut, 30
rhubarb-rose, 30

coffee, Keoke, 30
Collins, peach, 25
cosmo, pineapple, 22
gin, green, 22
mai tai, classic tiki, 25
margaritas, Sunset, 25
shake, California date, 29
sidecar, watermelon, 26
smoothies
citrus, 29
persimmon, 29
vodka, fresh pineapple, 22
Duck, Pinot-braised, with spicy
greens, 110
Dukkah (Egyptian nut-and-spice
blend), 164
Dumplings
pork and shrimp (shu mai), 234
rice balls, spicy, 234
shrimp and chive, naked, 234
Dutch ovens, 78

E, F

Eggplant
ratatouille, grilled, 165
Eggs
and asparagus toasts, 225
Benedict with crab, 225
burritos, New Mexican red chile
breakfast, 229
chiles rellenos, baked, 233
Hangtown fry, 230
huevos rancheros, speedy,
with the works, 226
pasture-raised, 233
Enchiladas
chicken, green chile, 102
turkey, 116
Farro, green olive, and feta
salad, 151
Fennel
salad, spinach, mushroom,
and, with warm bacon
vinaigrette, 49
and tepary bean ragout, 56
Figs
coffee cake, 220
jam, blackberry-orange-, 241
pork shoulder roast with
garlic, Pinot Noir,
and, 95
tart, Black Mission, 187

Fish
ahi tuna
citrus salad, grilled, 129
poke, sesame, 18
anchovy fries with smoked
paprika mayo, 18
bass, grilled, with salsa
verde, 131
halibut
chilled poached, with fresh
apricot salsa, 123
kebabs with grilled bread and
pancetta, 123
sablefish, sake and birch syrup–
roasted, with fresh peas
and chard, 124
salmon, 119
cedar-planked, 119
grilled, with cucumber
salad, 120
grilled king, with asparagus,
morels, and leeks, 119
shioyaki, 120
smoked, pan-fried trout
with, 128
sardines
grilled, with cold bean
salad, 127
pan-fried, with caramelized
onions, pine nuts, and
raisins, 131
tacos, Baja, 127
trout
crispy, with capers, 128
pan-fried, with smoked
salmon, 128
Fortune cookies, homemade, 213
French bread, sourdough, 174
Frito pie, 61
Fro-yo, tart 'n' tangy, 201

G, H

Galettes
plum almond-cream, 183
rhubarb cardamom, 187
Garlic, 99
Gin
Bloody Mary, fresh, 26
green, 22
Grapefruit, avocado, and
spinach salad, 50
Gravy
rich brown, 115
Zinfandel, 112

Green Goddess salad, 46
Grilling, 83
Guacamole
    basic, 88
    Gabriel's, 13
Halibut
    chilled poached, with fresh
        apricot salsa, 123
    kebabs with grilled bread
        and pancetta, 123
Hangtown fry, 230
Haupia (coconut triangles), 209
Hazelnuts, 169
    apricot nut tart, 180
    -butter muffins, 220
    dukkah (Egyptian nut-and-spice
        blend), 164
    herb salad, 34
    honey crisp, blackberry, 189
Honey caramel nut bars, 213
Huckleberry skillet cobbler, 189
Huevos rancheros, speedy, with
    the works, 226

I–L

Ice cream. *See also* Sherbet;
        Sorbets
    chocolate, Mexican, 206
    coconut avocado, 205
    pie, apricot almond swirl, 202
    shake, California date, 29
Jams, quick
    cherry-rhubarb, 238
    fig-blackberry-orange, 241
    peach-raspberry-lavender, 241
    plum, spiced, 238
Kahlúa
    Keoke coffee, 30
Kale
    crispy grilled, with creamy
        sesame dressing, 163
    lentil stew with winter
        vegetables, 65
Kebabs
    Armenian-style, 99
    halibut, with grilled bread
        and pancetta, 123
Keoke coffee, 30
Ketchup, golden tomato, 247
Kimchi
    and avocado quesadillas, 151
    burgers, Korean, 82

Laksa, chicken, 58
Lamb
    kebabs, Armenian-style, 99
    leg of, grilled apricot-stuffed, 96
    shoulder chops, grilled, with
        pimentón rub, 96
    stew with roasted red peppers,
        99
Lemons, Meyer, 194
    cake, 194
    –shallot sauce, roast chicken
        with, 106
Lentil stew with winter
    vegetables, 65
Lettuce
    baby romaine, green bean
        Caesar salad with, 40
    Cobb salad, classic, 37
    crab Louis, deviled, 38
    Green Goddess salad, 46
    grilled, with manchego, 48
    hazelnut herb salad, 34
    salad, spring, Chez Panisse's
        baked goat cheese with, 34
Limes
    -chile beer, 22
    cosmo, pineapple, 22
    dressing, watermelon salad
        with, 50
    margaritas, *Sunset*, 25
Luaus, 87

M, N

Macadamia nuts, 185
    tart, 184
Mai tai, classic tiki, 25
Mango-coconut bubble tea, 30
Margaritas, *Sunset*, 25
Marionberries
    pie, 181
    salad, blue cheese, arugula,
        and, 45
Melons. *See also* Watermelon
    -berry *aguas frescas*, 26
    cantaloupe and prosciutto
        salad, 42
Mountain states, cuisine of, 129
Muffins, hazelnut-butter, 220
Mushrooms
    chanterelle
        risotto, 148
        roasted, 148

morels
    and asparagus quiche, 152
    salmon, grilled king, with
        asparagus, leeks,
        and, 119
    salad, spinach, fennel, and, with
        warm bacon vinaigrette, 49
    turkey Tetrazzini, *Sunset*, 116
Mussels
    paella, grilled seafood and
        chorizo, 140
    saffron steamed, 138
Nachos, chorizo-beef dinner, 85
Nanaimo bars, 214
Navajo fry bread, 176
Nettle and pine nut sauce, 147
Noodles. *See* Pasta and noodles
Nopales, grilled quesadillas with
    salsa slaw and, 151
Northwest, cuisine of, 124
Nu'ó'c châ'm (Vietnamese dipping
    sauce), 89
Nuts, 169. *See also individual nuts*

O, P

Olives
    dip, green-, 156
    oil, 49
    salad, farro, feta, and, 151
Onion dip, caramelized Maui, 13
Oranges
    chicken salad, best-ever
        Chinese, 109
    citrus salad, grilled ahi, 129
    jam, fig-blackberry-, 241
    margaritas, *Sunset*, 25
    navel, 109
    peels, candied, 217
Oysters, 17
    barbecued, with chipotle
        glaze, 17
    Hangtown fry, 230
Paella, grilled seafood and
    chorizo, 140
Pancakes
    cherry Dutch baby, 233
    corn, blue, 223
    mix, hearty whole-grain, 191
    sourdough, 223
Pancit (Filipino-style stir-fried
    noodles with vegetables
    and tofu), 147
Papaya-seed dressing, green
    salad with, 40

Parfaits, chocolate liliko'i, 210
Parsley ravioli with brown butter
    sauce, 152
Parsnips, miso-glazed tofu with,
    two ways, 153
Passion fruit, 210
    chocolate liliko'i parfaits, 210
Pasta and noodles
    egg noodles
        turkey Tetrazzini, *Sunset*, 116
    rice noodles
        chicken *laksa*, 58
        cooked (*bun*), 69
        soup, Vietnamese beef
            (*pho bo*), 69
        steak salad, Vietnamese-
            style, 84
        stir-fried, Filipino-style, with
            vegetables and tofu
            (*pancit*), 147
        soba noodle bowl, warm, 70
        tagliatelle with nettle and
            pine nut sauce, 147
    wheat noodles
        stir-fried, Filipino-style, with
            vegetables and tofu
            (*pancit*), 147
Pastel de chocolate y chile pasilla
    (pasilla chile chocolate
    cake), 200
Peaches
    cobbler, dutch-oven, 191
    Collins, 25
    and ginger glazed riblets, 93
    jam, raspberry-lavender-, 241
Pears, 205
    chutney, 238
    and pecan upside-down
        cake, 199
    sorbet, 205
Pea shoots, quick-cooked, 159
Pecans
    honey caramel nut bars, 213
    and pear upside-down cake, 199
Persimmons, 29, 50
    -currant bread, 199
    salad with dates, cashews,
        and honey, 50
    smoothies, 29
Pesto
    basil, classic, 246
    lemon, basil, and walnut, 246
    pumpkin seed–mint, 56

Pho bo (Vietnamese beef noodle soup), 69
Pies
  apricot almond swirl ice cream, 202
  blueberry, spiced, 183
  crust, best all-purpose, 192
  marionberry, 181
  pumpkin, ancho chile, 192
Pineapple
  cosmo, 22
  and pork buns, *char siu*-glazed, 87
  satays with coconut caramel, 191
  vodka, fresh, 22
Piñon and pine nuts, 169
  brittle, spiced, 207
  sauces
    hot fudge, 207
    nettle and, 147
  toasted, quinoa with, 165
Pizzas
  bianca, 144
  broccoli rabe, Delfina's, 142
  dough
    Delfina's, 143
    stretching, 142
  grilled, 144
  margherita, 144
  sauce, ripe tomato pizza, 144
Plums
  almond-cream galette, 183
  jam, spiced, 238
Poke, sesame ahi, 18
Popsicles, triple-berry, 208
Pork. *See also* Bacon; Prosciutto; Sausage
  burritos grandes, *Sunset's*, 88
  crêpes, sizzling Saigon (*bánh xèo*), 89
  and pineapple buns, *char siu*-glazed, 87
  riblets
    Chinese glazed, with garlic and Thai basil, 90
    peach and ginger glazed, 93
  rice balls, spicy, 234
  sandwiches, Hoi An-style oven-crisped (*bánh mì thit Hoi An*), 91
  shoulder roast with figs, garlic, and Pinot Noir, 95

and shrimp dumplings (*shu mai*), 234
  stews
    green chile (*chile verde*), 70
    red chile (*carne adovada*), 71
    shot-and-a-beer, 95
  tamales, Lupe's, 92
Posole, speedy chicken, with avocado and lime, 65
Potatoes
  golden olive oil–roasted, 166
  Makah Ozette, with bacon cream, 166
Prosciutto
  asparagus and egg toasts, 225
  and cantaloupe salad, 42
Pumpkin, 192
  bowls, mini, 56
  pie, ancho chile, 192
  purée, 192
  soup with pumpkin seed–mint pesto, 56

Q, R

Quesadillas
  grilled, with *nopales* and salsa slaw, 151
  kimchi and avocado, 151
Quiche, asparagus and morel, 152
Quinoa with toasted pine nuts, 165
Raspberries, 203
  aguas frescas, melon-berry, 26
  jam, peach-lavender-, 241
  popsicles, triple-berry, 208
  sherbet, berry buttermilk, 203
  tres leches cake with, 196
Ratatouille, grilled, 165
Ravioli, parsley, with brown butter sauce, 152
Rhubarb
  bubble tea, rose-, 30
  galette, cardamom, 187
  jam, cherry, 238
Rice
  balls, spicy, 234
  burritos grandes, *Sunset's*, 88
  California rolls, 135
  Mexican red, 229
  paella, grilled seafood and chorizo, 140
  risotto, chanterelle mushroom, 148

salad, black, with butternut squash and pomegranate seeds, 116
  stuffing, Chinese, 170
Romanesco broccoli, roasted, 159
Rum
  mai tai, classic tiki, 25

S

Saag (Indian spinach), 160
Sablefish, sake and birch syrup–roasted, with fresh peas and chard, 124
Salad dressings
  Caesar, 40
  deviled Louis, 38
  Green Goddess, 46
  papaya-seed, 40
  soy-ginger, spicy, 109
Salads
  ahi citrus, grilled, 129
  asparagus herb, 46
  avocado-poblano, spicy, 42
  bean, cold, grilled sardines with, 127
  blooming, 37
  calamari herb, Vietnamese, 136
  cantaloupe and prosciutto, 42
  celery Victor with watercress and capers, 38
  Champagne cabbage, 14
  chicken, best-ever Chinese, 109
  Cobb, classic, 37
  corn and avocado, fresh, 45
  crab Louis, deviled, 38
  cucumber, grilled salmon with, 120
  endive apple, 47
  farro, green olive, and feta, 151
  green, with papaya-seed dressing, 40
  green bean Caesar, with baby romaine lettuces, 40
  Green Goddess, 46
  hazelnut herb, 34
  lettuces, grilled, with manchego, 48
  marionberry, blue cheese, and arugula, 45
  persimmon, with dates, cashews, and honey, 50
  ruby grapefruit, avocado, and spinach, 50

spinach, mushroom, and fennel, with warm bacon vinaigrette, 49
  spring lettuce, Chez Panisse's baked goat cheese with, 34
  steak, Vietnamese-style, 84
  tomato, heirloom, with pomegranate drizzle, 47
  watermelon, with lime dressing, 50
Salmon, 119
  cedar-planked, 119
  grilled, with cucumber salad, 120
  grilled king, with asparagus, morels, and leeks, 119
  shioyaki, 120
  smoked, pan-fried trout with, 128
Salsas
  fresca, classic, 88
  ranchera, 226
  Santa Maria, 74
  spring, roasted baby artichokes with, 11
  verde, 131
Sandwiches. *See also* Burgers
  pork
    Hoi An–style oven-crisped (*bánh mì thit Hoi An*), 91
    and pineapple buns, *char siu*-glazed, 87
  turkey and cheese, Golden Gate grilled, 117
Sardines
  grilled, with cold bean salad, 127
  pan-fried, with caramelized onions, pine nuts, and raisins, 131
Sauces. *See also* Pesto; Salsas
  apricot, 201
  avocado, herbed, 132
  blackberry-orange, 101
  brandy-peppercorn, 101
  chile
    green (*chile verde*), 105
    red (*chile colorado*), 105
  chipotle barbecue, 82
  chocolate, 210
  hot fudge piñon, 207
  nettle and pine nut, 147
  Vietnamese dipping (*nu'ó'c châ'm*), 89

Sausage
 chili beans, 176
 Chinese
  rice stuffing, 170
 chorizo
  -beef dinner nachos, 85
  burritos, New Mexican red
   chile breakfast, 229
  chiles rellenos, baked, 233
  -cornbread dressing, 172
  paella, grilled seafood
   and, 140
  pinto beans, La Super-
   Rica, 164
  refried beans, 226
Seafood main courses, 132–140
Shake, California date, 29
Shallots
 caramelized, and walnuts, 169
 and cauliflower, roasted, with
  chard and *dukkah*, 164
 fried sliced, 91
 –Meyer lemon sauce, roast
  chicken with, 106
Sheepherder's bread, 177
Sherbet, berry buttermilk, 203
Shrimp
 and chive dumplings, naked, 234
 cioppino, 62
 Green Goddess salad, 46
 paella, grilled seafood and
  chorizo, 140
 and pork dumplings
  (shu mai), 234
Shu mai (pork and shrimp
  dumplings), 234
Sidecar, watermelon, 26
Simple syrup, 22
Smoothies
 citrus, 29
 persimmon, 29
Sopaipillas, 216
Sorbets
 green apple Sauvignon
  Blanc, 206
 pear, 205
Soups
 artichoke, creamy, 54
 carrot, with Dungeness crab, 57
 chicken *laksa*, 58
 corn, chilled, 58
 pumpkin, with pumpkin seed–
  mint pesto, 56

soba noodle bowl, warm, 70
tomato, tiered, 54
tortilla, 61
Vietnamese beef noodle
 (pho bo), 69
Sourdough
 bread, French, 174
 pancakes, 223
 starters, 173, 175, 223
 stuffing, artichoke parmesan,
  172
Southwest, cuisine of, 162
Spinach
 Green Goddess dressing, 46
 Indian *(saag)*, 160
 salads
  mushroom, fennel, and,
   with warm bacon
   vinaigrette, 49
  ruby grapefruit, avocado,
   and, 50
Squash
 butternut
  with green chile and mustard
   seeds, 169
  lentil stew with winter
   vegetables, 65
  rice salad, black, with
   pomegranate seeds
   and, 148
 summer
  beef, dutch oven–braised, and
   summer vegetables, 78
  ratatouille, grilled, 165
Starters, sourdough, 173, 175, 223
Strawberries, 203
 aguas frescas, melon-berry, 26
 popsicles, triple-berry, 208
 tart, brown sugar, 184
Stuffings and dressings
 artichoke parmesan sourdough,
  172
 cornbread-chorizo, 172
 rice, Chinese, 170
Sushi, 135
Syrup, simple, 22

T

Tacos
 beef, cola shredded-, 81
 fish, Baja, 127
 topping, 176

Tamales, Lupe's pork, 92
Tangerines
 olive oil cake, 195
 smoothies, citrus, 29
Taquitos, bean and chicken, 10
Tarragon aioli, 14
Tarts. *See also* Galettes
 apricot nut, 180
 butter pastry for, 181
 chocolate, dark, with cherries
  and almond whipped
  cream, 188
 fig, Black Mission, 187
 macadamia nut, 184
 strawberry, brown sugar, 184
Tea. *See* Bubble tea
Tequila
 margaritas, *Sunset*, 25
 shot-and-a-beer pork stew, 95
Toffee, almond, 217
Tofu
 and herb curry, 66
 miso-glazed, with parsnips
  two ways, 153
 noodles, Filipino-style stir-fried,
  with vegetables and, 147
Tomatillos
 poblano chipotle salsa,
  roasted, 14
 salsa verde, 131
Tomatoes, 54
 Bloody Mary, fresh, 26
 canned heirloom, 241
 chili, smoky beef-and-bacon, 62
 cioppino, 62
 ketchup, golden, 247
 pizza sauce, 144
 ratatouille, grilled, 165
 rice, Mexican red, 229
 salad, heirloom, with
  pomegranate drizzle, 47
 salsas
  fresca, classic, 88
  ranchera, 226
  Santa Maria, 74
 slow-roasted, 163
 soups
  tiered, 54
  tortilla, 61
Tortilla chips
 nachos, chorizo-beef dinner, 85

Tortillas. *See also* Burritos;
  Enchiladas; Quesadillas;
  Tacos
 chilaquiles, 230
 soup, 61
 taquitos, bean and chicken, 10
Tres leches cake with raspberries,
  196
Trout
 crispy, with capers, 128
 pan-fried, with smoked
  salmon, 128
Tuna. *See* Ahi tuna
Turkey
 barbecued glazed, 111
 and cheese, Golden Gate
  grilled, 117
 cooking, 115
 enchiladas, 116
 heritage, with crisped pancetta
  and rosemary, 115
 Tetrazzini, *Sunset*, 116
 wine-smoked, 112

V–Z

Vegetarian main courses, 142–153
Venison loin roast, 101
Vodka
 Bloody Mary, fresh, 26
 Collins, peach, 25
 cosmo, pineapple, 22
 pineapple, fresh, 22
Walnuts, 169
 burgers, Lia's, 144
 fig coffee cake, 220
 pesto, lemon, basil, and, 246
 shallots, caramelized, and, 169
Watercress
 celery Victor with capers
  and, 38
 Cobb salad, classic, 37
 quick-cooked, 159
Watermelon
 salad with lime dressing, 50
 sidecar, 26
Wine, 24
Yogurt
 fresh homemade, 247
 fro-yo, tart 'n' tangy, 201
Zucchini
 beef, dutch oven–braised, and
  summer vegetables, 78
 ratatouille, grilled, 165